Bloody Sunday and the Rule of Law in Northern Ireland

Also by Dermot P. J. Walsh

THE CONFISCATION OF CRIMINAL ASSETS: Law and Procedure (*editor with J. Paul McCutcheon*)

THE IRISH POLICE: A Legal and Constitutional Perspective

THE USE AND ABUSE OF EMERGENCY LEGISLATION IN NORTHERN IRELAND

Bloody Sunday and the Rule of Law in Northern Ireland

Dermot P. J. Walsh
Barrister at Law
Chair of Law
Director, Centre for Criminal Justice
University of Limerick
Ireland

First published in Great Britain 2000 by
MACMILLAN PRESS LTD
Houndmills, Basingstoke, Hampshire RG21 6XS and London
Companies and representatives throughout the world

A catalogue record for this book is available from the British Library.

ISBN 0–333–72287–6 hardcover
ISBN 0–333–72288–4 paperback

First published in the United States of America 2000 by
ST. MARTIN'S PRESS, INC.,
Scholarly and Reference Division,
175 Fifth Avenue, New York, N.Y. 10010

ISBN 0–312–23058–3

Library of Congress Cataloging-in-Publication Data
Walsh, Dermot, 1957–
Bloody Sunday and the rule of law in Northern Ireland / Dermot Walsh.
p.   cm.
Includes bibliographical references (p.) and index.
ISBN 0–312–23058–3 (cloth)
1. Londonderry (Northern Ireland)—History.   2. Demonstrations—Northern
Ireland—Londonderry—History—20th century.   3. Political violence—Northern
Ireland—Londonderry—History—20th century.   4. Massacres—Northern
Ireland—Londonderry—History—20th century.   5. Northern Ireland—History–
–1969–1994.   6. Law—Northern Ireland.   I. Title

DA995.L75 W35   2000
941.6'210824—dc21
                                                                99–053147

This book is printed on paper suitable for recycling and made from fully managed and sustained
forest sources.

10   9   8   7   6   5   4   3   2   1
09   08   07   06   05   04   03   02   01   00

Printed and bound in Great Britain by
Antony Rowe Ltd, Chippenham, Wiltshire

To my mother and father
Edward and Sarah Walsh

Contents

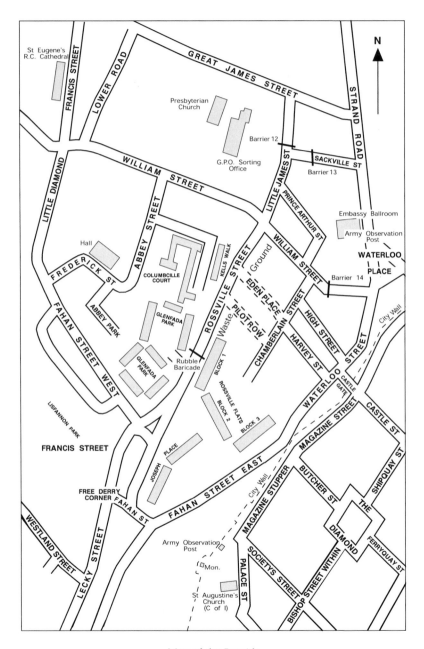

Map of the Bogside

Preface

The conflict in Northern Ireland has produced a whole catalogue of incidents and events which, many years later, still evoke powerful emotions both locally and nationally. Few, however, are so deeply ingrained in the mass consciousness of a whole community as the events in Derry on 30 January 1972; generally known as Bloody Sunday. On that day British soldiers shot dead 13 and wounded 15 unarmed civilians in the context of a protest march against internment without trial in Northern Ireland. Of course Bloody Sunday was not an isolated incident. From one perspective it was simply the latest episode in a conflict which since August 1969 had produced many violent deaths at the hands of both the security forces and terrorists. These continued long after Bloody Sunday and include many more examples of the mass slaughter of innocent civilians, primarily at the hands of terrorists. Nevertheless Bloody Sunday stands out from all the rest.

Bloody Sunday represents the classic example of a state resorting to the might of its armed forces, and the use of lethal force in particular, to crush public protest against the implementation of oppressive and discriminatory policies by that state. In Ireland, of course, memories of the atrocities committed by the forces of the crown at regular intervals over the past three or four centuries are never too far below the surface. In January 1972 these memories were very much alive and potent among the nationalist community in Northern Ireland as a result of their treatment at the hands of the government and the security forces in general since the province was established in 1921, and particularly since August 1969. Not surprisingly, therefore, nationalist reaction to the slaughter on Bloody Sunday was immediate, explosive and far-reaching. Violence broke out across Northern Ireland and in Dublin on a scale rarely witnessed before. Irish communities throughout the world staged public protests against the British government. Within the nationalist community in Northern Ireland the opinion that the state was irreformable began to spread. The Provisional IRA (more than any of the other nationalist paramilitary organisations) attracted recruits, resources and support, which have enabled it to continue an armed campaign against British sovereignty over the six counties of Northern Ireland up to the current ceasefire. That campaign, in turn, has involved many atrocities.

Twenty-seven years later Bloody Sunday has a critical bearing on the success of the peace agreement in Northern Ireland. The failure of the law and justice system to punish those responsible and provide redress for those who had been injured and the families of the deceased dealt a shattering blow to nationalist confidence in the rule of law. Nowhere was this felt more acutely than among the relatives and the victims themselves, who had campaigned fruitlessly for justice for more than 25 years. For the nationalist community as a whole it confirmed an established pattern of security force excesses going unpunished; a pattern which has continued from Bloody Sunday right up to the current peace process. If the peace agreement is to succeed one of the vital prerequisites is the restoration of nationalist confidence in the capacity of the law and justice system to prevent excesses by the security forces and to punish them when they do occur. Given the magnitude of the failure of the law and justice system in the case of Bloody Sunday it would make a huge contribution to the restoration of nationalist confidence if, even 27 years after the event, justice was finally seen to be done.

As might be expected there is already a body of literature on Bloody Sunday, although its volume hardly matches the importance of the subject. Apart from the official report of the Widgery Tribunal into what happened on Bloody Sunday the first significant work to be published was Professor Samuel Dash's report 'Justice Denied: A Challenge to Lord Widgery's Report on Bloody Sunday', which was published by the International League for the Rights of Man in 1972. Based on the evidence presented to the tribunal, Dash offers a damning critique of the tribunal's conclusions. It was followed just over a year later by Professor Bryan McMahon's article 'The Impaired Asset: A Legal Commentary on the Widgery Tribunal', which was published in *La Domaine Humain* in 1974. Not only does McMahon subject Lord Widgery's reasoning on key issues to a powerful and damaging critique, but he also exposes fundamental flaws in Widgery's interpretation and application of the law. Nine more years were to pass before Dr Raymond McClean published an account of his personal experiences of Bloody Sunday in his book *The Road to Bloody Sunday*. Dr McClean had attended to several of the dead and wounded on Bloody Sunday and had been present on behalf of Cardinal Conway at the postmortems on the deceased. Incredibly he was not called as a witness at the Widgery Tribunal even though he had very pertinent evidence to offer. A few months before the twenty-fifth anniversary of Bloody Sunday Don Mullan published *Eyewitness Bloody Sunday: The Truth*, which has now gone into its second edition. It contains an edited collection of statements dictated in 1972 by eyewitnesses to the events of Bloody Sunday. It also contains a new and compelling theory about the location from which some of the fatal shots were fired on that day. My own report, *The Bloody Sunday Tribunal of Inquiry: A Resounding Defeat for Truth, Justice and the Rule of Law*, was launched at a press conference on the twenty-fifth anniversary of Bloody Sunday. Exactly one year later the Irish government published its own analysis under the title *Bloody Sunday and the Report of the Widgery Tribunal: The Irish Government's Assessment of the New Material*. Now that the Saville Tribunal has been established to conduct a fresh inquiry into Bloody Sunday it can be expected that the literature on the subject will grow significantly over the next few years.

The present book has grown out of the research I conducted for my report *The Bloody Sunday Tribunal of Inquiry: A Resounding Defeat for Truth, Justice and the Rule of Law*. That research consisted of a painstaking analysis of soldiers' evidence to the Widgery Tribunal in the light of the original statements they had made to the military police on the night of Bloody Sunday. The nature and extent of the discrepancies between their original statements and their subsequent evidence, coupled with the fact that the soldiers were not cross-examined about the discrepancies when they gave their evidence to the tribunal, meant that the tribunal's confidence in the reliability and veracity of the soldiers' evidence was fundamentally misplaced. This in turn meant that the tribunal's report and conclusions were fundamentally flawed.

This book aims to develop this research more fully by examining in particular the role of the law and the justice system in failing to prevent Bloody Sunday from happening in the first place and in compounding the injustice by conferring a spurious legality on the shootings after the event. It reveals that from at least August 1969 the law was used as a tool of executive expediency in responding to the challenge posed by civil rights protests, sectarian violence and violence against the state. Not only did it function as a vehicle for oppressive security policies but it also proved spectacularly inept at correcting many of the worst excesses. Even the European Convention for the protection of Human Rights and Fundamental Freedoms proved a relative disappointment in this regard. The net result was the creation of an environment in which members of the security forces could believe that they were not subject to the rule of law for actions taken in furtherance of the immediate security and political objectives of the government. Bloody Sunday unquestionably offers the most extreme example of the consequences. It cannot, however, be explained away as an isolated aberration. The subordination of the rule of law and justice to the immediate demands of the executive and security policies which allowed Bloody Sunday to happen were well established by January 1972 and continued unabated right up until the current peace process began to take effect. The damage which has been done to public confidence in the rule of law, particularly among the nationalist community, has been profound. Restoration of this confidence is a vital prerequisite for the successful implementation of the peace agreement and establishment of a just and lasting peace in Northern Ireland.

The book does not attempt to determine the full truth of what happened on Bloody Sunday. It focuses instead on the conduct of the Widgery Tribunal's inquiry into Bloody Sunday and the contents of the tribunal's report. This includes the results of primary research on the statements and evidence of those soldiers who fired the shots on Bloody Sunday. The critique of the Widgery Tribunal's performance is set in the broader context of the security policies of the Stormont and British governments, the contents and operation of the emergency legislation, the practices of the security forces and relevant rulings of the Northern Irish courts, the British courts and the European Commission and Court of Human Rights from at least the 1960s up to the adoption of the Good Friday Peace Agreement in 1998.

For me the book reflects one of the primary reasons why I was attracted to a career in law. It all began with my horror at witnessing the television coverage of the excessive and brutal force used by the police on the civil rights marchers in Derry in October 1968. Even though I was only ten years of age at the time the events sparked a very deep sense of commitment to challenge such injustice in whatever way I could. That commitment was fuelled by the experiences of my secondary school years in Belfast (St Malachy's College) from 1969 to 1976. My memories of those years are dominated by scenes of little terraced streets being patrolled by armed soldiers in full battle fatigues; the cries and protests of women and children as their houses were searched by the soldiers; the personal experience of being stopped and searched regularly by those same soldiers; the sight and eerie high-pitched scream of small field tanks and armoured troop carriers moving along the narrow residential streets, almost dwarfing the little houses which fronted onto the footpaths; the drone of army helicopters as they hovered stationary in the sky for hours on end; the sight of fortified army observation posts perched on top of residential flats; the threatening presence of heavily fortified army bases in residential areas, including one immediately adjacent to my school; the smell of CS gas and smouldering buildings and cars from the previous night's rioting; the sound of gun shots and bomb explosions as I sat in the classroom;

the vibrations of the classroom as huge bombs exploded in the vicinity of the school; the sense of loss and helplessness over the death of class-mates, blown up or shot by loyalists; the terrible sense of foreboding of loyalist and security force retaliation in the wake of fatal bombings and shootings by republicans; the sense of anarchy as the school was caught up in student protests against the use of internment without trial; and, ultimately, the almost communal sense of outrage and rebel-lion as the full horror of Bloody Sunday became apparent.

As those years progressed I realised that the oppressive security poli-cies and practices I was witnessing would not be remedied by either the government or the legislature. Indeed they were more likely to be the source of many of the excesses. Retaliatory violence, whether in the form of street rioting or armed resistance, only seemed to provoke further abuses from the security forces, supplemented by the actions of loyalist paramilitaries, leading inevitably to a vicious spiral of self-perpetuating violence. The law, however, seemed to offer a powerful alternative. Surely the oppressive actions of the executive, and the security forces in particular, could be challenged effectively by recourse to the law? Equipped with a sound knowledge of the law and a profes-sional legal qualification I could at least make a practical and meaning-ful contribution to remedying the abuses and promoting human rights, equality and justice in Northern Ireland. It was with that ideal in mind that I commenced my career in law at The Queen's University of Belfast in 1976. After graduation and under the auspices of the Cobden Trust Studentship I embarked upon research into the operation of the emergency legislation in Northern Ireland. This resulted in 1983 in the publication of my book *The Use and Abuse of Emergency Legislation in Northern Ireland*. Since then I have continued my research on the interaction between law and security policy in Northern Ireland with the aim of promoting what I consider to be one of the primary functions of the law, namely to protect the weak against victimisation and oppression at the hands of the powerful. This book is an impor-tant milestone in that work. As will become apparent from its con-tents, however, one of the lessons I have learned is that there are limits to the capacity of the law to deliver justice. Indeed in Northern Ireland over the past thirty years it might not be unfair to say that its capacity to deliver justice has been overshadowed by its equal capacity to func-tion as a vehicle and a cover for injustice.

When researching and writing this book I benefited from the cooper-ation of a number of individuals and bodies. Before listing them, how-ever, I must pay tribute generally to the relatives and friends of those shot dead on Bloody Sunday and to their legal advisers and supporters, who have campaigned tirelessly over 27 years to secure justice. The sense of loss, grief and helplessness which the relatives of the victims undoubtedly suffered in the immediate aftermath of Bloody Sunday would have deterred most other persons from even making the attempt. Those lawyers and human rights activists who have stood with the relatives and campaigned energetically on their behalf deserve the thanks of all of us who believe in the sanctity of human rights and the need for a just and lasting peace in Northern Ireland. In particular, therefore, I am indebted to the relatives of those shot dead on Bloody Sunday, the Bloody Sunday Trust and their solicitors Madden and Finucane. If I had not been engaged by the Bloody Sunday Trust to conduct research on the statements and evidence of the soldiers who fired the shots on Bloody Sunday it is quite likely that this book would never have been written in its current form. Jane Winter, director of British Irish Rights Watch, and Patricia Coyle of Madden and Finucane deserve a special mention. It was largely due to Jane's hard work and persistence that the original statements made by the soldiers were eventually released by the Home Office. Patricia personally transported these voluminous documents from Derry to my base in Limerick and was always available to respond to any query I might have about them.

I am especially grateful to the University of Limerick for giving me the time, space and resources necessary to research and write the book. In particular I am indebted to Pattie Punch, humanities librarian in the University of Limerick, who worked her usual wonders in supplying me with Northern Irish and European case reports as and when I needed them. John Moroney, Faculty of Education in the University of Limerick, also deserves a special mention and thanks. His moral encouragement and support at critical times ensured that the project stayed on course until completion. I would also like to thank Alison Howson (and her predecessor Sunder Katwala), who has done a superbly professional job as commissioning editor, and Keith Povey for his meticulous editing. Finally, and most especially, I wish to thank my wife Alice and our children Orla and Niall. Their support and patience throughout my work on the book were treasures which could not be purchased. My only hope is that they, and all the others who have assisted me in the project, will see some merit in the final product. As always, of course, they bear no responsibility whatsoever for the views expressed or any shortcomings that may be found in the work. That responsibility is entirely mine.

Lisnagry, County Limerick   DERMOT P. J. WALSH

1
Bloody Sunday

Derry city is the archetypal divided city. Even its name reflects division. For Irish nationalists (largely catholic) it is Derry, while for British unionists (largely protestant) it is Londonderry. The city itself is divided by the River Foyle, which separates the predominantly unionist east from the predominantly nationalist west. The city centre is located on the west bank. Bordering the city centre to the west is the Bogside, the scene of Bloody Sunday. At the time of Bloody Sunday the Bogside was an area of terraced housing dating mostly from the turn of the century, coupled with 1960s high-rise flat complexes. To the west of the Bogside, on a hill overlooking the city, is the Creggan estate. This is a large sprawling estate of high-density public housing built in the 1960s primarily to accommodate the overflow from the Bogside and other neighbouring areas. Derry as a whole had traditionally suffered from high levels of unemployment, low investment, overcrowded housing, environmental deprivation and anti-Catholic discrimination by the state. The Bogside and Creggan areas, which were overwhelmingly catholic and nationalist, suffered more than most from these ills. Nevertheless they were characterised by a very developed sense of community. The population was anchored by a high incidence of long-established, extended families. The high levels of deprivation and discrimination to which they were subject seemed only to strengthen their communal resolve to improve their situation.

In the late 1960s Derry was at the forefront of the struggle for basic civil rights for Catholics in Northern Ireland. Many of the major civil rights protest marches from that era were held in Derry. By the same token most of the rioting and brutal excesses of the security forces were experienced in Derry, and in the Bogside in particular. As the civil rights campaign gradually gave way to an armed struggle against

British and unionist rule in Northern Ireland Derry was once more in the vanguard. The Bogside and Creggan areas in particular became major IRA strongholds and the battleground for many armed confrontations between the IRA and the security forces. After the Northern Irish government introduced internment in August 1971 the IRA effectively took control of large parts of the Creggan and the Bogside. They established permanent armed checkpoints on all access routes and the security forces were effectively excluded from these 'no-go areas'. From these bases the IRA launched bombing attacks on commercial and security targets in other parts of the city.

The concept of no-go areas from which the official forces of law and order were excluded provoked an intensely hostile reaction from the unionist majority in Northern Ireland and the government came under intense pressure to move against them. Eventually, in October 1971 the British Army moved in force against the no-go areas. The operation in Derry was conducted by the 8th Infantry Brigade. Their instructions were to regain the initiative from the IRA and reimpose the rule of law on the Creggan and the Bogside. In this context the rule of law meant the imposition of law and order by the security forces. This entailed the removal of the barricades and IRA checkpoints, arrest and search operations, the establishment of permanent military checkpoints on all access roads from the city centre into the Bogside and Creggan, the establishment of permanent military observation posts and regular street patrols by armed soldiers in armoured vehicles. In other words the areas in question were placed effectively under a state of military siege.

The military strategy provoked a hostile response from the local community. On the streets this was expressed primarily in the form of minor rioting. Small groups of youths stoning British soldiers at the permanent checkpoints were a frequent, sometimes daily occurrence. The soldiers would respond by firing rubber bullets and CS gas cannisters and by organising snatch squads to chase and arrest the ringleaders. These street skirmishes were occasionally organised as a diversion or cover for an IRA sniper attack on the soldiers. Indeed by 1972 the threat of IRA sniper attacks was so severe that the army was not able to mount patrols during the day in the Bogside area south of William Street. The army's capacity to function in the Bogside and Creggan at night was compromised by the practice of switching on searchlights and sounding car horns on any occasion that soldiers appeared in the vicinity. The IRA was gradually driving the security forces back out of the Bogside and Creggan.

Another significant feature of the street skirmishes was the fact that they were threatening to spread beyond the immediate Bogside area. For some time the soldiers had pursued a policy of containing the rioters in the Bogside south of the William Street boundary (see map, p. viii). However as the frequency of car hijackings and burnings in the context of these riots increased, this strategy became more and more difficult to sustain. Inevitably the commercial premises and other properties in the area north of William Street were at risk of succumbing to the rioters. The traders and commercial interests concerned became increasingly alarmed that the whole of this shopping area was in imminent danger of being wiped out. Accordingly they lobbied the political and security establishments for more resolute action. The political and security interests were also concerned that the IRA writ was threatening to extend beyond the confines of the Creggan and Bogside areas and into the city centre. The scene was set, therefore, for a major change of strategy by the security forces aimed at reversing the IRA advance and reimposing the writ of the security forces in these areas. At the root of this strategy would be a severe crackdown on the street rioters, whose activities were perceived as a vital element in facilitating the IRA advance.

An opportunity for launching such a crackdown was presented by an anti-internment march organised for 30 January 1972. Internment without trial had been introduced by the Northern Irish government in August 1971, resulting in the arrest of hundreds of nationalists in dawn swoops by the security forces throughout Northern Ireland. Most of those arrested in the initial operations had no involvement whatsoever in terrorist activity and many of them were subjected to brutal treatment at the hands of the security forces.[1] Primarily because of its brutal and discriminatory application internment made a greater contribution to the scale and intensity of violence in Northern Ireland than any other previous military operation or strategy. It had a huge impact on the alienation of the nationalist community from the forces of law and order and the state, and led indirectly to Bloody Sunday itself.

As an integral part of the internment policy the government imposed a ban on all parades and processions throughout Northern Ireland from 9 August 1971. Nevertheless many civil rights marches were held in protest against internment in the ensuing months in defiance of this ban. The security forces generally did not attempt to break up these marches despite the fact that they were technically unlawful. They were content to pursue a policy of preventing the marches from proceeding into certain areas and photographing the participants with a view to future prosecution in the courts. For the most part, therefore, the marches passed off peacefully with only minor skirmishes between rioters and the security forces, usually after the marches had ended. There was never any hint of the dramatic change in policy that was to be imposed on such a march planned for Derry on 30 January 1972.

The Northern Ireland Civil Rights Association (NICRA) notified the authorities that they planned to hold a march in Derry on Sunday 30 January 1972. The purpose of the march was to protest against the policy of internment without trial and the brutality inflicted on those who had been detained in internment operations. It was intended that the march would assemble in the Creggan estate and proceed from there to the city centre, via the Bogside, for a rally in Guildhall Square. The organisers were advised that the march would be unlawful, but that did not affect their decision to proceed. After their intentions had been disclosed, the Reverend Ian Paisley announced plans for a counter-demonstration by unionists to be held at roughly the same time in Guildhall Square. This was part of a general strategy being pursued by unionists to pressurise the government into using force to suppress the unlawful civil rights marches.

The government's security committee met to consider what policy to adopt in order to deal with the threat to public order presented by the possible clash between the march and the counterdemonstration. Exactly what was decided by this committee remains shrouded in doubt. The official position is that a decision was made to stop the march from proceeding beyond the Bogside into the city centre so as to prevent rioting and damage to commercial premises and shops. The Commander of the 8th Infantry Brigade was put in charge of the operation to implement this policy. The operation order drawn up for this purpose relied heavily on the standard method of erecting army barricades across all access routes from the Bogside to the city centre; effectively sealing off the Bogside with a military cordon. These barriers, 26 in all, consisted of wooden knife rests reinforced with barbed wire and concrete slabs. At some of them an armoured personnel carrier was stationed at either side of the street close behind and almost parallel to the barrier in order to provide reinforcement and cover for the troops stationed behind. Each barrier was manned by an army platoon with representative RUC officers in support. Reinforcements and reserves were provided by the 1st Battalion of the Parachute Regiment, the 1st Battalion of the Kings Own Border Regiment, two companies of the 3rd Battalion of the Royal Regiment of Fusiliers and two water cannon.

The operation order stipulated that the march should be dealt with in as low a key as possible for as long as possible. If it took place entirely within the Creggan and the Bogside it should go unchallenged. No action was to be taken against the marchers unless they tried to breach the barriers or used violence against the security forces. CS gas was not to be used except as a last resort if troops were about to be overrun and the rioters could no longer be held off with water cannon and rubber bullets. An arrest force was to be held centrally behind the barriers and used to launch a 'scoop-up' operation to arrest as many rioters as possible. The 1st Battalion of the Parachute Regiment was given the specific responsibility of maintaining a 'brigade arrest force' to conduct a scoop-up arrest operation. Such an operation was to be launched only on the orders of the brigade commander and was to be conducted on foot. The clear implication was that the scoop-up operation would follow the standard pattern of soldiers rushing out to grab the ringleaders in the immediate vicinity of the barricades. There was no suggestion that the soldiers would go in on military vehicles and pursue the rioters and marchers deep into the Bogside. Indeed not only was it envisaged that the operation would be conducted on foot, but the order to commence the operation specifically stated that the soldiers were 'not to conduct [a] running battle down Rossville Street'.[2] This order, coupled with the contents of the operation order, suggested that the march and any associated rioting would be contained in the standard manner.

Although the organisers of the unionist counterdemonstration would not have been satisfied by such a low-key strategy they surprisingly called off their demonstration. The official reason given was that they were satisfied by assurances that the civil rights march would not be allowed to proceed to the city centre. In some quarters, however, the unionist reaction was interpreted as evidence of behind-the-scene assurances from unionist sources high up in the political and security establishments that the real strategy would involve the deployment of maximum force against the marchers and that it would be safer for the unionist counterdemonstrators not to be anywhere near the immediate vicinity. Indeed it was strongly suspected in nationalist circles that the official security strategy was nothing more than a smokescreen to conceal the real strategy, which was to use the march as an opportunity to inflict severe punishment on the rioters and, if the opportunity presented itself, IRA gunmen in the area. This would be achieved by resorting to the use of lethal force. The obvious objective would be to halt the spread of violence beyond the William Street boundary and restore the hegemony of the security forces in the area. A useful political spin-off would be the mollification of unionist demands to unleash the security forces against the IRA.

Several key decisions and subsequent events lend credence to the unofficial version. From the outset the RUC commander in the area, Chief Superintendent Lagan, had been advocating a low-key containment policy. It was his opinion that a direct confrontation between the security forces and the marchers would be disastrous. He advised that the march should be allowed to take its course unhindered and that the leaders should be photographed with a view to being prosecuted later in the courts. In the usual course of events the advice of the police commander in the area would be followed in such matters. In this case, however, a political decision was taken at a high level, after consultation with the chief constable of the RUC and the commander of land forces in Northern Ireland, to overrule Chief Superintendent Lagan. The clear implication was that the political and security establishment were pursuing an agenda which went beyond coping with this march with the minimum of disruption to the local peace and public order.

The nature of that other agenda was reflected by the unusual decision to deploy the 1st Battalion of the Parachute Regiment to conduct the scoop-up operation against rioters. Prior to Bloody Sunday the regiment had not seen service in Derry. Indeed they had to be brought in specially for the event from Belfast, with some members flying in from Malta only the night before. The official, and implausible, explanation for deploying the 1st Battalion was that it was the only experienced uncommitted battalion in Northern Ireland at the time. Even if this explanation is accepted it does not explain the decision to deploy them specifically for the scoop-up arrest operation. They could have been used purely for barrier and other incidental security duties, thereby freeing up the regular 8th Infantry Brigade to conduct the arrest operation; an operation with which they were quite familiar in this area. The deployment of the 1st Battalion Parachute Regiment by contrast was entirely inconsistent with a policy of minimum force and containment. The Parachute Regiment has the deserved reputation of being the toughest in the British Army, trained to use maximum firepower as a first resort when confronted with a threat to life or personal safety. This is clearly reflected in the following description of them in the report of the inquiry into Bloody Sunday by Lord Chief Justice Widgery:

> In the Parachute Regiment, at any rate in the 1st Battalion, the soldiers are trained to take what may be described as a hard line upon these questions. The events of 30 January and the attitude of

individual soldiers whilst giving evidence suggest that when engaging an identified gunman or bomb-thrower they shoot to kill and continue to fire until the target disappears or falls. *When under attack and returning fire they show no particular concern for the safety of others in the vicinity of the target. ... Further, when hostile firing is taking place the soldiers of 1 Para will fire on a person who appears to be using a firearm against them without waiting until they can positively identify the weapon* (emphasis added).[3]

Any impartial observer could have predicted the likelihood of brutal and even maximum force being used against the marchers and rioters as a result of their deployment on the scoop-up operation. Indeed it is difficult to avoid the suspicion that that is exactly what the political and security establishment desired.

Another telling factor was the blatant failure of the soldiers to abide by the clear terms of the operation order for the march. As will be seen below, their departure from the low key and minimum force strictures of the operation order was so widespread and consistent that it must have resulted from a prior understanding that the real objective of the operation was to inflict a crushing defeat on the rioters and any active IRA personnel in the area. Ultimately, of course, the clearest indication of the real political and security intent is provided by the devastating results of the operation.

The Sunday afternoon of 30 January 1972 was fine and sunny. The marchers assembled in the Creggan estate. As they made their way through the Creggan their numbers began to swell. The participants included many women and children and there was generally a carnival and relaxed atmosphere. By the time they reached William Street in the Bogside, estimates of their number varied from 10 000 to 25 000. Their direct route to Guildhall Square in the city centre lay along William Street, but it was blocked off by army barrier 14 just beyond the junction with Rossville Street (see map). When the march reached the junction between William Street and Rossville Street the leaders turned and headed up Rossville Street away from the city centre and away from a direct confrontation with the army at barrier 14. The stewards were very active in ensuring that the body of the march followed this route. The march proceeded up Rossville Street, passed Rossville Flats to Free Derry Corner, where a rally was held. It was apparent, therefore, that the marchers' strategy from the outset had been to accept their exclusion from the city centre and thereby avoid a direct confrontation with the army.[4]

Given the huge size of the march and the relatively small area within which it had to make its U-turn there was an inevitable confrontation between the marchers and the soldiers in the cul-de-sac created by the William Street barrier (see barrier 14 on map). Considerable pressure was applied on the barrier for a period by the sheer weight of numbers pushing into the confined space. This was accompanied by a consider-able volume of catcalling and jeering. As the front of the march made its way up Rossville Street the pressure of numbers at barrier 14 began to ease. As often happened with such marches a small number of youths took advantage of the opportunity to throw stones at the sol-diers. Indeed there were minor skirmishes between these youths and the soldiers as the march passed by a number of barriers en route to William Street. The soldiers responded with volleys of rubber bullets. One of the water cannons was brought up from behind the barriers and it proceeded to drench the rioters with water coloured with a pur-ple dye. A CS gas canister exploded beneath the cannon, disabling the crew, who were not wearing their gas masks. The water cannon was withdrawn while the gas cleared and more rubber bullets were fired. When the water cannon was brought into action a second time it began to have some effect and the rioters began to disperse.

While the rioting was going on the march had proceeded on up Rossville Street to Free Derry Corner. Not all the marchers, however, followed this route. Many began to make their way home up Rossville Street to Rossville Flats and Glenfada Flats and places beyond. As was usually the case at the end of these events, many people milled around in groups in conversation or simply taking in the afternoon's events. Rossville Street in particular was still quite crowded with people who either had not taken part in the march or who had not proceeded to the rally at Free Derry Corner. It must be emphasised, however, that none of these people were involved in stoning the soldiers at the barriers. Their presence, however, was to be a vital factor in what happened next.

At 3.55 pm the commander of the 1st Battalion of the Parachute Regiment, Lieutenant Colonel Wilford, was keen to conduct a scoop-up operation to arrest and disperse the remaining rioters. He had three companies available to him for this purpose: A Company, C Company and Support Company. The Support Company was reinforced by a composite platoon from Administrative Company. All three companies were brought forward at the same time, but only C Company and Support Company actually participated in the scoop-up arrest opera-tion which followed.

At 16.07 the order was given to launch the arrest operation. The contents of that order and the identity of the officer who gave it are critical to an assessment of the ensuing events. Both, however, are hotly contested. The official version is that the operation was authorised by the commander of the 8th Brigade, as envisaged by the operation order. The authorisation, apparently, was in terms which permitted Lieutenant Colonel Wilford to employ all three companies. The problem with this version is that it does not accord with the evidence. A much stronger case can be made out that Lieutenant Colonel Wilford actually acted on his own initiative and in defiance of orders. The brigade log, which was maintained in the brigade operations room as a minute by minute record of events and messages, contained the following entries for the critical times:

> Serial 147, 1555 hours from 1 Para. Would like to deploy sub-unit through barricade 14 to pick up yobbos in William Street/Little James Street.
>
> Serial 159, 1609 hours from Brigade Major. Orders given to 1 Para at 1607 hours for one sub-unit of 1 Para to do scoop-up through barrier 14. Not to conduct running battle down Rossville Street.

Quite clearly, therefore, the brigade log conflicted with the authorisation supposedly given by the brigade commander. The latter had purportedly permitted the use of three companies, while the brigade log clearly records authorisation for one (a 'sub-unit' is a company). Further support for the view that Lieutenant Colonel Wilford acted on his own initiative was forthcoming from Chief Superintendent Lagan. He had been in the brigade commander's office at the time the scoop-up operation was launched. In his evidence to the Widgery Tribunal he was firmly of the opinion that the operation had been launched without authorisation from the brigade commander.

Of more consequence, perhaps, was the whole issue of whether Lieutenant Colonel Wilford had exceeded his orders in the conduct of the operation, or whether in fact he was acting in furtherance of a strategy which had been secretly agreed and for which the formal instructions were merely a smokescreen. Whatever the answer, there can be little doubt that he greatly exceeded his formal orders to devastating effect. The brigade operation order had envisaged that the arrest operation would be conducted on foot along two axes of advance, namely William Street/Little Diamond and William Street/Little James Street (see map). It was never contemplated that Rossville Street would be used as an axis of advance. This is also reflected in the brigade log, which recorded the specific instruction 'Not to conduct running battle down Rossville Street'.[5]

In the event, Support Company went in through barrier 12 (see map) in a convoy of ten vehicles, including armoured personnel carriers, two fourton lorries and a Ferret scout car. This of course was totally at odds with the normal procedure in scoop-up operations, where the soldiers go in on foot. It was also clearly in breach of the brigade order. They advanced at speed up Rossville Street in complete defiance of the brigade order and the instructions recorded in the brigade log. The leading armoured personnel carrier veered left and stopped on waste ground near Eden Place, covering the entrance to the courtyard of Rossville Flats and an entrance to Chamberlain Street. The second armoured personnel carrier proceeded past the first and stopped in the actual courtyard of Rossville Flats near the north end of Block 1. The remainder of the vehicles initially stopped along Rossville Street, although another armoured personnel carrier and the scout car later moved on to join the armoured personnel carrier at Block 1 of Rossville Flats. Not one of these movements could be justified on the basis of the brigade order.

At the same time as Support Company went through barrier 12, C Company went through barrier 14 on foot. They advanced along Chamberlain Street in a direction which, once again, bore no relationship to the planned axes of advance. Their action had the effect of flushing people out into the courtyard of Rossville Flats and into Eden Place, where the armoured personnel carriers of Support Company had deployed. On any interpretation this looked very much like a carefully preplanned exercise which bore no relationship to the formal terms of the brigade order.

As soon as the armoured vehicles of Support Company broke through barrier 12 the remaining rioters and others in the immediate vicinity ran off down Rossville Street, where they merged with the few hundred people still milling around there. Panic ensued when to everyone's surprise the vehicles sped aggressively down Rossville Street. Everyone scattered for refuge. Most ran for the courtyard of Rossville Flats, some ran further down Rossville Street while others ran in the direction of Glenfada Park. Their numbers were swelled by the crowds driven out onto the Rossville Flats courtyard and Eden Place by the advance of C Company up Chamberlain Street. It was in this confusion and panic that the first shots rang out, adding to the pandemonium and terror among the crowd. In the space of about ten minutes 13 civilians were shot dead[6] and a further 13 were wounded.[7] Two more civilians had been wounded about 15 minutes earlier by shots fired by soldiers in a derelict house on William Street.[8] All of the dead were shot by soldiers, as were all of the wounded with one possible exception. Most of the deaths and injuries occurred in the general area of Rossville Street, Rossville Flats and Glenfada Park, although some army shots were fired outside that immediate area.

The circumstances in which the civilians were shot and wounded are hotly disputed. The Widgery Tribunal found that the soldiers fired a total of 108 bullets. Later it will be seen that even that figure is disputed. The soldiers claimed that they fired only at gunmen and bombers in circumstances where they had come under a veritable fusillage of bombs and bullets. Lord Widgery was of the opinion that as many shots were probably fired at the soldiers as were fired by them. However no guns were recovered from any of the victims and the only bombs recovered were four nail bombs, allegedly found on the body of Gerald Donaghy in disputed circumstances. No photographic evidence was produced showing a gunman or bomber despite the fact that there were many photographers operating in the area, including at least two army photographers. There was some civilian evidence to the effect that the occasional gunman was spotted. Some civilians also reported seeing and hearing gunfire which did not come from the army. However no civilian or journalist reported seeing anyone throw a bomb at the army. Forensic tests on all of the deceased (with the exception of Gerald Donaghy, on which see later) proved negative for handling bombs. They also proved negative for the handling of weapons for five of the deceased, and were inconclusive with respect to the rest. There was a huge body of civilian and journalist evidence that soldiers fired at unarmed civilians in circumstances where there was no real threat to the lives of the soldiers.

Whatever the truth about these shootings there could be no doubting the profoundly serious and disturbing nature of their consequences. At one level there were the violent consequences. Rioting and shooting broke out in nationalist areas all over Northern Ireland as the nationalist community vented their anger at what they saw as mass murder inflicted on their community by the armed forces of the British crown. This violent reaction spilled over into the Republic of Ireland, where many street demonstrations resulted in attacks on British-owned commercial property and the burning of the British embassy in Dublin. Public protest marches and demonstrations were held in many cities around the world. Of greater long-term significance for the violence in Northern Ireland was the impact on IRA recruitment. Young men and women all over Ireland were queueing up to join the IRA in numbers that had not been witnessed before and have not been experienced since. Indeed Bloody Sunday might be cited, alongside internment and the H-Block hunger strikes, as one of the most influential events in provoking nationalist alienation from the state in Northern Ireland, and sustaining a long drawn-out and bloody war of insurrection which proved to be beyond the capacity of the state to quell.

At a deeper level Bloody Sunday had implications for the very legitimacy of the state of Northern Ireland. As will be seen in greater detail in Chapter 2, nationalist confidence in the capacity of the state to grant them equality of respect with the unionist community in political, economic and cultural matters was already teetering on the brink even before Bloody Sunday. For many nationalists the events of Bloody Sunday sent out the stark message that the state would not even respect their right to life should they choose to engage in a show of public dissent against state policy. What they saw was the armed forces of the state engaging in mass killing and wounding in order to suppress a largely peaceful demonstration against the repressive policies of the state. In their eyes this was the ultimate proof of the illegitimacy of the state. Even in neutral circles the events of Bloody Sunday rocked public confidence in the rule of law and the integrity of government to the core. If there was any truth to the allegations being made about the actions of the army it was absolutely essential that they should be investigated quickly and in a manner which would persuade the sceptical that the inquiry was thorough, independent and impartial. If it discovered wrongdoing then it was equally essential that those responsible should be held accountable in an appropriate manner and the necessary remedial measures taken. Any failure to deliver on these requirements would simply compound the damage done to the rule of law and the integrity of the state in Northern Ireland. For nationalists it would be yet more confirmation, if more was needed, that the state was not capable of accommodating them.

The British government responded to this challenge by deciding the very next day to appoint a judicial inquiry into the events of Bloody Sunday. This inquiry was to be established under the Tribunals and Inquiries (Evidence) Act 1921 and would be chaired by Lord Chief Justice Widgery. This tribunal issued its report ten weeks later, only for it to be castigated bitterly by the nationalist community as a biased and unashamed attempt to protect the army against any claims of serious wrongdoing. Instead of placing the blame for the deaths and injuries on the army the report blamed those who had organised the illegal march for creating 'a highly dangerous situation in which a clash between the demonstrators and the security forces was almost inevitable.' The report praised the decision to contain the march within the Bogside and concluded that it had been perfectly proper to deploy the 1st Battalion of the Parachute Regiment for the scoop-up arrest operation. It concluded that the arrest operation had been launched and conducted in accordance with the brigade order. Critically, the report concluded that the soldiers had opened fire only after they had come under fire and that there had been no general breakdown of discipline among them. They had fired only at targets which they had identified as gunmen in circumstances where they believed such action was justified. While the report acknowledged that none of the deceased or wounded were proved to have been shot while holding a firearm or bomb, it went on to declare that there was a strong suspicion that some of them had been firing weapons or handling bombs in the course of the afternoon and that others had been closely supporting them.[9]

On any interpretation these conclusions represent a resounding victory for the army and a serious indictment of the organisers of the march and the dead and wounded. Even those conclusions which were critical of the army were couched in language which downplayed the extent of the army's culpability. The decision to launch the arrest operation despite the fact that the danger had passed was described as follows: 'If the Army had persisted in its "low-key" attitude and had not launched a large scale operation to arrest hooligans the day might have passed off without serious incident.'

There was the merest hint of criticism of the commander of the 8th Brigade for his assessment of the dangers involved in conducting an arrest operation in the circumstances which prevailed on Bloody Sunday. It was considered that he may have underestimated the hazard to civilians in the area. Even the shooting by some soldiers which the tribunal described as bordering on the reckless was explained away as a result of their training, which made them aggressive and quick in decision, a reflection of differences in their character and temperament. Such efforts at shielding the army from criticism strengthened the perception of the inquiry and the report as an exercise in exonerating the army from blame.

The very fact that the British government took the unprecedented decision in January 1998 to establish a second tribunal of inquiry into Bloody Sunday is in itself a major vote of no confidence in the Widgery Report. This book will address the extent to which nationalist criticisms of the Widgery Inquiry and its report are justified, the role which the law and justice system has played in the whole Bloody Sunday experience and the progress, if any, which has been made since in restoring respect for law and justice in Northern Ireland. In order to set the scene, however, it is necessary to explain how Bloody Sunday could have happened and why it is so deeply seared into the consciousness of the nationalist community in Northern Ireland.

2
The Road to Bloody Sunday

The state of Northern Ireland

Establishing the state

The road to Bloody Sunday begins at least as far back as the establishment of Northern Ireland as a distinct political entity in 1921. Between 1800 and 1921 the whole of Ireland had been governed directly from London under the terms of the Act of Union 1800. As the nineteenth century had drawn to a close the British government had come under increasing pressure to restore a measure of autonomy to the Irish over their own political affairs.[1] By 1914 this pressure bore fruit in the form of the Government of Ireland Act. While the enactment of this measure represented a victory for the majority of Irish MPs who made up the Irish Home Rule Party, it also exposed the communal division which had been present in Ireland for the previous two centuries and still survives today at the very heart of the conflict in Northern Ireland. On the one hand there was the majority community, largely Catholic, who demanded 'Home Rule' for Ireland, and on the other hand there was the minority community, largely Protestant and concentrated in the north-east of the country, who wished to remain under direct rule from London. Broadly speaking the former might be termed nationalists and the latter unionists. Both sides demonstrated the strength and depth of their feelings on the issue between 1910 and 1914 by organising themselves into paramilitary bodies which engaged regularly in public displays of military drilling and marching.[2]

The implementation of the 1914 Act, and the accompanying prospect of military confrontation between the opposing camps, was suspended with the onset of the First World War.[3] By the time the war had drawn to a close the political and security situation in Ireland had changed dramatically.[4] The intervening years had witnessed the nationalist uprising against the British Forces in 1916 and the British government's execution of its leaders. Nationalist opinion had hardened to the extent that the objective of Home Rule was swept aside in favour of complete independence from Britain. This was reflected in the withdrawal of the majority of Irish MPs from the Westminster parliament to form the first Dail (Irish parliament) in 1919. This first Dail sanctioned the commencement of the War of Independence, which resulted in the secession of 26 of the 32 Irish counties from the rest of the United Kingdom in 1922. These 26 counties today constitute Ireland (sometimes referred to, less accurately, as the Republic of Ireland or Eire). The remaining six constitute Northern Ireland.

The unionists were also active in protecting their interests during this period.[5] Through adroit use of their considerable political influence at Westminster they managed to persuade the British government to modify substantially its plans for Irish Home Rule. Instead of the establishment of a single devolved government for the whole country there would be two governments: one for the 26 counties, which were overwhelmingly Catholic and nationalist, and one for the six counties of Northern Ireland, which contained a 2 : 1 protestant and unionist majority over the nationalists. These arrangements were enshrined in the Government of Ireland Act, 1920. Before this act came fully into effect, however, it was superseded by the Anglo-Irish Treaty of 1921.[6] This treaty made provision for the establishment of an Irish Free State, but it also included a provision which permitted the six north-eastern counties to opt out of the Free State; an option they exercised. These counties remained part of the United Kingdom and were officially designated Northern Ireland. Those provisions of the Government of Ireland Act, 1920, which provided Northern Ireland with its own institutions of devolved government came into effect in 1921.

The institutions of state

The 1920 Act adopted a variant of the Westminster model for the government of Northern Ireland.[7] It provided for a legislature consisting of the crown, represented by the governor general, a House of Commons directly elected by adult universal suffrage and a senate, most of the members of which were elected by the House of Commons.[8] The primary legislative power rested with the House of Commons. Despite appearances, however, the Stormont parliament was not a sovereign parliament. Its legislative powers were conferred by an Act of the UK parliament. Accordingly they were limited in scope and their exercise was amenable to judicial review under the terms of the 1920 Act.[9] Ultimately these powers could be curtailed or even abolished altogether by a simple Act of the UK parliament. In practice the Stormont parliament enjoyed very substantial autonomy from Westminster. The Government of Ireland Act defined its powers in very extensive terms by stipulating that it could 'make laws for the peace, order and good government' of Northern Ireland. Certain matters, such as defence and foreign affairs, were reserved to the sovereign government at Westminster, but for the most part the provincial parliament had the power to make laws on most matters affecting the people of Northern Ireland. In the fifty years from 1922 to 1972 it was the primary source of legislation on economic, social, property, justice, public order, educational and cultural matters affecting Northern Ireland.[10] During this period a convention gradually developed that the Westminster government did not interfere in matters within the compass of the Stormont parliament.[11]

Although the executive power in Northern Ireland was technically vested in the crown there was provision for executive powers in respect of matters within the competence of the Stormont parliament to be delegated to the governor.[12] Powers so delegated were to be exercised by departments established by the governor or the Stormont parliament. The departments were placed under the charge of ministers. The ministries were incorporated and specific powers were conferred upon them. Each minister was responsible in law and to parliament for the manner in which his ministry exercised its powers and discharged its executive function. Although the list of ministries or departments varied from time to time the main ones were the Prime Minister's Department, Finance, Home Affairs, Labour, Commerce, Agriculture, Education, Health and Local Government. There was also an attorney general. In line with the Westminster model, the formation of a government and the appointment of ministers was dictated by that party which enjoyed a majority of seats in the House of Commons in the Stormont parliament. The leader of that party in the House of Commons would be elected prime minister by a majority of his fellows MPs. He, in turn, would normally appoint the ministers in his cabinet from among the senior members of his party in parliament.

Prior to the Government of Ireland Act, 1920, Ireland had its own court system.[13] The 1920 Act reserved to the Westminster parliament all matters relating to the Supreme Court of Judicature in Northern Ireland and constituted the court in two divisions: the High Court and the Court of Appeal.[14] The enactments which had previously applied to the Supreme Court of Judicature in Ireland were applied with the necessary adaptations to the Supreme Court of Northern Ireland. Appeal lay, and still lies, from the Court of Appeal to the House of Lords in London. On constitutional matters appeal lay to the Judicial Committee of the Privy Council in London. The power to legislate in respect of the lower courts vested in the Stormont parliament. The judges sitting in these lower courts were appointed by the governor on the advice of the prime minister of Northern Ireland. The attorney general was also appointed on the advice of the prime minister. He had ultimate responsibility for the initiation and prosecution of all criminal offences. In serious cases the files would be sent to him for direction and advice.[15] This is of critical importance because the attorney general also held ministerial office in the Stormont government and was almost invariably a senior member of the Unionist Party. An independent office of director of public prosecutions was not established statutorily until 1972 for the specific purpose of protecting the prosecution process from the appearance of political bias.[16] Nevertheless it would appear that the decision not to prosecute in the Bloody Sunday cases was taken ultimately by the attorney general.

A divided society

From its inception Northern Ireland was a divided society.[17] The fact that it was established at all reflected the deep divide in Ireland between the Protestant/unionist and Catholic/nationalist traditions. The border was devised and drawn to convert the Protestant/unionist minority in Ireland as a whole into a secure majority within its own self-governing province within the United Kingdom. Inevitably the Catholic/nationalist population within these six counties found their status transformed from being part of a majority in the island as whole to that of a sizeable minority in a province cut off politically, socially, economically and culturally from the rest of the country.

The communal division was evident at several levels. For example parts of the province were populated almost exclusively by one side or the other, and the same applied to many streets and housing estates within urban areas. Not surprisingly this division found its way into government.

Initially elections to the Stormont parliament were conducted on a proportional representation basis in which the state was divided up into multimember constituencies in which each elector had a single transferable vote. The specific purpose of this arrangement was to protect the interests of minorities.[18] In 1929, however, the Stormont parliament exercised its power under the Government of Ireland Act to replace the proportional representation system with single-member constituencies in which each elector had a single non-transferable vote.[19] The candidate who scored the highest votes in a constituency was elected to represent that constituency. This electoral model is biased in favour of larger parties whose support is concentrated in particular constituencies. In Northern Ireland the beneficiaries were the Unionist Party and the Nationalist Party. In a normal democracy this Westminster model of government should, over a period of time, result in a see-saw transfer of power between the two largest parties. A critical and distinctive feature of the Northern Irish 'democracy', however, was that elections never produced this see-sawing of power. Northern Ireland had been specifically created as a separate political entity in order to secure a permanent unionist majority over their nationalist opponents. It was hardly surprising, therefore, that elections always provided the unionists with a substantial majority in the Stormont parliament.[20] This in turn meant that they held the reins of power in government without a break for the fifty years of devolved government in Northern Ireland. Every prime minister and every government minister during that period were members of the Unionist Party. The Nationalist Party was consigned to the wilderness of a permanent opposition in which there was never any realistic hope of acceding to power.

Despite their impregnable position within the government of Northern Ireland and their support within the British government the unionists suffered from a deep-seated insecurity. At the southern and western borders of Northern Ireland lay an independent state which they perceived as Catholic and nationalist, and therefore as anti-Protestant and hostile to the continued existence of Northern Ireland as a separate entity. These fears were crystalised in provisions of the 1937 Irish constitution which recognised the special position of the Catholic church in the Irish state[21] and which asserted the jurisdiction of the Irish state over Northern Ireland.[22] The primal fear of unionists was that they would be swallowed up by the Irish state, which would set about suppressing their political and religious liberties, privileges and traditions.[23] They never fully trusted Britain to protect them fully against this perceived threat. Accordingly the defence of the borders and the very constitutional existence of Northern Ireland was a fundamental imperative for all unionist governments from 1922. The siege mentality always lurked close beneath the surface, ready to be summoned up at the merest whiff of a nationalist threat.

The greatest source of insecurity for the unionists, of course, was the perceived enemy within the borders of Northern Ireland itself. At least one third of the population was Catholic and the majority of these were perceived as nationalists who felt no political or cultural allegiance to Britain or Northern Ireland as a separate political entity. They desired reunification with their fellow citizens in Ireland, from whom they had been separated in 1921 by the creation of Northern Ireland. Successive unionist governments responded to the presence of the nationalist community by subjecting them to systematic discrimination in the local government electoral system, employment, public sector housing allocation and economic investment, and by the suppression of nationalist political and cultural expression.[24] Inevitably such tactics accentuated the nationalist perception that they were second-class citizens in a state which barely tolerated their presence. More significantly in the immediate context, they provided a focus for the civil rights campaign which culminated ultimately in Bloody Sunday. It is therefore necessary to dwell a little on the nature and extent of this discrimination and the suppression of the nationalist community.

The local government electoral system produced some of the most perfidious and brazen examples of unfair discrimination. The proportional representation system of elections which had been applied in Ireland was replaced in Northern Ireland by the single majority system in 1922.[25] To qualify for a vote in local government elections one had to reside as occupier of a dwelling house or occupy land with a rateable property to the value of at least £10. This discriminated against catholics not just because they were less likely than Protestants to have property of that value, but also because they were more likely to have two or more families living under the one roof. In addition voters either had to have been born in Northern Ireland or have resided in the United Kingdom for the previous seven years. The net effect was that Protestants enjoyed an even larger share of the local government vote than their proportion of the local population justified. Indeed unionist majorities on local councils accentuated this latter problem by allocating public housing in a discriminatory fashion to favour their own electoral prospects. Compounding the prejudice was the fact that business owners could qualify for multiple votes. A company occupying premises valued at more than £10 might nominate electors in respect of each £10 of that value, subject to a maximum of six electors per company. Since the business class in Northern Ireland was largely Protestant this meant that their share of the local government vote was artificially inflated even more. The net effect was that Protestants enjoyed an even larger share of the local government vote than their proportion of the population in certain local government areas justified. Not surprisingly the injustice inherent in this situation was a particular source of grievance for the burgeoning civil rights movement. Indeed it provided the inspiration for one of their most distinctive rallying cries 'One Man – One Vote'.

A full appreciation of the frustration which fuelled the civil rights movement in these days also requires some reference to the gerrymandering of the local government constituencies.[26] Given the political/religious demography of Northern Ireland it was only to be expected that some councils would be under nationalist control in spite of the bias inherent in the voting system. This was particularly true of Derry City itself. Although the city had a nationalist majority in terms of both the local population and registered voters, the local electoral wards were drawn in such a way that nationalists were always a minority in the local governing bodies. The message for nationalists was stark. Even in what they perceived to be their own city they were denied the civic pride and responsibility which was their due. Instead they had to accept being ruled by a minority of unionists. The maintenance of this artificial arrangement required a policy of herding Catholics into certain local electoral wards, resulting in the creation of nationalist ghettoes characterised by overcrowding, poor housing, high unemployment and poverty.

Derry also suffered more than its fair share of another major grievance of the civil rights movement, namely discrimination in economic investment. Throughout the fifty-year period of Stormont rule the Northern Ireland economy and general standard of living was much healthier than in the rest of Ireland. This was due, at least in part, to generous subsidies from the British exchequer. Unfortunately the British government did not exercise closer scrutiny over the discriminatory manner in which the Stormont government spent this money. Industry, commerce, agriculture and infrastructure in the east of the state, which was largely Protestant, benefited from heavy investment compared with the west, which was largely Catholic.[27] Even within these two regions there was a noticeable disparity in investment between Catholic and Protestant areas. Derry suffered from this discrimination in line with other Catholic areas in the west. However there was one decision which particularly affected Derry and had a very marked effect on the strength of the civil rights movement within the city and throughout Northern Ireland as a whole. This decision concerned the location of Northern Ireland's second university. Derry was the natural home for this development on educational, demographic, commercial, historical and cultural grounds. The unionist government, however, balked at the prospect of awarding such a prize to a city with a nationalist majority. In 1965 it took the fatal decision to locate the new university on a greenfield site outside Coleraine, a town with a very strong Protestant population and, relative to Derry, a very weak claim to a university. The folly of this decision was realised in the 1970s, when the British government was forced to choose between closing the university or merging it with the Ulster Polytechnic at Jordanstown, Magee College in Derry and the College of Art and Design in Belfast. The more immediate effect was the psychological blow inflicted on the nationalist community in Derry and throughout Northern Ireland. The message for them was very stark. If they did not resort to positive action they faced economic, political and cultural poverty at the hands of the unionist government.

Closely allied to discrimination in economic investment is the tortuous issue of discrimination in employment. Systematic anti-Catholic discrimination in employment practices in the public and private sectors has been a distinctive feature of Northern Ireland for much of its existence.[28] It was a primary target of the civil rights campaign and it persists as a running sore fuelling the community conflict today.[29] The fact that central and much of local government were permanently in the hands of the Unionist Party throughout the Stormont era created the opportunity for heavy bias in favour of Protestant employment in the public sector. The statistics and public pronouncements of senior unionist politicians leave no room for doubting the fact that this opportunity was used to the full. It must also be said, of course, that there were other contributing factors to the serious imbalance in public sector employment between the two communities. For example Catholics of a strong nationalist persuasion would not incline towards employment in the institutions of a state from which they were politically and culturally alienated. Moreover employment in certain key institutions of the state, such as the RUC, would be heavily discouraged by some nationalist communities.

Discrimination against Catholics in the private sector was made possible by the fact that the major companies were either owned or managed by Protestants. It was perhaps inevitable that they would follow the lead of their political leaders in employment practices. A contributing factor was the heavy concentration of commercial, industrial and agricultural investment in predominantly Protestant areas. That, of course, was itself a by-product of the anti-Catholic discrimination in economic investment. Since employment opportunities were to be found primarily in Protestant areas, it was only to be expected that Protestants would be overrepresented in the workforce. It must also be remembered that, in both the public and the private sector, discrimination operated not just at the point of recruitment. Catholics who did manage to surmount this hurdle generally found it more difficult to secure promotion than did their Protestant counterparts. This in turn helped perpetuate the discriminatory practices at the point of recruitment, as those making the key recruitment decisions were much more likely to be Protestant.

The final important example of anti-Catholic discrimination concerned public sector housing allocation.[30] Catholics, particularly in urban areas, were more heavily dependant on public sector housing than their Protestant counterparts. This imbalance was due partly to the fact that the former were less able to afford private housing and partly because they tended to have larger families than Protestants. Up until the early 1970s public housing provision and allocation were the responsibility of local government. The unionist councils displayed little enthusiasm in their response to the demand in Catholic areas. Indeed they regularly adopted a deliberate policy of allocating public sector housing to favour their own electoral prospects. The net result was that Catholic areas suffered from exceptionally long waiting lists for public housing allocation and a disproportionately large share of substandard housing in both the public and the private sector. In these areas it was quite normal for two families to share a small terraced house while one of them (sometimes both) waited for a suitable house to become available in the locality.

The living conditions in the overcrowded Catholic areas was not helped by some of the housing schemes provided by the councils. Concrete, multistorey flat complexes with no green spaces or public amenities, so redolent of the 1960s, were features of both Derry and Belfast, and to a lesser extent of some of the provincial towns throughout Northern Ireland. Most, but by no means all, of these disastrous developments were sited in Catholic areas, the most notorious being the Divis Flats and the Unity Flats of Belfast. Less well-known but no less depressing were the Rossville Flats in Derry, the scene of the Bloody Sunday shootings. The inherent problems attached to these developments were exacerbated in Catholic areas by the attendant problems of exceptionally high unemployment, severe economic and social deprivation and the preponderance of families with a large number of children.

Poor standards of building, materials and design only added to the misery of the residents. It was not long before this cocktail of problems produced a degree of alienation and resentment which was extreme even by the standards of nationalist areas in Northern Ireland.

Nationalist frustrations about the housing situation were fuelled by the well-founded perception that the unionist councils did not always act with complete propriety in the allocation of public housing. There were many examples of Catholic families on the waiting list being jumped by Protestant applicants who had not been in the queue for as long and whose needs were not as urgent as those of their Catholic counterparts. Some highly publicised cases provoked fury in Catholic quarters. Indeed one such housing case in Dungannon might be considered as the trigger which sparked the civil rights movement into life.[31] Two homeless Catholic families were squatting in two adjacent houses. One of the families left their house and the unionist council allocated it to a single 19-year-old Protestant woman who happened to be secretary to the local council's solicitor, who in turn happened to be a unionist parliamentary candidate. A few days after the new tenant moved in the council evicted the Catholic family squatting next door. A nationalist MP, Austin Currie,[32] occupied the house in protest, only to be evicted by a policeman who happened to be the brother of the 19-year-old Protestant woman who had been allocated the house next door. To complete the saga this same policeman was subsequently allocated the house by the council. The events attracted press and television coverage and led directly to a civil rights march from Coalisland to Dungannon in August 1968. Such discriminatory housing policies and practices were felt even more keenly in Derry City, where another civil rights march was organised in October 1968. This particular march was declared unlawful and the marchers were batoned off the streets with brutal severity by the unionist police force and its part-time B Special constabulary.[33] That set the pattern which was eventually to culminate in the Bloody Sunday civil rights march.

The cumulative effect of discrimination in the electoral system, employment, economic investment and public sector housing allocation was instrumental in providing the conditions for the growth of the civil rights movement in the 1960s. The circumstances in which the State of Northern Ireland was established were such that the nationalist minority was always going to be infected by a natural resentment and alienation. Unquestionably this predisposition was fuelled by the unionist monopoly on power and their cynical manipulation of the local government electoral system to ensure their hegemony even in nationalist areas. The birth and growth of the civil rights movement, however, would suggest that it was the anti-Catholic discrimination in economic and social matters that provided the catalyst for the nationalist resentment to express itself in the form of direct action on the streets.

Nowhere was this resentment and alienation felt more than in Derry. The gross deprivation inflicted on the city by way of high unemployment, substandard housing, neglected environment and discrimination in employment, housing allocation and economic investment was exceptional even by the standards of nationalist areas in Northern Ireland. To make matters worse Derry also provided the classic example of gerrymandering by the unionists. The social and psychological impact of these factors was accentuated partly by Derry's stark demography and partly by its status as the second city of Northern Ireland after Belfast. The River Foyle divides the city between the Protestant east bank and the Catholic west bank. Not only did this facilitate discrimination on sectarian grounds but it also created the conditions in which the effects of that discrimination would have been starkly visible. The fact that the city centre was located on the nationalist and more heavily populated west bank of the city did not result in any fairer, let alone more favourable, treatment for the nationalist areas of the city. The net effect was that the higher expectations of residents who lived in an important city and shared the west bank of the river with the city centre were dashed. The investment which they could legitimately have expected in terms of infrastructure, industry, housing, education, culture and environmental improvement was denied them. Not only were they worse off than their neighbours on the east bank but they were even worse off than the residents of other smaller provincial towns in Northern Ireland. The source of their problem was that they were a nationalist majority in a city in Northern Ireland.

Police and public order

Parliament, the courts and public protest were the three non-violent options which the nationalist community might have been expected to use to challenge their discriminatory treatment at the hands of the unionist government. Throughout the 50-year history of the Stormont government the parliamentary option always proved the weakest.[34] For much of that period the nationalist representatives were ambivalent about being seen to acknowledge the Stormont parliament by participating in its processes. This ambivalence, combined with internal squabbles, ensured that they were unable to present any sort of unified and coherent challenge to the unionist government. It was not until the late 1960s that they managed to construct a relatively disciplined and professional party in the form of the Social and Democratic Labour Party (SDLP). The leaders of this party were adept at using the parliamentary processes to attack the policies and actions of the unionist government with reasoned and articulate arguments. They were no more successful in achieving reform, however, than their fractious and demoralised predecessors. The inbuilt unionist majority in the parliament and the country meant that, irrespective of the justice and potency of the arguments being put, the government never felt itself under any real pressure to respond meaningfully to nationalist complaints. Parliament was not a realistic option for remedying nationalist grievances.

The courts in Northern Ireland have not fared much better as a source of redress for nationalist grievances. This, however, should not automatically be attributed to an inbuilt judicial bias in favour of unionists and against nationalists. It is true, of course, that appointments to the bench in Northern Ireland, particularly to the most senior positions, were heavily weighted in favour of judges with a pro-unionist background.[35] Nevertheless the reasons for the relative failure of the courts to offer a remedy for some of the patently unjust policies and actions of the unionist government go much deeper. Up until the 1960s it was not generally recognised in Britain or Northern Ireland that the law could be used to challenge policy decisions taken by government ministers or by the government as a whole. Since the United Kingdom lacked a written constitution the whole concept of judicial review of legislative and administrative action was largely alien to its courts and the lawyers practising in them. Over the last quarter of a century this whole scene has changed emphatically and a very large and sophisticated body of legal principles governing the judicial review of administrative action has been developed, and continues to be developed, at a furious pace by the UK courts. Increasingly the courts are being considered as a viable option to challenge government policies which discriminate unfairly against distinct sections of the population. In the 1960s, however, such a strategy would have been novel and unlikely to succeed in the absence of very special circumstances. It follows that the legal advice being proferred to nationalist representatives at this time would have been pessimistic about the chances of using the courts to seek a remedy for their grievances. The Dungannon housing case described earlier, for example, resulted in court action which failed to secure a remedy for the Catholic family involved. The judge, Justice Gibson, concluded that the evidence did not establish that the council allocated houses in a capricious way or from motives of discrimination. Inevitably this reinforced nationalist pessimism about the capacity of the courts to deliver justice. As will be seen later, however, the *coup de grâce* was reserved for a major case in which a judicial challenge to a ministerial prohibition on the formation of 'Republican Clubs' went all the way to the House of Lords only to be defeated. The courts were not a serious option for the redress of nationalist grievances.

The third option, public protest, inevitably created the potential for confrontation between the nationalist community and the forces of law and order on the streets. This path was taken by sections of the nationalist community from 1968. The result was perceived by many as the most heinous and inflammatory aspect of Stormont rule and the ultimate proof for the argument that Northern Ireland was a Protestant state for a Protestant people and that nationalists had no place there. To understand how the policing of public protests in Northern Ireland could have had that effect, it is necessary to look briefly at the police and public order structures and practices from the establishment of the state in 1921 up to the late 1960s. This is critical to an understanding not just of the nationalist anger which fuelled the civil rights movement in the late 1960s and early 1970s but also of the events which culminated in Bloody Sunday itself.

Special constabularies

Policing in Northern Ireland has always been an integral part of the unionist domination over the nationalist community in Northern Ireland. Prior to its establishment as a separate state, Northern Ireland was policed in common with the rest of Ireland, outside Dublin, by the Royal Irish Constabulary (RIC).[36] The unionists, however, were never fully content with this arrangement.[37] Despite the fact that the force had earned the designation 'Royal' and had played a leading role in combatting Irish nationalism, unionists were never fully confident that it could be relied upon to protect their political interests in the northern counties. The facts that the RIC was controlled from Dublin and that its membership was over 70 per cent Catholic were viewed with suspicion and unease by the unionists. Their sense of vulnerability deepened as the militant nationalist challenge to British rule in Ireland began to increase in scope and intensity throughout the country. They responded by launching a persistent and effective campaign for a separate police force for the northern counties.[38]

Unfortunately the unionist strategy depended very heavily on the threat that if loyal Protestants were not recruited, trained, equipped and paid to protect their communities against the enemies of the king there was a very real danger that their constitutional leaders would not be able to prevent them from taking matters into their own hands. The clear implication was that ruthless Protestant paramilitaries such as the Ulster Volunteer Force (UVF) would take up arms and launch a violent and unlawful counteroffensive against the IRA. Some prominent unionist leaders actually proceeded to organise and arm the UVF and other Protestant paramilitary groupings, with the passive and occasionally active support of senior figures in the British government and the RIC.

Ultimately the British government caved in to the unionist demands. Between October 1920 and the transfer of responsibility for law and order to the unionist government in December 1921, no fewer than three bodies of special constabularies were established in the northern counties. The A Special Constabulary was a body of full-time special constables deployed to assist the RIC. The B Special Constabulary was a body of part-timers. Its members had to report for duty one night per week and could be called out for duty at any time as the occasion required. They were deployed primarily to police their own areas, thereby releasing the regular police and the A Specials for duty in the nationalist troublespots. The C Special Constabulary was a body of part-timers who were called out for duty only as needed.

Given the circumstances of their establishment it was always likely that these special constabularies would be viewed by nationalists as nothing more than Protestant paramilitary organisations dressed up with the uniforms and authority of the state. This perception was confirmed in practice by the fact that many of their leading figures had been active in the recruitment and organisation of the UVF and other unlawful Protestant paramilitary groupings, which in turn supplied a substantial proportion of the rank and file of the constabularies. Needless to say the membership was almost exclusively Protestant. Inevitably they perceived their function as protecting the state and the unionist community against nationalist subversion. In practice this meant keeping the Catholic community under close scrutiny and stamping down hard on any show of dissent to the British state. This involved the manning of checkpoints in and around Catholic areas, and conducting arrest, detention and public order operations primarily against Catholics. Significantly, many of these operations were conducted by the part-time B Special Constabulary, whose members operated primarily within their own localities in order to take maximum advantage of their local knowledge. This meant that Catholics frequently found themselves challenged at night at checkpoints or in their own homes by individuals whom they knew during the day as their neighbours or locals. The fact that these neighbours and locals were armed, uniformed, paid and entrusted with special police powers made a powerful and critical contribution to the nationalist perception of the police as simply the Protestant community armed, organised and sanctioned by the state to protect and promote the unionist cause. By definition this meant that the police were hostile and alien to the Catholic nationalist community. Since the B Specials remained a potent force in local policing right up to 1970, they continued to reinforce the nationalist perception of the police for almost the full reign of the Stormont government.

The negative impact of the B Specials on nationalist attitudes towards policing and the legitimacy of the state was fuelled by their frequent resort to oppressive and brutal methods when dealing with Catholics.[39] Harassment and humiliation were regular experiences for Catholics at B Special checkpoints. Constabulary intervention to restore public order in response to the frequent outbreaks of rioting between Catholics and Protestants in urban areas was almost invariably directed at the Catholic protagonists to the benign exclusion of the Protestants. The heavy-handed tactics employed included the use of lethal force and reprisal shootings against Catholics. The fear and disdain in which these special constables were held by Catholics were accentuated by the fact that the Catholic victims of their excesses often knew their tormentors by name or as their neighbours. An additional factor was the abject failure of the authorities to prefer charges against Specials in even the most clearcut of cases. One of the worst examples has echoes of Bloody Sunday itself.

On 23 June 1922 a party of A Specials, accompanied by British soldiers, drove into the nationalist village of Cushendall in County Antrim and opened fire on a crowd of people in the street. They proceeded to drag three youths up an alleyway before shooting them. Later the Specials claimed that they had been ambushed and that the youths had been shot in the ensuing gun battle. The British government established a judicial inquiry into the incident. The inquiry sat in private. The judge concluded that in his opinion one of the youths had been dragged up the alleyway by the Specials and shot through the mouth; that the Specials had shot dead a second youth who had put up his hands when the Specials had come into the shop where he was hiding; and that the Specials had shot the third youth in the alleyway after taking him out of the kitchen behind the shop. The judge also found that one of the Specials had threatened to shoot a local member of the regular police who had intervened to prevent the Specials from shooting a brother of one of the victims. The British government sent a copy of the inquiry's report to the Stormont government, urging action to identify and prosecute the Specials involved. The Stormont government, however, charged the newly appointed head of the RUC and the chief crown solicitor to conduct a second inquiry into the matter. They concluded that the Specials had been fired upon from four different points in the village. In a move which has striking parallels with the Widgery Inquiry into Bloody Sunday they dismissed all of the evidence of the local inhabitants and relied mainly on the evidence of one of the British soldiers. The attorney general for Northern Ireland endorsed the findings of the second inquiry in terms which, as will be seen later, bear an uncanny resemblance to Lord Widgery's analysis of the evidence submitted to the Bloody Sunday Inquiry:

> It is impossible to believe that this British officer was either mistaken or stating what he knew to be false. To anyone with experience of Irish witnesses there is nothing extraordinary in a number of civilians from a place like Cushendall, dominated up to recently by the IRA, coming forward to testify falsely against the crown forces... any statements [about the Specials] by the people of Cushendall should be received with the greatest caution. I can come to no other conclusion than that the crown forces were attacked and that they were justified in the steps they took to repel and overcome the attacks made on them.

The lesson for nationalists was simple. The special constabularies and the RUC were effectively above the law when dealing with nationalists, even when they resorted to the use of excessive and deadly force.

The establishment of the RUC

Despite the fact that the Catholic community was totally alienated from the special constabularies the British government transferred responsibility for law and order in Northern Ireland to the new unionist government in December 1921. The unionist leaders lost no time in consolidating their control over the Specials. A new C1 Constabulary was established with an overtly military function. They were organised and trained for deployment on counterinsurgency duties on the newly created border between the two Irish states. The nature and extent of their armoury made them appear less of a police body and more like a unit of the territorial army.

The unionist government also set about replacing the remnants of the RIC with an indigenous regular police force, the current Royal Ulster Constabulary (RUC). Although the government had entered into a commitment to the effect that one third of the RUC should be Catholic, reflecting the proportion of Catholics in the population of Northern Ireland at that time, it failed to take any meaningful steps to achieve this goal. Indeed the whole thrust of its policy was designed to produce a Protestant police force fully committed to serving and upholding a unionist state. A substantial proportion of the members of the A Special Constabulary were recruited directly into the new force, as were many of the B Specials and C1 Specials. Inevitably this ensured that the RUC, in both image and substance, retained a close affinity with the special constabularies and their Protestant paramilitary predecessors. Even those recruits who were drawn from the RIC came mostly with a strong unionist pedigree. Given this background and the force's distinct Protestant and unionist ethos the RUC was never likely to attract Catholics of a nationalist persuasion. Those Catholics who were favourably disposed towards serving in the force also had to contend with intimidation and threats from the IRA. The combination of these factors resulted in an initial Catholic membership of only 10 per cent, increasing to a high of 19 per cent by 1924 before falling gradually to an average of 11 per cent in 1969.[40] As only a small minority of the Catholics who remained in the force would have been of a nationalist persuasion and the bulk of the Protestant membership would have been of a unionist persuasion, there could be no doubt that the RUC was an overwhelmingly unionist body from top to bottom. Lest there be any doubt one has only to look at the oath of office which had to be taken from each member[41] and the strength of Orange Lodge membership within the force.[42]

Apart from its religious composition the new RUC looked very much like the old RIC. The bottle-green military-style uniform was retained, as was the militaristic structure and demeanour. If anything the RUC was even more heavily armed than its predecessor. It also had a stronger claim to the status of a centralised state police force as it was the sole police force for the whole of Northern Ireland. Most critically, however, the masters of this new state police force were the democratically elected government of Northern Ireland, as opposed to the British officials based in the Irish Office at Dublin Castle. The chief constable and senior officers were appointed, and could be removed, by the minister for home affairs. The chief constable was answerable directly to the minister for his management of the force, and the force was financed almost exclusively from central government funds. When this degree of control by the permanently unionist government is combined with the overwhelmingly Protestant/unionist composition of the force, its military structure and demeanour and its regular deployment on antinationalist security and public order duties, it is easy to see how it could be perceived as a unionist paramilitary force rather than a civilian police service for all the community.

Very little changed in policing between April 1922, when the RUC was established, and 1970.[43] Admittedly the A and C Special Constabularies were gradually wound down, largely because they were effectively made redundant by the advent of the RUC. Critically, however, the B Specials were retained, ready to exert control over Catholics in their localities when the need arose. Their supporting role ensured that the RUC could be deployed on border security and antisubversion and public order duties anywhere in Northern Ireland at short notice. By the same token, however, their active presence right up to 1970 was a constant irritant for Catholics and a key factor in maintaining Catholic alienation from the police and the state in Northern Ireland. Indeed the abolition of the B Specials was high on the list of demands of the civil rights marchers in the late 1960s. Their wish was eventually granted as the B Specials were disbanded in the wake of the recommendations of the Hunt Committee on policing in Northern Ireland.[44] However they were disbanded in name and uniform only as many B Specials became members of the Ulster Defence Regiment (UDR), which was established in the wake of the Hunt recommendations. That regiment has now been absorbed into the regular British Army under the title of the Royal Irish Regiment (RIR). Throughout the 1970s and 1980s, however, it equalled the reputation of the B Specials as an anti-Catholic force. Several of its members have even been convicted of the vicious sectarian murder of Catholics.

Special powers

Unionist fears about the threat to the existence of the fledgling state in 1922 were reflected in the enactment of the Civil Authorities (Special Powers) Act (generally known as the Special Powers Act) in that year. It was designed as temporary emergency legislation which would expire automatically after twelve months. In practice the Stormont parliament renewed the act for another twelve months in 1923 and every year thereafter until 1928, when it was renewed for a continuous five-year period. In 1933 it was made permanent by a legislative provision to the effect that it would remain in force until parliament determined otherwise. Accordingly it remained in force until replaced by the Northern Ireland (Emergency Provisions) Act in 1973.

The nature of this legislation can be gauged from the comments of a South African minister for justice, who is reported to have said that he would swap all the emergency legislation at his disposal for just one clause in Northern Ireland's Special Powers Act.[45] Presumably the clause that he had in mind was Section 1 as it conferred executive powers on the minister for home affairs which were both breathtaking and unprecedented in their scope. It empowered the minister for home affairs 'to take all such steps and issue all such orders as may be necessary for preserving the peace and maintaining order'. Incredibly this unbridled power carried with it the power to delegate the very same power unconditionally to any officer of the RUC. It would be difficult to envisage a more determined attempt to confer absolute power on executive officers. Certainly it left little scope for the rule of law, as opposed to executive diktat. As if that was not enough, Section 1 also empowered the minister for home affairs to make regulations 'for making further provision for the preservation of the peace and the maintenance of order'. Once again the intent to confer absolute power on an executive authority is obvious. On this occasion the power conferred was of a legislative nature. Effectively the legislature delegated its full legislative power to the minister for home affairs to use as he deemed fit in order to preserve the peace and maintain order.

The Special Powers Act was used by the Stormont government primarily to crush any show of nationalist dissent.[46] Initially, 35 regulations were issued under it and appended to the Act itself at the time of its enactment. These conferred on the police sweeping powers of stop, arrest, detention, interrogation, entry, search and seizure.[47] Some of the powers extended to the army. In addition internment was introduced periodically in response to upsurges in IRA activity. Regulations issued under the Act also enabled the minister for home affairs to impose restriction orders on individuals, confining their movements to a specified locality.[48] The death penalty was expressly provided for certain firearms and explosive offences, while flogging was available for others. In short the Act, coupled with the existence of the special constabulary and the paramilitary RUC, effectively placed the Stormont government in a position where it enjoyed powers similar to those current in times of martial law.[49] The only feature missing was military courts.

The Stormont government exercised its powers and deployed its paramilitary forces ruthlessly to suppress any show of violence from the nationalist community.[50] Even in times of peace, however, the government regularly resorted to its powers under the Act to deprive nationalists of the equal enjoyment of the most basic civil liberties. Attempts by the nationalist community to organise meetings and marches celebrating their Irish culture were regularly banned on the executive order of the minister for home affairs. Even the most innocuous events, such as a St Patrick's Day parade, sometimes fell foul of unionist paranoia. Anything at all which involved a public demonstration of Irish nationalist identity was likely to be banned if it offended the sensitivities of the unionist community.[51] The existence of a threat to the peace or public order did not seem to be a prerequisite. Nor was this suppression of nationalist culture confined to public events. Publications which sought to promote an Irish nationalist consciousness and identity were regularly censored. Similarly organisations which sought to promote political and social philosophies which the unionist government equated with nationalism were banned. Indeed it was a decision by the minister for home affairs to ban one such organisation which not only demonstrated the sweeping nature of the minister's powers under the Special Powers Act, but also helped convince nationalists that they could find no redress for their plight in the courts.

In March 1967 the minister for home affairs made a regulation under the Special Powers Act which proscribed 'the organisations at the date of this regulation or at any time thereafter describing themselves as "republican clubs" or any like organisation howsoever described'. In March 1968 Mr McEldowney was charged with being a member of the Slaughtneil Republican Club. The local magistrates dismissed the charge on the ground that the club in question did not constitute a threat to peace and order in Northern Ireland. The Northern Ireland Court of Appeal reversed this decision on the ground that it was for the minister for home affairs alone to decide whether a particular organisation should be deemed unlawful. Significantly the lord chief justice gave a powerful dissent, arguing that the regulation as a whole was too vague and wide and as such could not be considered necessary for preserving the peace and maintaining order as required by the Special Powers Act. The case eventually went to the House of Lords, where the decision of the Court of Appeal was upheld by a majority of three to two.[52] The majority ruled that, unless there was proof of bad faith on the part of the minister, it was for him alone to decide on the subversive nature of any organisation. This decision provided the ultimate proof, if proof was needed, that the minister enjoyed virtually absolute executive power under the Special Powers Act, and that the courts either could not or would not prevent him from using that power to suppress nationalist culture and identity. Boyle, Hadden and Hillyard comment that 'It is significant that the forces of law and order in Derry and Belfast broke down within weeks of the final rejection of the claim in the House of Lords.'[53]

Civil rights marches and violence

Failure to secure redress in the courts in respect of the Dungannon Housing case and the Republican Clubs case persuaded nationalists in the late 1960s that they would have to take to the streets to air their grievances, in imitation of the civil rights movement in the United States and the student protests in France. Indeed the outcome of the court cases fuelled the nationalist perception that the very institutions of the state, including the courts, were intent on suppressing their rights and identity in favour of maintaining unionist hegemony in the state. Accordingly the Northern Ireland Civil Rights Association (NICRA) was formed in 1967 to campaign for an end to discrimination against Catholics in voting and electoral matters, housing allocation and the oppressive security policies being enforced against the nationalist community.[54] The abolition of the B Specials and the repeal of the Special Powers Act were also high on the agenda.

Of course the strategy of taking to the streets in the form of marches and protest demonstrations ran a high risk of confrontation with the state in the guise of the B Special Constabulary, the RUC, and the extensive powers available to the minister for home affairs under the Special Powers Act. In addition both the police and the minister for home affairs had at their disposal a range of powers under public order legislation to control marches and street demonstrations. The primary provisions, apart from those in the Special Powers Act, were to be found in the Public Order Act (Northern Ireland) 1951. This measure enabled any police officer to impose whatever conditions on the route and conduct of a march as he deemed necessary for the preservation of public order.[55] The act also empowered the minister for home affairs to make an order prohibiting all, or any class of, public processions or meeting in any place for a period not exceeding three months.[56] Amendments to the act in 1970 enabled the minister to permit a march while at the same time banning any other march from taking place at the same time and place.[57] This power was aimed at dealing with the common practice of rival groups organising counterdemonstrations. Indeed it might have been exercised with respect to the

Bloody Sunday march had unionists not cancelled a counterdemonstration they had planned for Guildhall Square.

The first significant march organised by NICRA was from Coalisland to Dungannon in August 1968. This march passed off without significant incident, although it was rerouted in part by the police in the face of a counterdemonstration organised by unionists.[58] Its sequel in Derry on 5 October was an entirely different matter.[59] The plan was for the march to assemble on the Protestant east side of the river before marching across the bridge to the Catholic west side, ending in the Diamond within the walled section of the city. Counterdemonstrations overlapping in both time and place were planned by unionist bodies. The minister for home affairs responded by banning all marches from the east side of the city and within the city's walls. The organisers' attempts to proceed in defiance of the ban were thwarted by what can only be described as the brutal and indiscriminate use of batons and water cannon by the police. The message to NICRA and Catholics generally was very clear. The northern state would not tolerate public demonstrations of their grievances against the state and would resort to banning orders and brutal force to suppress them. On this occasion, however, the police excesses were captured on television and broadcast around the world. Within Northern Ireland they had an immediate inflammatory effect on nationalist and Catholic public opinion, leading inevitably to further and larger civil rights demonstrations.

The violent suppression of the Derry march on 5 October propelled Northern Ireland into a chain of events which would culminate in widespread sectarian violence and ultimately war between the IRA and the state. Further marches and demonstrations were held in Belfast and Derry throughout October and November. For the most part these passed off peacefully despite the use of limited banning and rerouting orders and the organisation of counterdemonstrations.[60] In Dungannon, however, public meetings in November and December were attacked by unionist mobs while the police adopted a relatively benign and passive stance. Indeed some members of the B Specials actually took part in the attacks.[61] Similarly in Armagh a civil rights march in November was prevented from proceeding owing to ineffective action by the police in controlling the actions of a large mob of unionists armed with a variety of weapons and acting under the leadership of the Reverend Ian Paisley.[62] A march from Belfast to Derry on 3–5 January was ambushed at several points by unionist mobs, most particularly at Burntollet Bridge, inflicting serious injuries on many of the marchers.[63] Once again the police were criticised for not affording sufficient protection to the marchers, and once again members of the B Specials actually took part in the attacks.[64] The media coverage of the events on this particular march had the major effect of raising the temperature within the Catholic community. The consequences were felt in Newry on 11 January, when a civil rights march was rerouted by the police in response to a counterdemonstration being planned by unionists.[65] In the event both the rerouting and the march organisation were bungled and serious violence broke out between some of the marchers and the police. The violence spread and continued sporadically that night in parts of Newry. In April the focus switched back to Derry. Rioting broke out between rival groups on 19 April after the minister had banned a civil rights march. The RUC drove the nationalist side back into the Bogside with the customary brutal and excessive force. Indeed in one incident a group of RUC men broke into a house in William Street and brutally beat the owner, Samuel Devenny, in front of his family.[66] He died three months later.[67] Consequential protests organised in Belfast and elsewhere mostly ended in violence between the protesters on the one hand and the police and unionist counterdemonstrators on the other.

The actions of the police in dealing with the public order situations associated with the civil rights marches and counterdemonstrations appeared to be heavily biased in favour of the unionists. This impression was compounded by the standard police actions in dealing with sectarian riots which were not uncommon during this period. Almost invariably the police would intervene between the rival factions with their face towards the nationalist rioters and their backs towards the unionist rioters. Not only did this mean that the nationalists were at the receiving end of police baton charges, water cannon and so on, but it also conveyed the impression that the police were taking the part of the unionist rioters. In other words it reinforced the nationalist perception that the police were an integral part of the hostile unionist establishment. This perception was already firmly established in Derry as a result of the events of October, January and April. Nevertheless it was to be strengthened even further by the events of the summer, which were to propel Northern Ireland into a state of civil war and result in the deployment of the British Army.[68]

The traditional orange parades on 12 July sparked off riots between the residents of the Bogside and the RUC. These lasted three days, in the course of which the RUC shot and wounded two civilians. Nevertheless this was merely a prelude to the violence that took place during the Apprentice Boys parade in Derry on 12 August.[69] On this occasion, however, the residents were prepared for the standard RUC tactic of driving them back into the Bogside with batons and bullets. Barricades were erected and manned by rioters using stones and petrol bombs. Over the next few days the RUC attempted unsuccessfully to breach the barricades with armoured cars and CS gas. The B Specials were deployed but to no avail. Meanwhile in other centres throughout Northern Ireland protest demonstrations were held in sympathy with the Bogsiders. These almost inevitably ended in violence, stretching the RUC and the B Specials to the limit. The rioting in Belfast was the most serious. Unionist mobs, accompanied by armed B Specials, surged into nationalist areas, attacking and burning Catholic homes. Whole streets were burned out. The RUC deployed Shorland armoured cars fitted with Browning heavy machine guns and fired into the Catholic Divis Flats, killing a nine-year-old boy and a British soldier who was home on leave. Catholics who were forced out of their homes in mixed areas retreated into the relative safety of the already overcrowded nationalist ghettoes in Belfast. Barricades were erected around these areas and the battle lines were firmly drawn between the nationalist community and the unionist state. As the RUC increasingly lost control in some parts of the state the British Army was mobilised in the worst trouble spots.[70]

Initially the army was welcomed by many in the beleaguered nationalist communities.[71] Despite the Stormont government's irrational belief that NICRA was a front for the IRA, the reality was that the official IRA was dormant in the late 1960s.[72] This was reflected by the failure of that organisation to protect the nationalist communities against the violent attacks by unionist mobs, the B Specials and the RUC. The British Army, therefore, was welcomed by the nationalist community as a protection against the state. The honeymoon period, however, was short-lived. Being deployed primarily in nationalist areas it was not long before the army was performing much the same role as the RUC, and seeking to root out an IRA that initially did not exist.[73] This policy was accompanied by the use of increasingly heavy-handed policing tactics by soldiers who were not trained in the art of civil policing, an escalating number of house searches for arms and even curfews in nationalist areas. These practices added to the potential for violence in nationalist areas and it was not long before soldiers found themselves on the front line, facing petrol bombs, stones, burning barricades and ultimately bullets. The army, like the RUC before it, responded in kind and the violence spiralled out of control once more.

This process was fuelled by the establishment of the Provisional IRA at the end of 1969.[74] The primary motivation for their establishment was to ensure that nationalist areas were never again left unprotected in the face of attack from unionist mobs and the police. As relations between the nationalist community and the British Army deteriorated throughout 1970, however, the IRA was increasingly drawn into armed conflict with the soldiers. A key event in this development was the curfew imposed by the GOC on the nationalist Falls Road area in July 1970.[75] This curfew lasted 35 hours and was the occasion for the indiscriminate searching of dwellings and persons throughout the area. In many cases the insides of houses were literally ripped apart by soldiers looking for arms. The courts upheld the legality of these actions in the prosecution of those who refused to obey army instructions to stay indoors, and in civil actions for damages for wrongful arrest. The searches produced a haul of 30 rifles, 24 shotguns and 52 pistols. The significance of these finds, however, was dwarfed by the effect that the whole operation had on nationalist alienation from the security forces and the growth of the IRA. These consequences were fuelled by the insensitive action of the security forces in taking Stormont ministers on a high-profile tour of the subjugated streets.

By the spring of 1971 the IRA tactics had extended to the bombing of commercial and strategic targets as well as armed offensives against the security forces.[76] Their objective at this point was to force the collapse of the Stormont government and to wring concessions for nationalists from the British government. The Stormont government responded to the escalating violence with ever tougher security measures, culminating in the introduction of internment on 8 August 1971.[77] In the initial operation hundreds of nationalists were arrested, most of whom had absolutely no connection whatsoever with violence. That fateful decision only had the effect of pouring petrol on the flames. In the succeeding days and weeks the violence spiralled out of control.[78] Young men and women queued up to join the IRA and even moderate Catholics generally withdrew their cooperation from the state. The intensity of the nationalist alienation increased as information began to leak out about the interrogation methods which were being used on many of those arrested. These involved covering the suspect's head with a black hood for a long period, exposing him to continuous and monotonous noise of a kind calculated to make any form of communication impossible, making him stand against a wall with legs apart and hands raised for periods of six or seven hours at a time, and depriving him of food and sleep. These methods, which came to be known as the five techniques, were designed to disorientate those being questioned and so to break their resistance.[79] Not only did they have a dramatic effect in galvanising the broad nationalist community they also resulted in the United Kingdom being found guilty of inhuman and degrading treatment by the European Court of Human Rights.[80]

Not surprisingly these developments provoked another phase of street protests. NICRA, which had been relatively quiescent since the army was first deployed in August 1969, began to organise civil rights and anti-internment marches and demonstrations.[81] It was one of these marches that was the occasion for the Bloody Sunday shootings.

Security policy and the law, 1970–72

One of the most critical and distinctive features of security policy in the late 1960s and early 1970s was the extent to which fundamental rights and freedoms, including the right to life, were subordinated to the operational demands of the police and the army. It has already been seen that the legislative intention behind the Special Powers Act was to delegate to the executive and the security forces maximum power to curb the basic freedoms of the individual. Equally significant, and perhaps unexpected, is the extent to which the judiciary were prepared to acquiesce in the excessive use and abuse of these powers by the security forces and their political masters. Indeed there can be little doubt that the combined actions and, on occasion, inaction of the legislature, the executive and the judiciary during this period sent a strong signal to the security forces that they would not be constrained by the law in their efforts to suppress rioting and deal with the perceived IRA threat. From this perspective the security forces were implicitly encouraged to resort to ever tougher and more oppressive measures until eventually they responded to a public order situation with the use of lethal force. Even then the executive and judicial institutions of the state conspired to clear them of wrongdoing.

To illustrate the extent to which the law was used as a pliable tool of security policy in the period leading up to Bloody Sunday it is necessary to consider some of the more significant police, army and executive powers in a little more detail. Before doing so, however, it would be as well to clarify the essential difference between soldiers and police officers in terms of legal status and function.

Status of the police and the army

Superficially the RUC bears all the hallmarks of a paramilitary body. Unlike British police forces it has always been organised, trained and equipped to function as a paramilitary police force. For most of the years of its existence it has been deployed primarily to quell by force any show of dissent to the authority of the state. Up until 1970 its rank structure, training and internal management systems were based primarily on a centralised military model. Its bases were referred to as police barracks, as opposed to police stations or police offices. Indeed for the past 30 years most of them, particularly those in or near nationalist areas, have looked more like heavily fortified military bases than police stations. Its members have always been armed, apart from a short period in 1970, and the force has always been well equipped with military hardware in the shape of machine guns and armoured landrovers. Nevertheless, all the members of the RUC have an essential attribute which they share in common with their British counterparts, and which distinguishes them from soldiers. They occupy the office of constable. Just like the members of British constabularies the RUC enjoy all of the peace-keeping powers, duties and privileges associated with the ancient office of constable. They are ministerial peace officers at common law. As such each member of the RUC is under a legal duty to keep the peace and preserve public order and is entrusted with a wide range of common law and statutory powers which can be used for this purpose.[82] The constitutional responsibility for enforcing the law, keeping the peace and preserving public order resides in the chief constable as the head of the force.

In contrast to constables, soldiers are not vested with any distinct peacekeeping powers, duties or privileges at common law by virtue of their status as soldiers.[83] In such matters they have exactly the same status as members of the public. Even when the army is called into active service in aid of the civil power, individual soldiers do not automatically acquire a body of powers, duties or privileges equivalent to those pertaining to constables. Insofar as they are called upon to restore the peace, maintain public order or otherwise assist in policing functions they must rely on the powers of the ordinary citizen, unless of course legislation is specifically enacted to confer special powers upon them. From the time they were deployed in Northern Ireland in 1969 the soldiers were vested with extensive powers of arrest, detention, stop and search. Initially some of these powers were shared in common with the members of the RUC, having been conferred pursuant to the Special Powers Act. With the enactment of the Northern Ireland (Emergency Provisions) Act 1973, however, separate provision was made for each.

As will be seen later, these statutory provisions conferred sweeping powers on the soldiers to intrude summarily on the individual's rights to liberty, bodily integrity and property. The powers in question were stretched to the limit and beyond by the army. While the courts occasionally made some effort to impose restraint, their interventions were wholly inadequate to impose any meaningful restrictions on the soldiers' freedom of action. Indeed it would appear that there was at least some judicial support for the proposition that the army's coercive powers were not limited to those conferred by legislation. For example the legality of the curfew imposed by the army in the Lower Falls area in 1970 was tested in a criminal prosecution of a person who refused to obey the curfew restrictions imposed by the army commander. The magistrate who heard the case ruled that the commander was entitled at common law to make what orders were necessary for the preservation of the peace in an emergency situation.[84] This supposedly was the position even in the absence of a declaration of military law. Although this decision is highly suspect, the fact that it went unchallenged suggested a widespread opinion that the army enjoyed whatever powers it considered necessary to restore and maintain public order in the circumstances that prevailed in Northern Ireland. This in turn was reflected in the security decisions taken by army commanders and the actions of individual soldiers on the ground.

Technically, in the absence of a declaration of military law the army is deployed in the aid of the civil authority.[85] In the case of Northern Ireland, however, that did not mean that the army was under the control of the minister for home affairs and the RUC. Indeed overall responsibility for security was given to the general officer commanding (GOC) in Northern Ireland when the army was deployed there in 1969.[86] Although it was later decided that the GOC should consult with the police through a security committee,[87] primary responsibility for security was not restored to the police until the mid 1970s. Nevertheless the minister for home affairs in the Stormont government purported to exercise his power under the Special Powers Act to confer security powers on soldiers. This raised the issue of whether such action was beyond his power, given that the legislative powers transferred to the Stormont parliament by the Government of Ireland Act 1920 did not extend to a power to legislate for the British armed forces. The point proved critical in the prosecution of five individuals[88] for their refusal to obey the order of an army officer.[89]

The individuals were engaged in a public sit-down protest against the behaviour of the British Army in Derry when the officer in question ordered them to move on. The officer was acting under Regulation 38, which had been issued by the minister for home affairs pursuant to the

Special Powers Act. This regulation purported to confer powers on British soldiers (and police officers) to disperse an assembly of three or more persons when they suspected that it might lead to a breach of the peace or serious public disorder or may make undue demands upon the police or army. The accused were convicted in summary proceedings by the local Magistrates' Court. However their convictions were overturned on appeal by the Northern Irish High Court, which ruled that in purporting to confer powers on the British Army the regulation went beyond the powers of the Northern Irish parliament and the minister for home affairs under the Government of Ireland Act 1920. Inevitably this decision raised major doubts about everything done by British soldiers purporting to exercise powers conferred upon them by regulations issued pursuant to the Special Powers Act. All of the arrests, detentions, searches, seizures and stops effected under the regulations were potentially unlawful. The practical significance of this decision, however, was short-lived. Within a matter of hours of it being handed down the Westminster parliament had rushed through legislation conferring retrospective validity on any actions taken by soldiers before the passing of the act which would otherwise have been invalid.[90] Moreover the act also authorised the Northern Irish parliament to legislate in respect of the British armed forces insofar as that was necessary for the maintenance of peace and order in Northern Ireland. This ensured that the Northern Irish government could continue to confer upon the army the sweeping discretionary powers over the liberty of the individual that from time to time it had traditionally conferred upon members of the RUC in response to nationalist unrest. The clear message being conveyed to both the police and the army was that even judicial restrictions on their freedom of action would be overridden swiftly by executive and/or legislative measures when necessary.

Police and army powers

The regulations issued by the minister for home affairs conferred sweeping powers of arrest on the police and soldiers. Regulation 10, for example, empowered all officers of the RUC, for the preservation of peace and maintenance of order, to authorise the arrest and detention of individuals for anything up to 48 hours. Officers could authorise a constable or a soldier to effect such an arrest. Incredibly it was not necessary for either the authorising officer or the constable or soldier effecting the arrest to suspect the individual arrested of any offence. It was quite sufficient that the authorising officer wanted to detain the individual for interrogation. It would therefore be quite lawful for officers to arrest individuals for the purpose of questioning them about their political views, their attitude towards the state, what they knew about other persons living in their area or whatever. The scope of the power was neatly summed up by Justice McGonigal (as he then was) in *In re McElduff* when he said that:

> the person arrested need not have committed any crime or offence nor even be suspected, reasonably or otherwise, of being about to commit one. It is sufficient that he is wanted for interrogation and for that reason, and for that reason alone, under this regulation he may be deprived of his liberty and held in custody for a period of not more than 48 hours.[91]

An arrest power of this nature is a total negation of the most fundamental principles that lie at the heart of the rule of law. The very notion that an officer of state could exercise such unrestricted power of arrest over citizens runs contrary to the concept of a state based on law. Nevertheless this power was regularly used in the early 1970s, particularly for the purpose of vetting individuals for an executive internment or detention order. Most of the actual arrests were effected by soldiers and the vast majority of those arrested were nationalists.

Regulation 10 effectively provided the police and army with all the legal cover they required to exercise almost total control over the liberty of the individual. Nevertheless it was not the only power of arrest conferred by the regulations issued pursuant to the Special Powers Act. Regulation 11(1) empowered constables or soldiers to arrest anyone whom they suspected of acting or being about to act in a manner prejudicial to the preservation of peace or the maintenance of order. Although exercise of this power was predicated on prior suspicion, it imposed only the mildest of constraints on the freedom of a constable or soldier to take an individual into custody. The suspicion did not have to relate to any specific action or offence on the part of the person arrested. Nor did it have to be based on reasonable grounds. It was quite sufficient that the constable or soldier honestly suspected that the person arrested was a threat to the preservation of peace or the maintenance of order. It did not matter that a reasonable person would not have formed a similar suspicion. Justice McGonigal, in *In re McElduff*, explained the nature of the suspicion required when he said that the power:

> deals only with a suspicion of certain things and clearly envisages a case where, although there are grounds for suspicion, there is no

proof of any act and, therefore, the arrest is not for the purpose of charge and trial but solely for detention in custody, what might be described as preventive detention.[92]

It follows, for example, that if constables or soldiers believed that a civil rights organisation was nothing more than a conspiracy to foment public disorder with a view to destabilising the state, it would be perfectly lawful for them to arrest under Regulation 11(1) anyone whom they believed to be an active member of that organisation. The practical significance of this illustration lies in the fact that in the late 1960s and early 1970s many in the unionist community, including the RUC and the government itself, perceived NICRA as nothing more than a front for a republican conspiracy to overthrow the state. It should come as no surprise, therefore, that many members of NICRA fell victim to this power of arrest.

Although the power of arrest under Regulation 11(1) was not as broad as that available under Regulation 10 it was nevertheless clearly incompatible with the most basic concepts of legality in a liberal democracy. Incredibly, however, the sheer scope of the power was not its most heinous feature from a civil liberties perspective. That accolade must be reserved for the power of detention that was automatically triggered by an arrest under Regulation 11(1). Anyone arrested under this power could be indefinitely detained without charge. Indeed the object of such an arrest was normally to vet the person arrested for an executive detention order under Regulation 11(2) and ultimately an internment order under Regulation 12. Needless to say the concept of an arrest power which permits the detention of a person without charge and for an unlimited period merely on the subjective suspicion that he or she poses a threat to public order is a total negation of the law and the hallmark of a totalitarian state which pays scant regard to the basic principles of legality. One of the basic functions of the law is to protect individuals against attempts by government officials to deprive them arbitrarily of their fundamental right to liberty. The mere fact that the government secures the enactment of legislation which appears to empower agents of the state to act in this manner does not mean that the powers conferred are thereby cloaked with the authority of law in the sense that that term is properly understood in a liberal democracy.

The regulations issued by the minister for home affairs pursuant to the Special Powers Act also extended to control of the streets. Soldiers and members of the RUC were conferred with powers to stop persons and vehicles.[93] Persons stopped under these powers could be frisk-searched and questioned about their identity and movements. Vehicles stopped could be searched and the occupants subjected to the same search and question as if they had been stopped on the street. Once again the power of stop and question did not depend on any requirement of prior suspicion, while the search powers were available on the basis of a suspicion that the person concerned was carrying any article or document which was prejudicial to the preservation of the peace or maintenance of order. In effect, individual constables or soldiers could exercise these powers on a case-by-case basis as they thought fit. These powers were used regularly in nationalist areas to check the identity and movements of individuals on the street. Nor did the sanctity of the home offer any protection. Both police and soldiers were vested with powers of entry, search and seizure, which could be exercised on the basis of a suspicion that the dwelling in question were being used for a purpose prejudicial to the preservation of peace or the maintenance of order.[94] These powers were used in the extensive searching of homes in planned operations which were such a distinctive feature of nationalist housing estates in urban areas in the early 1970s. Together with the powers to stop, question and search on the street these powers were a vital element of military control in nationalist areas, particularly when allied with resort to the curfew.[95]

The cumulative effect of these powers, coupled with their sweeping scope, created an environment in which it was considered useless to question anything that the police or army did by way of curtailing or denying the fundamental rights and freedoms of individuals. When confronted with a soldier who demanded evidence of identity, submission to a frisk search, entry and search of a vehicle or dwelling or even the arrest and detention of the individual concerned it seemed futile even to question whether the soldier was acting pursuant to a legal power. It was simply assumed that there was an obligation to comply. In such an environment the concept of the individual police officer or soldier being subject to the law was replaced by an understanding that he or she was the law. Inevitably this perception was shared as much by soldiers or police officers as it was by the people they controlled.

It did not follow that the exercise of the powers in question was totally immune to judicial scrutiny. In *In re McElduff*,[96] for example, the applicant was initially arrested by a soldier under Regulation 10 and taken into custody. He was then arrested by a police officer under Regulation 11(1) as a preliminary to executive detention under Regulation 11(2). The police officer did not give the applicant any reasons for the arrest, nor did he specify that he was effecting the arrest under Regulation 11(1) as opposed to Regulation 10 (or indeed Section 7 of the Act, which conferred an additional power of arrest). The applicant sought to challenge the legality of his arrest and detention by way of an application for *habeas corpus* on the ground, *inter alia*, that the arresting officer failed to comply with the common law requirement to inform the person arrested of the reason for his arrest.[97] The Northern Irish High Court ruled that when an arrest was being effected under a statutory power this requirement would generally be satisfied if the arresting officer informed the person concerned that he or she was being arrested under that statutory provision. A mere reference to the Act, however, would not normally be sufficient if it conferred more than one power of arrest, each with different requirements and consequences. It would be necessary to inform those arrested of the particular provision being applied in their case. Only then would they be able to make an informed assessment of their position. Since the Special Powers Act conferred more than one power of arrest, each of which differed in its requirements and consequences, it followed that it was not sufficient to tell those arrested that they were being arrested under the Special Powers Act. The actual provision, in this case Regulation 11(1), would have to be identified. Moreover, since arrest under Regulation 11(1) was predicated on the existence of a suspicion, those concerned would have to be told the basic reason for the arrest. As these requirements were not satisfied in the applicant's case, the court ruled his arrest unlawful and ordered his release.

Despite this apparent willingness of the courts to impose curbs on the exercise of these draconian powers when the opportunity presented itself, the government always moved swiftly to counter any consequential restriction on the freedom of the RUC and the army. The decision in *In re McElduff*, for example, meant that a substantial number of those arrested in the initial internment operation had been arrested and detained unlawfully. Nevertheless it did not result in the release of a single internee.[98] The authorities simply rearrested all concerned, taking care in each case to inform each individual that he or she was being arrested under Regulation 11(1), issued pursuant to the Special Powers Act. The applicant in *In re McElduff*, for example, was released from custody in Belfast Prison only to be formally rearrested at the door of the prison and taken back into custody. The sweeping powers available to the security forces under the Special Powers Act, coupled with the absence of an entrenched bill of rights in Northern Irish law, meant that such action was perfectly lawful. The only remedy available was an action for damages for the period of detention between the initial unlawful arrest and the subsequent lawful arrest.[99]

Interrogation and the admissibility of confessions

The impotence of the law to curb the excesses of the police and the army even extended to the brutal interrogation practices employed against many of those arrested and detained under the Special Powers Act in the early 1970s. Once again, however, the problem did not stem from any inadequacy in the law or the willingness of the judiciary to enforce it; quite the contrary. When the first charges were preferred on the basis of confessions obtained in the interrogation centres the courts did not shrink from applying the established common law rules on the admissibility of confessions.[100] At common law a confession was admissible in evidence against the person who made it only if the prosecution could prove that it was voluntary. In this context, voluntary means that it was not obtained by a fear of prejudice or hope of advantage exercised or held out by a person in authority or by oppression. Clearly, under this definition, if a police officer or soldier used force to extract a confession from a suspect in custody the confession would not be admissible in evidence against the suspect in subsequent criminal proceedings. Similarly a confession would be inadmissible if made as a result of threats against the suspect by his or her interrogators or otherwise as a result of fear instilled in him or her by the interrogators. It follows that confessions obtained by the use of the five techniques described earlier would not have been admissible against the victims in any criminal prosecution. The Northern Irish courts, however, went further and ruled inadmissible confessions obtained from suspects in certain circumstances which fell short of the use of violence, ill-treatment or threats.

In *R v Flynn & Leonard*,[101] for example, the two accused had been arrested under special police powers and interrogated by the RUC Special Branch at the Hollywood Detention Centre. Both confessed to offences for which they were subsequently tried before the Belfast City Commission (equivalent of the Crown Court). Although neither claimed that they had been physically ill-treated, both gave evidence that they had confessed out of fear of what might have happened to them in the interrogation centre. Lord Chief Justice McDermott excluded the confessions on the basis that they were not voluntary because of the oppressive circumstances in which they had been obtained. He explained this decision partly on the ground that 'the interrogation set-up was officially organised and operated in order to obtain information from persons who would otherwise have been less willing to give it'. The immediate effect of this decision was that the prosecution against both accused failed. Of greater import, perhaps, were the implications it had for the policy of using the special powers of arrest, detention and interrogation and for the regimes in the special interrogation centres to extract confessions which could be used to prosecute the individuals concerned in the ordinary courts. Ultimately, as will be seen later, the obstacle posed by the common law rules on the admissibility of confessions was overcome by the establishment of special no-jury courts, in which the common law voluntariness principle governing the admissibility of confessions was replaced by a statutory rule based on torture or inhuman and degrading treatment. In the interim the government and the security forces simply relied on internment without trial to detain those suspects against whom it had failed to secure convictions in the courts. Once again the fruits of a successful legal challenge to security abuses were neutralised by a combination of executive and legislative action. The law was not allowed to stand in the way of the direct and immediate application of security policy.

The interrogation of persons arrested under special police and army powers was not aimed solely at obtaining confessions which might be used in subsequent prosecutions. Intelligence gathering was probably the more immediate objective in most cases. This was particularly true with respect to the use of the 'five techniques' described earlier. Even if confessions were forthcoming in such cases they would have been excluded by the courts under the common law rules applicable at that time. As it happens, there is no record of the courts being presented with the opportunity to rule on the admissibility of confessions obtained by such techniques. Presumably this can be explained by a conscious decision on the part of the authorities not to expose the interrogation practices to the glare of public scrutiny when the outcome was virtually a foregone conclusion. That, however, does not explain why those police officers who resorted to the use of the five techniques were never prosecuted. It is inconceivable that prosecutions would not have been justified, at least in some of the cases, for offences such as assault, assault occasioning actual bodily harm and causing grievous bodily harm. The failure of the authorities to launch such prosecutions supports the argument that the security forces were permitted to operate above the law in their attempts to suppress nationalist violence against the state.

The government's ambivalence towards the brutal interrogation methods employed by the security forces was reflected in the fact that it actually set up an inquiry to consider whether interrogation by the use of the five techniques should be permitted to continue.[102] This Committee of Inquiry, under the chairmanship of Lord Parker, a senior law lord, was set up in the wake of the Compton Committee of Inquiry, which had found that the five techniques had been employed by the RUC in the interrogation of those arrested under their special powers.[103] By setting up the Parker Committee the government was clearly intimating that it did not accept that the use of such methods was patently unlawful in the circumstances. The committee acknowledged in its report that some of the practices described in the Compton Report might be unlawful. Incredibly, however, a majority of the committee members went on to recommend that the government should take the necessary measures to provide legal protection for members of the security forces engaged in the use of such methods. In their opinion the situation facing the security forces and the state was such that tough interrogation techniques were necessary. This is a stark illustration of the extent to which the security forces were being encouraged by those in high judicial and political office to believe that they were effectively beyond the reach of the law. If necessary, the law would be rewritten to suit their operational requirements. Equally, however, it must be said that a minority of the committee members, under the leadership of Lord Gardiner, another senior law lord, were of the view that the interrogation techniques were not only unlawful under domestic and international law but also could not be justified in the circumstances and were counterproductive. Eventually the British government accepted the minority view and the use of the five techniques was abandoned. Although many of those who had been at the receiving end of the five techniques subsequently received compensation, no prosecution was ever brought against any RUC officer involved.

The extent to which the security forces and the British government had acted beyond the law in using and permitting the use of such methods was highlighted by the European Court of Human Rights in a case brought by Ireland against the United Kingdom.[104] Ireland claimed that by permitting the interrogation practices, including the five techniques, employed in the RUC interrogation centres the United Kingdom was in breach of the prohibition on the use of torture or inhuman and degrading treatment, as laid down in Article 3 of the European Convention for the Protection of Human Rights and Fundamental Freedoms. The European Commission on Human Rights found that the interrogation practices amounted to torture. The European Court of Human Rights agreed that the United Kingdom was in breach of Article 3 but that the methods amounted to inhuman and degrading treatment and fell short of torture. Although this decision was not handed down until 1977, long after the use of the five techniques had been abandoned, it served as a potent reminder of the fact that no police officer had ever been brought to justice for using or permitting the use of such barbaric methods in the interrogation centres.

Internment

The backdrop to the use of the brutal interrogation methods and the related powers of arrest and detention was, of course, internment. No other feature of the special powers regime signified the predominance of executive expediency over the requirements of due process and the law more than internment without trial. The internment procedure formally subordinated the liberty of the individual to the absolute discretion of executive authority. In general it began with the arrest of an individual under regulation 11(1), which permitted arrest on the basis of a subjective suspicion that the individual had acted, was acting or was about to act in a manner prejudicial to the preservation of peace or maintenance of order. Anyone arrested under this power could be detained indefinitely. In practice they were either released shortly after arrest or served with an executive detention order under regulation 11(2). There was no judicial hearing or trial prior to an order being served. The individual was simply imprisoned on the diktat of the executive authority. The minister for home affairs could order the continued detention or internment of the individual under Regulation 12 if this appeared to be necessary for preserving the peace and maintaining order. The ultimate release of the individual was also in the hands of the minister for home affairs. Although the key decisions in the procedure rested with the minister, the Special Powers Act did make provision for the appointment of an advisory committee presided over by a senior judicial officer. The function of this committee was to review the cases in which the minister had made an internment order. While it could make a recommendation for release in any individual case, it was entirely a matter for the minister to decide whether to act on such a recommendation.[105]

Internment, of its very essence, leaves very little scope for the law to provide safeguards against the abuse of power. Indeed the subjective nature of the relevant powers, as defined in the Special Powers Act and associated regulations, left little room for judicial intervention. As has already been seen, what limited success there was in challenging the exercise of the arrest powers was based purely on procedural impropriety. Even then it was to prove a pyrrhic victory given the sweeping nature of the power in question. Attempts at challenging the legality of internment orders did not prove any more successful. Once again success in this regard was confined to technical or procedural matters. For example in *In re Mackey*[106] it was held that the common law rules of natural justice required that all interned persons appearing before the advisory committee should be provided with a written summary of the information upon which the suspicion against them was based. It was further held that they could be represented by a lawyer if they so wished. The value of these limited protections was undermined by the qualification that the written summary could be withheld when the disclosure of the relevant information would be contrary to public safety, either by prejudicing the work of the security forces or by revealing their intelligence system. In effect the law proved a very blunt tool in protecting the liberty of the individual against the demands of executive convenience. The requirements of due process had to give way to the achievement of security objectives.

The use of lethal force

The ultimate means of punishment and control available to the security forces is the power of summary execution. When inflicted without lawful justification it constitutes the most complete negation of legality and due process. It can be assumed, therefore, that in any democratic society based on the rule of law there will be clearly defined limits on the extent to which the security forces can resort to the use of lethal force, coupled with mechanisms to render accountable to the law any individual who exceeds those limits. In Northern Ireland these limits are laid down in a combination of statute and common law and the mechanisms are broadly the same as for any ordinary citizen who resorts to the use of lethal force without lawful excuse.[107] Nevertheless, between the outbreak of violence in 1969 and Bloody Sunday 48 civilians were shot dead by the security forces and two more were stabbed to death by a pitchfork.[108] The vast majority of these individuals were unarmed when they were killed and most of the killings occurred in disputed circumstances. The first five killings at the hands of the police in August 1969 were examined by the Scarman Tribunal, which found that all five victims had been innocent.

Surprisingly, no prosecutions were instigated against any of the soldiers and police officers involved in the fatal shootings examined by the Scarman Tribunal, or in any of the other 45 killings up to Bloody Sunday. The substance of the law governing the use of lethal force by the security forces is dealt with in some detail in Chapter 6. For present purposes it is sufficient to note that if the attorney general had initiated the prosecution of the police officers and soldiers involved in some of the fatal shootings from 1969 up to and including Bloody Sunday it is reasonable to suppose that they would have resulted in conviction for murder. The conventional understanding of the law during this period was that soldiers and police officers enjoyed no special powers to use force against the person beyond those available to the ordinary citizen. If they killed without lawful justification they would be exposed to the same criminal penalties as ordinary citizens. Their status as soldiers or police officers did not of itself provide a special defence or attract a different standard for assessing criminal culpability than that which was applicable to ordinary citizens. Although the regulations introduced under the Special Powers Act specifically conferred a wide range of coercive powers on police and soldiers, these did not extend to special powers to use force against the person. Even the emergency legislation which superseded the Special Powers Act did not confer such powers on the security forces.

Nevertheless, as the above survey of security policy and the law reveals, military expediency had clear priority over the most fundamental rights and freedoms. The law was used primarily as a tool to provide whatever powers were needed to give the security forces and the executive a free hand to deal directly and ruthlessly with violence or the threat of violence against the state. Peaceful protest demonstrations against the actions and policies of the state were suppressed by the expedient of declaring them unlawful and applying brutal force against those who defied the prohibition. Suspects were arrested and imprisoned without recourse to due process or even a trial. The use of brutal and lethal force by the security forces without justification did not result in criminal prosecutions. Overall the courts were surprisingly quiescent in the face of this prostitution of the law to the oppressive demands of the executive. On the few occasions when they did move to curtail the actions of the security forces and the executive on technical grounds, the legislature and the executive reacted swiftly to cancel out the effects. The inevitable signal being sent to the security forces was that their freedom to resort to force, including the use of lethal force, in the course of military operations would not be curbed by the law. Undoubtedly this helped create the environment in which Bloody Sunday could happen.

3
The Widgery Inquiry

Introduction

On 31 January 1972 the British government responded to the public outcry which followed the Bloody Sunday shootings by announcing that a tribunal of inquiry would be set up under the sole chairmanship of the lord chief justice, Lord Widgery. The tribunal's terms of reference were to inquire into 'a definite matter of urgent public importance, namely the events on Sunday 30 January which led to loss of life in connection with the procession in Londonderry on that day'.[1] The tribunal interpreted these terms of reference to mean that its purpose was 'to reconstruct, with as much detail as was necessary, the events which led up to the shooting of a number of people in the streets of Londonderry on the afternoon of Sunday 30 January'.[2]

The limits of the inquiry in spatial terms were the streets in which the disturbances and the shooting had taken place. The time period started with the moment when the marchers had first become involved in violence and ended with the death of the deceased and the conclusion of the affair. This was later clarified to include the plans that had been made to deal with the march and the orders that had been given to the soldiers before the march. The tribunal specifically excluded moral judgements from its remit, holding that these were a matter for others acting on the basis of the facts found by the tribunal.[3]

The tribunal conducted 17 public sessions between 21 February and 14 March 1972 in which it heard 117 witnesses, including priests, 'other people from Londonderry', press and television reporters, photographers, cameramen and sound recordists, soldiers, police officers, doctors, forensic experts and pathologists. Three further sessions were held from 16 to 20 March to hear the closing speeches of the counsels

acting on behalf of the relatives of the deceased, the army and the tribunal. Further evidence considered by the tribunal included over two
hundred statements and a large number of photographs.[4] Significantly
the tribunal did not examine the scene of any of the shootings, nor did
it commission any engineers' reports of the locations of any of the
shootings, nor did it take evidence from victims who were still in
hospital.

The tribunal completed its report on 10 April 1972, just ten weeks
after the events in question. The material part of the report runs to
only 36 pages. The report itself was published on 18 April 1972.
Although the transcripts of the public sessions of the tribunal have
been made available for public inspection, a very substantial body of
the material considered by the tribunal has not been made available.

Tribunals of inquiry

Status

The Widgery Tribunal of Inquiry was set up under the Tribunals of
Inquiry (Evidence) Act 1921. The exceptional nature of the tribunal is
indicated by the fact that only 21 tribunals have ever been set up
under the Act in Britain;[5] the twenty-first being the tribunal of inquiry
into the Dunblane massacre. A tribunal can be established under the
Act when it is resolved by both houses of parliament that 'it is expedient that a tribunal be established for inquiring into a definite matter
described in the Resolution as of urgent public importance'.[6] They are
reserved for those rare occasions when the purity and integrity of
public life has been threatened by a crisis of public confidence.[7] The
purpose of such a tribunal of inquiry is not to establish the guilt or
innocence of the parties allegedly involved, but to establish the truth,
if any, behind the allegations which led to the crisis. If its report
exposes wrongdoing, the task of taking the necessary corrective action
falls elsewhere. The tribunal's value lies in its capacity to persuade the
public that the full facts have been established, and generally to assist
in restoring public confidence in the integrity of government.

To comprehend fully the status and role of tribunals of inquiry
appointed under the 1921 Act, it is necessary to begin with the 1921
Act itself. When the instrument appointing a tribunal deems that the
1921 Act applies, the effect is to vest the tribunal with all the powers,
rights and privileges of the High Court or a judge of the High Court in
respect of compelling witnesses to attend and submit to examination,

and compelling the production of documents and the examination of witnesses abroad. Any person who refuses to attend when summoned, refuses to take an oath, fails to answer any question or produce any documents required by the tribunal, or does any other thing which amounts to a contempt of court is at risk of being proceeded against for contempt in the High Court.[8] Witnesses before a tribunal are entitled to the same immunities and privileges to which they would be entitled as witnesses in civil proceedings in the High Court.[9]

A Tribunal established under the 1921 Act must sit in public.[10] However it does have the power to exclude the public or a section of the public when it is of the opinion that it is in the public interest to do so for reasons connected with the subject matter of the inquiry or the nature of the evidence to be given. It also has the power to authorise the legal representation of any person appearing before it.[11] By the same token it can refuse such representation.

Inquisitorial as opposed to adversarial

It is clear from these provisions that a tribunal appointed under the 1921 Act is a very powerful instrument for inquiring into the matters referred to it. However the frequent references to the High Court should not be interpreted as meaning that the tribunal will function in a manner similar to the High Court when exercising its criminal or civil jurisdiction. Indeed it must be emphasised that the function of the tribunal is fundamentally different in some critical respects from that of the High Court. Under our adversarial system of justice, when the High Court is hearing a case between two opposing parties it does not play an active role in adducing evidence to determine the factual truth of a matter in dispute between the parties. Its primary role is to make a final determination on the basis of the evidence presented to it by the opposing parties. In discharging this role it relies on the parties to present all the relevant evidence and to subject the evidence of their opponents to searching scrutiny. The High Court itself will not pursue this task. Its input is confined largely to ensuring that the parties respect the rules of procedure in adducing the evidence and scrutinising each other's evidence. At the end of the day the primary function of the High Court is to decide in favour of one side or the other in accordance with the rules of the game. It is not concerned first and foremost with establishing the truth. It may be, of course, that the adversarial procedure and the attendant rules applied by the court are best suited to producing a final determination which accords with the truth in any case. That, however, is not necessarily the same thing as saying that the High Court is actively engaged in a search for the truth.

A tribunal of inquiry, by contrast, is set up specifically to find the truth. It is expected to take a positive and primary role in searching out the truth as best it can. Certainly, it will seek the assistance of any interested party who has evidence to give or has an interest in challenging the evidence offered by another party. It must be emphasised, however, that it is the tribunal, and not the parties, which decides what witnesses will be called to give evidence. Indeed strictly speaking there are no parties, no plaintiff and defendant, no prosecutor and accused, only an inquiry after the truth. It is the tribunal which directs that inquiry. All the witnesses are the tribunal's witnesses, not the witnesses of the parties who wish them to be called. Whether any individual witness will be called is a matter for the tribunal. Moreover the tribunal can be expected to act on its own initiative to seek out witnesses who may be able to assist in the quest for the truth. Ultimately the task facing the tribunal is to establish the truth, not to make a determination in favour of one party engaged in an adversarial contest with another.

Rules of procedure

It follows from this description of the tribunal's task that it is not necessarily bound by the rules of evidence and procedure applicable to adversarial proceedings in the High Court. Indeed, apart from the provisions mentioned above, the 1921 Act does not impose any constraints on the tribunal's control over its own procedure. Technically it is free to determine its own procedures and rules of evidence. There is always the danger, of course, that the inquisitorial approach will result in serious allegations being made against an identifiable individual during the proceedings, without that individual being afforded a realistic opportunity to answer those allegations and generally defend his or her reputation. In 1966 the report of the Royal Commission on Tribunals of Inquiry (the Salmon Commission) specifically addressed this problem and came up with six cardinal principles which ought to govern the conduct of inquiry proceedings:[12]

1. Before any person becomes involved in an inquiry the tribunal must be satisfied that there are circumstances which affect him or her and which the tribunal proposes to investigate.
2. Before any person who is involved in an inquiry is called as a witness he or she should be informed of any allegations against him or her and the substance of the evidence in support of them.

3. (a) He or she should be given an adequate opportunity to prepare his or her case with the help of legal advisers. (b) His or her legal expenses should normally be met out of public funds.
4. He or she should have the opportunity to be examined by his or her own solicitor or counsel and to state his or her case in public at the inquiry.
5. Any material witnesses he or she wishes called at the inquiry should, if practicable, be heard.
6. He or she should have the opportunity to test by cross-examination, conducted by his or her own solicitor or counsel, any evidence which may affect him or her.

Salmon considered that observance of these six principles is of the highest importance in safeguarding witnesses and interested parties in tribunal proceedings.[13] He also considered that their effective observance requires less haste in the conduct of tribunal proceedings. While he recognised the urgency of establishing what has happened as speedily as possible, he specifically recommended that when allegations are made against witnesses they should be given adequate time to prepare their case. The delay which will ensue is a 'small price to pay in order to avoid injustice'.[14]

The adoption of Salmon's principles would clearly promote fair treatment for individuals who become the subject of serious allegations during an inquiry. They would also convey the appearance of adversarial proceedings, at least when witnesses are called by an individual and examined by counsel for that individual. This appearance would be strengthened by witnesses being cross-examined by counsel representing other individuals. Nevertheless the recommendations do not, and were never meant to, fundamentally alter the inquisitorial nature of the proceedings. Despite the appearances, all the witnesses remain witnesses of the tribunal and the tribunal retains its primary responsibility for directing the proceedings and seeking out the truth. Salmon's recommendations were merely designed to provide a measure of fair play for those individuals who are at risk of being the subject of serious allegations during the proceedings.

The government accepted the bulk of Salmon's recommendations on these matters. Although they were never framed in a statutory code of procedure, Salmon's recommendations have been largely followed in subsequent inquiries. Before departing from them in any given instance, the inquiry concerned normally offers a detailed explanation.

The nature of the Widgery Tribunal's task

The Widgery Tribunal was appointed to investigate the most serious allegations that had ever been made in peace time concerning the activities of the modern British Army within the United Kingdom. It was alleged that soldiers had shot dead 13 and wounded 15 unarmed civilians in the context of street rioting which had taken place in the aftermath of a 'civil rights' march. Inevitably such allegations rocked public confidence in the state to the core, not just in Britain and Ireland but in all other democratic countries throughout the world. It is difficult to conceive of more serious and disturbing allegations being made against a democratic state whose institutions of law and order are subject to the rule of law. The restoration of public confidence in the state, its institutions of law and order and its international respectability depended on the truth being established by an investigation which was independent in both substance and appearance. In the event of the investigation finding that the deaths and injuries were unlawful or could have been avoided, then those responsible would also have to be punished in accordance with their culpability, and measures taken to ensure that similar events could not happen again. The vital and weighty task of establishing the truth fell to the Widgery Tribunal of Inquiry.

Of course the establishment of the truth is not simply an end in itself. It must be established in a manner which convinces the public and restores public confidence in the integrity of government. In other words the tribunal has a vital accountability function to discharge. Indeed accountability lies at the heart of the role of a tribunal appointed under the 1921 Act. A tribunal is only appointed under this Act on the rare occasions when it is essential that a matter of grave public concern be investigated thoroughly to the full satisfaction of the public. Lord Salmon explains the heavy burden of responsibility that rests on such tribunals as follows:

> There are, however, exceptional cases in which such [tribunals] must
> be used to preserve the purity and integrity of our public life without which a successful democracy is impossible. It is essential that on the very rare occasions when crises of public confidence occur, the evil, if it exists, shall be exposed so that it may be rooted out; or if it does not exist, the public shall be satisfied that in reality there is no substance in the prevalent rumours and suspicions by which they have been disturbed.[15]

There can be no doubt that the events of Bloody Sunday constituted one of these 'very rare occasions'. Indeed it is difficult to think of an occasion this century in which there has been a greater need for the public to be satisfied either that there was no foundation for their 'suspicions' or that the 'evil' which existed should be exposed and rooted out. The Widgery Tribunal was the primary means through which this public satisfaction was to be achieved. In short it was a fundamental exercise in public accountability. Its success or failure would have a vital impact on public confidence, at home and abroad, in the commitment of the government to the fundamental tenets of democracy and justice.

In the context of Bloody Sunday, the tribunal could not discharge this accountability mission simply by investigating and reaching conclusions on how each of the deceased came to be shot, and whether the individual soldiers had acted recklessly in shooting them. Accountability in this context also required a full and transparent investigation of all the factors which contributed to the deaths. In order to restore public confidence in the government and the army, the public would need to be satisfied that the deaths were not, for example, simply the price that had to be paid to put a new political/security strategy into effect or the result of an ill-prepared or misconceived military operation. Equally, of course, if the deaths were the result of any such factors then the public would want to be satisfied that they and the persons responsible were fully exposed so that others could take the necessary punitive measures and whatever further measures were necessary to ensure that such as incident would not happen again.

In the light of the foregoing the tasks of the Widgery Tribunal can be summarised as follows:

1. To establish the truth about what happened during the events within its terms of reference.
2. To satisfy the public that the full facts had been established, and thereby to help restore public confidence in the integrity of the government.
3. To conduct the inquiry in a manner which was best suited to achieving the tasks set out in 1 and 2 above, while at the same time according fair procedures to those individuals who were at risk of becoming the subject of serious allegations in the course of the inquiry.

Bias

From the outset the tribunal was affected by the appearance of bias in favour of the party whose actions were the primary subject matter of its investigation, namely the soldiers involved in the Bloody Sunday operation. This could have severely undermined its capacity to discharge one of its most vital functions, namely to satisfy the public that the full facts had been established. If the tribunal reached conclusions which effectively exonerated the army from culpability for the shootings, any appearance of bias in favour of the army would not only render the findings unacceptable but would also compound the lack of public confidence in the government that had been generated by the shootings in the first place. Moreover there was a very real danger that allegations of bias could call the legality of the tribunal's findings into question.

It is a fundamental principle of fairness that a body must not be affected by bias when discharging a judicial function.[16] Not only does this mean that the body must be free from actual bias in the discharge of its function, but also that it must not convey the appearance of bias in the discharge of that function. In this context the mere appearance of bias is just as fatal as actual bias. Indeed a decision taken by a body in the exercise of a judicial function will normally be declared unlawful if it can be shown that the decision was affected by actual bias or the appearance of bias.

It can be argued, of course, that a tribunal of inquiry appointed under the 1921 Act is not a judicial body in the sense that it has not been established to reach a final judgment on an issue in dispute between two adversarial parties. It is essentially an investigative body whose primary task is to establish the facts of what happened in an event for which the actual facts are hotly contested. It issues a report on the facts rather than a judgment or decision in favour of one party and against another. While this argument may be relevant in protecting the tribunal's report from a formal judicial review on the grounds of bias, it does not mean that the issue of bias is irrelevant to the tribunal's proceedings. The fact of the matter is that one of the fundamental reasons why a tribunal of inquiry is appointed under the 1921 Act is to secure public confidence in the truthfulness and fairness of its findings. If the manner in which the tribunal approaches its fact-finding mission is tainted by the appearance of bias in favour of an individual party who has a vested interest in a certain outcome, its capacity to achieve this fundamental aspect of its task will be irreparably compromised. This danger is particularly apposite to the Widgery Inquiry as it took on so many of the trappings of a judicial body: it was chaired by the lord chief justice, it identified two adversarial protagonists at the outset, it left the presentation of the evidence largely to these two parties, it conducted its proceedings along the lines of an adversarial trial and it delivered its report in a judicial style which found in favour of one party or the other on most issues.

Nevertheless, there are very strong reasons for believing that from the beginning the British political and security establishments managed to influence the inquiry in a manner and to a degree sufficient to disqualify the inquiry from the task for which it was appointed. This is evident from the contents of a confidential memo of a meeting between the Prime Minister, Ted Heath, the Lord Chancellor, Lord Hailsham and Lord Widgery on the evening of 31 January 1972.[17] Despite the fact that the inquiry was supposed to be public, independent and judicial, the purpose of that meeting appeared to be to discuss how the inquiry would be conducted. Minutes were recorded in the memo by Robert Armstrong, the principal private secretary to the Prime Minister. The tone and content of the discussion and the decisions taken reflect an agenda designed to steer the inquiry in a direction favourable to the interests of the army and the British establishment generally. The impact of these decisions was compounded by decisions taken by the tribunal itself which appeared unduly favourable to the army. The resultant bias against the victims and their relatives is a recurrent theme throughout the remainder of this chapter which deals with the structure and conduct of the inquiry, and in the following three chapters which deal respectively with the inquiry's report, the soldiers' evidence and the application of the criminal law to the shootings on Bloody Sunday.

Composition of the tribunal

The Tribunals of Inquiry (Evidence) Act 1921 does not lay down any specifications on the qualifications of the person or persons chairing a tribunal appointed under the Act. In practice, of course, the chairman will normally be a senior judge. He or she may be assisted by one or more persons. The critical factor is for the public to be confident that the members of the tribunal will seek out the truth efficiently, successfully and without fear of or favour to any vested interest.

It would appear that the chairman of the tribunal of inquiry into Bloody Sunday was chosen because he was the lord chief justice of the day. As such he could be expected to bring to the tribunal the intellectual skills and legal experience necessary to root out the truth efficiently and successfully. His position would also place him above any hint of fear or favour. Unfortunately, however, Lord Widgery also happened to be a former British Army officer. The inquiry, of course, was concerned with establishing the truth of the most serious and shameful allegations that were ever likely to be made against the British Army in peacetime. Findings against the army on any significant aspect of the allegations would very seriously damage the proud image of the army at home and abroad to an extent unparalleled in its history. Moreover it would represent a very serious political and military setback in the fight against militant Irish nationalism. Seen in this light the memo of the meeting between the prime minister, the lord chancellor and Lord Widgery takes on a telling significance when it actually records the prime minister advising Lord Widgery that: '[i]t had to be remembered that we were in Northern Ireland fighting not only a military war but a propaganda war'.

It is not being argued here that Lord Widgery, as a former member of the British Army, was actually swayed by any of these considerations in his investigation and exposition of the truth. However bias is not simply a matter of actual prejudice. Critically, it is also a matter of appearances. The reality is that many of those aggrieved at the actions of the British Army on Bloody Sunday will see not the lord chief justice, with his distinguished record of judicial service, chairing the tribunal. Instead they will see a former British soldier investigating very serious allegations against British soldiers in circumstances where adverse findings would be seriously damaging not just to the individual soldiers concerned but also to the entire image of the British Army. It is virtually inevitable that these people would have no confidence in a report which exonerated the soldiers from any serious wrongdoing. In these circumstances it was a grave error to appoint the lord chief justice as the chairman of the tribunal. Indeed it is respectfully submitted that the appointment brought with it an unfortunate appearance of bias which precluded the tribunal from fulfilling the mandate with which it was charged.

Terms of reference

From the outset the tribunal was determined to impose a very narrow interpretation on its terms of reference. It was adamant that only the events which occurred on the streets of the Bogside on the Sunday afternoon in question were relevant. When pushed, it was prepared to accept that these events could not sensibly be considered without taking into account the operational plans that were made to deal with the march and the orders that were given to the soldiers before the march. The tribunal specifically excluded moral judgements from its remit, holding that they were a matter for others acting on the basis of facts found by the tribunal.

Of course this narrow interpretation may accord with one of the primary functions of a tribunal of inquiry established under the 1921 Act, namely to establish the facts of what happened. An equally important function, however, is to restore public confidence in the integrity of the government. To achieve this objective it will be necessary in many situations to point the finger of blame at those responsible. Certainly, given the events of Bloody Sunday the one question which most people wanted answered was who was culpable, either legally or morally, for the deaths and injuries. Indeed given the fact that the tribunal was investigating the use of lethal force by the armed agents of the state the whole issue of the legal and moral limits on the use of such force was centre stage. It was imperative, therefore, that the tribunal should address this crunch issue and offer its findings on whether the soldiers or their superiors were culpable. By focusing narrowly on who was shot where by whom and in what circumstances the Widgery Tribunal shirked one of its most important responsibilities. It is submitted that the effect was to protect the role and activities of the army against damaging analysis.

The tribunal's biased approach to its terms of reference is also evident in the fact that it excluded the political input to the events that led to the deaths. Despite the efforts of counsel for the relatives, the tribunal refused to call as witnesses members of the security committee, which was ultimately responsible for the decision to stop the march. The tribunal also refused to examine the reasons behind the security committee's decision, despite the fact that it was taken in the face of advice to the contrary from the senior police commander for the area. The tribunal's refusal to consider this critical issue meant that one of the fundamental questions affecting the events was never answered; namely, was a political decision taken to use the march as an excuse to restore the hegemony of the security forces in the Bogside? The refusal to provide an answer to this question meant, of course, that the tribunal had shirked an important aspect of one of its fundamental tasks, namely to establish the full truth and satisfy the public that the full truth had been established. It also, however, displayed the appearance of not wanting to dig too deeply into the reasons why so many civilians should have been killed in a single army operation which, at least on the surface (apart from the deaths), was no different from many similar operations which had preceded it. If the answer to the question posed was in the affirmative it would have lent considerable support to allegations that the primary objective of the army was not a 'scoop-up' arrest operation but a deliberate tactical device to inflict a decisive defeat on the rioters and any IRA gunmen who were goaded into an armed response. At the very least the tribunal would have been forced to address the link between the political direction behind the Bloody Sunday security operation and the cost in terms of civilian deaths which resulted. In short the tribunal's refusal to consider the admitted political involvement conveyed the appearance of protecting the British government and the army against the risk of adverse and potentially explosive conclusions.

The tribunal's narrow interpretation of its terms of reference also served the interests of the army by excluding consideration of some of the shooting incidents. The tribunal interpreted its remit as being confined to those shootings which resulted in fatalities. So, for example, it did not consider those shootings which occurred on the fringes of the Bogside, presumably because of the location in which they occurred and because they did not result in fatalities. It is worth noting, however, that the tribunal did receive oral evidence about these shootings. As will be seen later, this clearly established that the soldiers fired at unidentified targets in some of these incidents. Also, some of them involved claims by the soldiers concerned that they actually hit identified targets, despite the fact that there was no independent evidence of casualties. Excluding these incidents from the scope of the inquiry therefore served the interests of the army by shielding the soldiers concerned from the inevitable adverse conclusions about their conduct.

Most of those who were injured by army gunfire were also excluded from consideration in the tribunal's report, presumably because the terms of reference were confined to the deaths. Since the wounded were injured by the same general firing that caused the deaths, their exclusion is inexcusable. Indeed it is difficult to imagine a more blatant example of bias than the exclusion of most of the injured victims. Since there was no evidence to connect any of them with firearms or bombs it was clearly in the interests of the army to have them excluded. Moreover their exclusion had the automatic effect of concealing the full gravity and recklessness of army gunfire during that ten-minute period.

Another element of bias resulting from the tribunal's interpretation of its terms of reference concerned its inconsistent application of its own interpretation. This is primarily concerned with sections in the report which deal with the background to the events on Bloody Sunday and assessments about who was responsible. The significance of these elements is considered in the following chapter, which deals with the report itself.

Location of sittings

Since the events occurred in Derry and the large majority of civilian witnesses lived in Derry, the obvious and most suitable location for the tribunal to sit was Derry. The Guildhall, the seat of Derry City Council, would have been admirably suited for the purpose and was within easy walking distance for most of the witnesses living in Derry. This latter point was significant because of all the witnesses who gave evidence at the tribunal, those from the Bogside and the Creggan faced the greatest practical difficulty travelling to an out-of-town venue. They also happened to be the witnesses most critical of the army.

The tribunal decided to sit in Coleraine instead of Derry. Coleraine is a Protestant unionist town about 35 miles to the north-east of Derry. It had featured prominently in the northern political conflict in the mid 1960s when the Stormont government selected it instead of Derry as the preferred location for Northern Ireland's second university. Derry, of course, would have been the natural and obvious choice had the decision been taken on the basis of objective educational, social, cultural and economic criteria. The psychological blow inflicted by the choice of Coleraine over Derry played a major role in alienating nationalist Derry from the state and ultimately preparing the ground for the violence which erupted only a few years later. The decision to choose Coleraine over Derry as the venue for the inquiry, therefore, was both insensitive and provocative. It did little to engender a sense that the inquiry was going to be independent and objective.

According to the tribunal's report, the decision to locate the inquiry in Coleraine was taken on the grounds of 'security and convenience'.[18] These grounds did not receive any further elaboration. It was never made clear whose convenience was being served by sitting in Coleraine. It was certainly not the convenience of those witnesses from the Bogside and Creggan who had made highly critical statements about the security forces. A decision in favour of the Guildhall would have enabled them to give evidence virtually on their doorsteps. Forcing them to embark on a 70-mile round trip to a town which many of them would have considered alien and dangerous was about as inconvenient as it could get. The inevitable effect would have been to undermine both physically and psychologically their resolve to persist with the full force of their evidence. For the military witnesses, however, Coleraine would have been a much more suitable location as it was a town in which they would be welcome. There would also be the added advantage, from their perspective, of distance in space and cultural environment from the scene of the events which were under scrutiny.

In the absence of convincing justification it would be difficult not to conclude that the decision to sit in Coleraine was taken deliberately to convenience the army and inconvenience the civilian witnesses critical of the army. At the very least it conveyed the appearance of bias in favour of the latter. The only other justification proffered was 'security'. However no attempt was made to explain how sitting in the Guildhall would have been a greater security risk than sitting in Coleraine. Significantly Lord Widgery admitted during the tribunal proceedings that Derry would have been a better location, but that he had been advised that Coleraine would be preferable on the grounds of security. Although he did not say it specifically, this advice must have come from the security forces. An earlier draft of the report makes it clear that the advice was given by 'Army commanders'. Since the inquiry was to be into the conduct of the security forces, this only adds to the suspicion that the decision to locate in Coleraine as opposed to Derry was infected with bias in favour of the army. Indeed it is worth noting that the memo of the meeting between the prime minister, the lord chancellor and Lord Widgery states that:

> The Prime Minister said that it would have to be decided where the Tribunal should sit. It probably ought to be somewhere near Londonderry; but the Guildhall, which was the obvious place, *might be thought to be on the wrong side of the Foyle*. One possibility would be to find a suitable place a little distance away from Londonderry. The Lord Chief Justice said that he thought that the Tribunal would have to be held in Londonderry, so that people were not inhibited from giving evidence to it (emphasis added).

This clearly suggests that there was both political and military pressure to prevent the tribunal from sitting in the Guildhall. The 'wrong side of the [River] Foyle' is a reference to that side on which the shootings took place and in which the majority of civilian witnesses were living. It is also, of course, a reference to the fact that the Guildhall is located on the nationalist west bank of the Foyle as opposed to the unionist east bank.

It is worth contrasting the approach of the Widgery Tribunal on the question of location to that of the Scarman Tribunal of Inquiry into the acts of violence and civil disturbance which occurred in diverse parts of Northern Ireland during the summer of 1969. The latter did not let oversensitivity about security fears expose its proceedings to the risk of being seen to be biased in favour of one side or another. It had to investigate acts of violence which occurred at diverse times in Belfast, Derry, Dungiven, Armagh, Coalisland, Dungannon, Newry and Crossmaglen. In order to facilitate the submission of oral evidence from civilian parties the tribunal actually moved from one location to another. It sat in Belfast to hear witnesses from Belfast, in Armagh for the convenience of witnesses from Armagh, Newry, Coalisland, Dungannon and Crossmaglen and, most significantly in this context, in Derry to hear witnesses from Derry and Dungiven.[19] If the Scarman Tribunal could sit in Derry there is no apparent reason why the Widgery Tribunal could not have done likewise. Since the tribunal did not offer any convincing justification for its failure to do so, it would seem legitimate to conclude that the decision was taken to convenience the army and, by the same token, to inconvenience those witnesses from the Bogside and Creggan who were critical of the army.

Treasury Solicitor

A tribunal of inquiry appointed under the 1921 Act requires its own team of solicitors and counsel to function effectively. The reasons for this are succinctly summarised in the following passage from the Salmon Report:

> the Tribunal's function is not only to report upon but to inquire into the matters which are disturbing the public. It is the Tribunal alone which is entrusted by Parliament to carry out this important duty on the public's behalf. And it is in the Tribunal alone which, for this purpose, the public reposes its confidence. The nature of the task of the Tribunal is therefore inescapably inquisitorial. In carrying out this task it cannot and should not be deprived of the services of solicitor and counsel, for their services are essential. But for them the Tribunal would have to interview the witnesses personally before hearing their evidence and descend into the arena at the hearing as they did in the Budget Leak Tribunal. This would in our view be in the highest degree undesirable.[20]

The practice has always been for a tribunal of inquiry appointed under the 1921 Act to rely on the services of the Treasury Solicitor. The Salmon Report observed that the Treasury Solicitor had 'vast experience of public administration and also the entrée into all government departments'. It considered that this would prove of tremendous benefit in the course of a tribunal's investigation where it was important to have detailed knowledge of how government administration actually functions. The Salmon Report recognised that the Treasury Solicitor comes into close contact with the government of the day. This of course might prove problematic if a tribunal had to investigate a matter which could prove politically embarrassing for the government of the day. However the Salmon Report also observed that governments come and go whereas the Treasury Solicitor and his staff are civil servants who carry out their duties impartially, irrespective of which party is in power. Accordingly there is no danger that reliance on the services of the Treasury Solicitor would bias a tribunal investigation of a politically sensitive matter in favour of the political party that happened to be in power.

What the Salmon Report did not consider was the propriety of a tribunal of inquiry relying on the services of the Treasury Solicitor when the subject of the inquiry was allegations made by Irish citizens about the actions of a central institution in the British establishment which enjoyed the firm political allegiance of both government and opposition. The Treasury Solicitor is in fact a body of solicitors who work full-time in the government service. They are civil servants whose primary function is to give legal advice and assistance to government departments, including the Ministry of Defence. Indeed the Treasury Solicitor has acted for the ministry in civil actions arising out of the fatal shooting of civilians by soldiers in Northern Ireland.[21] Accordingly it would be difficult for an impartial observer to feel satisfied that the Treasury Solicitor was a suitable choice of solicitor to service a tribunal whose function it was to investigate very serious allegations by Irish people against the government's armed forces. At the very least the independent observer might suspect a conflict of interest.

Further problems with reliance on the Treasury Solicitor emerge from the contents of the memo of the meeting between the prime minister, the lord chancellor and Lord Widgery: 'The Lord Chancellor suggested that the Treasury Solicitor and the Cabinet Office should provide the secretariat for the Tribunal, and *the Treasury Solicitor would need to brief counsel for the Army*' (emphasis added). The implications of this are profoundly disturbing. If accurate, the most senior figure in the British legal establishment suggested that the solicitor appointed to serve the tribunal, appointed by parliament with all of the powers and privileges of the High Court and chaired by the lord chief justice, should also brief counsel for the very party whose actions were supposed to be investigated by the tribunal. A deeper and more disturbing conflict of interest would be difficult to imagine. When it is considered that the party being investigated was the British Army and that it was being investigated for shooting dead 13 unarmed civilians in the context of a protest demonstration against government security policy in Northern Ireland, the conflict of interest takes on very sinister implications. Indeed it smacks of the British legal and political establishments engaging in a conspiracy to pervert the course of justice in order to protect the political and security establishments from having to accept responsibility for the events of Bloody Sunday. This scenario is so bizarre, unprecedented and unbelievable that one would be tempted to conclude that the memo is an inaccurate record of what was actually said at the meeting. Unfortunately it has never been clarified or corrected.

It is not being suggested here that the Treasury Solicitor acted with anything but the utmost professional integrity and impartiality during the course of the tribunal. That, however, is not the issue. If his participation can reasonably be interpreted as conveying the appearance of bias in favour of the army then that would have been sufficient to disable the tribunal from fully discharging the task it was set. It is submitted that the status and image of the Treasury Solicitor, coupled with the nature of the inquiry to be carried out by the tribunal, were sufficient in themselves to convey the appearance that the tribunal would be biased in favour of the army and, by implication, against those making the allegations critical of the army.

Once again the contrast with the Scarman Tribunal is both stark and instructive. The Scarman Tribunal acknowledged the practice and the value of appointing the Treasury Solicitor to act for a tribunal appointed under the 1921 Act. However Lord Scarman also recognised the significance of the fact that the police were involved in the disturbances which his inquiry had to investigate. Accordingly he felt that it would not be fitting for the tribunal to rely on the Treasury Solicitor to conduct the investigation. Although he did not spell it out, it is clear that Lord Scarman was concerned that the use of the Treasury Solicitor might convey the appearance that the tribunal would not be totally independent and impartial in its investigation of alleged police wrongdoing. Given that the Widgery Tribunal was concerned with allegations against the army, and that those allegations were much more serious than those against the police in the Scarman Inquiry, it might reasonably have been expected that the Widgery Tribunal would have followed the example of the Scarman Tribunal. It certainly must have been aware of the fact that Lord Scarman had felt it necessary to depart from the traditional practice of engaging the Treasury Solicitor. At the very least, therefore, the Widgery Tribunal should have explained its decision to engage the Treasury Solicitor and thereby to run the risk of appearing to be biased. Its failure even to acknowledge that there was an issue only fuels the appearance of bias that inevitably resulted from its reliance on the Treasury Solicitor.

The parties

Relevance

Another factor which undermined the capacity of the tribunal to discharge its task successfully was the manner in which it identified the parties and interests involved and organised their representation. Strictly speaking, of course, the inquiry was not to be conducted as an adversarial hearing. Nevertheless, in line with the Salmon recommendations, it was proper for the tribunal to permit legal representation of those parties against whom allegations were likely to be made. The obvious parties in question would be the soldiers involved, the injured and the next of kin of the deceased. In line with the Salmon principles, the legal representatives of these parties would be entitled to advance notice of the allegations made against them, and an opportunity to lead the evidence of their clients in examination, to examine material evidence against their clients and to cross-examine witnesses who give evidence against their clients. Beyond that it was the responsibility of counsel for the tribunal to ensure that all other relevant and accessible evidence was available to the inquiry and that all evidence was properly tested for reliability.

Legal representation

In the event the tribunal granted representation to the army and the deceased. One legal team acted for the army and another for the deceased. This arrangement obviously made sense in the case of the army, given the fact that on the day the individual soldiers were acting as a unit under military orders. The justification is less obvious in the case of the deceased. They did not form part of a closely knit organisation and had not been acting in concert on the day. Indeed most of them did not even know each other. They were all separate individuals. Given that the evidence of the soldiers was to the effect that they shot only at gunmen and bombers, it follows that their families were all entitled to their own separate legal representation. However the question of separate representation did not become an issue during the proceedings. When the proceedings opened a single legal team appeared for 12 of the 13 deceased as they anticipated that the tribunal would not permit separate representation. Their fears were confirmed at the outset by Lord Widgery, who declared that he saw no need for the individual deceased to be represented separately. The effect of this, of course, was that a single legal team consisting of a senior counsel, a junior counsel and a firm of instructing solicitors would have to carry the burden of representing the interests of a large number of separate individuals. It is worth noting here that no separate representation was considered for the wounded. The clear expectation of the tribunal was that the legal team for the deceased would cover the needs of the wounded, thereby more than doubling their burden.

A further, and perhaps more serious twist resulted from Lord Widgery's wish that the views of Derry people who might be critical of the army should also be represented, and that that representation should be provided by counsel for the deceased. The inevitable effect of this decision was that the single legal team representing the deceased also had to represent the wounded and the nationalist citizenry of Derry. This was a huge burden to place on such slender resources and could only result in the representation of the individual deceased being stretched beyond breaking point.

A two-party contest

An equally important consequence of Lord Widgery's approach, the significance of which cannot be overestimated, was that it effectively turned the inquiry into an adversarial contest between two opposing parties. What should have been an inquisitorial investigation conducted by the tribunal itself, with contributions from the affected parties, was shaping up to be an adversarial contest between unequal parties with the tribunal making a contribution. The significance of this, as will be seen later, was greatest during the vital cross-examination of the soldiers. This task was left almost exclusively to the counsel for the deceased. In its report the tribunal placed great store on its perception of how well the soldiers performed under cross-examination. The reality, of course, was that the counsel for the deceased were in a very weak position when it came to conducting this cross-examination. Not only did they not have the time and resources to prepare fully for this mammoth task, but they did not have copies of the critical statements made by the soldiers to the military police on the night of Bloody Sunday. As will be seen later, access to this vital evidence would have had a profound effect on the conduct of the soldiers' cross-examination and, by extension, the whole drift of the inquiry.

By contrast, counsel for the tribunal did have access to this critical material and could have used it to devastating effect in the cross-examination of the soldiers, which of course should have been the primary responsibility of counsel for the tribunal in such an inquiry. Incredibly, however, counsel for the tribunal hardly featured at all in the cross-examination of the soldiers. This most critical aspect of the inquiry was left to counsel for one of the 'parties'. That, of course, is what one would expect in an adversarial proceeding, but not what should happen in an inquisitorial inquiry appointed under the 1921 Act.

It is apparent, therefore, that Lord Widgery's approach to representation at the inquiry had the effect of steering the inquiry away from an inquisitorial approach and towards an adversarial approach. Not only did this conflict with the terms of appointment of the tribunal, but it also meant that the tribunal's focus was less on establishing the truth of what had happened and more on picking the winner of a legal contest between unequal opposing parties.

The British Army versus Irish nationalists

An equally important consequence was the characterisation of the inquiry as a contest between the British Army on the one hand and militant Irish nationalists on the other. The subtext, of course, was that the former were risking their lives to protect the integrity of the United Kingdom from the violent and subversive activities of the latter and generally to keep the peace, protect property and maintain public order on the streets of Derry. The other side, by contrast, were Irish nationalists who gave no allegiance to the state and either engaged in violent and murderous attacks on the security forces and the wanton destruction of property or, at best, refused to give their allegiance to the security forces in combatting such activities. Lord Widgery actually fuelled this perception of the nationalist community in Derry by his partisan background account of the lead-up to Bloody Sunday. By characterising the deceased, the wounded and the nationalist citizenry of Derry as one side in a two-sided contest Lord Widgery was surreptitiously shifting the sympathy of British, unionist and non-aligned public opinion away from the deceased and wounded in favour of the army.

Order of the closing speeches

The characterisation of the proceedings as a two-party adversarial contest made it virtually inevitable that there would be conflict over the order of the closing speeches. It was never in doubt that the final address would be made by the counsel for the tribunal. However neither the counsel for the army nor the counsel for the deceased wanted to make the first closing address. Each was acutely aware of the value of being able to respond to points made by their opponent in his closing address. This advantage was only going to be available to one party, namely the party who went second. In the end Lord Widgery settled the matter, and it may come as no surprise to learn that the decision was in favour of counsel for the army. It is not being suggested here that this decision actually had a substantial impact either on the outcome of the inquiry or on the fairness of the procedures. Although counsel for the army did make full use of the advantage to respond to many of the points made by his adversary in his closing address, it would be difficult to assert that this had any significant impact on the tribunal's conclusions. The real significance of the decision emerges when it is placed in the context of the other quasi-procedural decisions that the tribunal had to make – location of sittings, representation, use of the Treasury Solicitor and the status of the statements taken by the Northern Ireland Civil Rights Association (see later). All of these, without exception, went in favour of the army. The decision on closing addresses therefore made it a clean sweep in favour of the army. That, of course, does not necessarily establish actual bias, but it certainly conveys a very strong appearance of bias.

Evidence and procedure

Gathering evidence

Since the tribunal of inquiry was inquisitorial in nature the task of adducing evidence fell on the tribunal itself, as opposed to the respective parties. In effect this meant that one of the primary tasks of the Treasury Solicitor was to seek out relevant evidence to present to the tribunal. Of course their task was made considerably easier by the fact that the tribunal was being conducted essentially in adversarial mode. Counsel for the deceased and the counsel for the army were active in identifying and securing sources of evidence which they wished the tribunal to consider. For the most part this took the form of compiling witness statements, which were sent together with the names and addresses of the witnesses to the Treasury Solicitor. Other material sent included photographic and video evidence and sound recordings. The Treasury Solicitor also made a public appeal for relevant evidence and sources of evidence to be communicated to him for the purposes of the inquiry. This attracted a further substantial body of statements and material evidence from third parties for the tribunal's consideration.

The Treasury Solicitor's team had to examine all the evidence submitted with a view to sifting out the relevant from the irrelevant. Once they had determined which evidence should be submitted to the tribunal their next task was to take formal statements from those witnesses whom they considered should be called formally to give evidence to the tribunal. Equally they had to identify those material exhibits which should be presented in evidence to the tribunal. Those that were already in their possession were classified and given serial numbers for the purpose of identification at the tribunal. They also had to take steps to obtain those which were not already in the custody of the tribunal. Since the tribunal had all of the powers of the High Court it could subpoena witnesses who refused to cooperate voluntarily and the production of material evidence when that was not produced voluntarily. However there is no record of the tribunal having to resort to such coercive measures.

The tribunal had access to scientific evidence such as medical reports and the results of forensic tests on guns, clothing and the bodies of the deceased. It could also have commissioned engineer's reports on any of the scenes of the fatal shootings. It will be seen later that in at least one case a dispute over the circumstances in which individual shots were fired could have been resolved by an engineer's report of the scene. The tribunal, however, failed to commission any such reports. Indeed it did not carry out any on-the-spot investigations. While Lord Widgery did go on a walkabout in the area, that was more of a public relations exercise than an attempt to assess the circumstances of individual shootings. Given the fundamental conflict over the circumstances in which the shootings occurred, it is submitted that detailed assessments of the physical layout of the scenes of the individual shootings would have been very useful in reaching a judgment on whether there was any justification for the shootings.

Admissibility of evidence

In any investigation which will lead ultimately to a judicial trial it is quite normal to amass evidence which cannot be presented in court because it does not satisfy the rules on the admissibility of evidence. Nevertheless the evidence will often prove useful in making a factual determination of what happened in the disputed matters. This in turn can prove useful in deciding whether to proceed with the trial. Equally the evidence might prove useful in the formulation of an appropriate strategy to employ at the trial. Technically inadmissible evidence can play an even more significant role in a tribunal of inquiry. The tribunal is not bound by the strict rules of evidence which apply in a court of law. The tribunal's function is to seek out the truth of what happened in a disputed matter. A court of law, by comparison, is primarily concerned with whether one party has proved his or her case against the other in accordance with the rules governing the proceedings, including the rules of evidence. In the latter, therefore, the rules of the proceedings assume a much greater importance than they do in the former. For the tribunal the truth is the key issue, not who wins. Accordingly the rules of evidence and procedure do not play the central role that they play in a trial. It can be therefore expected that the Treasury Solicitor will not feel hampered by the technical legal rules of evidence in the process of gathering material evidence. Anything that can shed light on the truth of what actually happened will be relevant and must be considered even if it does not satisfy the technical legal rules of evidence governing a judicial trial.

The relaxed attitude towards the rules of evidence and procedure carries through to the formal tribunal proceedings themselves. The tribunal is the master of its own procedure subject, of course, to the overriding requirement of fairness to all the parties involved. Equally it is not bound by the formal rules of evidence applicable in a court of law. It can accept evidence which would be inadmissible in the latter. Indeed there is no absolute requirement for the tribunal to base its findings purely on the evidence formally presented in its public sessions. Ultimately its task is to establish the truth and there is nothing in law which prohibits it from taking into account evidence it has received but has not been presented and tested in the public sessions. In practice, of course, fairness to individuals will normally require the presentation and examination of evidence in public sessions. Equally the tribunal's special responsibility to restore public confidence in the integrity of government by convincingly establishing the full facts of what happened will normally require the public presentation and examination of all evidence taken into account by the tribunal in reaching its findings.

Rules of evidence and procedure in the Widgery Tribunal

The extent to which the Widgery Tribunal was bound by formal rules of evidence and procedure was complicated by the fact that Lord Widgery took the irregular course of conducting the inquiry on an adversarial as opposed to an inquisitorial basis. In other words he conducted the proceedings more like a contest between two opposing parties. It might have been expected, therefore, that the formal rules of evidence and procedure applicable to a trial in a court of law would be applied. Indeed for the most part that is exactly what happened. Each side made opening statements. Witnesses were examined, cross-examined and re-examined by each side as if they were witnesses being called by one side or the other. Admittedly witnesses were also examined and cross-examined by the tribunal, but this did not alter the essentially adversarial nature of the contest. Even technical rules such as those governing the asking of leading questions in examination were largely followed in practice.

Critically the tribunal's perception of the proceedings as an adversarial contest between two parties carried over into the rules governing the admissibility of evidence. Incredibly Lord Widgery refused to consider some very cogent evidence offered on behalf of the deceased, purportedly because it did not satisfy the technical rules governing the admissibility of evidence in a court of law. The evidence in question concerned tapes of British Army and RUC radio messages on the afternoon of Bloody Sunday. The vital significance of this evidence from the perspective of the deceased was that it offered substantial proof that soldiers had fired from the Derry Walls, despite the fact that the army denied that any shots had been fired from that location. Lord Widgery purported to exclude the tapes on the ground that the radio messages had been intercepted unlawfully. Not only was his application of the rules governing the admissibility of unlawfully obtained evidence totally out of place in a tribunal of inquiry, but his interpretation of the rules themselves was surely flawed. Indeed had the tapes been presented as evidence in a court of law it is highly unlikely that they would have been ruled inadmissible on account of the fact that they contained radio messages which had been unlawfully intercepted.

Another significant body of evidence which the Widgery Tribunal refused to accept was over 700 eyewitness statements made to the Northern Ireland Civil Rights Association (NICRA) in the aftermath of Bloody Sunday. Lord Widgery refused to call even a single one of these eyewitnesses to give evidence because, as he saw it, their statements had been submitted late in order to cause him maximum embarrassment. Why this should be a relevant factor in the proceedings of an inquiry whose primary mission was to establish the truth is difficult to fathom. However they were not the only vital witnesses who were not called to give evidence before the tribunal. Incredibly Lord Widgery did not take evidence from those who had been wounded on Bloody Sunday and who were still in hospital at the time of the tribunal sittings. No explanation for their omission was offered apart from the fact that Lord Widgery did not think it was necessary to call them.[22] Equally strange was the failure to call Dr Raymond McClean to give evidence. He had attended to many of the dead and wounded on Bloody Sunday and had been present at the postmortems on the dead at the request of Cardinal Conway. No explanation was given for his omission. Given that he was a potentially vital witness it might be deduced that he was excluded because his evidence on several critical matters contradicted the official version being offered by the army.[23]

It must be remembered, of course, that just because witnesses were not called to give evidence at the tribunal it does not follow that their statements were not taken into account by the tribunal in its assessment of the truth. Indeed it will be seen later that the tribunal did in fact consider some of the material that it refused to admit in the formal public hearings. The problem with this, of course, is that it may prove difficult to assure the public that all relevant evidence has been taken into account when a huge body of evidence, all of which is identified with the one side, has either been publicly rejected on technical grounds or simply ignored by the tribunal. The scale of this credibility problem is apparent from the following account of the tribunal's treatment of the NICRA statements.

The NICRA statements

The Northern Ireland Civil Rights Association collected over 700 statements from witnesses in the aftermath of Bloody Sunday. These were delivered to the Treasury Solicitor's office in London on 3 March 1972, although they were not referred to Lord Widgery until 9 March 1972. Commenting on these statements in a memorandum (dated 10 March) the secretary to the tribunal said 'It is likely however that had these statements been received at an earlier stage the Treasury Solicitor would have thought it worthwhile to take statements with a view to the writers giving evidence'. According to the same memorandum it seems that Lord Widgery was not prepared to call any of the witnesses to make formal statements. He considered that the statements were submitted at a late stage in order to cause him maximum embarrassment. Lord Widgery did, however, read 15 statements which counsel for the tribunal thought worthwhile to draw to his attention. Nevertheless he refused to call these witnesses to make statements on the ground that they could not 'bring any new element to the proceedings of the Tribunal'. Counsel for the tribunal subsequently advised Lord Widgery that he would like to see four of these statements given in evidence bearing on the death of three of the deceased. He advised that at least two of these statements were likely to be more reliable than evidence already presented to the tribunal on these matters by another witness (Miss Richmond). The memorandum records, incredibly, that the lord chief justice still refused to budge. The secretary proceeded to advise Lord Widgery that:

> It is important that the LCJ's report should not include references to the deaths of these four [*sic*] men which could be criticised as contradicted by evidence which was available to the Tribunal but not considered by it. If the Chief refers for example to Miss Richmond's evidence he will need also to refer to having seen statements which present another possibly more reliable account of the same events.

Interestingly, in the report itself Lord Widgery did refer to the evidence of Miss Richmond and to another person's statement, which he preferred, namely that of Sean McDermott.[24] Since Mr McDermott was not called as a witness during the proceedings it would seem reasonable to conclude that his was one of the statements that the counsel for the tribunal wished to have called. In any event it is apparent that Lord Widgery preferred the statement of a witness who was never called to appear at the tribunal over that of a witness who was both examined and cross-examined during the tribunal proceedings.

The secretary also claimed in the memorandum that he advised Lord Widgery on the desirability of taking evidence from at least a few of these potential witnesses in order to avoid subsequent heavy criticism. He further described how Lord Widgery intended to deal with the issue in his report:

> He was quite prepared to say in the report that the Tribunal had taken note of all the statements, on the basis that they had all been inspected by Counsel for the Tribunal or by Treasury Solicitor's officers. Indeed, in the last resort he was prepared to read them all himself, though Mr Stocker assured him that this was not necessary.

Interestingly the report states that:

> The Northern Ireland Civil Rights Association collected a large number of statements from people in Londonderry said to be willing to give evidence. These statements reached me at an advanced stage in the Inquiry. In so far as they contained new material I have made use of them.[25]

In the light of the secretary's memorandum and the tribunal report itself, however, it would appear that Lord Widgery only made use of one statement, namely that of Sean McDermott. Moreover there must be a strong suspicion that this was done to satisfy the secretary's misgivings about referring to the evidence of Miss Richmond without disclosing that the tribunal had seen statements that presented a different account of the incident in question, one which the tribunal preferred.

This cavalier attitude towards a very substantial body of evidence that was critical of the army reflects poorly on the manner in which the tribunal approached and discharged its task. A tribunal appointed under the 1921 Act is expected to adopt a positive and inquisitive attitude towards digging out the truth. Effectively dumping a whole body of relevant evidence that had been painstakingly put together hardly fulfils that expectation. The excuse that the statements were produced at a late hour is weak. They were produced just ten days after the start of the tribunal proceedings. If the work of the tribunal was considerably advanced by that stage, that is more a reflection of the inappropriate haste at which it was conducting its business. In any event a tribunal appointed under the 1921 Act should not refuse to hear relevant evidence simply because it was submitted late in the proceedings. Even if it is accepted that the tribunal counsel and the Treasury Solicitor adequately vetted the material, the fact remains that they considered some of the statements highly pertinent in the light of other evidence received by the tribunal. The failure to have all these particular statements considered publicly by the tribunal cannot be excused because the tribunal chairman considered them in private and concluded that they added nothing new. If they contradicted evidence already given in public, they should at least have been scrutinised in public.

Inevitably the tribunal's refusal to call any of these witnesses must fuel the suspicion that it was looking at only part of the picture. The part presumed missing was associated with the deceased and injured. This in turn is likely to raise suspicions of bias. If the tribunal secretary's memorandum is accurate on this point, then it must also be said that these suspicions will be fanned even further by the very clumsy and misleading attempt by the tribunal to conceal the fact that it did not make any substantial use of the statements.

Police files

Among the evidence obtained by the tribunal were police files on all the deceased and 13 of the 15 civilians who were admitted to

Altnagelvin Hospital with gunshot wounds. These files were in addition to the nine pages of criminal records on the deceased and injured which were also obtained by the tribunal. The first question that must be asked with respect to these files and records is why the tribunal was interested in them at all. They provided no evidence of what had happened on Bloody Sunday. At best (from the army's perspective) they could only reveal whether any of the deceased had been convicted of firearms offences, or were suspected by the police of being involved in paramilitary activity. Either way they could not provide any credible evidence as to whether they had been shot justifiably on Bloody Sunday. Their prejudicial effect against the deceased and injured would be so great as to outweigh any possible probative value that they might have. It is therefore very worrying that the tribunal saw fit to obtain these files and records and, presumably, took them into account.

Of course it could be argued that the tribunal was conducting an inquisitorial investigation and not an adversarial trial, and therefore it was justifiable and necessary for it to make use of any available evidence that it considered relevant, including police files and records on the deceased and injured. This argument would carry more force if the tribunal had demonstrated a similar zeal with respect to other more cogent evidence, such as the eyewitness statements gathered by the Northern Ireland Civil Rights Association. Much more disturbing, however, is the fact that the tribunal does not appear to have obtained police and army files and criminal records on the soldiers who took part in the Bloody Sunday operation. It is submitted that these would have been more relevant than files and records on the deceased and injured. The inquiry was supposed to have been an investigation into the events which resulted in the 13 deaths. Surely background information on those who did the killings is more relevant for this purpose than background information on those who were killed. It may be, of course, that there were no police files or criminal records on the army personnel in question. All of them, however, must have had an army record. It is difficult to avoid the conclusion that the tribunal's failure to obtain these records reflects a bias in favour of the army. Indeed it conveys the impression, which is evident in various other aspects of the tribunal's work, that the tribunal was unduly concerned to build a case against the deceased and injured and thereby cast a more favourable light on the army's actions.

There is an interesting side issue as to why the police should have maintained files (as distinct from criminal records) on so many of the deceased and injured, and whether the individuals in question were aware of the existence of these files. Counsel for the army actually admitted during the tribunal proceedings that, contrary to information released by the army to the media, none of the deceased were on the wanted list. Since none of the wounded were arrested it must follow that they too were not on the wanted list. Of more immediate importance, however, is the fact that the tribunal did not alert counsel for the deceased and injured that it had access to these files. This contrasts with the fact that the criminal records of four of the deceased were openly discussed during the tribunal hearings. With respect to the police files, however, the tribunal's silence meant that counsel for the deceased and injured did not have an opportunity to challenge the probative value of information in them which may very well have been highly prejudicial to their clients. The only party that could benefit from this silence, of course, was the army. Once again, therefore, it is difficult to avoid the conclusion that the tribunal's approach to its task was unnecessarily biased in favour of the army.

Speed

One of the most remarkable features about the whole tribunal of inquiry is the speed with which it completed its task. Just ten weeks after it had been appointed the tribunal purported not just to have investigated but also to have published the truth of the events that led to the deaths in Derry on Bloody Sunday. Given the unprecedented nature of the events it was investigating and the enormity of the vested interests at stake, it is almost absurd even to think that the tribunal could have confidently established the truth of what happened in the space of only ten weeks. Such a feat would hardly have been possible if all the deaths and injuries had occurred in one incident for which there was copious video evidence. The deaths and injuries on Bloody Sunday, however, occurred in several different incidents, of which the video and photographic evidence was very limited. Moreover there were literally hundreds of witnesses whose statements had to be sifted through and whose evidence had to be heard and tested. To make matters worse their evidence often provided several different versions of the same events. For the tribunal to claim that it had received, analysed, digested and drawn confident and reliable conclusions about what had happened in these circumstances in the space of less than ten weeks was to stretch credulity to the limit. Such a claim was hardly likely to inspire that public confidence in its findings which was so vital for the restoration of public confidence in the state and its institutions of public order.

In partial defence of the Widgery Tribunal it must be said that it was under considerable pressure to complete its task as soon as possible. In the parliamentary debate on the motion to appoint the tribunal the point was made again and again that the tribunal must not become a device to push the horrific events of Bloody Sunday into the background until public and international concern had died down. It was considered that the best means of avoiding this outcome was to have the matter investigated quickly. It is apparent that Widgery himself fell into this trap. In the introduction to his report he said that the value of the inquiry would 'largely depend on its being conducted and concluded expeditiously'.[26] There may be contexts in which this perspective is valid. Given the profound importance of the matters that Widgery had to investigate and their sheer complexity, it can only be described as misguided in this instance.

Significantly Lord Salmon made some reflections on the element of speed in an inquiry appointed under the 1921 Act.[27] He acknowledged the importance of revealing the truth to the public as soon as possible, and in particular that there should be no dilatoriness in starting an inquiry and pushing it to its conclusion. Equally, however, he was of the opinion that too much haste can result in unfairness to the parties concerned, and he specifically denounced the speed at which some postwar tribunals had conducted their inquiries.

Although each inquiry is wholly unique, some useful comparison might be made in this context with the Scarman tribunal. This was appointed under the 1921 Act to inquire into 'the acts of violence and civil disturbance which occurred' in Belfast, Derry, Dungiven, Armagh, Coalisland, Dungannon, Newry and Crossmaglen during the summer of 1969 and 'resulted in loss of life, personal injury and damage to property'. It submitted its report around the same time as the Widgery Report despite the fact that it had been appointed almost two and a half years before the Widgery Tribunal. In other words the Scarman proceedings were more than ten times longer than the Widgery proceedings. Some of the difference might be accounted for by the fact that the former had more incidents to examine than the latter. However this must be set against the fact that the gravity of the matters being investigated by the Widgery Tribunal were much more profound and therefore should have attracted much more careful deliberation. It must also be acknowledged that the long gestation period for the Scarman Report meant that it had been overtaken by events by the time it was published. Given the unprecedented nature of the events that the Widgery Tribunal was investigating, that was hardly likely to have been a problem for it. The overriding requirement for the Widgery Report was public confidence in its findings. That could not be bought by speed, but it could surely be lost through haste. Indeed it is worth noting that a lack of public confidence in its findings was not something that dogged the Scarman Report.

In short it is difficult to avoid the conclusion that as a result of the undue haste in which it investigated the most serious allegations that have been made in peacetime against agents of the state, the Widgery Tribunal severely compromised its own capacity to achieve one of the most vital aspects of its task, namely to inspire public confidence in the truth and fullness of its findings.

Closely associated with the issue of speed is the length of the tribunal's report. Indeed the length of the report might be considered a direct and inevitable consequence of the speed of the inquiry. The main body of the report runs to a mere 36 pages. Given the speed at which the inquiry was conducted this is hardly surprising. Nevertheless it is a further significant indication that the events of Bloody Sunday were not investigated with the care, patience, diligence and thoroughness that might have been expected given the gravity and complexity of the issues involved. Public confidence in the conduct of the investigation and the reliability of its findings could hardly be boosted by such a lightweight product. An immediate and justifiable assumption would be that the report is simply too short to offer a full and accurate analysis of the evidence, the facts and the issues that had to be examined in order to satisfy public concern. The Scarman Report offers a telling comparison. It runs to no fewer than 245 pages.

4
A Flawed Report

Introduction

The extent to which the Widgery Tribunal of Inquiry had achieved the vital and onerous task entrusted to it would be determined by the contents of its report. Would this report satisfy the public that the full facts about Bloody Sunday had been established convincingly? Did it identify those who were culpable, and the extent to which they were culpable, in a manner which would restore public confidence, and the confidence of the nationalist community in particular, in the integrity of government? Alternatively, did it convincingly prove that neither the soldiers nor their masters in the political and security establishments were at fault for the deaths and injuries inflicted that day? If it did expose wrongdoing or failures at any of these levels, did it clear the way for the necessary remedial and/or punitive action to be taken to ensure that justice was not only done but also seen to be done? These are the basic questions which have to be asked in order to determine whether the tribunal was a success.

Twenty-seven years later it would be perverse even to suggest that the tribunal was successful in fulfilling its official mandate. The very fact that an unprecedented second tribunal of inquiry had to be appointed to investigate the very same matters is in itself powerful testimony of the failure of the Widgery Tribunal. However the tribunal's report represents much more than a failure to get to the truth of the matter. Indeed it confirms what many had already begun to suspect during the course of the inquiry, namely that the tribunal was more concerned with exonerating the soldiers and the security and political establishments from blame than it was with exposing the full extent of the truth. Factors such as the composition of the tribunal, the terms of reference and the narrow interpretation imposed on those terms by the tribunal, the appointment of the Treasury Solicitor to service the tribunal, the location of the tribunal sittings, the characterisation of the inquiry as an adversarial contest between the British Army and the Bogsiders, the refusal to call evidence from members of the security committee who were ultimately responsible for the key decisions in the planning of the Bloody Sunday operation, the refusal to call evidence from the individuals who had submitted 700 statements to NICRA, the failure to call evidence from Dr McClean or the wounded who were still in hospital and the speed with which the proceedings were conducted conveyed the clear message that the tribunal was not determined to investigate what had happened thoroughly and without fear of or favour to the British establishment. Nevertheless even the nationalist community was ill-prepared for the extent to which the Widgery Report reflected a bias in favour of the army in its analysis and conclusions of what had happened on Bloody Sunday.

The appearance of bias permeates the whole report to the extent that a reader would find it difficult to avoid the conclusion that Lord Widgery had been set the task of producing a report effectively to exonerate the army from any serious wrongdoing and protect it against the risk of any damaging press coverage or legal action. The extent of the apparent bias is such that it renders the report fundamentally flawed. Throughout Lord Widgery seems to display an unjustified preference for the evidence of army witnesses over that of civilian witnesses; he focuses narrowly on some shooting incidents to the exclusion of others in a manner which clearly protects the army against the risk of adverse findings; he adopts a low-key approach to clear evidence of unjustifiable shootings which resulted in several deaths and injuries; he draws conclusions favourable to the army which are not supported by the evidence; he ignores the critical policy issues surrounding the use of lethal force in the sort of circumstances that prevailed on Bloody Sunday; and he takes an inconsistent approach to his interpretation of the terms of reference in a manner which distinctly favours the actions of the army.

These fundamental weaknesses are sufficient in themselves to deprive the report of any credibility that it might otherwise have had. They also, of course, render the inquiry and the report part of the problem instead of the solution. By straining to clear the army of any serious wrongdoing in the face of all the evidence to the contrary, the inquiry and the report actually compounded the deep sense of outrage and injustice felt by the nationalist community and many others in the wake of Bloody Sunday. The fact that a tribunal of inquiry vested with all the powers and privileges of the High Court and chaired by the lord chief justice could produce such a report had a devastating effect on nationalist confidence in the rule of law and the integrity of the state. If they could not depend on the judicial arm of the state to deliver justice when they were shot on the streets en masse by British soldiers, why would they withhold support from those within their community who would use force of arms in an attempt to overthrow that state? It was not as if the state had treated them up to that point with equality and fairness in economic, social, cultural, political and security matters. The Widgery Report into Bloody Sunday therefore might be interpreted as the final straw which pushed a large section of the nationalist community into the IRA camp, thereby laying the foundations for the perpetuation of an armed struggle which the British authorities would find impossible to defeat by military or civil means over the next quarter of a century.

Incredibly the bias which permeated the inquiry and report went much deeper than that which was apparent on the face of the proceedings and the report itself. In addition to the memo of the meeting between the prime minister and Lord Widgery and others on the eve of the tribunal, the inquiry papers released in 1996 reveal further disturbing evidence of bias in favour of the army. The nature and extent of this evidence is sufficient to dispel any benefit of the doubt to which the Widgery Report may have been entitled in respect of its credibility and impartiality. This material includes extensive memos by the secretary to the tribunal concerning the compilation of the report itself and the original statements made to the military police on the night of Bloody Sunday by the soldiers who had fired the shots.

This chapter will deal with the fundamental weaknesses which are apparent in the report, together with the invidious role played by the secretary to the tribunal in the compilation of the report. The subsequent chapter will deal with the original statements made by the soldiers on the night of Bloody Sunday. It will reveal how they, more than any other single factor, destroyed any credibility that may otherwise have been attached to the Widgery Report.

Terms of reference

It was seen in Chapter 3 that the tribunal imposed a very restrictive interpretation on its own terms of reference. It made it clear that the spatial limits of the inquiry were the streets in which the disturbances and shootings had taken place. In terms of time, the inquiry was limited to the period beginning with the moment when the marchers first became involved in violence and ending with the deaths of the deceased and the conclusion of the affair. Subsequently the tribunal accepted that the contents of the military orders and the decision to deploy the 1st Battalion of the Parachute Regiment were also relevant. However it also made clear that the inquiry was purely a fact-finding exercise. Its task was to try to form an objective view of the events and the sequence in which they occurred so that others would have a firm basis upon which to reach conclusions. It was emphatically no part of the tribunal's function to make moral judgments. Unfortunately the tribunal's report does not always stay within its own self-imposed constraints. More disturbing, however, is the fact that on those occasions when it does stray beyond them it almost invariably makes findings or judgments which are heavily biased in favour of the army.

The security background

The first major example of the tribunal straying beyond its own self-imposed constraints occurred early in the report when it embarked on a survey of the background security situation in the Bogside and Creggan during the previous six months. At no point during the inquiry proceedings was it ever made clear that the tribunal would feel the need to make findings on such matters. Nevertheless the report included five substantial paragraphs containing very contentious and biased findings on the security situation in Derry during this period.[1] Highly selective material and grossly misleading statistics were used to paint a picture of the Bogside as an expanding nest of snipers and vicious rioters who were gradually engulfing the commercial areas in the immediate vicinity and goading the army into violent confrontation at every opportunity. Precise figures were quoted for the number of shots and bombs fired at the security forces, the number of explosions and the valuation of property damage. Curiously, however, these figures related to the period 1 August 1971 to 9 February 1972. Very conveniently for the army's case, this period goes back far enough in time to capture the massive escalation in violence which erupted in the days and weeks immediately following the introduction of internment on 8 August 1971. More disturbing perhaps is the fact that it extends beyond Bloody Sunday itself to capture the massive upsurge in violence that the events of Bloody Sunday provoked. In effect the tribunal was using events which would not have happened but for the actions of the soldiers on Bloody Sunday as a means of explaining why the soldiers acted in the way they did on Bloody Sunday. It is difficult to avoid the conclusion that the tribunal was striving to present the security situation in a light most sympathetic to the army. Further support for this conclusion is forthcoming from the distinctly unsympathetic presentation of the 'other side' in this contest.

No attempt was made to balance the security picture by presenting the political, security, economic and social policies which had impacted harshly upon the local population, thereby alienating them from the state and the security forces. Amazingly no explanation was offered as to why 'civil rights' marches were being organised in defiance of the ministerial ban. Similarly no attempt was made to place the Derry civil rights march in the context of other civil rights marches. It is submitted that this issue was at least as significant to an understanding of the events of 'Bloody Sunday' as any account of the security situation in the six-month period in question. If previous civil rights marches in defiance of the ban had passed off without the loss of 13 lives and 15 wounded, the tribunal should at the very least have considered why the Derry march should have been any different. These serious omissions were compounded by the distinctly hostile and unfair light in which the people of the Creggan and the Bogside were presented. No serious attempt was made to distinguish them from the gunmen or those who regularly engaged in rioting. The following is a particularly telling passage:

> Though parts of the Bogside and Creggan were patrolled, no military initiative was taken except in response to aggression or for specific search or arrest operations. The improvement hoped for did not, however, take place. *The residents of the Bogside and Creggan* threw up or repaired over 50 barricades, including the one in Rossville Street which figured prominently in the proceedings of the Inquiry; frequent sniping and bombing attacks were made on the security forces; and the IRA tightened its grip on the district (emphasis added).[2]

The emphasis throughout this and associated passages is the depiction of the security forces as reasonable and flexible operators who were being relentlessly attacked by a vicious community for whom violence, death and destruction were a way of life.[3]

The effect of focusing on the government's perspective of the security situation and ignoring the perspectives and experiences of the local population and the civil rights lobby was clearly biased in itself.

The significance of this bias can be seen at several points in the tribunal's report. The most obvious, of course, is the fact that Lord Widgery chose to characterise the tribunal proceedings primarily as an adversarial contest between the security forces and the people of the Bogside and Creggan. From the outset, therefore, the reader is not too subtly steered in the direction of sympathy for the army. However there are also plenty of specific examples in the report where the biased presentation of the security situation openly favours the army. The most striking examples are when the tribunal considered the plan to contain the march and the question of whether the arrest operation should have been launched at all. On both of these important issues the tribunal's analysis is conducted against the background of the situation in which the soldiers found themselves. That situation, however, is a highly misleading one which resulted from the tribunal's biased account of the background. The net effect is that the tribunal is able to convey to the reader that the critical decisions to stop the march and to launch the arrest operation were beyond reproach. A more balanced presentation of the background would have rendered such a perception much more difficult to sustain.

The bias in the background presentation also helps to present the army shootings in a much more favourable light than would otherwise have been warranted. The distorted focus on sniping and rioting in the Bogside area conveys to the reader a picture of the soldiers' lives being under direct and immediate threat from the moment they started the arrest operation. Before the reader ever gets to the point where the soldiers open fire he or she is already being steered unfairly in the direction of a defence of justification. Worse still is the fact that the deceased and wounded, as residents of the Bogside, are tainted with suspicion before the reader ever gets to the point where they are shot.

There was no need for this bias in the background presentation. Indeed there was no need for the background presentation at all. If the tribunal had applied its own interpretation of its terms of reference it would not have embarked upon this review of the background security situation. The report would have been no worse for its omission. Indeed it would have been considerably strengthened as a substantial and damaging element of bias would have been avoided. It is submitted that a Tribunal of Inquiry which goes beyond its own interpretation of its terms of reference to indulge in a very one-sided presentation of material that impacts substantially on important sections of its report, is guilty of a bias which renders it impossible for it to achieve the fundamental objects for which it was appointed.

Moral judgments

Although Lord Widgery considered his function simply to be to establish the facts of what had happened, there are places in the report
where he proceeds to make judgments about the soundness of certain
decisions or the justification of certain actions. Indeed it could hardly
be otherwise. The very nature of the events which had to be investigated required judgments to be made in order to render the report
meaningful and intelligible. The very choice of what facts needed to be
established with respect to any particular decision or incident presup-
posed an understanding of the nature of the judgment that would
have to be made with respect to it. For example the facts surrounding
the launching of the scoop-up operation could not be investigated in
isolation from the judgmental issue of whether the 1st Battalion of the
Parachute Regiment should have been sent in at the time they were
sent in. It is hardly surprising, therefore, that Lord Widgery did express
a judgment, albeit a highly tentative and guarded judgment, about the
wisdom of launching the arrest operation in the circumstances which
prevailed at the time. Indeed there are other clear examples throughout the report of judgments being made, including the justification for
individual shootings, the decision to stop the march, the deployment
of the 1st Battalion of the Parachute Regiment as an arrest force and
the issue of whether orders were exceeded.

It is therefore apparent that Lord Widgery did not feel precluded
from making judgments about individual decisions, actions or policies.
What he did very definitely consider to be outside the tribunal's remit
was the whole issue of moral or legal culpability for the day's events.
This was a matter for others. It is therefore strange that he devoted a
whole section to the question of responsibility.[4] Within the section on
responsibility there is even a subsection under the heading 'Were the
Soldiers Justified in Firing?',[5] where he concluded that 'in the majority
of cases the soldier gave an explanation which, if true, justified his
action'.[6] While this was not presented as a finding on the question of
legal culpability it is unquestionably aimed at preventing the prosecution of the soldiers concerned. In terms of moral responsibility it is
difficult to interpret the conclusion as anything other than a moral
judgment that the soldiers were not to blame. This of course is something which Lord Widgery had determined at the outset that the
tribunal had no jurisdiction to consider.

A truly astounding example of Lord Widgery exceeding the self-
imposed constraints on the remit of the tribunal is his conclusion that
'There would have been no deaths in Londonderry on 30 January if

those who organised the illegal march had not thereby created a highly dangerous situation in which a clash between the security forces was almost inevitable.'[7] This patently moral judgment on culpability appeared for the first time in the summary of conclusions at the end of the report. The foundations for it were not presented in the body of the report, nor was it even discussed in the report or in the public proceedings of the inquiry. Indeed the findings in the report clearly show that the organisers of the march set out to avoid a violent confrontation between the marchers and the security forces, and in fact they were successful in achieving that objective. The march had passed on and the fringe rioters were beginning to disperse when the arrest operation was launched. If anything the actual cause of the deaths was the arrest operation and the deployment of the 1st Battalion of the Parachute Regiment to conduct that operation. Indeed it is difficult to avoid the impression that Lord Widgery only included this unwarranted and unsupported judgment in order to deflect public attention away from the true causes of the deaths and injuries. This is supported by the fact that it is placed in a prime position at the very head of the summary of conclusions. Professor Bryan McMahon explains the significance of this as follows:

> placing this statement first on the Summary of Conclusions could bear the interpretation of being a political tactic. It could very well have been an attempt to suggest the headlines for the British Press and by doing so reassuring the British conscience. This interpretation could well be borne out by the *Sunday Times'* allegation that the Summary of Conclusions was leaked in advance to the newspapers. If true, this kind of tactic is unworthy of a judicial tribunal, and must cast doubt not only on the present Tribunal but also as to the future independence of such tribunals.[8]

Policy judgment

Although Lord Widgery allowed himself the luxury of making a sweeping judgment about who was ultimately responsible for the deaths on Bloody Sunday, he was not so forthcoming on the critical policy issue of armed soldiers engaging with gunmen and bombers (assuming for the moment that there were some) in a confined space where there were large numbers of people. The scenario described repeatedly to the tribunal by witnesses across the board was that of soldiers shooting to kill in situations where large numbers of civilians were at risk. On several occasions soldiers described themselves as pursuing rioters while dodging bricks and bottles and then breaking off to shoot at a gunman or someone holding what looked like a nail bomb. When it is considered that the bullets they were firing had a range of over two miles and that they were firing in relatively confined spaces, such as the courtyards of Rossville Flats and Glenfada Park, with large numbers of people about, there must be cause for concern. That concern can only be heightened by the statement given by many soldiers that they considered themselves entitled to shoot at a gunman or bomber even if civilians were in the vicinity and at risk. Moreover, their training was such that their instinctive reaction in such situations was to shoot to kill first.

The inevitable question arises as to whether there should be a serious rethink about whether soldiers trained to think and act in such a manner should be sent in, fully armed, to enforce law and order in a riot situation where there are a large number of civilians about. In the heat of the moment bricks and bottles can so easily be mistaken for nail and acid bombs. Inevitably there must be a very high risk that these soldiers will react with lethal force and disastrous consequences not just for stone throwers but also for innocent civilians who happen to be in the vicinity. Is this risk acceptable?

Lord Widgery was clearly aware of the relevance and importance of the issue. The report does include a subsection under the heading 'Should the Arrest Operation have been Launched at all?'[9] It defines the risks posed by the arrest operation as follows:

> In view of the large numbers of people in the area the arrest operation presented two particular risks: first, that in a large scale scoop-up of rioters a number of people who were not rioters would be caught in the net and perhaps roughly handled; secondly that if the troops were fired upon and returned fire innocent civilians might well be injured.[10]

It might well have added the risk posed to unarmed civilians by a strategy of using heavily armed soldiers to conduct an arrest operation in a riot situation when those soldiers were trained to react quickly to a perceived threat to life or safety. In any event the report does not offer an analysis of the principles or policies which should govern this situation. It confines itself to a statement on the explanation offered by the brigadier for his decision to send in the soldiers from the 1st Battalion of the Parachute Regiment and a finding that the decision was 'made in good faith by an experienced officer on the information available to him, but he underestimated the dangers involved'.[11]

The issue arose again later in the report when Lord Widgery was considering whether the soldiers had been justified in their actions. Once again it is obvious that Lord Widgery was aware of the underlying policy considerations. The discussion focuses on the contents of the 'Yellow Card', which sets out the rules governing the circumstances in which soldiers can open fire (see Chapter 6). Lord Widgery specifically acknowledged that these rules are vague about the extent to which soldiers can resort to lethal firepower in crowded places. However, he did not proceed to offer an analysis of what policies and principles should inform the resort to lethal force in such circumstances. Instead he contented himself with a finding that the circumstances prevailing on Bloody Sunday were such that 'the soldiers were entitled to regard themselves as acting individually and thus entitled to fire under the terms of [the rules] without waiting for orders'.[12] He went on to state that 'in the majority of cases the soldiers gave an explanation which, if true, justified his action'.[13] Nowhere is there any discussion of the broader issues which were very pertinent to the Bloody Sunday situation: should a large body of soldiers engaged in an arrest operation engage gunmen (assuming for the moment that the army's version is true) in circumstances where a large number of civilians are at risk? Should the soldiers concerned withdraw to cover until the civilians are out of danger and/or call in specialist marksmen? Should there be a tightening up of the rules governing the use of firearms in such circumstances to avoid the attendant risk to civilians? These are issues that the tribunal did not address despite the fact that there would be further marches and riots in which the army would be called in to conduct arrest operations and enforce order. What use is a tribunal of inquiry if its investigation and report do nothing to contribute to a means of avoiding a repeat of the events it has had to investigate?

The closest that Lord Widgery came to addressing the underlying policy issues can be found in the following astonishing passage on how individual soldiers are likely to interpret the requirements of the Yellow Card:

> Soldiers will react to the situations in which they find themselves in different ways according to their temperament and to the prevailing circumstances. The more intensive the shooting or stone-throwing which is going on the more ready they will be to interpret the Yellow Card as permitting them to open fire. The individual soldier's reaction may also be affected by the general understanding of these problems which prevails in his unit. In the Parachute Regiment, at

any rate in the 1st Battalion, the soldiers are trained to take what may be described as a hard line upon these questions. The events of 30 January and the attitude of individual soldiers whilst giving evidence suggest that when engaging a gunman or bomb-thrower they shoot to kill and continue to fire until the target disappears or falls. When under attack and returning fire they show no particular concern for the safety of others in the vicinity of the target. They are aware that civilians who do not wish to be associated with violence tend to make themselves scarce at the first alarm and they know that it is the deliberate policy of gunmen to use civilians as cover. Further when hostile firing is taking place the soldiers of 1 Para will fire on a person who appears to be using a firearm against them without always waiting until they can positively identify the weapon. A more restrictive interpretation of the terms of the Yellow Card by 1 Para might have saved some of the casualties on 30 January, but with correspondingly increased risk to the soldiers themselves.[14]

In effect Lord Widgery is saying that when soldiers resort to the use of lethal force their actions must be judged in accordance with their individual temperament and the standards applicable within their particular regiment. It would be difficult to conceive of a greater perversion of the rule of law. The notion that soldiers should generally be judged by standards different from those applied to any other person is anathema to the most fundamental principles of the common law. That individual soldiers should be judged in accordance with their own temperaments and the standards of their own regiments is simply ludicrous. It is inconceivable that such a position could be adopted by a lord chief justice, unless of course he was attempting to present the actions of soldiers in the most sympathetic light possible. The only thing that can be said in Lord Widgery's favour is that he was not purporting to define the strict legal position on how the use of lethal force by a soldier should be judged. Nevertheless he was setting criteria which would be used by himself and others to judge the actions of soldiers. Since these criteria are so patently flawed it must follow that conclusions based upon them are equally flawed.

Looking at only part of the picture

It has already been seen in Chapter 3 that the inquiry did not fully address all the relevant evidence. Inevitably this resulted in the tribunal's report being less complete and accurate than it otherwise would have been. In addition there are two prominent and related features of the report which also suggest that the tribunal did not fully ascertain what had happened with respect to the events within its terms of reference. First, the report did not offer an analysis of each of the shots fired by each of the soldiers. Second, the tribunal's analysis of the events on Bloody Sunday was distorted and rendered incomplete by virtue of the fact that it approached its task from the perspective that the single most important issue it had to determine was who had fired first. Each of these points will be considered in turn. A third point that must be addressed concerns evidence which has emerged in recent years that some of the dead were shot by soldiers positioned on the Derry walls. This issue was raised at the inquiry itself. Indeed it was seen in Chapter 3 that the tape recording of intercepted radio messages suggested that some of the firing had come from the Derry walls. The security forces, however, have always denied that there was any firing from the Derry walls and Lord Widgery refused to allow the issue to be pursued at the inquiry.

The individual shots

The tribunal's report did not offer an analysis of the circumstances in which each shot had been fired by each soldier. Insofar as the firing by each soldier was analysed at all in the report, it was done indirectly pursuant to an examination of the issue of who had fired first and the circumstances in which each of the deceased had been shot dead. This was supplemented by a superficial and generalised discussion of whether the soldiers had been justified in firing. The finding was that 'in the majority of cases the soldier gave an explanation which, if true, justified his action', and that 'in general the accounts given by the soldiers of the circumstances in which they fired and the reasons why they did so were, in my opinion, truthful'. The report did not support these findings with an analysis of the evidence it accepted and rejected in each individual case. Nor did it even clearly identify and substantiate the minority of cases in which it felt that the soldiers had not been justified in shooting or those cases in which it felt the soldiers had not told the truth. It did say that the shots which killed the four men in Glenfada Park had been fired without justification. However it made no attempt to place these in a different category from any of the other shots fired by the soldiers in the park. Since almost 30 per cent of the 108 shots fired by the Army had been fired in that park, the tribunal's finding that the majority of the firing by the soldiers had been justified has a very hollow ring about it. Indeed it can even be said that it is downright misleading.

Not only is this whole approach likely to convey an incomplete and possibly inaccurate picture of the full circumstances in which the deceased were shot, but it also fails to deliver a full account of the events which led to the deaths that afternoon. Apart from the cases of John Johnson and Damien Donaghy it does not even provide an account of the circumstances in which each of the wounded came to be shot. Similarly it fails to address those instances in which shots were fired which cannot be attributed to any of the known deaths. Indeed it is doubtful that the analysis of the circumstances in which each of the victims were shot dead conveys much useful information about the conduct of the soldiers in firing.

The forensic evidence with respect to the 13 deaths was such that it was possible to match up an individual soldier with a specific fatal shooting in only two instances. For each of the remainder the tribunal attempted to identify the soldier or soldiers responsible by considering: the evidence of each soldier about his location(s) and the circumstances in which he had fired each shot; civilian and material evidence about where and how each victim had been shot dead; and medical evidence about the wounds suffered by each such victim. In a few cases the tribunal felt that it could identify the soldier responsible with a degree of confidence. For the rest, however, it could do no more than identify several soldiers, any one or more of whom could have been responsible.

In order to identify the soldier(s) responsible in each individual case, the tribunal began by using medical evidence to chart the likely line of fire of the fatal bullet(s). It then examined the soldiers' evidence on the time and location of the instances in which they had fired bullets and their description of their target(s). By matching up the medical evidence and the actual description of the victim with the soldiers' accounts, the tribunal sought to identify the soldier who was most likely to have fired the fatal shot in each case. Incredibly the report made no attempt to examine each shot in the context of all the shots fired by the soldier concerned. Equally it made no attempt to examine the fatal shootings in the context of the woundings.

As a result of this peculiar approach the report put more focus on the movements of the victims immediately prior to their death than on the conduct of the soldiers that afternoon. It failed to offer a complete picture of the circumstances in which each soldier had fired each shot. This is particularly disappointing because the tribunal received a very large body of evidence on the circumstances in which each shot had been fired. This evidence included oral evidence given during the tribunal sessions, statement evidence given to the Treasury Solicitor and statements from the soldiers to the military police. Significantly, many of the soldiers who gave evidence about firing at and or hitting targets described those targets in terms that could not be matched with any of the known dead and injured. This, of course, seriously undermined the value of the tribunal's focus on which soldier killed which victim. At the very least it could be expected that the tribunal would use the evidence available to it to present an analysis of the circumstances in which each soldier had fired and to reach findings on the same. Such analysis and findings are the whole object of appointing a tribunal. The public concern which led to the appointment of the tribunal was evoked by the widespread feeling that soldiers may have fired without justification at unarmed civilians, killing and wounding 28. This concern could not be assuaged by a report which deliberately omitted to address each instance in which each soldier had fired and which failed to present reasoned findings on whether each soldier had been justified in his actions. Generalisations are simply not good enough, especially when they are not based on a full and transparent analysis of the evidence.

Interestingly, two early drafts of sections of the report drawn up by the secretary to the tribunal (see later) did attempt to address all the shots fired by each soldier. These sections were missing from the published version. It therefore follows that the tribunal was at least aware of the importance of considering the overall conduct of each soldier who had fired shots, including the circumstances in which he came to fire each shot. At some point, however, a deliberate decision was taken to omit that vital aspect from the report. It is not immediately apparent why the tribunal would have wanted to omit this material. The drafts drawn up by the secretary were actually quite sparse and did little more than offer a potted version of the explanations given by the soldiers concerned.

Before leaving the issue of each shot fired by the soldiers it is necessary to say something about evidence which recently emerged that the soldiers actually fired many more bullets on Bloody Sunday than the 108 officially acknowledged. If shots were fired from the Derry walls then clearly they have not been counted among the 108. This matter is pursued further below. It has also been alleged that at least some of the soldiers who participated in the arrest operation on Bloody Sunday had their own unofficial stocks of bullets. These allegedly included dum dum bullets, which have been outlawed by the Geneva Convention.[15] The primary source of these allegations is an individual who claims to be a member of the 1st Battalion of the Parachute Regiment and to have taken part in the arrest operation on Bloody Sunday. His account has featured in articles in the *Sunday Business Post* and a Channel Four news documentary.[16] As yet his identity has not been officially confirmed so it would be premature to draw firm conclusions from the profoundly disturbing contents of his statement. Nevertheless, vital aspects of his evidence do accord with accounts given by civilian witnesses. Moreover the medical evidence on the wounds sustained by Bernard McGuigan are consistent with the injurious caused by dum dum bullets. If it transpires that the soldiers did have their own personal supply of bullets in addition to their official supply, the whole substance of the Widgery Report will be rendered virtually worthless.

The 'most important single issue'

The second related point which suggests that the tribunal's report may not offer a complete picture of the events which led to the deaths that afternoon concerns the question of who fired first. In its report the tribunal described this question as 'probably the most important single issue' the inquiry had to determine. The tribunal did not actually explain why it considered this to be the single most important issue. However it clearly implied that it was vital in apportioning responsibility for the deaths and injuries suffered that day.

Undoubtedly the question of who fired first is relevant to an objective and complete determination of the events that led to the deaths that afternoon. Moreover if all the shots fired that afternoon were fired in the context of a pitched battle between the army and a unit of the IRA then it may well have been the single most important issue. However there is no suggestion that all the shots were fired in these circumstances. The reality is that at least 21 soldiers fired at least 108 shots in a ten-minute period at different locations. According to the soldiers' version they fired at 40 identified targets. The mere fact (which is disputed) that the first shots were fired at the army does not offer a general justification for the shots fired by each soldier over the next ten minutes. Certainly the legality of each soldier's actions would have to be established individually on the basis of what each saw and believed when he opened fire. The key task for the tribunal, therefore, was to determine whether each individual soldier had been justified in firing each individual shot. Instead of discharging this critical task the tribunal contented itself with general findings about the soldiers' actions which were heavily coloured by its perception of what was the single most important issue the inquiry had to determine.

Shooting from the Derry walls

The evidence suggesting that some of the fatal shots fired on Bloody Sunday were fired from the Derry walls has been steadily mounting in recent years. Don Mullan's book, *Eyewitness Bloody Sunday: The Truth*, published in January 1997, reproduces 114 of the NICRA statements given by civilian witnesses whom Lord Widgery refused to call as witnesses at the inquiry. Some of these statements clearly assert that some of the shots were fired from the direction of the Derry walls. Mullan supports these assertions by reference to medical and ballistics evidence. The reports of the postmortem examination of three of the deceased who had been shot at the same location and time reveal that their wounds all had a remarkably similar 45-degree downward trajectory. This would have been consistent with the deceased having been shot from a position on the Derry walls and totally inconsistent with Widgery's findings to the effect that they had been shot by soldiers on the ground further down Rossville Street. Further ballistics analysis of bullet impact marks on buildings at the entrance to Glenfada Park and Rossville Street support Mullan's thesis that shots were fired from the Derry walls. It would also appear that at least one former soldier in the Royal Anglian Regiment is prepared to confirm that some of the fatal shots were fired from the vicinity of the Walls.

Until all of this evidence has been fully examined and tested by the new inquiry it is not possible to reach any firm conclusions on whether shots were fired from the Derry walls. What is not in doubt is that even in 1972 sufficient evidence was available to present a strong *prima facie* case that soldiers had fired from the vicinity of the walls. The mere fact that Lord Widgery chose to ignore this important issue during the inquiry and in the report indicates a major flaw in the whole proceedings. If it transpires that shots were fired from the Derry Walls then once again the whole substance of the report will be rendered virtually worthless.

Reliance on army evidence

One of the most striking features about the tribunal proceedings was the extent of the conflict between the evidence of army witnesses on the one side and that of civilians and journalists on the other. Broadly speaking it would be fair to say that the evidence of the civilians and journalists was that the army had opened fire on unarmed civilians in circumstances where the lives of soldiers had not been seriously at risk. The evidence from army sources was largely that a legitimate and necessary decision had been taken to effect an arrest operation against rioters, and that individual soldiers had opened fire only when they had identified a gunman or bomber who was threatening their lives or the lives of their comrades. Of course this conflict was evident in the immediate aftermath of the shootings and it was a significant factor in prompting the decision to set up the tribunal of inquiry. The fundamental task of the tribunal was to determine objectively and authoritatively where the truth lay among these conflicting versions.

It has already been seen in Chapter 3 that the inquiry seriously prejudiced the interests of the deceased and injured by refusing to hear evidence from those who had submitted statements to NICRA, by declaring the taped radio messages inadmissible and by failing to call Dr McClean as a witness. These decisions served the interests of the army by reducing the weight of evidence that innocent civilians had been shot without justification. Nevertheless the testimony and material which was formally presented to the tribunal during its public hearings provided a huge body of evidence, much of it from unimpeachable sources, suggesting that many soldiers had indeed shot innocent civilians without justification. This evidence, of course, was in direct conflict with the version of events presented by army witnesses. The critical question, therefore, was how the tribunal was going to resolve this conflict in its report.

It is no exaggeration to say that Lord Widgery based his report almost exclusively on the self-serving testimonies of the soldiers. A major example concerns the issue of who fired first in the courtyard of Rossville Flats, a matter which the tribunal misleadingly elevated to the 'single most important issue' it had to determine. The report dealt with this issue by offering a representative sample of the civilian evidence (including that of journalists), all of which pointed the finger of blame at the army, followed by a summary of evidence from 'Major 236', all of the soldiers who had fired in and around the courtyard and a number of other soldiers who claimed to have witnessed firing in the area at the time. Most but not all of the soldiers testified that the army had come under fire first. Next, most significantly, Lord Widgery included a lengthy section on civilian evidence that gunmen had been present in the Bogside that afternoon. This section covered just about every piece of civilian evidence there was about gunmen in the Bogside that afternoon. Very little of it actually concerned whether shots had been fired at the soldiers in the courtyard of Rossville Flats before the soldiers had themselves opened fire. Nevertheless it was sufficient to convey a misleading impression of the soldiers being subjected to substantial hostile fire when they arrived in Rossville Street. What is missing, however, is any reference to the substantial number of military witnesses who claimed in evidence that they had heard no hostile firing nor seen any nail bombs being thrown during this crucial period. Also missing is any reference to the lack of army reports about hostile fire at that time.

In short the tribunal report piled up the evidence in favour of the army being fired on first in the courtyard of Rossville Flats, including much irrelevant but seriously prejudicial evidence, while at the same time minimising the evidence to the contrary. Consequently Lord Widgery felt able to draw the following conclusions:

> I am entirely satisfied that the first firing in the courtyard was directed at the soldiers. Such a conclusion is not reached by counting heads or by selecting one particular witness as truthful in preference to another. It is a conclusion gradually built up over many days of listening to evidence and watching the demeanour of witnesses under cross-examination. It does not mean that witnesses who spoke in the opposite sense were not doing their best to be truthful. On the contrary I was much impressed by the care with which many of them, particularly the newspaper reporters, television men and photographers, gave evidence. Notwithstanding the opinion of Sergeant O I do not think that the initial firing from the Flats was particularly heavy and much of it may have been ill-directed fire from pistols and like weapons. The soldiers' response was immediate and members of the crowd running away in fear at the soldiers' presence understandably might fail to appreciate that the initial bursts had come from the direction of the Flats. The photographs already referred to in paragraph 7 confirm that the soldiers' initial action was to make arrests and there was no reason why they should have suddenly desisted and begun to shoot unless they had come under fire themselves. If the soldiers are wrong they were parties in a lying conspiracy which must have come to light in the rigorous cross-examination to which they were subject.[17]

This extract is particularly significant in that it identifies all the factors which enabled the tribunal to be 'entirely satisfied' that the army had not fired first. Clearly the key factor is the tribunal's complete acceptance of the soldiers' version of events. This acceptance, however, was based only partly on the soldiers' performance in the witness box. Disturbingly the tribunal also found support for its conclusion in the notion that the soldiers would not have ceased the arrest operation and opened fire if they had not been shot at first. Reliance on this notion is disturbing because it is the very allegation which the tribunal was supposed to be examining. Instead of examining it objectively in the light of all the evidence, the tribunal actually treated it as confirmation of its finding that the army had not opened fire without proper justification.

In a similar vein is the fact that the tribunal found support in the notion that if the soldiers' evidence had not been truthful, then they had been engaged in a lying conspiracy which would have come to light under cross-examination. The tribunal might just as easily have concluded that if the civilian witnesses and journalists had not been telling the truth then they had been engaged in a lying conspiracy which would have been exposed under cross-examination. The naivety of the tribunal in this matter has been exposed, of course, by events since Bloody Sunday, which strongly suggest that cross-examination is not always an effective tool to expose a group of witnesses who are less than truthful in the witness box. It is also worth mentioning at this point that, as will be seen later, virtually all the soldiers concerned had made statements shortly after the shootings which did not accord in many respects with the evidence they gave to the tribunal. Had these earlier statements been available to counsel for the deceased then it is reasonable to assume that their cross-examination would have been much more damaging. The earlier statements were known to counsel for the tribunal, but inexplicably they were not used to conduct a damaging cross-examination of the soldiers. In these circumstances it was, to say the least, disingenuous of the tribunal to consider the soldiers' performance under cross-examination as corroborative of the truth of their evidence.

In the light of the large body of civilian and independent evidence in conflict with the army's version, one might have expected the tribunal to express at least some doubts or uncertainty about who had fired first. Once again, however, the awkward evidence which contradicted the army's version was explained away as mistaken. It is difficult to accept, however, that so many civilians and independent journalists could all have reached the same mistaken conclusion about the same incident based on their own independent powers of observation. To remain 'entirely satisfied' about the army's version in the face of such a large body of evidence to the contrary from independent persons who were 'doing their best to be truthful' suggests an exceptional degree of confidence in the honesty and reliability of the army witnesses.

The other major point of conflict in the evidence presented to the tribunal concerned the central issue of whether the soldiers had been justified in firing. In dealing with this matter Lord Widgery left no doubt that he preferred the self-serving testimony of the soldiers to the conflicting accounts offered by civilian and other independent witnesses:

> Those accustomed to listening to witnesses could not fail to be impressed by the demeanour of the soldiers of 1 Para. They gave their evidence with confidence and without hesitation or prevarication and withstood a rigorous cross-examination without contradicting themselves or each other. With one or two exceptions I accept that they were telling the truth as they remembered it.[18]

Later he went on to say that 'in general the accounts given by the soldiers of the circumstances in which they fired and the reasons why they did so were ... truthful'.[19] It is notable that in both these quotations Lord Widgery implicitly acknowledged a few exceptional cases in which he was not convinced of the veracity of the soldiers' testimonies. Presumably one of the soldiers he had in mind was soldier H, who claimed to have fired 19 shots at a gunman in a flat. Earlier Lord Widgery had concluded that soldier H's version was not credible and that the 19 shots, were therefore unaccounted for. It is also worth noting that soldier H fired 22 shots altogether, one fifth of the total shots officially fired by the soldiers on Bloody Sunday. Moreover he was one of the four soldiers involved in the shootings in Glenfada Park, about which, uniquely, Lord Widgery was unable to draw any firm conclusions because the testimony was so confused and conflicting.[20] These soldiers fired a total of 29 shots in Glenfada Park (including H's 19 which were unaccounted for), killing four and wounding three. It is therefore apparent that on the basis of his own findings Lord Widgery's confidence in the veracity of the soldiers' testimony was misplaced. Moreover the manner in which he declared his belief in that testimony was calculated to conceal the doubts that Widgery himself patently entertained about the soldiers' account of four of the deaths.

The persuasiveness of Lord Widgery's confidence in the testimony of the soldiers is further undermined by the sheer implausibility of that testimony. The most obvious problem in this context is the fact that in most cases there were no dead and wounded to correlate with the accounts given to the tribunal by the soldiers. That in itself raises a huge doubt about the reliability of their evidence. This doubt is accentuated by the fact that there was an almost complete lack of physical, photographic and video evidence to support the soldiers' claims that the persons they had shot had been in possession of guns and bombs and their accounts of the nature and level of hostile shooting and bombing. Lord Widgery's comment on these serious discrepancies and omissions conveys an almost desperate attempt to impart some credence to the soldiers' testimony:

> There is a widely held belief that on some previous occasions when shots have been exchanged in Londonderry, casualties amongst the IRA and their supporters have been spirited away over the border into the Republic. Even a remote possibility that this occurred on 30 January increases the difficulty of trying to match a soldier's account of why he fired with other evidence of the conduct of an individual deceased.[21]

Not surprisingly there was absolutely no evidence to suggest that anything like this occurred with respect to persons killed and injured on Bloody Sunday.

It is also worth noting that there was no evidence of any civilian or military casualties from sources other than the army. With the controversial exception of Gerald Donaghy (see Chapter 5), no guns or bombs were recovered either from the bodies of the dead or from the streets. Nor were any of the deceased or wounded photographed in possession of a gun or a bomb. This was despite the fact that the soldiers claimed that they had come under sustained gun and bomb attack and had only returned fire at identified gunmen and bombers. The soldiers' regular explanation for their failure to recover any guns and bombs was that they had been removed by accomplices. Indeed the evidence of the soldiers regularly depicted an unreal picture of civilians engaging in suicidal behaviour by picking up guns and bombs dropped by the gunmen and bombers on being shot. Given the overwhelming risk to life inherent in such actions, the army's accounts must be treated with the greatest scepticism.

The inherent weaknesses in the soldiers' testimony are sufficient in themselves to call into question the enthusiasm with which Lord Widgery relied upon it. When these weaknesses are added to the conflicting testimony of independent witnesses, Lord Widgery's faith in the soldiers' testimony becomes untenable. This apparent bias in favour of the army permeates his interpretation and presentation of the evidence throughout the report. On the launching of the arrest operation, for example, he was happy to accept the self-serving testimony of three officers despite the fact that it blatantly conflicted with the evidence contained in the brigade log and the testimony of Chief Superintendent Lagan. In no instance did he come down categorically in favour of civilian evidence over army evidence. With respect to the shooting of Damien Donaghy and John Johnson, whom he accepted had been totally innocent civilians, he found it impossible to reach any conclusion on whether explosive substances had been fired at the soldiers. Similarly he found it impossible to reach firm conclusions about the events in Glenfada Park. This contrasted markedly with his ability to reach firm conclusions in favour of the army on many other issues despite the presence of cogent independence evidence to the contrary.

It has already been seen that Lord Widgery's presentation of the evidence seemed unduly favourable to the army. Another example of this can be found in his treatment of the alleged hostile firing of the first high-velocity shot, which had hit a drainpipe on the side of the Presbyterian church. With respect to this incident the report states that:

> [a] large number of witnesses gave evidence about this incident, which clearly occurred and which proves that at that stage there was at least one sniper, equipped with a high velocity weapon, established somewhere in the vicinity of the Rossville Flats and prepared to open fire on the soldiers.

What the report does not reveal is that all of these witnesses were soldiers! Moreover not one of these soldiers actually mentioned this shot in the statements they made to the military police on the night of Bloody Sunday itself. So not only did the report conceal the fact that it accepted the self-serving testimony of the soldiers at face value, but it also concealed the fact that there were grounds to question the reliability of the soldiers' testimony on the matter in question.

A particularly disturbing example of Lord Widgery's approach to resolving the conflict of evidence is actually to be found outside the report altogether. As will be seen below, the documents released by the Home Office in the summer of 1996 included memos from the tribunal secretary to Lord Widgery concerning diverse aspects of the draft report. One such memo contained advice on how Lord Widgery should approach certain issues when drafting his report. In particular the secretary drew Lord Widgery's attention to the remarkable coincidence that the soldiers say they fired at gunmen behind the barricade and that the swab tests on all the people behind the barricade were positive. The secretary recorded Lord Widgery's response as follows: 'LCJ will

pile up the case against the deceased, including the forensic coincidence and the willingness of local people to remove guns, but will conclude that he cannot find with certainty that anyone of 13 was a
gunman.' This is capable of a number of interpretations. At its very
worst and most shameful it could be interpreted as evidence that the
Lord Chief Justice himself was intent on presenting the case against
the deceased in the strongest possible terms; that is, he was consciously
biased in favour of the army. That interpretation is not being relied
on here. Nevertheless, at the very least it suggests that Lord Widgery,
presumably under the influence of the secretary's communication,
adopted an unfair approach to the presentation of the evidence upon
which he based his conclusions. Irrespective of whether or not he
adopted an unfair approach, it is submitted that this appearance is sufficient in itself to impugn the credibility of the tribunal's report. This,
coupled with all of the other examples of bias in favour of the army in
the interpretation and presentation of the evidence, destroys any credible claim that the report might otherwise have had to being an impartial, objective and accurate account of what happened on Bloody
Sunday. It also lends support to the deeply disturbing proposition that
the inquiry and the report were part of a cynical exercise to protect the
British Army and the security and political establishments against the
awful truth and consequences of what happened on Bloody Sunday.
Further support for this proposition can be found in the actions of the
secretary to the tribunal.

The secretary to the tribunal

One of the most shocking and damning aspects of the material
released for public inspection in the summer of 1996 was the revela-
tion of the extent to which the secretary to the tribunal had privately
influenced the substance and presentation of the tribunal's report. It is
to be expected, of course, that the secretary would have assisted Lord
Widgery in his work on the report. It is equally to be expected, however, that his assistance would have been confined to administrative
tasks such as checking out details and references requested by Lord
Widgery. Certainly, it would have been beyond his remit actually to
advise Lord Widgery on the substantive contents of any of his conclusions, or on how those conclusions should be presented or supported,
in order to convey a particular point of view. Similarly it would not
have been his job to identify issues and review the evidence relevant to
those issues. That task was discharged, very properly, by counsel for the

tribunal in his closing address to the tribunal. It is outrageous, there-fore, to find cogent evidence that the secretary may have exerted quite a substantial influence over key issues in the report.

The materials released in the summer of 1996 include a number of memos from the secretary dealing with various aspects of the report and the secretary's comments on various drafts of the report. These reveal that the secretary:

- Identified certain issues that would have to be covered in the report in order to deflect criticism of its contents from quarters hostile to the army; for example 'Discrepancies between the evidence of the journalists and that of the soldiers when the report is published. The journalists will be on to it like hawks. For instance, there is a clear discrepancy between what Winchester says and what soldier F says. The LCJ should deal with this.'
- Flagged aspects of the arrest operation that would have to be addressed in order to deal with the evidence suggesting that it was bungled.
- Presented arguments to undermine the success of counsel for the deceased in undermining the forensic evidence against some of the deceased (indeed he even went so far as to misrepresent the forensic evidence against the deceased in pressing his objective); for example 'Mr McSparran succeeded in throwing doubt on the significance of the paraffin swab tests. But surely it should be said that it is a remarkable coincidence that the soldiers say that they fired at gun-men behind the barricade and that the swab tests on all the people behind the barricade were positive. Dr Martin's scrupulous fairness under cross-examination had the effect of giving a large slice of the benefit of the doubt to the deceased.'
- Added a gloss (favourable to the army) on parts of the counsel for the tribunal's summing up; for example 'There is no point in recapitulating Mr Stocker's analysis. But points which stand out in consideration of the attitude of mind of the soldiers are as follows:

  a) Very active fire was going on when the Composite Force took up their positions.
  b) Sergeant K fired at the two men crawling away from the barri-cade on the strength of the glimpse of a rifle butt. But he had a telescopic site. Furthermore it is recorded at page 87F of Day 15 that he was content with one shot, viz: he was content to stop the man from using his gun again.

c) L himself saw the rifle being pulled along by one of the crawlers and was also ordered to fire by his Platoon Sergeant. He was going forward to the aid of the wounded older man on the barricade when he was called back by his Platoon Sergeant.

d) Soldier M consulted soldier 039 before deciding one of the crawlers was carrying a rifle and opening fire.

e) Soldier C and Lance Corporal D confirmed one another's sighting of a gunman before firing at the window in Block 1 of the Rossville Flats.'

- Advised Lord Widgery on the slant (favourable to the army) to put on parts of the report's conclusions, and actually offered a draft version of some parts; for example:

  – 'There is a good deal of evidence that the initial firing on the soldiers included firing from sub-machine guns, probably Thompson sub-machine guns. The TSMG is a low velocity weapon, but it could hardly be described as a "light weapon". I wonder whether without invalidating your conclusion that the initial firing was not particularly heavy you could amend it to include a reference to some automatic firing.'

  – 'Here is an alternative version for the final paragraph of your Summary of Conclusions. I am not at all proud of it! "There was no general breakdown in discipline. For the most part the soldiers acted as they did because they thought their orders required it. No order and no training can ensure that a soldier will always act wisely, as well as bravely and with initiative. The individual soldier ought not to have to bear the burden of deciding whether to open fire in confusion such as prevailed on 30 January. But that is only another way of saying that it is highly regrettable that the Army has to operate in support of the civil power. Responsibility for the tragedy lies at the door of those in Northern Ireland who systematically employ violence to try to make their views prevail".'

  – 'May I also suggest a strengthening of the second sentence of paragraph 9 as follows: "Some are wholly acquitted of complicity in such action; but there is a strong suspicion that some others had been firing weapons or handling bombs in the course of the afternoon and that yet others had been closely supporting them." My reason for suggesting the change is that I think that you thought that one at least of the men on the barricade had been firing, rather than that all three of them had been close to someone else who had been firing. There is also a minor objection to the text as it stands that it is open to the macabre comment "Of course they were in close proximity to the discharge of firearms. They were close to the Paras".'

• Actually wrote drafts of whole sections of the report and made revisions to some drafts written by Lord Widgery.

The mere fact that the secretary to the tribunal should even attempt to influence the substance of the report and its conclusions in this manner and to this extent is shocking. The whole purpose in appointing a tribunal of inquiry under the 1921 Act was, apart from the fundamental need to establish the truth, to ensure the public that the investigation would be carried out in an impartial, independent, professional and fearless manner. This assurance was essential to achieve that other primary objective in establishing the tribunal, namely public confidence that the full truth would be exposed. It is expected that, insofar as it is possible, the proceedings of such a tribunal would be carried out in public. That, of course, is a vital element in the tribunal's capacity to satisfy its obligations to the public. It therefore follows that the secretary of the tribunal should not work behind the scenes, hidden from the public view and from counsel for the parties and the tribunal itself, to influence the tribunal's interpretation of the evidence, the substance and presentation of the report and the report's conclusions. Such actions are hardly compatible with the obligations placed on the tribunal and the manner in which they are expected to be discharged.

What is even more disturbing is the fact that most of the secretary's suggestions were reflected in the published report. Indeed with respect to some of the secretary's suggestions there is clear evidence that Lord Widgery accepted and acted upon them. For example, with respect to the point above concerning the conflict between journalist and army evidence, the secretary recorded Lord Widgery's response as follows: 'He accepts this. May deal with it by some selected examples (eg Winchester and F) of insoluble clashes between military and civilian evidence. This would follow on the analysis of the charge that Army was trigger happy.' As noted earlier, the point above concerning the forensic evidence is recorded by the secretary as drawing the following response: 'LCJ will pile up the case against the deceased, including the forensic coincidence and the willingness of local people to remove guns, but will conclude that he cannot find with certainty that anyone of 13 was a gunman.'

It is of course disturbing that Lord Widgery should accept and act upon the secretary's suggestions, as that implies that the tribunal's findings were influenced by arguments that were not made in the course of its public hearings and tested in cross-examination by the parties affected. What is more disturbing, perhaps, is the fact that many of the secretary's contributions seem to have been motivated by the desire to present the army's case in a more favourable light than might otherwise have been the case in Lord Widgery's drafts. In the material that has been released for public inspection no example can be found of contributions from the secretary that would have had the effect of putting the case for the deceased or injured in a more favourable light. In short, by accepting and acting upon the secretary's recommendations the tribunal failed to fulfil its obligation to be totally impartial in ascertaining and presenting the full truth of what happened.

Conclusion

The tribunal's report can be interpreted largely as an assertion that there was no 'evil' to be rooted out in the light of events on Bloody Sunday. Even though it concluded that the firing of some soldiers 'bordered on the reckless' it merely attributed this to 'differences in the character and temperament of the soldiers concerned'. Moreover it clearly implied that all of the firing had been in accordance with the limits of the standing orders of the Yellow Card, which it considered satisfactory. The only possible hint of criticism of the army in the report's conclusions was to the effect that if the soldiers had maintained a 'low-key' attitude the day might have passed off without serious incident, and that the army may have underestimated the risk posed to civilians by the circumstances of the arrest operation. However these were more than offset by the very first (and bizarre) finding in the summary of conclusions: that those who organised the march were responsible for the deaths. The findings on every other allegation against the army were resoundingly in favour of the army. As well as those mentioned above these include the finding that the decision to contain the march within the Bogside 'was fully justified by events and was successfully carried out,' that the use of 1 Para as an arrest force had been sincere; that there had been no breach of orders in the launching and conduct of the arrest operation; and that there had been no general breakdown in discipline. The question therefore arises whether the tribunal had discharged its task successfully by investigating and concluding that there was no 'evil' to be rooted out. Could these findings in favour of the army restore public confidence in 'the purity and integrity of our public life without which a successful democracy is impossible'?

It is a sad fact of life in Northern Ireland that there is a section of public opinion which would not be unduly concerned if the army had fired on unarmed civilians in the Bogside. There is an even larger section who would simply refuse to believe that the British Army would do any such thing. There are also those who would be only too willing to believe it irrespective of the evidence. It is axiomatic that these sections of the public would not be profoundly influenced by the contents of the tribunal's report one way or the other. The success of the report cannot be judged by the extent to which it mollified or confirmed their prejudices. It must be judged against its capacity to satisfy any reasonable person who would be appalled by the notion that the army of a democratic state founded on the rule of law could fire on its own unarmed civilians, killing 13 and wounding 15, while they were engaged in a public protest against the government of the day.

This and the preceding chapter have exposed aspects of the tribunal, the manner in which it conducted its inquiry and the substance of its report which suggest that a reasonable person could not place his or her confidence in the tribunal's findings. The immediate implication, of course, is that the tribunal did not discharge the vital task for which it was appointed. Its findings were not sufficient to restore public confidence in the integrity of the government. Indeed there are substantial grounds for believing that the whole exercise merely compounded the deep sense of injustice and fundamental lack of confidence in the integrity of government which were generated by the events of Bloody Sunday. Any lingering doubt there may be about this will surely be dispelled by an analysis of the evidence given by the soldiers to the tribunal in the light of the original statements they made on the night of Bloody Sunday.

5
The Soldiers' Statements

Reliance on army evidence

One of the most striking features of the Widgery Report is the extent to which it relied on the self-serving testimony of the soldiers. It is to be expected, of course, that the tribunal of inquiry would have accepted and acted upon the soldiers' testimony if it was satisfied that that testimony was credible and reliable. By the same token it is to be expected that the tribunal would have accepted and acted upon civilian testimony and other material evidence which was found to be credible and reliable. Where evidence from these respective sources conflicted, despite appearing to be both credible and reliable, it is to be expected that the tribunal would have looked to independent sources of evidence to help establish the facts. A critical weakness of the Widgery Tribunal, however, is the fact that it clung stubbornly to its belief in the integrity of the soldiers and the veracity of their testimony, despite the existence of a substantial body of evidence from impeccable and independent sources which directly contradicted the soldiers' testimony in most of the key issues. Nor was this belief shaken by the fact that the testimony of some of the soldiers was clearly incredible. Lord Widgery himself was unable to accept the testimony of the soldiers involved in the Glenfada Park shootings, which accounted for four of the dead and three of the wounded and nearly 30 per cent of all of the shots officially fired on Bloody Sunday. Similarly he declared that Soldier S's firing of 12 shots at a suspected gunman in an alleyway between the flats had been 'unjustifiably dangerous' in the circumstances. When these are added to the shots fired by the soldiers in Glenfada Park it transpires that Lord Widgery had serious concerns about the justification for at least 40 per cent of the shots fired on

Bloody Sunday. This is not however, reflected, in the substance of his report.

Throughout the report it is evident that Lord Widgery's unshakeable and seemingly irrational trust in the soldiers' testimony was based on the impression they made upon him in the witness box. Early on in the report he cursorily set aside the evidence of the army's own brigade log and the supporting sworn testimony of Chief Superintendent Lagan, simply because three officers went into the witness box and offered sworn testimony that the entry in the log did not accurately record the critical events surrounding the launch of the arrest operation. It is also worth quoting again the comments of Lord Widgery on how the soldiers generally impressed him in the witness box:

> Those accustomed to listening to witnesses could not fail to be impressed by the demeanour of the soldiers of 1 Para. They gave their evidence with confidence and without hesitation or prevarication and withstood a rigorous cross-examination without contradicting themselves or each other. With one or two exceptions I accept that they were telling the truth as they remembered it.[1]

The report went on to conclude that 'in general the accounts given by the soldiers of the circumstances in which they fired and the reasons why they did so were ... truthful'. Clearly Lord Widgery based his findings on what he considered to be the impeccable performance of the soldiers in the witness box. It therefore follows that if it can be established that the accounts given by the soldiers in the witness box did not always accord with their original accounts, and that the circumstances of their examination and cross-examination were such that the differences were unlikely to be exposed and tested, the whole credibility of the Widgery Report and its findings will be severely undermined.

The reliability of the soldiers' testimony and the manner in which they withstood cross-examination in the witness box must now be reassessed in the light of the statements they submitted to the military police on the night of Bloody Sunday. The contents and indeed the very existence of these statements were not revealed until the summer of 1996. It is submitted that the following analysis of the statements and their significance for the testimony offered by the soldiers to the tribunal reveal that the soldiers' testimony cannot be relied upon as a complete and accurate account of the circumstances in which the shots were fired on Bloody Sunday. The tribunal failed to expose the inherent untrustworthiness of the soldiers' testimony. Perhaps even more disturbing is the possibility that the tribunal may not have been acting in good faith when it declared its confidence in the honesty and accuracy of the soldiers' testimony. Indeed it would appear that the tribunal concealed the very existence of the soldiers' original statements.

The soldiers' statements

Among the documents released in the summer of 1996 were 41 statements made to the military police by soldiers who participated in the Bloody Sunday operation. All of the soldiers who opened fire in Derry that afternoon made a statement to the military police that night. In the course of the few days immediately after 30 January some of these soldiers also made supplementary statements. Of the 41 statements available for public inspection 13 are supplementaries (two from one soldier). Statements were also taken by employees of the Treasury Solicitor acting on behalf of the tribunal from all those soldiers who were subsequently called to give evidence to the tribunal (from here on these statements are referred to as statements to the Treasury Solicitor). Most of these were taken in early March. It is also apparent that many of the other soldiers and police personnel involved in the events of Bloody Sunday made statements to the military police on 30–31 January 1972. Not all of them, however, are among those which have been released. There must therefore be a suspicion that the documents were removed by the Home Office before the decision on public access was taken.

The partial release of these statements provided an additional and significant source of material on the circumstances surrounding the firing of each bullet on the afternoon of Bloody Sunday. With respect to each shooting incident, the actual evidence given to the tribunal has now been supplemented by at least two statements from each of the soldiers who fired the shots: one made to the military police on the night of 30–31 January (plus supplementaries) and the other made to the Treasury Solicitor in early March for the purposes of the tribunal proceedings. Significantly counsel for the relatives did not have access to these statements. Now, however, it is possible to consider the testimony given to the tribunal by each soldier in the light of the statement made by that soldier on the night of 30–31 January 1972. If this exercise reveals serious and relevant discrepancies between the two, the trust that the tribunal placed in the soldiers' testimony will be very severely challenged. Given the extent to which the inquiry's findings depended on the reliability and veracity of the soldiers' testimony, the unavoidable conclusion will be that the inquiry's findings were fatally flawed.

Unfortunately for the tribunal and for those who placed their trust in the reliability of its findings, an assessment of the soldiers' evidence reveals, for most soldiers, serious differences between the accounts they gave to the military police and the accounts they gave to the tribunal. Each soldier's account is considered in turn; a feature which is noticeably missing from the tribunal's report. It is also worth noting that counsel to the Saville Tribunal has carried a detailed comparison of the accounts offered by each soldier in his statements to the military police and employees of the Treasury Solicitor and his testimony to the Widgery Tribunal. The results of this exercise are set out in tabular form highlighting discrepancies among the accounts offered by each soldier.[2] Instances where a soldier included details in his testimony which did not appear in his original statement to the military police are also noted, although they are not described as discrepancies. Counsel to the tribunal makes no attempt to interpret the significance of any of these discrepancies, although he does draw attention to instances where his view of the existence of a discrepancy differs from that of the findings of the author as presented in *The Bloody Sunday Tribunal of Inquiry: A Resounding Defeat for Truth, Justice and the Rule of Law*. Nevertheless, the results of counsel's exercise clearly illustrate the extent to which the testimony of many soldiers differed from the accounts they had originally offered to the military police.

The William Street shootings

Soldiers A and B had been the first soldiers to open fire on alleged targets. Indeed their shots had been separate in both time and place from the main shootings. They had been stationed in a three-storey derelict building on William Street just to the west of some open land near the Presbyterian church. Soldier A had been in an upper room and B had been on the ground floor. Both claimed in oral testimony that they had seen two smoking objects flying past the building in which they were stationed and then heard two explosions which they had presumed to be nail bombs. This had happened just before 4 pm. Both claimed that they had identified a nail bomber. Both had fired independently at this target, with A firing two shots and B firing three (while wearing his gas mask). B claimed that his target had always been in his sights and that there had been about eight people immediately behind the target. A, on the other hand, claimed that the target had been darting in and out from the corner of a building at a different spot from that identified by B. Moreover A had not seen any other persons in the immediate vicinity. Despite these differences in their testimony to the tribunal, both claimed to have shot and hit the same target, namely Damien Donaghy. Neither admitted to having shot John Johnson, although it is clear that he had been shot in the same incident. Significantly A claimed to have received orders to shoot from his platoon commander. B, on the other hand, had shot without communicating with his commander even though he had been in the same room. Another significant feature is that there is no record of this shooting in the brigade log. It follows that, contrary to established practice, it was not reported immediately after the event.

The tribunal accepted that both Donaghy and Johnson had not been throwing nail bombs and were innocent of any wrongdoing.[3] Nevertheless it also accepted that both soldiers A and B honestly believed that they had fired at a man who was about to throw a nail bomb at them. In reaching this conclusion it also accepted that they believed they had seen and heard nail bombs being thrown in their vicinity, despite the fact that all non-army evidence refuted the claim that nail bombs had been thrown in the vicinity. The tribunal made no attempt to determine how a second innocent man had come to be shot when both soldiers had apparently fired at and hit the same innocent target. Nor did it seriously address the discrepancies between the soldiers' accounts of the firing, nor the admitted failure by soldier B to report the presence of the nail bomber to his commander before firing or to report the firing immediately to his base.

The statements made by A and B on the night of the firing differ on some critical points, and A's statement differs in some vital respects from the account he gave to the tribunal. A's original account placed his target at a different spot from that in B's account. Also, in A's original account the target was holding the alleged nail bomb in his right hand and striking it against the wall, at which point it ignited. In B's original account, by contrast, the target was holding the bomb in his right hand and striking a fuse match against the wall with his left hand. Interestingly in A's later statement to the Treasury Solicitor he made two critical corrections to his original statement. The first changed the location of his target to bring it more into line with that of B's target. The second revised his description of the actions of the target in lighting the alleged nail bomb to make it identical to B's account. This correction was vital not just in order to make A's statement consistent with B's, but also because it was highly improbable as it stood. Nail bombs are not ignited by striking them against the wall. If all that A had seen was a man striking an object against the wall, he would hardly have been justified in shooting to kill that man.

The vital question, of course, is why A changed his account in these critical respects. Was it the result of mature reflection, or was it the result of advice that his original account might not afford sufficient justification for his action given that two persons had been wounded and both were objectively innocent of any wrongdoing? An additional or alternative possibility might have been a desire to avoid the difficulties that would arise from substantive differences between the accounts of A and B. Soldier A explained that the correction of the bomber's location had been necessary because the map he had used when he made his original statement had not been sufficiently detailed for him to pinpoint the exact position of the bomber. He also claimed that his original hand-written statement had stated that the bomber had struck a match against the wall with his left hand and brought it towards a round object (which he had presumed to be a nail bomb) in his right hand. He suggested that a mistake must have been made in typing up his original hand-written version. It is not possible, of course, to reach any definite conclusions on these issues. Given the manner in which the corrections were made, however, there is at least the appearance that soldier A was advised about the discrepancies between his statement and that of B either when or immediately before he made his statement to the Treasury Solicitor. It is also worth emphasising that the critical differences between the original statements of A and B and those between A's original account and the evidence he gave to the tribunal were not revealed during examination in chief nor probed during cross-examination. Counsel for the deceased would not have been aware of the contents of the original statements by the soldiers.

The first shots on Rossville Street

Soldier N had been the commander of Mortar Platoon. His platoon had been the first to debus in Rossville Street. Significantly he had heard no shots at all until he fired himself. He claimed in his testimony to the tribunal that he had fired three shots over the head of a crowd that was advancing threateningly towards him from an alleyway leading from Chamberlain Street. This of course was the crowd that had been stampeded in panic by the advance of C Company up Chamberlain Street. Soldier N described firing the first two of these shots into the wall of

13 Chamberlain Street at about two feet above head height, and the third into the east wall of 14 Chamberlain Street at head height. All three shots are significant for at least two reasons. First, there is a very strong case for believing that they were the first shots fired on Rossville Street. It is difficult to see how soldiers in any of the other vehicles would have had time to debus and commence making arrests before these shots were fired. If shots had been fired at the vehicles before the soldiers in any of the other vehicles had had time to debus it is difficult to see how they had not been seen or heard by Soldier N. However it is quite feasible that the three shots fired by Soldier N were heard by other soldiers but they did not immediately presume that they had come from an army source. Whatever the correct explanation the tribunal ignored the strong possibility that these shots had been the first shots fired on Rossville Street when making its determination on who had fired first.

The second significant feature about these shots was the fact that they were fired contrary to the terms of the Yellow Card. The tribunal did not attach much importance to the strict terms of the Yellow Card *per se*. It was more concerned to consider whether the soldiers had engaged collectively in undisciplined or unjustified shooting. In its brief consideration of the instances when warning shots had been fired over the heads of a crowd it did not conclude that there were grounds for admonishing the soldiers concerned.[4] This position is particularly startling in N's case as he actually admitted in testimony to the tribunal that one of the shots had been fired at head height. Moreover the evidence of a journalist who would have been in the immediate vicinity of the warning shots fired by N was that a bullet had hit the wall about 5–10 inches above his head. The timing and location of this incident suggests very strongly that this had been one of the bullets fired by N. Incredibly the tribunal did not consider this aspect of N's warning shots. This omission is particularly significant not just because it suggests a reluctance to address evidence of unacceptable conduct by individual soldiers, but also because N claimed that shortly after firing these warning shots he had fired at and hit an alleged nail bomber.

N claimed that he had spotted a person about to throw a smoking object, which he had taken to be a nail bomb. He had fired one shot at this person, hitting him in the leg. The victim had then staggered out of sight behind a wall. N had not seen or heard the alleged nail bomb explode. Since the tribunal did not examine all the wounding cases (with the exception of Donaghy and Johnson) the propriety of N's actions in this matter was not considered.

There are some discrepancies between the account given by N in his original statement and that offered to the tribunal. In his original statement he claimed that he had fired one shot high into the east wall of 14 Chamberlain Street and two high into the north wall of 13 Chamberlain Street. This was the reverse order to that given in testimony to the tribunal. The version given to the tribunal appeared for the first time in the statement made to the Treasury Solicitor. The discrepancy was neither explained nor disclosed during the tribunal proceedings.

Strangely, in an additional statement the next day he said that after firing the first shot he had thought that his rifle had not recocked, whereupon he had ejected a live bullet before firing again. This meant that he had used one more bullet than accounted for in his original statement. While this addendum does not disclose any impropriety when considered in isolation, it nevertheless contributes to a general trend of soldiers making subsequent additions to their statements in order to make them more consistent with the facts and/or consistent with each other. Although Soldier N did mention the ejection of the live bullet in testimony to the tribunal, it was not disclosed that it had not been included in his original statement.

Rossville Flats courtyard

Overview

The general thrust of the soldiers' testimony on the firing in and around the courtyard of Rossville Flats is that they had come under sustained gunfire from several gunmen, nail bombing from several nail bombers, acid bombs from the flats, at least one petrol bomb and other missiles. They claimed to have identified no fewer than six or possibly seven gunmen. Three soldiers had fired at five or possibly six of these gunmen in all and claimed three or four strikes. Two soldiers also claimed to have shot at two nail bombers and one petrol bomber, while one soldier claimed to have shot at one acid bomber.

It must be said at the outset that the soldiers' testimony on these matters lacked credibility. For a start there was only one known casualty, and his description and the location of his shooting did not match any of the accounts given by the soldiers. Furthermore there is no doubt that a large number of civilians ran through the courtyard during these events. It is unlikely, to say the least, that gunmen and bombers could go into action with the degree of ferocity alleged without causing a substantial number of casualties and without the civilians and journalists present being aware of it. In fact there had been only one casualty and he had been shot by the soldiers in the presence of numerous and reliable civilian witnesses.

The civilians and journalists in question were virtually unanimous in claiming that the soldiers had chased the crowd into the courtyard of the flats and opened fire without any obvious or serious provocation. No-one (apart from the soldiers) had seen anyone fire shots or throw nail, acid or petrol bombs. The veracity of the soldiers' allegations was seriously undermined by the fact that they were not supported by independent sources of evidence. It was further undermined by the fact that it did not fit easily with the known facts. For example no bodies or wounded people were found at the spots where the soldiers claimed to have hit gunmen and bombers. None of the dead or wounded (wherever they were found) could be matched with the descriptions of the alleged gunmen and bombers that the soldiers claimed to have shot. The only person to have been shot dead in the courtyard was John Duddy. Neither the place where he was shot nor his description matched any of the victims the soldiers claim to have shot in the courtyard. Moreover there is ample reliable evidence to establish that Duddy had been shot dead while running away, along with many others, from the advancing soldiers. The forensic evidence established that there was no suspicion that he might have fired a gun or thrown a nail bomb. This was confirmed by all the witnesses to his shooting.

In the light of this evidence to the inquiry one might have expected the tribunal to conclude, at the very least, that no serious credibility could be attached to the soldiers' testimony of their firing in the courtyard. Incredibly, however, the tribunal did not even examine the circumstances in which each individual soldier had opened fire. Instead it attempted to determine who had fired first and who had shot John Duddy. Bizarrely, the tribunal concluded that Duddy had probably run into a line of fire directed at a gunman or bomber. No attempt was made to determine where this gunman or bomber might have been, or exactly what evidence there was for his existence. Instead the tribunal contented itself with the dubious finding that the soldiers had been fired on first in the vicinity of the courtyard and that they had returned shots at identifiable targets (that is, gunmen or bombers). The tribunal did not examine on a case-by-case basis the testimony of each soldier who had fired shots in the courtyard. It simply reached the general conclusion that the evidence of the soldiers as a whole was honest and reliable, and that they genuinely believed that they had fired at legitimate targets in each instance. This was despite the fact that the tribunal itself expressed doubts about Soldier O's testimony on the severity of the hostile fire directed at the soldiers. The failure of the tribunal to examine the evidence of each of the soldiers on a case-by-case basis was a serious weakness in its procedure and raises substantial grounds for doubt about the credibility of its findings. These doubts are considerably enhanced by the discrepancies between the accounts given by the soldiers concerned in their original statements and the testimony they offered to the tribunal.

Soldier Q

Soldier Q had been in soldier N's platoon. In his testimony he claimed to have heard shots about one minute after debussing, but he did not know where they had come from or at whom they had been fired. If these shots had not been fired by the army then his testimony on this point does not accord with N's. He claimed that he had seen a person throwing what appeared to be nail bombs at soldiers. He further claimed that one of them had exploded and that he had shot the bomber as he was about to throw another. This other bomb had rolled away without exploding. However the tribunal was not able to identify a victim who accorded with Q's account. Moreover none of the civilian witnesses or journalists had seen a nail bomb explode in the courtyard.

In his original statement Q claimed that the person whom he had shot had been throwing nail bombs at soldiers taking cover behind a military vehicle about 50 yards from the corner of Block 1. In his testimony, however, he said that the person had been throwing the bombs at soldiers at the entrance to Chamberlain Street. The version given in testimony first appeared in the statement given to the Treasury Solicitor. No explanation was offered for the discrepancy, nor was it revealed during the tribunal proceedings. One possible explanation for the change is that the soldiers sheltering behind the military vehicle would have been beyond the range of a bomber located at the position where Q claimed that the bomber had been located. Accordingly some alteration would have been necessary in order to protect Q's original account from being discredited under cross-examination. In his original statement Q also said that the bomber had thrown only one nail bomb before he shot him, while in testimony he said that he had thrown several.

Soldier S

Soldier S had been in N's vehicle. He claimed in his testimony that they had come under fire immediately upon debussing. This plainly contradicts N's testimony. S had taken shelter at the back of the houses on Chamberlain Street and had spotted a gunman firing from between Blocks 1 and 2. He had returned fire on four separate occasions, firing three shots on each occasion. He believed he had struck his target twice, although it might not have been the same gunman on both occasions as he had kept moving in and out of S's vision. The tribunal was unable to identify any person who had been killed or injured in circumstances that accorded with S's account.

There are several discrepancies between S's original statement and the testimony he gave to the tribunal. First, there was no mention in the original of coming under fire immediately after debussing. Given N's evidence to the tribunal this omission is particularly significant. It raises a serious question about the credibility of S's testimony on this point to the tribunal. His claim that they had come under fire was first mentioned in S's statement to the Treasury Solicitor, but no explanation was offered as to why it was first disclosed at that point. Its absence from the original statement was not disclosed during the tribunal proceedings. It is worth recalling in this context that S's testimony was specifically cited (and presumably relied upon) during the tribunal's consideration of the 'vital issue' of who had fired first.

Interestingly, S claimed in his original statement that he had first cocked his weapon when he took up position at the back of Chamberlain Street. This would suggest that he had not come under fire immediately upon debussing. In his statement to the Treasury Solicitor (and in testimony to the tribunal), however, the original version changed to the effect that he had cocked his weapon as soon as he had come under fire, which in the context of this statement (and testimony) meant immediately after debussing and before taking up position at the back of Chamberlain Street. It is difficult not to conclude that at some point after making his original statement a deliberate decision was taken to change the original version of events to include a false assertion that he had come under fire immediately after debussing. The discrepancy about when he cocked his weapon was not disclosed during the tribunal proceedings.

Second, S said in his original statement that a section of the crowd had opened up to reveal the gunman and closed again immediately after S had returned fire. S claimed that this pattern had repeated itself on each of the four occasions on which he had fired at the gunman's position. This account was not repeated in testimony. It is almost inconceivable that unarmed civilians would repeatedly put themselves in the line of fire between a soldier and a gunman, particularly when it was generally agreed that the crowd had been trying to escape through the alleyways between the flats. No explanation was offered of why S's testimony on this point should have changed from his original statement. One obvious possibility is that he had been advised that it was barely credible as it stood and that it would probably come under attack for that reason at the tribunal. The discrepancy between S's original statement and his testimony on this point was not disclosed during the proceedings.

Third, in his original statement he claimed that nail bombs and acid bombs had been raining down from the flats, while in his testimony to the tribunal he only mentioned the acid bombs. In his statement to the Treasury Solicitor he admitted that his earlier claim about nail bombs raining down from the flats had not been correct. He explained the discrepancy rather weakly by saying that he had heard distant bangs and assumed that they were nail bombs. Neither the alteration nor the explanation was disclosed during the tribunal proceedings.

It is also worth mentioning in this context that after making his original statement on 30–31 January, S made a further statement on 4 February. It is not entirely clear why he made this additional statement because it relates not to any of his actions but to the actions of Soldier O. In it he claimed that he had seen a gunman open fire from a ground-floor window in the flats and that O had engaged this gunman. Oddly, O's version of this incident differed in some respects. S also claimed in the additional statement that he had seen nail bombs and acid bombs being dropped from the flats. In fact he specifically mentioned seeing five nail bombs. This claim was made a full four days after his original statement. Given that S subsequently admitted to the Treasury Solicitor that he had not seen any nail bombs, a serious doubt is obviously raised about the truthfulness of his evidence in general. Nevertheless these facts about the nail bombs were never disclosed to the counsel for the deceased, nor were they adverted to during the tribunal proceedings.

Fourth, in his original statement S claimed that the shots fired at him by the gunman between Blocks 1 and 2 had passed about 5–10 metres from him and struck the wall about 50 metres behind him, while in his statement to the Treasury Solicitor he stated that the shots had hit the wall about 5–10 metres behind him. Once again, this discrepancy was not disclosed during the tribunal proceedings.

Soldier V

Soldier V had been in N's vehicle. In his testimony to the tribunal he claimed that he had heard two explosions before debussing with S. He had heard and seen rifle fire landing near them just after debussing.

His testimony on both these points was obviously not supported by N's and it did not accord fully with S's. V had fired one shot at a person who was about to throw a petrol bomb with a lit fuse. He had hit his target and spotted the fuse burning some distance away. He had assumed that the person concerned had thrown the bomb and that the fuse had become detached. The circumstances of the shooting and the description of the victim as given by V could not be matched up with any of the casualties.

V claimed that after shooting the bomber he had taken up position behind S at the back of Chamberlain Street. This is strange because in testimony S said that a gunman had fired shots at him which struck the wall behind him. V did not report seeing or hearing these shots. Moreover S did not report seeing V firing at the alleged petrol bomber. The testimony of S and V also differed on the question of the number and movement of people in the immediate vicinity. More serious problems with V's testimony are revealed when it is compared with his original statement to the military police.

In his original statement V said that he had seen a person throw a bottle with a fuse attached to it. The bottle had hit the ground but had not exploded. V had then fired one shot at the bottle thrower. On the basis of this statement there were grounds for charging V with murder or attempted murder, depending on whether his target had been killed or not. It is therefore highly significant that the version given in testimony was substantially different. In testimony he claimed to have fired as the bomber was about to throw. This would make a charge of murder or attempted murder much more difficult to sustain. The difference first appeared in V's statement to the Treasury Solicitor, but no explanation was offered apart from his assertion that the version he gave to the Treasury Solicitor was correct. Once again the change was not disclosed during the tribunal proceedings. It is difficult to believe that such a critical change was merely the product of V recalling the sequence of events more accurately at a later date. There must at least be a suspicion that he had been advised to revise his original version in order to protect himself against the threat of criminal proceedings.

There are other discrepancies between V's original statement and the account he offered in testimony. In the former he claimed that he had heard two explosions as he debussed. In testimony he said that he had heard these before debussing. In his statement he said that the rioters had thrown petrol bombs and acid bombs. In testimony he mentioned only one petrol bomb and made no mention of acid bombs being thrown. In his statement to the Treasury Solicitor he admitted that he had not seen any petrol bombs being thrown. However he did not offer any explanation for his earlier statement to the contrary. Furthermore in his original statement V said that firing had been directed at them from several different directions. He did not make this claim in testimony.

Taking all these discrepancies into account, including the disparities between his testimony and that of others such as S and N, it would be difficult to place much trust in V's testimony.

Soldier O

Soldier O had been in the second vehicle of N's platoon. In his testimony he said that he had not heard any shots on debussing. However, after he had begun to make arrests they had come under fire from four or five different positions in the flats. He claimed that about 80–100 shots had been fired at them in a very short space of time. It was the most intense he had ever experienced over a few minutes. O claimed that he had fired three shots at a man firing a pistol from behind a car parked in the forecourt of the flats. He claimed that he had missed with his first shot and struck with the other two. The gunman had been carried away by three or four men and a Knight of Malta. O had then seen a gunman on the lower catwalk between Blocks 2 and 3. He had fired three shots at him. The first one had missed but he had hit the target with the next two. The gunman had been dragged away by people on the balcony. A few minutes later he had fired two shots at a gunman between Blocks 2 and 3, but he did not know if he scored a hit.

The reliability of O's testimony is suspect in at least two important respects without ever having to compare it with his original statement. First, his account of the intensity of the hostile firing in the forecourt was so far-fetched that the tribunal itself felt the need expressly to discount it.[5] Second, his account of the circumstances in which he had shot his victims did not accord with the circumstances in which any of the dead or wounded had been hit. The significance of these points is enhanced by the many discrepancies between the account given in his original statement and that given in testimony.

In his original statement he made no claim that the hostile firing was the most intense he had ever experienced. He also said that he had been at the rear of the military vehicle when the firing started, while in testimony he said that he had been returning to it. In the original statement he said he had fired two shots at the gunman on the catwalk, while in testimony he said it was three. He corrected his original statement on this point the next day by making an additional statement. However he did not explain why he did not mention firing the three shots in his original statement. In his original statement he said that he had not seen the gunman on the catwalk after he shot him, but he had seen people dragging something along the catwalk before they disappeared and reappeared shortly afterwards at ground level. In testimony, however, he said that he had seen people dragging the body of the gunman into the cover of an archway and made no mention of them reappearing at ground level. In his original statement he claimed that they had come under attack from several acid bombs and petrol bombs. In testimony, however, he said that he had seen only one acid bomb and did not mention seeing any petrol bombs. In his original statement he made no mention of giving an order to shoot anyone who threw acid bombs from the flats. In testimony he claimed that he had given this order. None of these discrepancies were disclosed during the tribunal proceedings.

It is also worth noting that O's weapon had been cocked from the time they left Little James Street. He claimed that N had given them permission to cock their weapons at that point. This suggests that the soldiers had been expecting to engage gunmen even before they moved through the barriers.

Soldier R

Soldier R had been in the second vehicle of N's platoon. He had debussed in the company of soldiers O and T. He claimed in his testimony to have heard one or two explosions shortly after debussing, and as they had moved into the forecourt of Rossville Flats they had come under intense gunfire from around the flats. He claimed that he had spotted a man about to throw a lighted nail bomb. He had shot the man and the bomb had dropped to his feet but had not exploded. Then he had been splashed by one of two acid bombs thrown from the flats, but he had not sought immediate medical attention. He had seen O fire at a man by a car in the carpark. Then he had seen a man between Blocks 2 and 3 fire a pistol. He had returned three shots but did not know if he hit the target.

There are problems with the testimony that R gave to the tribunal. His claim about coming under intense fire as they advanced into the forecourt raises the question of why the soldiers should have continued to advance in such circumstances. It also suffers from the weakness common to other such testimony, namely that no civilian or military casualties resulted from the allegedly intense firing despite the fact that it supposedly occurred in a confined space where a substantial number of people were present. His shooting of the alleged nail bomber provides yet another example of a lighted nail bomb failing to explode. Also, none of the victims match the circumstances in which R claimed to have shot the nail bomber. Further weaknesses are revealed by comparing his original statement with his testimony to the tribunal.

In his original statement he said that acid bombs had been thrown at them, one of which had 'splattered' across his legs. In an additional statement made on 4 February this was changed to two bombs actually 'striking' him on the legs and staining his denims. He also claimed in this statement that another soldier had thrown water over his legs to prevent him from being burned. In his statement to the Treasury Solicitor he stated that the water had not been thrown on him until later. In his original statement there was no mention of O firing at the gunman at the car. He did not mention this incident until the additional statement. It is also significant that in his statement to the Treasury Solicitor he changed his original story in order to bring it into line with the statements of O and T. However at no point in any of his statements did he mention T firing, or being ordered to fire, at the alleged acid bomber. He did however, make these assertions in his testimony. No explanation was offered for any of the discrepancies between R's statements and his testimony, or for any of the additions. Their existence was not disclosed during the tribunal proceedings.

It is also worth noting that in his testimony to the tribunal R claimed that he was entitled to shoot when confronted by a gunman or bomber, even if there were innocent people in the vicinity.

Soldier T

Soldier T had been in the second vehicle in N's platoon. He had debussed in the company of O and R. Unlike R, he had not heard or seen any explosions or nail bombs shortly after debussing. He claimed in his testimony, however, that he had been splashed by acid from bombs thrown from the flats. On the order of O he had fired two shots at a person he claimed had been about to throw an acid bomb, but did not claim a hit. His identification of the bomber was based on the fact that he had already seen him throw what he took to be an acid bomb on account of its colour. He had fired at him when he saw him with another bottle in his hand. Even if T's account is true, it means that he fired in circumstances where the threat to life was highly speculative.

There was also a significant difference in the account that he gave of this incident in his original statement.

In T's original statement he said that he had taken aim as the alleged bomber had been bringing his arm back to throw the second bottle, and he had fired just as the target let go. In his statement to the Treasury Solicitor this had changed to firing after the second bottle had been thrown and before it hit the ground. The second version allows T to claim that he had had the opportunity (which was not present in the first version) to see the colour of the contents of the second bottle. No explanation was given for this change, nor was its existence disclosed during the tribunal proceedings.

Another significant feature of T's original statement was the fact that he did not mention any shots being fired after debussing. This, of course, conflicted with the accounts given by O and R. It is interesting, therefore, that by the time T came to make his statement to the Treasury Solicitor it included a claim that he had heard a burst of gunfire after debussing. Once again, T's testimony about hearing the burst of gunfire was specifically cited (and presumably relied upon) during the tribunal's consideration of the 'vital issue' of who had fired first. The tribunal, however, clearly ignored the fact that this vitally significant piece of evidence was not contained in T's original statement.

The barricade shootings

Overview

Eight of the deceased were shot at or around the barricade in Rossville Street. On the basis of the soldiers' testimony any of at least ten soldiers could have been responsible for one or more of these deaths. Only in the case of Michael Kelly was it established with certainty that Soldier F had fired the fatal shot.

In its assessment of the shootings at or around the barricade the tribunal rejected the allegation that the soldiers had fired indiscriminately into the backs of a large crowd of people as they tried to scramble to safety across the barricade.[6] On the basis of eyewitness and forensic evidence there were grounds upon which the tribunal could reasonably have come to this conclusion. However that does not answer the question of whether the soldiers had been justified in firing at targets at or around the barricade and, in particular, at the victims who were shot dead. There was seriously conflicting evidence about the circumstances in which each of the victims had been shot at the barricade. Each of the soldiers claimed that all their shots had been

aimed at persons who were firing guns or nail bombs or were in possession of guns or nail bombs. All the civilian and journalist witnesses
claimed that they had not seen anyone at the barricades with either
guns or nail bombs. Those who had actually seen individuals being
shot denied that they had been armed. There was no photographic evidence of anyone at the barricades possessing guns or nail bombs and
no guns or nail bombs were recovered. With respect to some of the victims, the forensic evidence held out the possibility that they might
have either fired a gun or been in the immediate vicinity of a gun
being fired. However the tribunal decided that this evidence was not
strong enough to warrant a finding that any particular individual had
fired a gun. There was no forensic evidence to suggest that any of the
victims may have thrown a nail bomb.

In the light of all this evidence it would have been very difficult for
the tribunal to be satisfied that the soldiers had fired with justification.
Indeed it is significant that at no point did the tribunal make a specific
finding about the propriety of the actions of the soldiers who were
responsible for the deaths at or around the barricade. It contented itself
with a finding that the soldiers had not fired into the backs of a fleeing
crowd. When considering the circumstances in which each of the
deceased had been shot, the tribunal totally avoided making a finding
on the propriety of the soldiers' actions (with the possible exception of
an expression of confidence in Soldier K's evidence, which is dealt with
later). The tribunal's failure to make any clear findings on this issue
must be seen in the light of the fact that in several important respects
the testimony of some soldiers did not always match the testimony
of other soldiers, and on some occasions did not match the actual
facts. This conflict and mismatch of evidence is disturbing given that
the primary reason offered by the tribunal for relying on the soldiers'
testimony was the extent to which they impressed the tribunal by
sticking to their version of events without contradicting themselves or
each other while under cross-examination. What is even more disturbing is the fact that the testimony of each of the soldiers who spoke
about firing in the general direction of the barricade differed in some
very important respects from the statements they gave to the military
police on the night of 30–31 January. Not only were these serious discrepancies not disclosed to the counsel for the deceased, they were not
disclosed during the tribunal proceedings. Had they been disclosed the
cross-examination of these soldiers might have taken a very different
course, with all the implications that would have had for the tribunal's
declared confidence in the evidence of the soldiers concerned.

Soldier P

Soldier P had been in the second vehicle of N's platoon. He had debussed with a partner at the north end of Block 1 before the vehicle proceeded into the carpark at Rossville Flats. In his testimony he claimed that they had come under fire from the barricade on Rossville Street. He claimed that he had seen a man at the barricade lighting a nail bomb in his left hand with a match in his right. He was unable to explain how the man had actually lit the match. He had fired two shots a him, missing with the first and hitting him with the second. The bomb had fallen still fizzing at his feet but had not exploded. The fact that the bomb did not explode (thereby providing objective evidence of P's account) is of course suspect. Further suspicion is raised by the fact that neither P nor his partner made any attempt to take cover, despite the fact that they had supposedly come under fire. It is also significant that the partner was closer to the alleged bomber than P but did not take any evasive action.

Shortly after this P claimed that he had fired four shots at a man behind the barricade who had a pistol. The first shot had hit the barricade and the other three had hit the target. If P's evidence was accurate, then the victim could have been any one of those found dead at the barricade itself, with the exception of Michael Kelly. It is worth noting, however, that none of the victims behind the barricade suffered three bullet wounds.

Shortly after this, he claimed that he had felt threatened by a crowd advancing towards him and had fired three shots over their heads. Such shots are of course not covered by the Yellow Card. In any event, his account of this incident is highly improbable due to the fact that there were armed soldiers between him and the advancing crowd. Not only does this cast doubt on his claim to have felt threatened, but it is barely conceivable that an unarmed crowd would have advanced on a soldier who had just demonstrated his preparedness to shoot to kill and while there were other armed soldiers between the crowd and their target. It is also significant that no other soldier made any reference to such an incident, or indeed to the existence of a crowd behaving in this fashion. The veracity of P's testimony is further called into question by the major discrepancies between it and the contents of his statement to the military police.

In his original statement P claimed that he had cocked his rifle before they actually went through the army barricade to conduct the arrest operation. In his statement to the Treasury Solicitor he changed this to the moment of debussing on Rossville Street. He also said that all the soldiers had debussed from the vehicle at the same time, while in testimony he admitted that only some had done so. In his original statement he said that he had operated with two partners, while in his statement to the Treasury Solicitor he changed this to one. In his original statement he placed the alleged nail bomber on the army side of the Rossville Barricade while in testimony he said that he had been on the opposite side. He also said that he had fired while lying on the ground, but in his statement to the Treasury Solicitor he changed this to kneeling. In the original statement he said that he had seen the first shot hit the ground at the feet of the nail bomber, while in testimony he implicitly acknowledged that it could have gone on to Free Derry Corner. In his original statement he said that a crowd had moved up and removed the body of the nail bomber, while in his statement to the Treasury Solicitor he said that he had not actually seen this happen.

Perhaps the most significant discrepancy was that in his original statement he claimed that he had fired five shots over the heads of the crowd in order to disperse them. He changed the five to three in an additional statement made the next day. When he made his statement to the Treasury Solicitor, however, he changed his original version to firing over their heads because he had felt threatened by them. While this corrected version did not accord readily with the facts described above, it served to protect P against the allegation that his actions had been reckless and undisciplined. There must be more than a suspicion that the change was made deliberately for this purpose. No explanation was given for this or any of the other changes from the version presented in P's original statement to the testimony he actually gave to the tribunal. Nor were the discrepancies disclosed during the tribunal proceedings.

Soldier U

Soldier U had been in the second vehicle of N's platoon. It is very difficult to know what to make of his testimony as the accounts given in his original statement, his statement to the Treasury Solicitor and his evidence to the tribunal differ from each other in several important respects. In the light of this it is difficult to see how any serious credibility can be attached to his testimony.

In his testimony he claimed that he had heard a long burst of gunfire as his vehicle moved along Rossville Street. None of the other soldiers in the vehicle reported this. Moreover it was not mentioned in his original statement. He said in testimony that he had cocked his weapon after delivering an arrested person to the arresting point. By contrast he claimed in his original statement that he had cocked his weapon immediately on debussing. He said in testimony that he had been fired at while bringing in the arrested person, but there was nothing about this in his original statement. In his statement to the Treasury Solicitor he claimed that he had heard four or five shots as he went to arrest the rioter. There is nothing about this either in his original statement or in his testimony to the tribunal. In his original statement he claimed that he had come under fire while at the north end of Block 1 of Rossville Flats. This was not mentioned in his statement to the Treasury Solicitor nor in his testimony to the tribunal. In his statement to the Treasury Solicitor he said that he had seen a soldier at the entrance to Rossville Flats firing at a gunman. This was not mentioned in his original statement nor in his testimony to the tribunal.

In testimony to the tribunal U claimed that he had seen a group of people on the other side of the barricade on Rossville Street. One of them had had a pistol. U had fired one shot at him and had hit the target. This story was fairly consistent in all three accounts.

Perhaps the most bizarre aspect of U's testimony concerned his claim of what had happened to William Nash and Alexander Nash. In his testimony he said that he had seen both of them at the barricade. The former had had a stomach wound and the latter had been attending to him. As U watched he had seen an arm holding a pistol emerge from a door in the flats. Two shots had been fired from this pistol. The first had struck the ground in front of the barricade and ricocheted into Alexander Nash, wounding him in the shoulder. The second had struck William Nash in the head. All of this is highly suspect. According to U none of the other soldiers in the vicinity of Kells Walk had fired around that time. This, of course, creates a difficulty about how William Nash came to be wounded in the stomach. Much more problematic is the fact that William Nash had not received a bullet wound to the head at all. He had been killed by a shot to the stomach.

The tribunal nevertheless effectively accepted U's account by finding that Alexander Nash must have been shot by an unknown gunman behind the door in the flats.[7] It supported this conclusion with medical evidence that the bullet which wounded Nash may have been a low-velocity shot, such as that fired by a pistol. The bullet, of course, was not recovered and the medical evidence was based only on the notion that an army bullet could normally be expected to cause more damage than was caused to Nash's shoulder. In reaching this conclusion the tribunal ignored the fact that U's account was patently wrong as far as William Nash was concerned. The credibility of the tribunal's conclusion is also seriously weakened by the other inconsistencies in U's accounts generally. In this respect it is worth noting that U did not even mention the incident in question in his original statement. No explanation was ever given for the discrepancies in U's statements and testimony, nor was their existence disclosed during the tribunal proceedings.

Soldier C

Soldier C had been in the composite force (drawn from different platoons). At one point he had taken up position on a ramp leading up to the first balcony of the flats overlooking the barricade on Rossville Street. In his testimony he claimed that he had seen a man fire a shot from a doorway in the flats. The gunman had reappeared and fired two more shots from an automatic weapon. C had returned fire and hit his target. The weapon had fallen to the ground. Then he had noticed a man firing shots from a pistol at an open window on the third floor of Rossville Flats. C had returned one shot, which had missed. He had been joined at that point by Soldier D. The gunman had reappeared and fired twice. C had fired two shots at him and D had fired one. The gunman had been hit.

There were some minor discrepancies between this testimony and C's original statement. In the latter for example, he said that he had seen a flash of light at the window where the second gunman had been located. In the statement to the Treasury Solicitor he said that this had been the flash of the window being opened, while in his testimony he said that it had been the flash of a weapon being fired. This has some significance in that there is compelling evidence that a reporter taking photographs from one of the windows was fired on.

The credibility of C's testimony was very severely undermined in cross-examination. He had claimed in his testimony that he had been lying down when he spotted and fired at the two gunmen. Counsel for the deceased produced compelling evidence that there was a three-foot wall around the ramp where C had been lying and that this would have rendered it impossible for him to see the gunmen. Significantly the model the soldier had been looking at and the photographs he had tendered in evidence did not reveal this wall. This raised the strong possibility that C had not been where he claimed to be when firing these shots. However he persisted in his claim that he had been able to see the gunmen over the wall, and bizarrely the tribunal seemed to accept his claim. Incredibly the tribunal did not commission an engineer's report of this wall and the effect it would have had on C's capacity to see the alleged gunmen from his prone position. It was quite happy to accept C's word on the matter despite the fact that the evidence to the contrary could easily have been checked.

C's testimony on the shots fired at the second gunman conflicts in certain respects with D's testimony.

Soldier D

Soldier D had been a member of the composite force. D's testimony was to the effect that he had heard pistol fire and C returning fire. He had joined C at that point and C had told him that there was a gunman on the third floor of Rossville Flats. D had fired at this gunman on two occasions and claimed that C had fired only on the second occasion. This was a clear contradiction of C's account.

Soldier K

Soldier K had been in the composite force. In his testimony he claimed that he had seen two men behind the barricade crawling in the direction of Rossville Flats. The one at the rear had appeared to have something under his body which looked like a rifle. K had fired one shot at him, as had soldiers L and M. He was not sure if he had hit his target. The man had kept crawling until he reached the door of the flats, at which point he had been dragged inside by others, as had the second man. In his original statement K said that he thought he may have hit the target although he had not observed a strike.

The tribunal specifically praised the credibility and reliability of K's testimony.[8] Surprisingly the tribunal made no mention of the propriety of K firing at someone who only may have been carrying a rifle and who was not posing an immediate threat to anyone. It does not appear that any warning was shouted before K fired. In these circumstances there are grounds for arguing that the shooting was unjustifiable. At the very least the tribunal could be expected to have considered further whether a warning should have been given before opening fire. It is worth noting in this context that K said in testimony that he had not heard any explosions at that time.

The full implications of the tribunal's trust in K's testimony becomes apparent when L and M's evidence is considered. If K's testimony is accepted as accurate then it poses some difficulties for that of L and M, and *vice versa*.

Soldier L

Soldier L had been in the composite force. In his testimony he claimed that he had seen two men behind the barricade crawling in the direction of Rossville Flats. The one in front had had what appeared to be a rifle below his body (K said it was the one behind). L had fired one shot and thought that he had hit the target. The front man had kept crawling and as the man behind him overtook him the rifle had become clearly visible. L had fired another shot and reckoned that he had hit both men. He did not say anything about others dragging the two men into the flats. However he did say that a man had come out of a doorway in the flats and fired a few shots. Later another soldier had warned him about a building at the other end of Kells Walk. He had seen a man with a rifle at the building and fired two shots at him, but he did not think that he had hit his target.

The comments made above with respect to K's shooting of the man behind the barricade also applies to L's shooting of both men behind the barricade. The conflict between his account of what happened and that of K also raises some doubt about the reliability of their accounts. It is also worth noting that the independent and medical evidence suggests that only one man was shot while crawling behind the barricade in the direction of Rossville Flats. L's credibility is further called into question by the material discrepancies between his testimony and the account he gave in his original statement.

In his original statement L claimed that both men behind the barricade had had a weapon underneath their bodies. Moreover he claimed that he had been ordered to fire at the two men. He also said that the second man had reached the doorway and had been pulled inside. He said nothing about a man coming out and firing a few shots. Furthermore he also claimed that as they had withdrawn they had been fired on from a side street off Rossville Street and he had returned two shots. All of this was really quite different from the account he gave in his testimony.

The credibility of L's evidence is even further undermined by the fact that his statement to the Treasury Solicitor differed in some respects from both his original statement and his testimony. In his statement to the Treasury Solicitor he claimed that he had already shot the man crawling behind the barricade when he saw the second man crawling. He also said that the second man had taken possession of the rifle left by the first man. Both of them had managed to make it to the door but L reckoned that the first man had died at that point. There was no mention of a man coming out and firing a few shots. He also said that

K had gone into Glenfada Park. K did not say this in testimony and no-one else said that K had entered the park. No explanation was offered for the discrepancies in L's statements, nor were they disclosed during the tribunal proceedings.

Soldier M

Soldier M had been a member of the composite force. In his testimony he claimed that he had seen two men behind the barricade crawling in the direction of Rossville Flats. Both had had what appeared to be a weapon underneath their bodies. He had fired one shot at the first man and had struck his target. He had then fired a shot at the second man and had hit the target. He claimed that the first had managed to reach the door of the flats and had been dragged inside, and that 10–15 people had come out and dragged the second man inside.

The comments made above with respect to K's testimony apply equally to M's. It is also worth noting that M's version differed in some important respects from both K's and L's. It was even more at odds with the independent evidence applicable to these events than either L's or K's.

Ironically, the account M offered in his original statement did not differ significantly from that given in testimony. However, in a bizarre twist he made a further statement on 4 February. In it he stated that as they had moved along Kells Walk they had come under fire from Rossville Flats. He had located the gunman on the top floor balcony of Flat 2. The gunman had been engaged by another soldier whom he could not identify. M proceeded to say that he had hit two gunmen during the action, but did not clarify whether these were the two he had described in his original statement. If they were it is not entirely clear why it was necessary for M to make this further statement. To confuse matters further the statement was signed (in print) by Soldier K although it purports to be M's statement. No explanation was offered for these discrepancies, nor were they disclosed during the tribunal proceedings.

The Glenfada Park shootings

Overview

Of all the shootings, those in Glenfada Park are probably the most controversial. Four civilians were shot dead and three were wounded. There is a compelling body of evidence to suggest that most if not all of those killed in the park were killed unlawfully. The case against the army was considerably strengthened by the fact that the six soldiers who gave evidence about events in the park offered versions which not only conflicted with civilian and independent evidence, but also conflicted in many important respects with each other. In addition the testimony of at least one soldier (Soldier H) was so bizarre that the tribunal specifically singled it out as being unreliable.[9] It was therefore hardly surprising that the tribunal found that the shots which killed the four victims had been 'fired without justification'.[10] However a distinctly unsatisfactory aspect of this finding is the fact that it was made only on a balance of probability. The nature of the evidence offered was such that any impartial judicial body should have been satisfied beyond reasonable doubt that the soldiers had unjustifiably fired their guns in Glenfada Park. This is confirmed by the soldiers' original statements. The soldiers' evidence to the tribunal, coupled with a comparison between it and their original statements, demonstrate beyond question that the testimony of the soldiers to the tribunal was inherently unreliable.

Soldier E

Soldier E had been in the antitank platoon. In testimony he claimed that he had heard firing from Rossville Flats after debussing on Rossville Street. He said that he had spotted a gunman at the window of one of the flats and fired one round at him. Later he had seen a crowd move from the barricade into Glenfada Park. On his own initiative he had proceeded into the park (taking about four others with him) to arrest them. In the park one of the crowd had thrown a petrol bomb. When he had gone on to throw a nail bomb E had fired two shots at him. The first one had missed and the second had hit the target. The nail bomb had exploded. Under cross-examination he claimed that a second nail bomb had been thrown and landed not far in front of him. It too had exploded. He had seen two other persons fall, but did not know how they had been hit. The crowd had still been aggressive and he and his colleagues had moved forward and arrested about 30 of them.

E's account of what happened in Glenfada Park differed substantially from that of his colleagues (none of whom gave similar versions). Moreover the platoon commander, Lieutenant 119, claimed not only to have given the order to go into Glenfada Park, but also to have followed his men in. E's account of the nail bombs exploding was not supported by any evidence of injury or damage from the explosions. Further discrepancies are evident from his original statement.

In his original statement he claimed that the crowd in Glenfada Park had bombarded them with petrol bombs and nail bombs. In his testimony he mentioned only one of the former and two of the latter. In the statement he said that he had seen the rioter light a nail bomb before throwing it in his direction, while in testimony he said that he had not seen him lighting it. Also, in his statement he said that he had seen the other two rioters fall before he fired, while in testimony he said that they had fallen after he fired. He did not mention anything about the arrests in his original statement. No explanation was offered for these discrepancies, nor were they disclosed during the tribunal proceedings.

Soldier F

Soldier F had been in the second vehicle of the antitank platoon. In his testimony he had said that he had heard shooting from Rossville Flats on debussing. He had also seen two explosions about 40 yards in front of the barricade. He had seen a person about to throw a nail bomb from the barricade. He had fired one shot at the bomber and had hit his target. He had then seen a man with a rifle go from the barricade with a group of others into Glenfada Park. On the orders of E, both he and G had gone into Glenfada Park to intercept them. On entering he had seen a group of three persons, one of whom had been about to throw a nail bomb. He had fired two shots at the bomber and hit his target. The bomb had fallen at the bomber's feet and had not exploded. Then he had gone to the corner of the park to investigate firing from the direction of Rossville Flats. He had fired two shots at a gunman between the flats and Joseph Place. He had hit his target. He had then spotted about 20 people huddled together at the wall. He had arrested them and retreated to his vehicle on Rossville Street. The radio operator in the vehicle had seen a gunman at a window on the second floor of the Rossville Flats. F had got out and fired three shots at a movement which he took to be a rifle at the window in question. He had moved forward to the front of the vehicle and fired three shots at a gunman with a weapon sticking out of the adjacent window. He had then seen a gunman at a window on the top floor and fired two rounds at him.

F's testimony about what happened in Glenfada Park differed substantially from that of his colleagues (none of whom gave similar versions). He also claimed that he had gone in on the orders of E, although Lieutenant 119 claimed that he had given the order. A particular feature of F's testimony is his admission to the tribunal that his original version of events had been quite different in some respects. In particular he admitted that he had forgotten to mention having shot dead the alleged gunman between Rossville Flats and Joseph Place. This omission can only be described as bizarre. A further twist is that he originally accounted for the two shots expended on the gunman by adding them to the shots he had fired at the alleged gunmen at the windows of Rossville Flats. This, of course, severely undermined the credibility of his evidence about these alleged gunmen. In any event, on the basis of the accounts given by F to the tribunal it is apparent that there were grounds for concluding that F had not fired at clearly identifiable, legitimate targets. Whatever credibility remained of F's testimony must surely have been extinguished by some further bizarre contradictions between his original statement and the version he gave in oral testimony.

In his original statement he claimed that he had heard shots from a window in Rossville Flats before going into Glenfada Park. Incredibly, he had fired three shots at the window from where he estimated that the shots had come. In other words he had fired without having a clearly identifiable target. There was no mention at all of this incident in his testimony. One can only assume that it related to one of the incidents in which he fired at a window after coming out of Glenfada Park. Either way, the admitted circumstances of the firing were a clear and reckless breach of all rules governing the discharge of firearms. Equally strange was the absence of any reference in the original statement to the shooting of the nail bomber at the barricade; nor was it mentioned in the additional statement he made later. This did not appear until his statement to the Treasury Solicitor.

In his original statement he claimed that 30–40 rioters had left the barricade and entered Glenfada Park. There was no mention of this in his testimony. He said that he had shot the nail bomber in the park while there was a riot going on. There was no mention of this riot in his additional statement. He also said that after shooting the nail bomber in the park he had advanced towards the rioters and they had scattered. There was no mention of this in his testimony. As discussed above, he made no mention in either his original statement or his additional statement of shooting the alleged gunman between Rossville Flats and Joseph Place. It did not appear until his statement to the Treasury Solicitor.

In his original statement he gave an even more incriminating version of shooting at alleged gunmen at the windows of Rossville Flats. Of the first such shooting, F claimed that the radio operator had seen something move at a window and F had fired four shots at it. The reck-lessness of such action speaks for itself.

Finally it is worth noting that the markings on the map showing the positions from where F fired were totally at odds with his testimony. He claimed that he could correct these positions with the benefit of aerial photography. It should also be said that F was one of the few sol-diers from whom the military police found it necessary to take an almost complete second statement. The credibility of his testimony was not helped by the fact that even this second statement did not accord with his testimony. His second statement was actually signed (in print) 'soldier G', but presumably this was a misprint.

Not all of the serious discrepancies in F's statements were disclosed during the tribunal proceedings. It is particularly worth noting that those which suggested that F had fired recklessly and without lawful authority were not disclosed.

Soldier G

Soldier G had been a member of the antitank platoon and F's partner. In his testimony he claimed that after debussing and taking cover beside a wall at Kells Walk he had heard someone shout that there was a gunman down an alley. He had looked down the alley and seen a man dodging from side to side and carrying what appeared to be a weapon of some sort. G had immediately fired two shots at him but had not hit his target. After going into Glenfada Park he had seen two gunmen at the south-west corner. He had immediately fired three shots at one of them. Both had fallen. He had assumed that F, who had fired beside him, had shot the second. A crowd had run past and picked up the weapons. After returning to his vehicle on Rossville Street the dri-ver had reported shots being fired from a window in Rossville Flats. G had seen the window move and shots come from it. He had fired back at someone who had moved at the window.

G's testimony about events in Glenfada Park differed in several respects from the versions given by his colleagues (none of which were similar). He accepted in his testimony that there was a difference between his recollection of events in Glenfada Park and that of F. He claimed that he had first realised this when they discussed the events afterwards. It was also disclosed during his testimony that he had ear-lier claimed that the person he had shot had been throwing a nail bomb. He claimed in testimony that he did not know how this had come about as he did not remember making that statement. There was also a significant difference between his and F's account of firing at the window in Rossville Flats. However when the counsel for the deceased attempted to pursue this discrepancy in cross-examination, Lord Widgery cut it short on the basis that it was not possible to establish that both were talking about the same window, despite the fact that both had clearly described the same window.

It is also worth noting that when G had fired at the man down the alleyway his life and safety had not been in immediate danger, he had not clearly established that the man was carrying a gun and he had not shouted any warning. Similarly, on his own evidence, it appeared that the two alleged gunmen in Glenfada Park had not been immediately threatening his life or that of his colleagues. Nevertheless he had fired without shouting a warning. In such circumstances a charge of murder or attempted murder might be appropriate.

In his original statement he claimed that he had fired at the alleged gunman in the alley in order to give cover to a colleague who had been running across open ground. There was no mention of this in his testimony and it must be said that it is difficult to see how the alleged gunman could have been posing any threat to his colleague in the circumstances. In his original statement he said that after shooting the alleged gunmen in Glenfada Park he and F had given chase to those who had picked up the weapons. In his testimony he said that he advanced into the park in order 'to find where the weapons had gone.' In his statement to the Treasury Solicitor G said that he had gone down the western side of the park and F down the eastern side. For the first time he also said that he had seen F firing shots at a gunman. Contrary to what he said in his original statement G also said that F had arrested about 20 civilians just before he joined him.

Bizarrely G made an additional statement the next day which totally contradicted his original description of the circumstances in which he had shot the gunman in Glenfada Park. In the additional statement he claimed that the target had been throwing nail bombs. As explained above G claimed in testimony that he did not remember making this claim.

It appears that G made a further statement on 14 February. This statement does not appear to have been released. In it, however, it seems that G claimed that he had actually shot both gunmen and a third man who had been throwing nail bombs. In his statement to the Treasury Solicitor he confirmed that his statement of 14 February had been read back to him before he signed it, however he did not remember it saying that he had shot all three men. In his statement to the Treasury Solicitor he claimed that he might have shot both gunmen and that F might have shot a third man. All this is totally bizarre and it is impossible to know what to make of it, except of course that it renders G's testimony totally unreliable. Significantly these extraordinary circumstances were not disclosed during the tribunal proceedings.

Soldier H

Soldier H had been a member of the antitank platoon. Of all the evidence given to the tribunal his must rank as the most incredible, partly because it was so unbelievable and partly because the version of events he gave to the tribunal was dramatically different from his original version.

In his testimony H claimed that as he and his colleagues had advanced towards the barricade on Rossville Street he had seen two gunmen at the barricade. He had also seen a youth throw what looked like a nail bomb, but had not seen it land nor heard it explode. He and his colleagues (F and G) had chased the youths into Glenfada Park, where he had seen one of his colleagues firing. H had spotted a youth about to throw an object which looked like a nail bomb, even though it had not been smoking or fizzing. H had fired two shots in quick succession, the first one missing and the second one striking his target. The bomb had fallen to the ground and had not exploded. Another youth had run forward and picked it up to throw it. H had fired a shot at him and hit the youth, who had then retreated, apparently wounded in the shoulder. H had then heard a shot and noticed the muzzle of a rifle sticking out of a frosted window of a flat at the southern end of the park. He had seen a silhouette behind the window. H claimed that he had fired a total of 19 shots at this alleged gunman over a period of one and a half minutes, taking time to reload once. Each time he had fired the gunman had stepped back out of view, but the muzzle had not moved from the window. On the nineteenth shot the gunman had fallen, the muzzle disappearing with him. Incredibly H claimed that the window had not shattered during this barrage so he had been unable to get a clear picture of the gunman.

H's testimony about what had happened in Glenfada Park did not accord with any of the versions of his colleagues, all of which differed in important respects. In H's case, however, the evidence about firing the 19 shots is simply beyond belief. Indeed the evidence shows that no window in Glenfada Park had been hit 19 times. One window in the flat that H claimed to have fired at suffered one strike, and that was a clear glass window. The flat in question belonged to an elderly couple. The tribunal specifically discounted H's testimony with respect to these shots, which meant of course that they must have been fired at one or more other targets and in different circumstances. However the tribunal did not proceed to determine what these targets or circumstances might have been.

H's testimony with respect to these 19 shots becomes even more bizarre when it is compared with the version he gave in his original statement. In this statement H described a virtual battle scene as the soldiers moved towards the barricade in Rossville Street. He said that they had been continually fired at, stoned, nailbombed and acid bombed. None of his colleagues described the scene in such dramatic terms and there was no photographic or other independent evidence to support this version. Indeed he did not repeat it himself in testimony. In his original statement he said that after chasing the youths into Glenfada Park he had spotted them hiding behind a car, but in his testimony it was the soldiers (not the youths) who had taken up position behind this car. He had seen three youths with nail bombs behind a wall. He had fired at the middle youth while F and G had fired at the other two. All three had fallen. Not only did this conflict with the versions given by F and G, but it also conflicted with the version H gave in testimony. In particular it is worth noting that in his original statement there was no suggestion that the youths had been about to throw the nail bombs. Since no warning had been shouted at them before they were shot, it would seem that H's original statement gives grounds for a charge of murder, or attempted murder as the case may be. He had then seen a fourth youth run forward and pick up an object dropped by one of the three youths and run away. H had fired one shot at the youth and had hit his target. In his testimony he changed this to the effect that the youth had been about to throw the bomb. The difference is critical because the version given in the original statement provides grounds for a charge of murder or attempted murder. It is also worth noting that H made a substantial amendment to his original statement, but repeated in it that the youths had merely been carrying the nail bombs (that is, they had not been in the act of throwing them) and he still did not mention that he thought the fourth youth had been about to throw the bomb. These elements did not appear until he made his statement to the Treasury Solicitor.

After shooting the fourth youth H claimed that the platoon commander had appeared and examined the bodies and confirmed that they were dead. This does not appear in his testimony even though he persisted with it in his substantial amendment. He then claimed that he and his colleagues had *continued along Rossville Street* (in testimony he said that they had been in Glenfada Park) towards the barricade, which they had broken up. He had then *returned along Rossville Street in a military vehicle, which had come under fire from flats extending east towards Chamberlain Street*. He had located the position of the gunman at a bathroom window (about 1 foot square) and returned 19 shots at him. The bizarre feature about this is that it places H in a military vehicle in Rossville Street when he fired these shots. He changed this in his substantial amendment (and in his testimony) to locate the gunman in a bathroom window in a flat at the southern end of Glenfada Park, and there was no mention of being in a military vehicle. In short he claimed in his original version that his firing of the 19 shots had occurred in a totally different place and in very different circumstances from those in his later versions.

In the substantial amendment H placed himself and his colleagues behind the car which in his earlier statement had been the refuge of the youths. His version of the shooting of the youths had also changed. This time he stated that two of the youths had had nail bombs. He had fired at one of them and had hit the target. His colleagues had also fired and four youths had been shot altogether. He then mentioned shooting a youth who had picked up an object from the shot youths. This of course would make a fifth victim. He also stated that his colleagues had been E, F and G. This was the first time that he mentioned E.

H's testimony clearly lacked any credibility and the tribunal was surely correct to conclude that it could not accept his version of the 19 shots. A much more disturbing feature, however, is the fact that the huge discrepancies in H's accounts were neither explained nor disclosed during the tribunal proceedings. In his case the nature of the conflicts are particularly significant as they raise the possibility that at least some of these shots may have killed or wounded some of the victims and that this may not even have happened in Glenfada Park. This, of course, would have profound implications for the tribunal's strategy of attempting to match up each of the deceased with the soldiers' accounts of the shots they fired. If there were at least 19 maverick shots floating about, it is difficult to see how the tribunal could reach any certain conclusions about the circumstances of a fatal shooting based on a soldier's account unless there was very strong, independent corroborative evidence of that account. Nevertheless the tribunal was content simply to ignore H's testimony of the 19 shots and not consider any further its implications for the Army's version of events in Glenfada Park and elsewhere.

Soldier J

Soldier J had been a member of the antitank platoon. In his testimony he said that after debussing he had heard a burst of automatic fire from Rossville Flats. As he and his colleagues had taken cover on Kells Walk some nail bombs had been thrown and he had heard one explode. They had moved towards the barricade on Rossville Street. Two gunmen behind the barricade had opened up with rifles. He had seen a person at the barricade about to throw a fizzing object which he had taken to be a nail bomb. J had fired one shot at him but did not think that he had hit the target. The crowd behind the barricade had begun to split up into the side streets. More nail bombs had been thrown. Two of these had gone off and about two had not. He had spotted someone at Rossville Flats with a fizzing object. J had fired one shot at him but did not think he had hit the target. Then he had heard the platoon commander order them to go into Glenfada Park to make arrests. He had heard an explosion as he went in behind F and G. He had seen them fire at two persons holding metallic objects, which he had taken to be nail bombs. Other civilians in the park had surrounded the bodies and must have picked up the nail bombs. He had made two arrests and withdrawn. Back at the vehicle one of his colleagues had returned fire at a gunman in Rossville Flats.

J's version of events as they approached the barricade was substantially exaggerated compared with that of most of the other soldiers. Moreover there was no independent evidence to corroborate his allegation about the number of nail bombs which were thrown and exploded. His version of events in Glenfada Park differed in several respects from those given by his colleagues, all of which differed from each other. A comparison of his testimony with the contents of his original statement discloses several serious discrepancies.

In his original statement he did not mention seeing or hearing any nail bombs explode. He also said that they had been ordered into Glenfada Park to escort a number of youths who had been arrested. In his evidence this became making arrests and then withdrawing from the park. The most striking feature about this is that there was no reference to an explosion nor to F and G firing at two persons with nail bombs. Nor was there any reference to making arrests. Also absent was any reference to one of his colleagues firing at the gunman in Rossville Flats who had fired at their vehicle after they returned from the park. In a very confusing amendment made in February he said that he had seen two persons in possession of nail bombs after taking up position in the park. These bombs had not gone off and F and G had fired at the persons holding them. He also mentioned the shots that had been fired at their vehicle on their return from the park. Once again, none of these alterations were either explained or disclosed during the tribunal proceedings.

Soldier 119

Soldier 119 had been the platoon commander of the antitank platoon. Since he had not fired any shots it is likely that he did not make a statement on the night of 30–31 January. However it appears that he did make a statement on 4 February which has not been released.

In his testimony 119 said that they had come under fire as they moved along Rossville Street. However he had not reported this on his radio and the credibility of his testimony on the firing was seriously undermined in cross-examination. He claimed that he had ordered two men into Glenfada Park in order to cut off gunmen. Under cross-examination he said that he had told them to take men with them. He had followed them into the park and admitted seeing E, F and G. Under cross-examination he also claimed to have seen J. He had seen F fire two shots but had not been able to see the target. He had seen three bodies on the ground but had not had a chance to examine them. He claimed that he had not reported these three bodies because of radio communication difficulties, although he also claimed that an order to withdraw had come over on the radio. In his statement to the Treasury Solicitor he did not mention seeing G and J in the park.

Soldier 119's account of the events surrounding the shootings in Glenfada Park conflicted with the versions offered by the others involved. Indeed when all the accounts are read as a whole one gets the distinct impression that Soldier 119 had not been in control of events in the park at all. There is a very strong likelihood that E, F, G and H had acted on their own initiative and that 119 was merely attempting to impart some legitimacy to their actions after the event.

Gerald Donaghy

A strange and disturbing sequel to the events in Glenfada Park concerned the case of Gerald Donaghy, who was one of the persons shot in the park. Shortly after being shot he was examined by Dr Swords, who found that he was still alive and recommended that he be taken to hospital immediately. He was driven away in a car which was stopped at an army checkpoint on Barrack Street, at which point the army took control of the car. Instead of being driven straight to the hospital he was driven to the army medical post on nearby Craigavon Bridge.

While there he was examined twice by an army medical officer, who pronounced him dead. Shortly after this examination and while Donaghy was still lying on the back seat of the car the nail bombs were found. There is disagreement over how they were found, and indeed where they were found. The version that seems to have become established is that a nail bomb was found in each of the two breast pockets of his jacket and one in each of two front trouser pockets, making a total of four.

Counsel for the deceased suggested that these bombs had been planted on Donaghy. Certainly there was very strong circumstantial evidence to suggest that the bombs had not been present until just before they were 'found' on him. One of the bombs in his jacket was so tightly squeezed into the pocket that it had to be cut out. Moreover his jeans were tight-fitting, with the pockets opening to the front. Any bombs in these pockets would have been clearly visible. Indeed when the first one was spotted it was actually sticking out of the top of his pocket. Nevertheless they had not been spotted earlier by Dr Swords when he examined him shortly after he was shot. It is worth noting here that Dr Swords had actually searched his pockets for identification. They had also not been spotted by the army medical officer, who had examined the body twice, opening the front of the trousers in the process. There was also compelling evidence that the body had been moved to a different position on the seat after the medical officer's last examination and the time when the bombs were discovered. Finally, there was ample opportunity for the bombs to have been planted after the body had been examined by the medical officer and before the bombs were found. All in all the case for the bombs being planted seems more credible than the reverse.

Surprisingly the tribunal concluded that the bombs had been in Donaghy's pockets all the time.[11] This of course was a clear finding that Donaghy was guilty of a criminal offence. It is respectfully submitted, therefore, that the tribunal should not have reached this categorical finding unless it was satisfied beyond reasonable doubt that the bombs had been there all the time. Given the nature of the bombs and the nature of Donaghy's pockets, coupled with the fact that the two doctors had failed to notice the bombs during their three examinations, there was surely more than reasonable doubt. The tribunal supported its positive finding with the argument that the evidence for planting the bombs was mere speculation. That in itself, however, does not mean that the only viable conclusion is that the bombs were there all the time. The onus was not on the defence to prove that they were planted, it was on the prosecution to prove beyond a reasonable doubt that they were there all along.

The tribunal's conclusions are rendered even more suspect by the fact that much of the army and police testimony on the matter does not add up. In his testimony, Soldier 104 claimed that he had seen the car at the bridge with its boot opened and what might have been a policewoman looking into the boot. He had looked through the window into the back seat and seen the deceased. He had noticed a bulging object in the deceased's front pocket with a small bit sticking out at the top. Then he had heard someone say that there were three nail bombs in the boot. It seems that he had earlier made two statement about this event, but neither were among the documents released. Nevertheless he admitted in testimony that his original statement about the location of the car had been mistaken. It also emerged is his statement to the Treasury Solicitor that in his original statement he said that he had first seen the deceased when the car was stopped at the checkpoint on Barrack Street and it was at that point that he had seen the nail bomb sticking out of his pocket. He changed this in his statement to the Treasury Solicitor to the effect that he had first seen the body at the bridge checkpoint and that he had not known that the object sticking out of the pocket was a nail bomb until he heard someone else say that nail bombs had been found in the boot. He was not able to explain the mistake. The most charitable interpretation that can be placed on all of this is that Soldier 104's evidence was neither credible nor reliable.

Soldier 150 had driven the car from the checkpoint on Barrack Street to the medical post on Craigavon Bridge. He had looked into the back seat and seen the body of the deceased with a gunshot wound to the lower abdomen. Interestingly the medical officer stated in testimony that he had not been able to find a wound on the body despite examining it twice. Soldier 150 had not noticed any nail bombs. He thought that the car had been checked by the RUC after he had driven it to the bridge.

PN7, a sergeant in the RUC, had checked the car at the bridge. He had not actually been in charge at the bridge but his superior had not been there when the car arrived and so PN7 had taken it upon himself to check for evidence of identity of the deceased. He had first checked a trouser pocket and found a nail bomb. He had immediately sent for an ATO, who had found three more nail bombs, one in the other trouser pocket and one in each of two breast pockets of the deceased's jacket.

An inexplicable aspect of PN7's testimony is the fact that he said he had never seen the medical officer who carried out the examination. This is peculiar because the medical officer is supposed to have carried out two examinations with an interval in between. According to the medical officer, about five minutes after the examination had been carried out he had heard someone say that nail bombs had been found on the body. PN7, however, said in testimony that he had seen the car being driven into the post and he had gone out more or less immediately to investigate. It is worth noting that PN7's general duties in the RUC involved working with explosives in quarries, so he would have had access to explosives.

It is evident that there were some serious discrepancies in the testimony of these army and police witnesses. While they are not sufficient in themselves to raise a strong case that the bombs were planted, they are sufficient to raise a suspicion. When this is combined with the fact that Donaghy's body had already been searched when it was put into the car the tribunal's conclusion would seem to be unwarranted. At the very least one would have expected an impartial and objective tribunal of inquiry to have concluded that there was sufficient doubt about the evidence of the bombs being there all along to prevent it from reaching a finding against Donaghy.[12]

Other shootings

Overview

There were a number of other army shootings on the west bank that afternoon. However they did not involve the Parachute Regiment and did not result in any identifiable victims. Despite the fact that oral and written evidence was submitted to the tribunal about these shootings they did not form part of the tribunal's report. This must be considered a serious omission. In all of the instances the soldiers engaged in hostile fire and in many instances claimed to have hit their targets. Their actions, therefore, were clearly relevant to the events that led to loss of life that afternoon. Moreover the soldiers' claims to have hit targets, coupled with the absence of any identifiable victims of their shootings, strike a clear parallel with much of the evidence given by the soldiers whose shootings were examined in the report. The tribunal's failure to examine these incidents and evidence must be interpreted as a clear dereliction of its duty as they were highly relevant to the events for which it was established to examine.

Soldier AA

Soldier AA, a member of the Royal Anglian Regiment, had been on duty at a checkpoint in Barrack Street. In his testimony he claimed that he had heard a single shot pass their position at 4 pm. Some civilians had told him about three gunmen behind the walls of Charlotte Place. As he had moved along Charlotte Place to investigate, a gunman had come round the corner of Columba's Walk and fired at him. He had returned one shot from the hip to save his life, but had not struck his target. Then he had come under fire from a 'gun port' in a bricked-up building. He had seen the flash of the muzzle and the silhouette of the gunman. One of the shots had gone into the flakjacket of a soldier behind him. AA had fired approximately three shots at the gunman, hitting his target. He had immediately switched fire to another gun port as he had heard a Thompson being fired up Long Tower Street. He had fired two shots into this gun port and two into another in the same building in which he believed the gunman to be. He thought that he had hit his target, although he had never actually seen who he was shooting at.

If AA's account is correct there is a serious question mark over the propriety of the last two sets of shots that he fired. He was simply firing into black holes in which there may or may not have been a gunman. The credibility of his account, however, is undermined by the fact that no identifiable victims were found to match the location of his shootings. There are also some serious discrepancies between the version he gave in his original statement and that given in his testimony.

In his original statement he made no mention of a warning from civilians, which was supposed to be his reason for proceededing along Charlotte Place. He did mention it in his statement to the Treasury Solicitor, but said it had occurred before he heard the first shot, which he timed at 16.15. He also said that he had cocked his weapon on seeing the first gunman, while in testimony he said that he had cocked it earlier, when he had heard the shot going past their position. Most significantly he made no mention of hearing the Thompson being fired from the other gunport before firing into it. This adds to the suspicion that he had acted recklessly in firing these shots. Even when he made an additional statement the next day, in which he clarified his earlier statement on the gun ports in question, he still made no mention of the Thompson. This did not appear until his statement to the Treasury Solicitor. No explanation was offered for the discrepancies in his statements and testimony, nor was their existence disclosed during the tribunal proceedings.

Soldier AB

Soldier AB, a member of the Royal Anglian Regiment, had been deployed at the junction of Charlotte Street and Barrack Street. In his original statement he claimed that he had been observing waste ground between Charlotte Street and St Columb's Walk at 4.15 pm when he had seen a man step around the corner of St Columb's Walk and Joyce Street junction and fire a shot at AA. Both AA and AB had fired at this man. AB had not seen his shot strike the target.

Soldier AC

Soldier AC, a member of the Royal Anglian Regiment, had been observing Celtic Park from a position in a derelict house at the junction of Long Tower Street and Howard Street. In his original statement he claimed that he had heard a shot come from a gap between two huts on the line of the ridge of Celtic Park at 4.45 pm. He had seen three men between the huts. One of them had been in the kneeling position and pointing a long stick-like object at AC's position. Soldier AC had fired two shots at the man, who had fallen to the ground and not moved again. The other two men had then dragged him behind the huts. About fifteen minutes later one of these two men had reappeared and adopted the aim position. Soldier AC had heard the sound of a shot and seen a puff of smoke at the end of a stick-like object the man was holding in his hands. The shot had passed over AC's position. Soldier AC had returned three shots. The man had fallen to the ground and lain motionless. Several minutes later the third man had appeared, picked up the weapon and dragged the body behind the huts.

Once again there were no casualties to match the incidents described by soldier AC. It must also be said that either his account was highly implausible or gunmen were acting with reckless disregard for their own safety.

Soldier AD

Soldier AD, a member of the Royal Anglian Regiment, had been stationed in the rear of a derelict house on the north side of Long Tower Street near to the junction with Howard Street. He had been observing Lecky Road. In his original statement he claimed that he had seen a man run out of the archway to the left of the Bogside Inn at about 4.45 pm. The man had jumped two or three feet and raised an object with both hands. The object had been long and straight and looked like a 0.303 rifle. Soldier AD had seen a flash and a puff of smoke from the end of the object and heard a round pass over his head. He had returned two shots at the man, the second of which had knocked him off his feet. A crowd had come forward and dragged the body behind the buildings into Meenan Square.

Yet again there was no reported casualty that corresponded with soldier AD's account of this shooting. It is also worth noting that if soldier AD had had a view of a gunman at the Bogside Inn he may also have had a view of the youths at the barricade on Rossville Street. Was he the source of some of the shots that killed one or more of the casualties at the barricade? Don Mullan provides a substantial argument that some of these shots must have been fired from a high elevation in the vicinity of the Derry walls. Lord Widgery, however, refused even to consider the proposition.

Soldier X

Soldier X had been stationed near a petrol-filling station on the Letterkenny Road, quite some distance away from the shootings in the Bogside. He claimed in his original statement that his position had come under fire sporadically throughout the day. At about 4.45 pm a burst of automatic fire had been directed at his position. The shots had come from the direction of a tunnel on the roof of a derelict building opposite the filling station. He had seen a figure silhouetted against the tunnel, and although he had not been able to see whether this person was carrying a gun he believed that he was the gunman who had just fired. Accordingly he had fired one shot at the target and seen him fall. Soldier X had kept the tunnel under observation for the next hour but had seen no further movement. Surprisingly he had not attempted to recover the body, nor had he radioed for assistance to recover the body. Once again there was no casualty to correspond with the soldier's version of the shooting.

Soldier Y

Soldier Y had been located at a post in the Brandywell. In his testimony he claimed that he had come under fire from a gunman in bushes in the direction of Creggan Heights. He had returned fire and seen the gunman fall back. There is no other evidence of a gunman having been killed or wounded at that location.

Soldier Z

Soldier Z, a member of 22 Lt AD Regiment, had been on Sackville Street near the junction with William Street at 4.50 pm. In his original statement he said that he had heard a shot strike the wall above his head. He had spotted a man at a window on the top floor of a derelict factory about 200 metres away from his position. The man had been holding a long straight object in one hand. Z had fired one shot, which had struck the man in the middle of the chest. The man had then fallen from sight, although his hand remained draped over the window sill. Z had been redeployed five minutes later and no attempt had been made to recover the body or the 'long straight object'. Not only did no casualty correspond to this shooting, but Z's own account of the incident affords scant justification for his opening fire.

Conclusion

It is evident from the foregoing analysis of the soldiers' evidence that for almost every soldier who fired one or more shots there were substantial discrepancies between the account offered in the statement made on the night of 30–31 January and the version given in oral testimony to the tribunal. The nature and extent of these discrepancies are sufficient in themselves to raise a serious doubt about the credibility and reliability of the testimony given by these soldiers. That doubt is only increased by the fact that in many of the cases where the soldiers were supposedly describing the same events their original accounts differed from each other, often fundamentally, in many respects. No fewer than 12 soldiers considered it necessary to make additional statements within the next few days. An even more sinister feature is the extent to which the accounts were changed again in the later statements to the Treasury Solicitor. It is hardly a coincidence that in many instances the effect of the change was to convert what had originally amounted to an unlawful or reckless shooting to a more justifiable one. Equally, many of the changes had the effect of reducing some of the conflicts between one soldier's version and another. Nevertheless the evidence the soldiers actually presented to the tribunal did not always add up to a coherent picture.

The extent of the inconsistency in the soldiers' statements and testimony is such that it would not be safe to rely on the army's version in virtually any instance where there was credible and cogent evidence to the contrary. It is truly incredible, therefore, that the tribunal should have so consistently based its conclusions on the army's version of events. For that reason alone the Widgery Report and its findings are hopelessly flawed. That, however, may not be the most disturbing aspect of the inquiry and its report. That accolade must be reserved for the fact that the tribunal did not disclose the existence of the original statements made on the night of Bloody Sunday and did not even attempt to cross-examine the soldiers about the discrepancies between those statements and the testimony they gave in the witness box. At the very least, therefore, the tribunal was guilty of bad faith in praising the testimony of the soldiers and basing its findings on that testimony in the face of credible and cogent evidence to the contrary. Indeed it might be no exaggeration to say that the tribunal effectively suppressed much of the truth about Bloody Sunday.

Counsel for the deceased was not provided with copies of the statements made by the soldiers on the night of 30–31 January, nor with copies of any additional or supplementary statements made in the succeeding days, nor with the statements made by the soldiers to the Treasury Solicitor. They had to conduct their cross-examination of each soldier on the basis of the account he had given to the tribunal. There was no advance notice of what the soldiers were going to say and in almost every case no notice was given of the inconsistencies in their earlier accounts. Clearly in such circumstances it would have been very difficult for counsel for the deceased to discredit an individual soldier's testimony in the witness box, particularly when that testimony was based on a statement which had been prepared and written well in advance to accord as far as possible with the versions given by other soldiers. It is worth remembering at this point that one of the reasons given by Lord Widgery for putting so much belief in the soldiers' testimony was the fact that they had stood up so well to rigorous cross-examination. The reality is that the soldiers were never exposed to the sort of cross-examination to which they would have been subjected had the contents of their earlier statements been disclosed to counsel for the deceased. As will become apparent below, Lord Widgery himself must have known this.

The disadvantage suffered by counsel for the deceased was not shared by counsel for the tribunal. The tribunal counsel, and Lord Widgery himself, did have copies of the earlier statements made by the soldiers.[13] It follows that they were in a position to know that the versions offered to the tribunal, and indeed those in the statements to the Treasury Solicitor, were often seriously at odds with the soldiers' original statements. At the very least one would have expected counsel for the tribunal to have put the irregularities to the soldiers in cross-examination. However this very rarely happened. In the few cases where it became apparent during the tribunal proceedings that a soldier had changed some aspect of his original statement it was because he had mentioned it in his statement to the Treasury Solicitor. For the most part the many and varied discrepancies outlined in the analysis above were never aired during the tribunal proceedings and were never communicated to counsel for the deceased. Even when the solicitor for the army asserted in his closing address that the testimony given by the soldiers to the tribunal did not differ from their original statements, apart from one admitted instance, counsel for the tribunal remained silent.

The conduct of the tribunal in this matter was totally inexcusable. A tribunal of inquiry is set up to search out the truth. It cannot confine itself to conclusions based on evidence presented in the examination and cross-examination of witnesses when other relevant evidence is available. It is its duty to dig out that other evidence and to scrutinise it with a view to ascertaining the whole truth. Given the contents of the tribunal's report, and in particular its findings, there can be little doubt that the tribunal ignored the damaging evidence of the soldiers' earlier statements when it was assessing the credibility and reliability of the testimony given by the soldiers in the witness box. It is this more than any other factor which totally discredits the tribunal's findings. Not only were they based on unreliable evidence, but the tribunal, by remaining silent when it was its duty to speak up, effectively concealed the existence of evidence which rendered the basis of its findings unreliable.

6
Lethal Force and the Law

Introduction

A cardinal feature of constitutional theory in the United Kingdom is
that police officers and soldiers are subject to the ordinary law of the
land even when acting in their official capacity.[1] If they are accused of
committing a criminal offence when effecting an arrest, acting to prevent a crime or seeking to restore public order, their liability will be
determined on exactly the same principles that would apply if they
were ordinary citizens. In other words they do not benefit from any
special privilege or immunity if they unlawfully kill or injure a person
while acting in the course of their duty. The standards set by the criminal law apply to them in exactly the same manner as they apply to
ordinary citizens. Of course the law does confer a range of powers on
police officers and soldiers which enable them to act coercively in situations which would be beyond the legal capacity of ordinary citizens.
That, however, does not detract from the general principle that if soldiers or police officers act beyond the limits of these powers in the
course of their duty their criminal liability will be assessed on the same
basis as that of ordinary citizens.

The purpose of this chapter is to review the law governing the exercise of lethal force by police officers and civilians, with particular
emphasis on how the relevant powers were interpreted judicially in
Northern Ireland in the 1970s. Consideration is also given to the internal army policy on the use of lethal force in operational situations (the
'Yellow Card'), the failure of the Widgery Tribunal to offer an analysis
of the law in the context of Bloody Sunday and the scope for prosecutions in the light of the Widgery Inquiry. It is necessary at the outset,
however, to identify the primary criminal offences which might be

relevant to a situation where a police officer or soldier fires real or plastic bullets in an operational situation.

Criminal offences

If soldiers or police officers fire an aimed shot without lawful justification and kill another human being they are likely to be charged with murder. Murder is committed when a person unlawfully kills another person with malice aforethought.[2] It used to be the case that the death had to occur within one year and a day of the last act of the accused which contributed to the death. This requirement has now been removed by the Law Reform (Year and a Day Rule) Act 1996. Malice aforethought is satisfied if the accused acted with the intention to kill or to cause serious injury to the victim. There is usually no difficulty satisfying this requirement when a soldier or police officer has fired a fatal shot at an identified target. Indeed arguments about the liability of the soldier or police officer in such cases typically focus on whether the killing was unlawful. For example it is lawful for anyone to kill in self defence, in defence of another, to effect an arrest, to prevent crime or to recapture a person who has escaped from lawful custody as long as it was reasonable to kill in the circumstances of the individual case. How this has been interpreted with respect to the fatal shootings by the security forces in Northern Ireland is considered in some detail below.

Manslaughter is another possibility if a soldier or police officer has killed in the course of duty. All unlawful homicides which are not murder are manslaughter.[3] By convention manslaughter is classified into two types: voluntary and involuntary. The former incorporates unlawful homicides, where the accused's state of mind was sufficient to satisfy murder but the presence of a certain mitigating factor reduces it to manslaughter. Involuntary manslaughter comprises all unlawful homicides committed by an accused who did not intend to kill or cause serious injury.[4] If the accused intended to kill or cause serious injury a charge of manslaughter would not normally be appropriate. If, however, without intending to kill or cause serious injury, he or she acts in a grossly negligent manner, thereby causing another's death, he or she will normally be guilty of manslaughter. A typical example might be a soldier discharging his weapon in a public place in order to frighten members of the public. If someone was killed as a result, and the soldier's action was without justification, it is likely that he would be found guilty of manslaughter.[5] It is also worth noting that a charge of manslaughter can arise if someone commits any inherently criminal act against another that is likely to cause some harm and in fact results in death. In practice, however, this variant is unlikely to feature in the prosecution of a soldier or police officer for discharging a firearm. As with murder, a prosecution for manslaughter will fail if the accused's action amounted to a use of force which was reasonable in the circumstances. This matter is dealt with below.

If a soldier or police officer fires a shot unlawfully in circumstances which do not result in death then clearly a charge of murder or manslaughter is not appropriate. However there are a range of other possible charges. The most serious would be attempted murder. This would be appropriate if the accused fired a shot at a target with the intention to kill (as opposed to injure) and either missed or inflicted a non-fatal wound on the victim. Other possibilities based on offences against the person include shooting with intent to murder, wounding with intent to cause grievous bodily harm, causing grievous bodily harm with intent to do some grievous bodily harm, wounding, inflicting grievous bodily harm, assault occasioning actual bodily harm, battery and assault. Firearms offences constitute another, albeit more remote and less appropriate possibility, At the time of Bloody Sunday possession with intent to endanger life or cause serious injury would appear to have been the most relevant firearms option.[6] It must be remembered, of course, that with all of these offences the action of the police officer or the soldier must have been conducted without lawful justification if an offence is to be established. The law on this critical issue is examined in detail below.

Before turning to possible defences based on the lawful use of force it is worth drawing attention to some other aspects of criminal liability which may prove of particular significance for the question of criminal liability for the events of Bloody Sunday. Firstly, it must be emphasised that the law in the United Kingdom does not recognise a defence of superior orders.[7] If soldiers or police officers fire a shot in circumstances which amount to one or more of the offences cited above it will be no defence for them to claim that they were ordered to do so by a superior officer. It does not follow, however, that only the soldier who fired the shot can be liable. If the superior officer gave an order to shoot in circumstances where there was no justification he or she could be liable either as a joint principal or as a secondary party to the offence committed, if any. Moreover in the case of manslaughter there is the possibility that senior officers could be liable if their orders, instructions or decisions were grossly negligent and resulted in a fatal shooting by a subordinate soldier or police officer. It therefore follows that those who planned and directed the security operation on Bloody Sunday are not necessarily exempt from criminal liability just because they did not actually pull the triggers.

Secondly, some of the soldiers who fired shots on Bloody Sunday will not necessarily escape criminal liability just because their shots cannot be linked to specific victims. In addition to possible charges such as attempted murder and shooting with intent to murder, they could be charged with murder if it can be established that they acted in concert in shooting at a victim who was unlawfully killed as a result. If they were acting in concert all of them will be considered responsible for the death even though it cannot be established which of them actually fired the fatal shot. In order to establish they were acting in concert it is necessary to show that at the time each of them fired shots they were acting in support of each other in a common enterprise.[8] It would not be necessary to show that the shooting had been preplanned. It would be quite sufficient that they joined with each other at a particular moment in time to shoot at a target or targets. So, for example, if a group of soldiers engaged in an arrest operation join with each other in unlawfully shooting an individual dead, they will all be guilty of murder even though it cannot be established which of them fired the fatal shot.

A third possibility worth mentioning is the joint enterprise. This is closely related to the notion of acting in concert. In a joint enterprise, however, it is not necessary to establish that all members of the group actually shot at the victim. It will be sufficient if one of them shot the victim and it can be established that they were all engaged in a common pursuit in which it was anticipated that unlawful force would be used.[9] If the members of the group were aware that there was a real or substantial risk that at least one of their number would resort to unlawful lethal force they will all be jointly liable if unlawful lethal force is used in the course of the common pursuit. It is at least arguable, therefore, that if a team of armed soldiers set out on an arrest operation in which each of them knows that one or more of them is contemplating the use of unlawful lethal force, all of them may be attached with criminal liability if unlawful lethal force is used, even if that force is used by only one of their number.

Criminal Law Act (Northern Ireland) 1967

The domestic law governing the use of force at the time of Bloody Sunday was contained in Section 3(1) of the Criminal Law Act (Northern Ireland) 1967 and the common law principles governing self-defence. If one person intentionally uses force against the person of another, resulting in the death of the latter, the former is normally guilty of murder unless he or she was acting within the scope of Section 3(1) of the 1967 Act or in self-defence. Given the central importance of these provisions for the legality of the actions of the soldiers on Bloody Sunday, it is essential to deal with them in some detail.

According to Section 3(1) of the Criminal Law Act (Northern Ireland) 1967, 'A person may use such force as is reasonable in the circumstances in the prevention of crime, or in effecting or assisting in the lawful arrest of offenders or suspected offenders or of persons unlawfully at large.' Although this statutory provision replaced the common law governing the use of force to prevent crime or to effect an arrest, it did not specifically replace the common law on self-defence. Nevertheless, it is generally accepted that Section 3(1) provides the essential test of when and how much force may be used, in self-defence as well as to prevent crime or effect an arrest.[10] At common law individuals are entitled to use as much force as is reasonable in the circumstances in order to protect themselves or another against attack. In most situations where one individual is acting in self-defence against an assailant he or she will also be acting to prevent a crime.[11] It should be no surprise, therefore, that the principles governing the amount of force, if any, that is reasonable in the circumstances for the purpose of a defence under Section 3(1) are the same as those governing the degree of force, if any, that is reasonable for the purpose of self-defence. The following exposition of the principles governing Section 3(1) is equally applicable to self-defence, and indeed will draw on self-defence case law where appropriate. Their interpretation and application in the case of the security forces in Northern Ireland will be dealt with in more detail later.

The decision maker

When someone is charged with murder the prosecution must prove beyond reasonable doubt that he or she has satisfied all the elements of the offence. Usually it is the jury which decides as a matter of fact whether the prosecution has discharged this burden. When the defence of the accused is based on self-defence or on Section 3(1), the prosecution must prove beyond reasonable doubt that the force used was unreasonable in the circumstances. The courts have consistently held that what constitutes reasonable force in this context is a question of fact. Accordingly it is a matter for the jury to decide in each individual case whether the force used was reasonable or unreasonable. However the trial judge will give the jury guidance on the factors it should take into account when making this determination. These factors will now be outlined under the following headings: the circumstances; subjective or objective test; excessive force; and justifying the use of lethal force. It must be remembered, however, that the 'shoot-to-kill' cases in Northern Ireland are heard before the Diplock Courts, which sit without a jury. All questions of fact (as of law) in these courts are decided by the judge alone. In these cases, therefore, it is judges who will decide, whether the force used was reasonable. Nevertheless, they will take into account the same factors they would expect the jury to take into account when deciding the issue.

The circumstances

Section 3(1) permits the use of such force as is reasonable in the circumstances. For the most part what is meant by the 'circumstances' does not give rise to difficulty in individual cases. The English Criminal Law Revision Committee, whose report resulted in the adoption of the equivalent to Section 3(1) in the British Criminal Law Act 1967, outlined the approach that the court should take:

> No doubt if a question arose on [Section] 3, the court, in considering what was reasonable force, would take into account all the circumstances, including in particular the nature and degree of force used, the seriousness of the evil to be prevented and the possibility of preventing it by other means.[12]

It follows that one of the circumstances the court must take into account is the gravity of the offence being prevented or for which the accused was arrested. There must be some proportionality between the degree of force used and the gravity of the offence. It would not be justifiable, for example, to shoot shoplifters even if the circumstances were such that that was the only method of preventing them from getting away. Similarly the courts will take into account other means which were available in the circumstances to effect an arrest or prevent a crime where those other means would have avoided the need to resort to the use of force or to the degree of force actually used.

Subjective or objective test

Closely related to the issue of the circumstances which must be taken into account in Section 3(1) is the question of whether a subjective or an objective test should be applied. In other words, should courts treat the accused on the basis of what the accused considered reasonable in the circumstances or on the basis of what a reasonable person would have considered reasonable. The difference can be critical. If courts take the objective approach the accused will lose the defence entirely if he or she used force in circumstances where a reasonable person would not have considered that the use of force was reasonable. It will make no difference that the accused honestly believed that resort to force was reasonable in the circumstances. Even if a reasonable person agrees that resort to force is reasonable in the circumstances, the accused will still lose the defence if he or she used more force than the reasonable person would have considered reasonable in the circumstances. For example, if the accused was being pushed forward in a queue by another person and he or she responded by punching the latter in the face, a reasonable person might well consider that this amounted to the use of more force than was reasonably necessary in the circumstances. That being the case the accused will lose the defence under Section 3(1). Under the objective test it will make no difference that the accused honestly believed that his or her response was appropriate and reasonable in the circumstances.

By contrast, a subjective test focuses on what the accused person honestly believed. If the courts take this approach the accused may have a good defence under Section 3(1) as long as he or she honestly believes that his or her use of force was reasonable in the circumstances. He or she will not lose the defence simply because a reasonable person would not have considered that resort to force (or the amount of force used) was reasonable in the circumstances.

In their interpretation of Section 3(1) the courts have been adopting what might be termed a mixed approach. That is, the test incorporates both objective and subjective elements.[13] Generally the court will consider whether the accused has used more force than a reasonable person would have considered necessary in the circumstances. In making this assessment it will place the reasonable person in the circumstances in which the accused found her or himself in at the time, including the facts which were known to the accused. This is neatly summed up in the following passage from the judgment of Justice Hutton in *R v Hegarty*:

> The decision whether the Crown has proved beyond reasonable doubt that the force used was unreasonable in the circumstances is a question of fact.... The appellate courts have clearly stated in deciding this question of fact the tribunal deciding it (whether it be a jury or judge sitting without a jury) must not decide it retrospectively

by sitting in the calm of the courtroom and debating with hindsight and in full possession of all the facts (including knowledge of the fatal consequence of the force used) whether the force used was reasonable or unreasonable. Rather the tribunal has to put itself in the position of the accused and to decide whether or not the force used was unreasonable taking account of the pressures and dangers to which the accused was then exposed (or the dangers to which others were exposed) and the time (which may be only a second or two) in which the accused had to come to a decision.[14]

It is also worth noting that when the circumstances are such as to justify the use of some force and the issue is whether excessive force has been used, the court's interpretation of what is reasonable will take into account the fact (where applicable) that the accused had only done what he or she honestly and instinctively thought was necessary in the circumstances. This is vividly conveyed in the following passage from the judgment of Lord Morris in *Palmer v R*:

> If there has been attack so that defence is reasonably necessary it will be recognised that a person defending himself cannot weigh to a nicety the exact measure of his necessary defensive action. If a jury thought that in a moment of unexpected anguish a person attacked had only done what he honestly and instinctively thought was necessary that would be most potent evidence that only reasonable defensive action had been taken.[15]

It may happen, of course, that the facts or circumstances are not what the accused believed them to be. In other words the accused may have been mistaken in his or her belief that the victim was posing a threat. Many of the fatal shootings by members of the security forces in Northern Ireland have occurred in circumstances where the policeman or soldier believed, wrongly, that the victim was armed or that he was a dangerous terrorist making good his escape. Policemen and soldiers in Northern Ireland must always be alive to the risk of armed attack. Their lives may depend on an instant and lethal response to the first sign of danger. This inevitably increases the risk of tragic mistakes being made. By the same token, however, soldiers or policemen who shoot dead an unarmed and innocent civilian have an obvious and compelling motivation for claiming, for example, that the victim had made a move which had led them to believe that the victim had been armed and about to shoot, or that they had believed that the victim was a dangerous terrorist making good his escape. These are claims which are very easy to make and very difficult to refute. What then does the law say about mistakes in this context? Is the accused treated on the basis of the actual facts known to him or her or on the basis of what he or she mistakenly believed the facts to be? Does it make any difference whether their mistakes were reasonable or unreasonable in the circumstances?

Up until the late 1980s the courts consistently adopted the objective approach on this issue.[16] In other words they considered whether the use of force was reasonable in the circumstances which the accused honestly and *reasonably* believed to exist. In *R v Fennell*,[17] for example, Lord Widgery himself espoused the objective approach when considering whether it was reasonable for a father to use force to protect his son from what he had mistakenly believed to be the wrongful arrest of his son. Referring generally to the role of mistaken belief in self-defence, Lord Widgery said 'Where a person honestly and *reasonably* believes that he or his child is in imminent danger of injury, it would be unjust if he were deprived of the right to use reasonable force by way of defence merely because he made some genuine mistake of fact'[18] (emphasis added).

Similarly, in a prosecution of a civilian who claimed to have been using force in self-defence against the police in the course of a riot in Derry in August 1969, Lord Chief Justice MacDermott proceeded on the basis that the objective test was appropriate.[19] In another Northern Irish case in the early 1970s, *R v Browne*,[20] Lord Chief Justice Lowry summarised the law on the use of lethal force in self-defence as follows: 'To justify killing or inflicting serious injury in self-defence, the accused must honestly believe *on reasonable grounds* that he is in immediate danger of death or serious injury and to kill or inflict serious injury provides the only reasonable means of protection'[21] (emphasis added). Clearly Lowry was adopting the objective approach as the appropriate standard for determining the relevant circumstances.

The first hint of a change from the objective to the subjective approach came in 1975 with the House of Lords landmark decision in *DPP v Morgan*,[22] a rape case where the accused claimed that he had believed (wrongly) that the victim had consented to intercourse. The House of Lords ruled that the accused would have a good defence to rape if he honestly believed that the victim had consented. So long as his belief was genuine it would not matter if it was mistaken and that a reasonable person would not have formed the belief in the circumstances. Applying this reasoning by analogy to the situation where lethal force is used in self-defence or under Section 3(1), it would seem that the objective approach must be discarded in favour of the subjective approach. In other words the accused should be treated on the basis of his mistaken view of the facts, even if a reasonable person would not have formed that view. If the accused honestly believed that the victim had been armed and about to shoot, his response in resorting to the use of lethal force would have to be assessed on the basis that his mistaken belief was true, even if it was an unreasonable belief in the circumstances. This view of the law was confirmed by the Court of Appeal in *R v Gladstone Williams*[23] and the Judicial Committee of the Privy Council in *Beckford v R*.[24] It has since been applied in Northern Ireland in at least two prosecutions for fatal shootings by members of the security forces.[25] The net result, of course, is to render it more difficult to secure a conviction against a soldier or a policeman in Northern Ireland for the fatal shooting of an unarmed civilian if the soldier or policeman claims that he believed (wrongly) that he was dealing with a dangerous terrorist who posed a threat to life.

Excessive force

It is clear, therefore, that when assessing whether the accused used no more force than was reasonably necessary in the interests of self-defence, preventing a crime or effecting an arrest, the courts will pay particular attention to the situation in which the accused found himself. If, on the facts known to him, the accused judges that his response was necessary the courts will be reluctant to find that he acted unreasonably unless his response is so out of proportion to the danger that he faced that no reasonable person could have contemplated it. If, however, the court does conclude that the accused did use more force than was reasonably necessary in the circumstances he will lose the defence entirely. This can have immense significance if the accused has used lethal force and is charged with murder as a consequence. If the court finds that he was justified in using some force but that his use of lethal force was more than reasonably necessary in the circumstances it will have to return a verdict of guilty of murder, which carries a mandatory life sentence. From time to time the argument has been made that the option of returning a conviction for manslaughter should be available if the accused thought, honestly but unreasonably, that his resort to lethal force was justified.[26] The attraction of manslaughter in this context is that it allows the court discretion over the nature and length of the sentence. The courts in the United Kingdom, however, have consistently rejected this argument.[27] The most recent and emphatic decision to this effect was handed down by the House of Lords in *R v Clegg*,[28] when a British soldier was convicted of the murder of a 'joyrider' who had been shot when driving through a security checkpoint in Northern Ireland. Accordingly, when Section 3(1) or the common law defence of self-defence is raised in response to a charge of murder it is an all or nothing situation. Either the accused will be convicted of murder or acquitted entirely, depending on whether or not the defence is made out. There is no half-way house of conviction for manslaughter if the accused honestly but unreasonably thought that the use of lethal force was justified.

Justifying lethal force

Resort to lethal force or potentially lethal force presents very acute problems for the interpretation of what amounts to reasonable force under Section 3(1) or in self-defence. Referring to the British equivalent of Section 3(1), the leading English text on criminal law suggests that it is not reasonable to resort to lethal force unless (1) it is necessary to do so in order to effect an arrest or prevent a crime; or (2) the evil which would follow from failure to prevent the crime or effect the arrest is so great that a reasonable person ought to think him or herself justified in taking another's life to avert that evil.[29] It would seem sensible to qualify this by saying that it would rarely, if ever, be justifiable to use lethal force solely in order to effect an arrest.[30] The whole purpose in effecting an arrest would be defeated if the person to be arrested was intentionally killed in the process. By contrast it is not difficult to envisage situations where resort to lethal force would be justified in self-defence or in order to prevent crime. Resort to lethal force for such purposes, however, would actually have to be necessary to prevent the crime or effect the arrest. It follows that if a less drastic alternative is available, the use of lethal force would not be justified under Section 3(1) or in self-defence. Even if the use of force is necessary to achieve a legitimate objective, there would have to be some proportionality between the force used and the evil which would follow if the crime was not prevented or the arrest effected. In other words the likely death of the victim would have to be the lesser of two evils. Shooting a shoplifter, for example, would not be justifiable even if that was the only means available to effect his arrest. It is therefore likely that the proportionality requirement can only be satisfied in an exceptional situation, such as when there is a substantial and immediate risk of death or serious injury if lethal force is not used against the offender.

Support for this restrictive approach to the lawful use of lethal force under Section 3(1) or in self-defence can be seen in the case of

Devlin v Armstrong.[31] Significantly this was the first case on the use of reasonable force to come before the Northern Irish courts in thirty years of violence. Moreover it concerned the unusual situation of a civilian attempting to rely on self-defence as a justification for the use of potentially lethal force against the police. Accordingly it provides a useful benchmark against which to assess subsequent cases in which members of the security forces relied on self-defence and Section 3(1) to justify the use of lethal force against civilians.

In *Devlin v Armstrong*, Bernadette Devlin[32] was convicted and sentenced to six months' imprisonment for riotous behaviour and incitement to riotous behaviour. The case against her was essentially that she had encouraged and participated in riots in the Bogside from 12–14 August 1969, which had ended with the deployment of British troops. Devlin appealed against her conviction primarily on the basis of self-defence. She argued that she had intercepted a police radio communication which suggested that the police were threatening to invade the Bogside, backed up by a unionist mob. Relevant excerpts from the communication revealed the police commander in question saying 'We have two hundred men and enough supporters to eat the place'; and 'We have enough men to polish them off once and for all'. Some months prior to these events the police had invaded the Bogside and violently attacked the local residents at random, resulting in the death of Samuel Devenny. Bernadette Devlin and others had feared a repetition of these events and had sought to protect themselves against it by building barricades and hurling stones and petrol bombs at the police lines and the unionist mob behind them.

In the Northern Irish Court of Appeal, Lord Chief Justice MacDermott did not rule out the possibility of a civilian relying successfully on Section 3(1) or self-defence as justification for the use of potentially lethal force against the security forces. However he did set a very high standard for determining the circumstances in which it would be reasonable to resort to the use of petrol bombs in self defence:

> However reasonable and convinced the appellant's apprehensions may have been, I find it impossible to hold that the danger she anticipated was sufficiently specific or imminent to justify the actions she took as measures of self-defence. The police were then in the throes of containing a riot in the course of their duty, and her interventions at that juncture were far too aggressive and premature to rank as justifiable efforts to prevent the prospective danger of the police getting out of hand and acting unlawfully which, as I have assumed, she anticipated.

Where force is used either in exercise of the right of self-defence or, under Section 3 of the Act of 1967, in the prevention of crime, it must be reasonable in the circumstances. This consideration alone seems to me to be fatal to the appellant's plea of justification. Whatever her fears and however genuine they may have been, to organise and encourage the throwing of petrol bombs was, I would hold, an utterly unwarranted and unlawful reaction. The night of 12 August had demonstrated the capacity of those lethal weapons to injure and destroy and nothing that had happened or was likely to happen could excuse the appellant in facilitating and encouraging their use.

Clearly MacDermott considered that the use of potentially lethal force would be reasonable only in exceptional circumstances. In the judge's view the use of petrol bombs constituted an overreaction to the nature of the danger anticipated by the accused in this case. The strong implication was that there would have to be a specific and immediate threat to the life or person of the accused or another person before it would be reasonable to resort to the use of such a potentially lethal weapon. It is worth bearing this standard in mind when the cases governing the use of force by the security forces are considered.

Before turning to Northern Irish case law it must be pointed out that Section 3(1) of the Criminal Law Act 1967 was enacted before the violence broke out in 1969. As such it was not designed specifically to deal with situations where heavily armed police officers and soldiers would be engaged on a permanent or semi-permanent basis in quelling major public rioting or combatting an armed insurrection against the state. It was intended to lay down the law generally on the justifiable use of force in order to prevent crime or effect an arrest. No distinction was made between a civilian using force against another civilian and a police officer (or soldier acting in aid of the civil power) using force against a civilian in the course of his or her duty to keep the peace, maintain public order and enforce the law. Exactly the same legal principles apply to the civilian, the police officer and the soldier. Similarly the common law governing the defence of self-defence draws no distinction between a citizen acting in self-defence and a policeman or soldier acting in self-defence. The same legal principles apply.

Northern Irish case law

The question which must now be addressed is how the principles governing the use of lethal force have been interpreted and applied to the actions of the security forces in Northern Ireland since 1969.

In particular it must be considered whether they have been interpreted and applied in a manner which has encouraged soldiers and police officers to believe that they are effectively beyond the reach of the law in situations where they deem it necessary to resort to lethal force. Has the criminal law been as weak and ineffective in controlling the use of lethal force by the security forces as it has been, at least up to Bloody Sunday, in protecting citizens against brutal interrogation practices, internment and arbitrary constraints on their liberty and freedoms? Did it create an environment in which the security forces were encouraged to resort to the use of lethal force when they considered that necessary to the pursuit of security policy?

The failure to prosecute offered the first sure indication that the law governing the use of lethal force would not always apply to the security forces in the same manner that it applied to ordinary civilians. Between 1969 and Bloody Sunday not one prosecution was taken against a member of the security forces for killing a civilian in the course of duty. This was despite the fact that the security forces killed 50 civilians during this period, the vast majority of whom were unarmed. The lack of prosecutions also meant that there was no opportunity for authoritative judicial analysis of the legal principles governing the use of lethal force by the security forces in Northern Ireland during this period. The first prosecution of a member of the security forces for the fatal shooting of an unarmed civilian did not occur until March 1974.[33] This case, however, concerned a charge of manslaughter against a soldier who had killed a 12-year-old boy after firing a shot, at night, allegedly without proper aim, into a street where civilians were present.[34] As such it did not afford an opportunity for the courts to pronounce upon the circumstances in which the security forces could lawfully resort to the deliberate use of lethal force in order to prevent a crime or effect an arrest. The first reported case in which the courts were presented with this opportunity did not arise until September 1974 in the case of *R v McNaughton*,[35] when a soldier was tried for the attempted murder of a civilian who allegedly had been attempting to escape from an army patrol.[36] A vital feature of this case was the significance which the trial judge, Lord Chief Justice Lowry, attached to the security factors surrounding the shooting.

The accused soldier had been in command of an eight-man patrol operating in the border area of South Armagh. As the soldiers had proceeded in the direction of an explosion heard earlier they had encountered the civilian in question walking across a field from the direction of the explosion. He had been carrying a sheet of plastic which at one time had been a bag for animal feed. He had explained that he lived in a nearby farmhouse and was coming back from feeding cattle. The accused had arrested the man on suspicion of being involved in the explosion and had compelled him to accompany the patrol in the direction of the explosion. The accused claimed that the man had attempted to escape over a fence. After shouting three warnings to stop the accused had fired a shot which wounded the victim. The vital issue, therefore, was whether this shooting had been reasonable in the circumstances. In considering the reasonableness of the accused's action the learned lord chief justice proceeded from the basis that the security forces had been operating in conditions with which the ordinary law was not designed to cope. Nevertheless the active service conditions experienced by the soldiers had to be taken into account in the application of the ordinary law. The range and substance of the conditions the lord chief justice considered relevant convey a very strong sense of deference to security interests. In addition to the accused's suspicion that he had been dealing with a dangerous terrorist who might have been involved in a recent explosion, the lord chief justice felt it necessary to consider:

> the fact that the patrol ... was traversing potentially hostile country where it needed good observation and a good tactical formation and to bear in mind also the orders that had been issued and the training which had been given with regard to such circumstances; thirdly, the consequences of [the victim] escaping successfully, and as they could appear to the accused; and fourthly, the burden which would be placed on the patrol if [the victim] proved difficult to handle. Fifthly, I must have regard to the fact that this patrol, which was about to set out on a three day mission (being carried in the first stage by helicopter), was heavily laden and not simply wearing battle order. Sixthly, I consider the undulating and enclosed nature of the country and the fact that [the victim] knew that country, as one assumes he did. ... Another factor is that, if the patrol were to be broken up through the need to run after the escaper or to send men in pursuit, then someone would be in the line of fire, if fire proved necessary.

One might be forgiven for thinking that the learned lord chief justice was treating the situation as though the security forces were operating under the laws of war rather than the ordinary law. Indeed he also endorsed what he considered to be the expert evidence of senior army officers, to the effect that: 'ordinary methods of recapturing an escaped prisoner which would be acceptable in peaceful conditions and different surroundings are just not practicable in the place and circumstances in which this escape was alleged to have been committed'. It is hardly surprising that the lord chief justice concluded that the prosecution had failed to establish beyond reasonable doubt that the shooting had been without justification. This conclusion, however, must be set against the undisputed fact that the accused soldier had not believed that the victim had been armed and had not felt there was an immediate threat to his own safety or that of members of his patrol.

The problem with the judicial approach in *McNaughton* is that it virtually left soldiers with almost absolute power over life and death in situations where they needed to apprehend someone whom they believed was a terrorist. Nevertheless, when the issue came before the courts again only a few months later in the context of a fatal shooting the judges defined the law in terms which were, if anything, even more sympathetic to security interests. Although this was more than two years after Bloody Sunday, it is critically important to an understanding of how the law failed so miserably to prevent Bloody Sunday from happening in the first place and also failed to punish those responsible after the event. It offered the strongest possible confirmation to security chiefs and the rank and file that in the course of their military duties the law would not subject them to the same high standards as it imposed on ordinary civilians, even when their objectives involved the use of lethal force.[37] The importance of the case is illustrated by the fact that it went all the way to the House of Lords, the highest court in the United Kingdom, thereby providing the most authoritative judicial statement of the relevant law.[38]

Patrick McElhone was a member of a farming family in County Tyrone. On 7 August 1974 an Army patrol questioned him while he was driving a tractor on the farm. Later that day, after McElhone had gone home for tea, the soldiers returned and he was taken out and questioned again. What happened next was the subject of a fundamental dispute between McElhone's parents and the soldiers. At the trial Justice MacDermott proceeded on the basis of the soldiers' version, which was that McElhone had walked down the road from the farm after the first questioning. The patrol sergeant had sent a soldier after him to bring him back for further questioning. The soldier had followed McElhone into a field and when McElhone failed to obey an order to halt the soldier had fired one shot at him from a distance of eight yards. The shot had proved fatal. McElhone had been unarmed at the time and neither he nor any member of his family had any connection with a paramilitary organisation or activity. The soldier who had fired the shot was tried for murder in the no-jury Diplock Courts (see Chapter 7). His defence was that he had honestly and reasonably believed that he had been dealing with a member of the IRA who was attempting to escape. He considered that it had been his duty to apprehend the deceased and he believed that firing at him had been a reasonable and proper way to discharge his duty in the circumstances. In other words the accused based his defence on Section 3(1) of the 1967 Act to the effect that he used such force as was reasonable in the circumstances in order to prevent crime or effect an arrest of an offender or suspected offender. The key issue, therefore, was whether his use of lethal force in the circumstances of this case was reasonable.

In defining the 'circumstances' in this case Justice MacDermott followed the lead of Lord Chief Justice Lowry in *R v McNaughton* and gave particular consideration to the wider security situation in which the soldiers were generally operating, including:

- The general wartime situation in Northern Ireland.
- The actual situation facing the soldier on the ground, for example whether he was operating in an area where there was a real risk of a life-threatening surprise attack.
- Whether or not the accused had reasonably suspected that the deceased might have been a terrorist.
- Whether the accused believed honestly and reasonably that it had been his duty to open fire.
- Whether alternative methods of stopping the deceased had been reasonably viable.

Superficially, this approach appeared to focus on the state of mind of the soldier and whether his belief had been reasonable. Under the law as it was believed to be at the time, the first requirement was that the soldier should have honestly believed that the deceased might have been a terrorist and that it had been his duty to open fire in order to apprehend him. The mere fact that the soldier had entertained this belief would not be sufficient in itself to afford a defence. The second requirement was that the soldier's belief would have to have been reasonable. In other words there would have to have been some basis upon which a reasonable person would have formed the same belief.

At first sight this objective element appeared to offer Northern Irish citizens protection against the overzealous use of lethal force by the security forces. Its value, however, was seriously compromised by the sort of factors which had to be taken into account when assessing the reasonableness of a soldier's belief. Basing what was reasonable on factors such as the general wartime situation in Northern Ireland, the local environment in which the soldier was operating and whether, given the soldier's state of mind, there were reasonably viable alternatives, robs the objective element of much of its meaning. The result was that the legality of a soldier's action in resorting to lethal force would depend substantially on how he, as a soldier, perceived the circumstances in which he was operating. This is starkly illustrated by the facts of the McElhone shooting.

Significantly Justice MacDermott found that the accused had not been acting in the belief that McElhone had been involved in acts of terrorism or was likely to be involved in any immediate act of terrorism. In other words, even in the mind of the soldier the deceased had not posed an immediate threat to his life or safety or to the lives or safety of others. Indeed there had been no terrorist activity in the area in the preceding days. The only suspicion against the deceased had arisen from the desire of the patrol sergeant to double-check whether the deceased had been on a list of suspected terrorists in the area, coupled with his failure to obey an order to halt for the purpose of being questioned a third time. Nevertheless the learned judge went on to conclude that the use of force had been reasonable in the circumstances. In reaching this conclusion he was clearly influenced by the 'general wartime situation' in Northern Ireland and, more particularly, the nature of the locality in question. Justice MacDermott described the latter as:

> an area in which troops had been attacked and killed; it was an area in which … soldiers … faced a real threat to their lives and where the element of surprise attack was a real threat. The said patrol had been briefed to expect attack and to be wary of being led into an ambush. [The patrol was] in an area which the men were perfectly entitled to regard as containing people who might be actively hostile.

This description could be applied to most nationalist areas patrolled by the army at the time. It follows from Justice MacDermott's analysis that it would have been reasonable for a soldier to resort to lethal force in a nationalist area against anyone whom he subjectively believed to be a terrorist and who failed to obey an order to stop. The fact that the suspect was not posing an immediate threat to the life or person of the soldier or anyone else would not render the use of lethal force against him unreasonable. Accordingly, the accused soldier was acquitted of the murder of McElhone despite the fact that McElhone had been an inno-cent, unarmed civilian with no paramilitary connections whatsoever.

Justice MacDermott's analysis, coupled with that of Lord Chief Justice Lowry in *McNaughton*, went well beyond what was understood to be the legal principles governing the use of force in order to prevent crime or effect an arrest. Indeed, Justice MacDermott specifically side-lined the analysis of the law presented in the leading criminal law text at the time as the discussion in it was 'very much in the context of the law as it appears in normal peaceful conditions'. It had never been con-templated that Section 3(1) of the 1967 Act could bear an interpreta-tion so favourable to the use of lethal force. Justice MacDermott's interpretation would permit the army (and the police) legitimately to use lethal force simply in order to apprehend anyone who was sus-pected of being a terrorist and who did not obey an order to stop, irre-spective of whether the suspect was armed or active at the time. From the McElhone case it would seem that the mere fact that an individual attempted to run away from an army patrol would in itself be sufficient grounds for a soldier in the patrol to form the belief that the individual was a suspect terrorist. Depending on the nature of the locality this would be sufficient justification for the soldier to resort to lethal force to apprehend the suspect. Given that nationalist areas were 'policed' exclusively by the army in the early 1970s it can be appreciated just how little protection Justice MacDermott's analysis afforded innocent civilians. By the same token it sent a message to the security forces that legal control on the use of lethal force in such areas was more relaxed than was the case in other areas or contexts.

The novelty of Justice MacDermott's interpretation is reflected in the fact that the attorney general referred the case to the Northern Ireland Court of Appeal for clarification of the law on the following issues: (1) 'whether a soldier commits a crime when he fires to kill or seriously wound an unarmed person because he honestly and reasonably believes that that person is a member of a proscribed organisation (in this case the Provisional IRA) who is seeking to run away, and the soldier's shot kills that person'; and (2) if it is a crime, whether the sol-dier is guilty of murder or manslaughter on the facts of this case.[39] Significantly Lord Justice Jones for the majority[40] specifically rejected the proposition advanced by the crown that the use of force would only be reasonable under Section 3(1) if (1) it was necessary to use force in order to prevent crime or effect an arrest; and (2) the evil which would follow from the failure to prevent crime or effect the arrest was so great that a reasonable man might think himself justified in taking another's life to avert that evil. Instead the learned judge considered that these were merely factors to be taken into account, as opposed to preconditions, when considering whether the use of force was reasonable. Ultimately it was a matter for the tribunal of fact to determine whether the use of force was reasonable. It is worth noting again that these cases were heard in the no-jury Diplock Courts, and as such the tribunal of fact was the trial judge.

A critical feature of the case, and one which distinguished it from *McNaughton*, was the fact that the accused had not believed that the victim might have been involved in a recent act of terrorism or that he was likely to be involved in an immediate act of terrorism. Would it still be justifiable in such circumstances for a soldier to shoot him dead if he tried to escape when the soldier did not believe that he might be armed and merely suspected that he might be a member of a proscribed organisation, an offence which at the time carried a maximum sentence of five years' imprisonment? The manner in which Lord Justice Jones dealt with this issue seems to imply greater importance being attached to the need to maintain the authority of the security forces than to innocent civilians' right to life:

> even if the deceased were not likely to be involved in any immediate act of terrorism, there was no reason to be sure, or even think, that he might not, either by giving information or otherwise, be involved after a short interval in acts which could have endangered the lives of the members of the patrol. This patrol was working in active service conditions, which the Lord Chief Justice said in McNaughton's case it was vitally important to remember, and if the deceased, on the basis of the respondent's belief, had been permitted to run away when legally called upon to halt, there might, consistent with what the respondent honestly and reasonably believed, have been a resultant discomfiture of the forces of law, and encouragement of the Provisional IRA to further resistance to the Army, and it could be seen by those in the area hitherto uncommitted to the IRA as a demonstration that the Army was ineffective to enforce its authority with possible extension of IRA influence and support, as has occurred in other parts of the Province.[41]

By contrast the powerful minority judgment of Lord Justice McGonigal sought to link the circumstances in which it might be lawful to use lethal force with the seriousness of the offence for which the soldier wished to stop or arrest the suspect. The question he felt he had to consider was whether shooting to kill or cause serious injury to an unarmed member of the IRA could be justified when he ran away to avoid having to answer questions.[42] Lord Justice McGonigal recognised that to accede to such a proposition would confer sweeping powers over life and death on the army even in cases where there was no immediate threat to the person: 'The possibilities of who may be shot legitimately, if the proposition is correct and one is entitled to speculate as to the future, are endless. It is giving an unlimited licence to the security forces.'[43]

He had little difficulty, therefore, concluding that the use of such force in these circumstances would be 'so manifestly disproportionate to the mischief sought to be prevented that no reasonable jury properly directed could do other than hold that the force used was excessive'.[44] The learned judge also dismissed the notion that a soldier's actions would be lawful if he thought that it was his duty to stop a suspect and that firing at him was a reasonable and proper way to discharge that duty in the circumstances. The soldier in the McElhone case had not been duty bound to use lethal force, but even if he had been it would have been so 'manifestly extreme that it could not be set up as a matter of justification or exoneration'.[45] It is also worth noting that Lord Justice McGonigal considered that the circumstances had not justified the use of any force. The soldier could and should have reacted by shouting further warnings to the victim. If that had failed the use of a warning shot should have been considered. The soldier's immediate resort to lethal force had not been necessary and therefore had not been reasonable in the circumstances.

Lord Justice McGonigal's more balanced approach was rejected not just by his colleagues in the Court of Appeal but also by the House of Lords. The leading judgment was handed down by Lord Diplock.[46] Unfortunately it did not offer any significant clarification beyond that provided by the Court of Appeal. It confirmed that the issue of whether the force used had been reasonable in the circumstances was a question of fact for the jury (in this case the trial judge). In answering that question the fact-finder should consider whether it was:

> satisfied that no reasonable man (a) with knowledge of such facts as were known to the accused or reasonably believed by him to exist (b) in the circumstances and time available to him for reflection (c) could be of opinion that the prevention of the risk of harm to which others might be exposed if the suspect were allowed to escape justified exposing the suspect to the risk of harm to him that might result from the kind of force that the accused contemplated using.

This bald statement clearly offered very little guidance on the fundamental question of when the use of lethal force by the security forces might be deemed reasonable. It is clearly apparent from other parts of the judgment, however, that armed soldiers operating in the unusual circumstances prevailing in Northern Ireland at the time had to be treated as a special case:

> There is little authority in English law concerning the rights and duties of a member of the armed forces of the Crown when acting in aid of the civil power; and what little authority there is relates almost entirely to the duties of soldiers when troops are called upon to assist in controlling a riotous assembly. Where used for such temporary purposes it may not be inaccurate to describe the legal rights and duties of a soldier as being no more than those of an ordinary citizen in uniform. But such a description is in my view misleading in the circumstances in which the army is currently employed in aid of the civil power in Northern Ireland. In some parts of the province there has existed for some years now a state of armed and clandestinely organised insurrection against the lawful government of Her Majesty by persons seeking to gain political ends by violent means – that is, by committing murder and other crimes of violence against persons and property.[47]

In other words the soldiers were to be considered as operating in a situation bordering on martial law. Indeed, Lord Justice Diplock specifically referred to the fact that a soldier was: 'under a duty, enforceable under military law, to search for criminals if so ordered by his superior officer and to risk his own life in the process'. For this purpose soldiers were armed with self-loading rifles from which a bullet, if it hit its human target, would almost certainly kill.

Lord Justice Diplock went on to confirm the view of the majority in the Court of Appeal that the soldier's power to resort to lethal force was not confined to situations in which there was an immediate threat to the person. The learned judge, however, specifically dealt with the McElhone case on the basis that 'the accused's honest and reasonable belief was that the deceased was a member of the Provisional IRA who, if he got away, was likely sooner or later to participate in acts of violence'. Accordingly any jury (or trial judge as the case may be) could find that it was reasonable for a soldier to shoot a suspect terrorist who was attempting to make good his escape. The learned judge also emphasised that the jury (or the judge) would have to take into account the highly charged circumstances in which the soldier would have to make the split-second decision. The net effect, of course, was that a soldier operating in Northern Ireland enjoyed immensely greater freedom to use lethal force than was the case with ordinary citizens.

The House of Lords' decision in the McElhone case left no room for doubt that armed soldiers operating in certain parts of Northern Ireland enjoyed very broad power to use lethal force against individuals who failed to obey an order to stop. This was the direct result of the courts' willingness to take a very broad interpretation of what circumstances should be taken into account when considering whether the force used in a particular incident was reasonable. Not only would they include the immediate circumstances in which the soldier found himself when he decided to open fire but they would also include such background circumstances as the general character of the area and the people living in it, as perceived by the security forces, as well as the general wartime situation in Northern Ireland. It would therefore, seem to follow that the planning behind a military operation which resulted in a fatal shooting would also be a relevant matter for consideration. Perversely, however, when the issue was raised in the second case of fatal shooting to reach the House of Lords from Northern Ireland, *Farrell v Ministry of Defence*,[48] these matters were considered irrelevant. Had they been included as part of the circumstances which had to be taken into consideration it is highly likely that the court would have concluded that the soldiers responsible had used more force than was reasonable in the circumstances. There are also obvious implications for the assessment of whether the force used on Bloody Sunday could qualify as reasonable.

The case in question concerned a civil action for damages arising out of the fatal shooting of three bank robbers in Newry, County Down in October 1971. The security forces had received advance information about a terrorist bomb attack on a bank. Consequently armed soldiers had been placed in position on the roof of a building opposite the bank to await the bombers. The bank robbers, however, had been unarmed and had no terrorist connections. They had attempted to run away when the soldiers had called on them to stop. Mistaking the robbers for the expected bombers the soldiers had duly shot them dead, that being the only means of apprehending them given that the soldiers had been positioned on the roof of a building. No criminal prosecution was taken against the soldiers or those involved in planning the operation. Mrs Farrell, the widow of one of the deceased, sued the Ministry of Defence for damages for the death of her husband. She lost at first instance in the High Court. However the Northern Ireland

Court of Appeal allowed her appeal and ordered a new trial on the grounds of a misdirection by the trial judge. One of the central issues in the case was whether the force used by the soldiers had been reasonable in the circumstances within the meaning of Section 3(1) of the Criminal Law Act (Northern Ireland) 1967. In particular, if the relevant circumstances were defined broadly to cover not just the actual shootings but also the planning of the operation there would be strong grounds for considering that the force used had been excessive in that no attempt had been made to arrest the suspects. Significantly Lord Chief Justice Lowry, in the Court of Appeal, felt that the circumstances should be interpreted broadly to include 'the circumstances in which an operation is conceived and planned and in which the preparatory steps are taken as well as those in which the final decisive act is performed'.[49] This would have been consistent with the approach of the Court of Appeal and the House of Lords in the McElhone case.

The Ministry of Defence appealed to the House of Lords. In upholding the appeal the House of Lords adopted an exceptionally narrow interpretation of the 'circumstances'. Only the immediate 'circumstances' surrounding the use of force were considered. Matters leading up to the shooting, such as the planning of the operation, were not taken into account. It is difficult, of course, to reconcile this with the approach of the courts, including the House of Lords itself, in the McElhone case. Nevertheless the effect was to insulate the soldiers against any legal liability for the overall planning of the operation. They had to be treated solely on the basis of the situation facing them from their position on the roof. The fact that it may have been grossly negligent not to deploy some of them on the ground where they might have been able to apprehend the offenders without resorting to lethal force was considered irrelevant.[50]

The House of Lords' decision in *Farrell v Ministry of Defence* had important implications for the criminal liability of those responsible for the deaths and woundings on Bloody Sunday. There are, of course, substantial grounds for believing that the soldiers would not have resorted to lethal force on the day if the security operation for the march had been sensibly planned and executed. The decision to stop the march from following its planned route to the city centre, the decision to deploy the Parachute Regiment for crowd control, the decision to send in two heavily armed mobile patrols to conduct a scoop-up arrest operation, the decision to penetrate so deeply into Rossville Street and Glenfada Park were all decisions which could be classified as negligent. Their collective effect was a strong probability that shots would be fired, resulting in death or serious injury to innocent civilians. In the light of the *Farrell* decision, however, the soldiers could excuse their actions on the basis that they had considered it to be both reasonable and their duty to engage suspected gunmen in the circumstances in which they had found themselves. The fact that they would not have found themselves in those circumstances had it not been for the negligent planning of their superior officers would not be sufficient to render them culpable for deaths and injuries which would not have occurred had the operation been planned sensibly. The superior officers responsible for the negligent planning would not be liable for murder or wounding since they had not fired the shots or ordered the shots to be fired in any individual case.

There is, of course, the remote possibility of pursuing those responsible for planning the Bloody Sunday operation for manslaughter. To succeed would require proof of gross negligence bordering on recklessness in the planning of the security operation. Nevertheless a majority in the Northern Ireland Court of Appeal in *Farrell v Ministry of Defence* were prepared to contemplate the notion that the ministry could be vicariously liable in tort for the negligence of the commanding officer in his planning of the whole operation.[51] The House of Lords, by contrast, totally ignored the point on the technical ground that it had not been specifically pleaded.[52] If, however, there are grounds to sue a commanding officer for negligence then it must follow that there could be grounds for prosecuting the commanding officer for manslaughter in a case where the negligence was sufficiently gross. Indeed in recent years the law has become more receptive to the notion of convicting the planners of an operation for manslaughter when deaths are caused by their negligent planning. Nevertheless successful cases are still rare, and there has yet to be a case where a death has been deliberately caused by a third party.[53] At the time of Bloody Sunday the very proposition was even more academic than real.

The combined effect of the decisions in the *McNaughton*, McElhone and *Farrell* cases left little doubt about the weakness of the law to impose tight constraints on the use of lethal force by the security forces in Northern Ireland. Indeed the message they conveyed was that the security forces could resort to the use of lethal force when their suspicions were aroused by civilians not submitting to their authority. When combined with the very extensive powers of stop and arrest available to the security forces this was tantamount to establishing them as the law, rather than as subject to the law. Certainly they had little to fear if they shot an unarmed civilian who might be a terrorist and failed to obey their order to halt. This message was driven home in some of the prose-cutions brought against members of the security forces for deaths resulting from their apparent 'shoot-to-kill' policy in the 1980s and early 1990s. Some of these cases are discussed in Chapter 7.

Although the law was interpreted and applied by the Northern Irish courts in a manner which gave immense discretion to the security forces in the use of lethal force it would not be true to say that they had absolute power over life and death. There have been cases, albeit only a few, of successful prosecutions for murder against members of the security forces who attempted to rely on the use of reasonable force as a defence for shooting unarmed civilians. These cases are discussed in Chapter 7. For the most part, however, they do not reflect a depar-ture from the law laid down by the Northern Irish courts and the House of Lords in the cases discussed above. The one possible excep-tion concerns the judgment of Lord Justice Kelly in *R v Fisher & Wright*.[54] In this case the two Scots Guardsmen were found guilty of the murder of an unarmed youth in the New Lodge Road area of Belfast in September 1992. In their defence they claimed that they believed, albeit mistakenly, that the youth had been armed with a 'coffee-jar' bomb and that he had been about to throw it at them. One of the soldiers also claimed that he had thought, mistakenly as it tran-spired, that the youth had been armed with a gun and had fired a shot at them. In rejecting their plea that they had used no more force than had been reasonable in the circumstances, Lord Justice Kelly applied the law as set out above under the heading of 'Subjective or Objective Test'. He was not persuaded beyond reasonable doubt that the two sol-diers had genuinely believed that the youth had been armed with a 'coffee-jar' bomb and/or a gun, and so he found them guilty of murder.

However the learned judge also took the opportunity to comment on the position taken by Lord Diplock in the House of Lords in the McElhone case, to the effect that it would be justifiable for a soldier to shoot simply if he believed that his target was a terrorist who, if he got away, was likely sooner or later to participate in acts of violence. Referring to this proposition Lord Justice Kelly said:

> I know of no criminal case in which the Diplock principle has been applied by the courts in Northern Ireland. For my part, I would, with great respect, be very slow to apply it. I would join those legal and other commentators in their expressions of reservation about the wisdom of applying it in its unconfined, indeterminate form. I see also dangers in its translation for use by those on the ground and considerable difficulty in its interpretation by the courts.[55]

While some encouragement can be drawn from this opinion of Lord Justice Kelly it does not, unfortunately, alter the law laid down by Lord Diplock in the House of Lords. Indeed the McElhone case was one in which a soldier shot the victim simply because he thought that he was a terrorist who might participate in acts of violence sooner or later if he got away. Moreover Lord Diplock's approach in that case was in line with that of the trial judge, Justice MacDermott, in the Belfast Crown Court. It is also worth noting that Lord Diplock's principle has since been applied at least twice in civil cases by the Northern Irish courts.[56] The European Commission on Human Rights has also ruled that it does not violate the right to life provisions of Article 2 of the European Convention for the Protection of Human Rights and Fundamental Freedoms.[57]

The Yellow Card

The broad discretion over the use of lethal force which the law has left to the security forces might be considered to be tempered by the terms of the 'Yellow Card'. These are the internal instructions issued to each soldier by the army command in Northern Ireland setting out instructions on when it is permissible to open fire. The contents of the card have been revised on at least two occasions and they have not always been a matter of public record. Indeed the version applicable at the time of Bloody Sunday itself is not publicly available. A revised version from November 1972, however, is available and is quoted in full below. It is submitted that it is substantially similar to the version that applied on Bloody Sunday, with at least one significant difference, which will be noted later. The second revision in 1980 produced a much shorter and simplified version.[58] The Revised November 1972 version reads as follows:

RESTRICTED
Army Code No. 70771

Instructions by the Director of Operations for
Opening Fire in Northern Ireland

1. These instructions are for the guidance of Commanders and troops operating collectively or individually. When troops are operating collectively soldiers will only open fire when ordered to do so by the Commander on the spot.

General Rules

2. Never use more force than the minimum necessary to enable you to carry out your duties.

3. Always first try to handle the situation by other means than opening fire. If you have to fire:

   a. Fire only aimed shots.
   b. Do not fire more rounds than absolutely necessary to achieve your aim.

4. Your magazine/belt must always be loaded with live ammunition and be fitted to the weapon. Unless you are about to open fire no live round is to be carried in the breech and the working parts must be forward. Company Commanders and above may, when circumstances in their opinion warrant such action, order weapons to be cocked, with a round in the breech where appropriate, and the safety catch at safe.

5. Automatic fire may be used against identified targets in the same circumstances as single shots if, in the opinion of the Commander on the spot, it is the minimum force required and no other weapon can be employed as effectively. Because automatic fire scatters it is not to be used where persons not using firearms are in, or may be close to, the line of fire.

Warning before firing

6. Whenever possible a warning should be given before you open fire. The only circumstances in which you may open fire without giving warning are described in paras 13, 14 and 15 below.

7. A warning should be as loud as possible, preferably by loud hailer. It must:

   a. Give clear orders to stop attacking or to halt as appropriate.
   b. State that fire will be opened if the orders are not obeyed.

You may fire after due warning

8. Against a person carrying what you can positively identify as a firearm,* but only if you have reason to think that he is about to use it for offensive purposes; he refuses to halt when called upon to do so, and there is no other way of stopping him.

9. Against a person throwing a petrol bomb if petrol bomb attacks continue in your area against troops and civilians or against property, if his action is likely to endanger life.

10. Against a person attacking or destroying property or stealing firearms or explosives, if his action is likely to endanger life.

11. Against a person who, though he is not a person attacking, has:

    a. in your sight killed or seriously injured a member of the security forces or a person whom it is your duty to protect and

    b. not halted when called upon to do so and cannot be arrested by any other means.

12. If there is no other way to protect yourself or those whom it is your duty to protect from the danger of being killed or seriously injured.

You may fire without warning

13. When hostile fire is taking place in your area and a warning is impracticable:

    a. Against a person using a firearm* against you or those whom it is your duty to protect

    b. against a person carrying what you can positively identify as a firearm* if he is clearly about to use it for offensive purposes.

14. At a vehicle if the occupants open fire or throw a bomb at you or those whom it is your duty to protect or are clearly about to do so.

15. If there is no other way to protect yourself or those whom it is your duty to protect from the danger of being killed or seriously injured.

Action by guards and at road blocks/checks

16. Where warnings are called for they should be in the form of specific challenges as set out in paragraphs 17 and 18.

17. If you have to challenge a person who is acting suspiciously you must do so in a firm, distinct voice, saying 'HALT – HANDS UP.'

    a. If he halts you are to say: 'STAND STILL AND KEEP YOUR HANDS UP.'

    b. Ask him why he is there, and if you are not satisfied call your Commander immediately and hand the person over to him.

18. If the person does not halt at once, you are to challenge again, saying 'HALT – HANDS UP' and, if the person does not halt on your second challenge, you are to cock your weapon, apply the safety catch and shout 'STAND STILL I AM READY TO FIRE.'

19. The rules covering the circumstances for opening fire are described in paragraphs 8–14. If the circumstances do not justify opening fire, you will do all you can to stop and detain the person without opening fire.
20. At a road block/check, you will NOT open fire on a vehicle simply because it refused to stop. If a vehicle does not halt at a road block/check note its description, make, registration number and direction of travel.
21. In all circumstances where you have challenged and the response is not satisfactory you will summon your Commander at the first opportunity.

Revised November 1972

*Note: 'Firearm' includes a grenade, nail bomb or gelignite type bomb.

One significant difference between this version and that applicable on Bloody Sunday concerns paragraph 13. In the version above soldiers are told that they may fire without warning in certain limited circumstances 'against a person carrying *what you can positively identify as* a firearm if he is clearly about to use it for offensive purposes'. (emphasis added). From the Widgery Report it would appear that the words in italics were missing in the version that applied at the time of Bloody Sunday. Under that version the soldier could fire without warning 'against a person carrying a firearm'. In other words the target actually had to be carrying a firearm for shooting to be permissible. In the revised version, therefore, the absolute standard is substituted by a subjective standard. What matters is not what the victim was actually carrying, but what the soldier himself had positively identified in the victim's possession. Increased subjectivity is also evident in another change effected in this provision. Under the Bloody Sunday version the soldier could fire if he had 'reason to think' that the person carrying the firearm was about to use it for offensive purposes. Under the November 1972 version, by contrast, the soldier could fire only if the person carrying what he could positively identify as a firearm was 'clearly about to use it for offensive purposes'. The former incorporated an objective reasonableness standard. There had to be some basis upon which the soldier had reason to believe that the victim was about to use the firearm for an offensive purpose. In the revised version it is at least arguable that it would be sufficient for the soldier actually to believe that the person was going to use for offensive purposes what he identified as a firearm.

Clearly the revised version allowed the soldier greater freedom to resort to the use of lethal force without a warning. He would not fall outside the scope of the Yellow Card simply because he mistakenly believed that his victim was carrying a firearm, or that he mistakenly believed that the victim was about to use it for offensive purposes. It must be emphasised, however, that the weaker, revised version did not apply on Bloody Sunday. Since none of the victims shot on that day were found to be carrying a firearm it seems likely that their shootings were in breach of the Yellow Card rules. Further support for this conclusion can be derived from the fact that none of the eye-witnesses, apart from the soldiers themselves, saw any of the victims carrying firearms. The most favourable interpretation of the evidence from the army's perspective is that the soldiers acted under the mistaken belief that they were firing at persons who were carrying firearms. That of course would not be sufficient to bring them within the scope of the version of the Yellow Card that applied at the time of Bloody Sunday. Indeed it is quite likely that the November 1972 revision was prompted by the realisation in security circles that the actions of many of the soldiers on Bloody Sunday did not come within the scope of the Yellow Card. The revision can therefore be interpreted as a conscious decision to lower the standards applicable to soldiers operating in Northern Ireland. Once again military expediency took priority over the need to protect innocent human life.

A vital feature of the instructions in the Yellow Card is the emphasis on 'minimum force'. The general rules stipulate that soldiers, individually and collectively, should use only the minimum force necessary to carry out their duties. Opening fire must be a last resort. The more specific rules make it clear that 'duties' are given a very limited interpretation in this context. It is permissible to open fire only when the target is posing an immediate threat to life, or where the target is escaping after having killed or injured and there is no other means of apprehending him, or if the target is about to use a firearm for offensive purposes and there is no other way of stopping him. Even when hostile fire is taking place in the immediate vicinity, a soldier can open fire against a person carrying a firearm only if he is clearly about to use it for an offensive purpose. It would appear, therefore, that a soldier would not be justified in opening fire if he merely suspects that the target is a member of a terrorist organisation who has failed to obey an order to stop. Similarly it would not be justifiable to open fire to disperse a hostile crowd when lesser measures, including retreat, are available to avoid a risk of serious injury to the soldier or others. Even if the target is armed it is not permissible to open fire on him unless he is using it for an offensive purpose.

The Yellow Card's emphasis on 'minimum force' and its restrictive interpretation of 'duty' contrasts with the legal standard of 'such force as is reasonable in the circumstances'. As has been seen, the latter has been interpreted by the courts as permitting the security forces to open fire in a broader range of situations than would appear to be permitted by their own Yellow Card. It is therefore necessary to examine how the judges have explained their failure to apply the standards set in the Yellow Card.

The status of the Yellow Card has been considered by the Northern Irish courts during several cases. On each occasion the court took the view that the card was nothing more than internal policy guidance with no legal force. In *R v McNaughton*,[59] for example, Lord Chief Justice Lowry explained that the contents of the Yellow Card 'are largely dictated by policy and are intended to lay down guidelines for the security forces but ... do not define the legal rights and obligations of members of the security forces under statute or common law.'[60] Technically, of course, that is correct. What is disturbing however is the readiness of the courts to dismiss the standard of 'minimum force' as prescribed in the card as a useful guide to what might be considered 'such force as is reasonable in the circumstances'. Given that the card was specifically formulated by the army to advise soldiers when they could open fire in the circumstances they were likely to face in Northern Ireland one might reasonably consider that the courts would be slow to ignore it in favour of a lower standard. Nevertheless in the McElhone case Justice MacDermott dismissed the relevance of the card as a measure of the appropriate legal standard governing the use of force:

> For my part, I consider this card to be something which exists for some reason of policy and is intended to lay down guide lines to the forces, but in my view it does not define the legal rights of the members of the Security Forces. No doubt it contains much sound advice, but I can readily understand that to many soldiers, and perhaps others too, it is to say the least of it a difficult document. The basic principles are that minimum force should be used and firing resorted to as a last resort. No one can gainsay the propriety and good sense of these propositions, but they must be considered in relation to the problem on the ground, and though a man who acts dutifully in accordance with the yellow card might easily establish his conduct as being justifiable, I do not accept that the failure so to act means, *ipso facto*, that his conduct is unlawful.[61]

In effect Justice MacDermott was saying that the army's own internal policy guidance set too high a standard for the soldiers themselves. Failure to meet those standards would not inevitably expose the soldier or soldiers concerned to criminal culpability. Lord Justice Gibson, in the Court of Appeal, went further and dismissed the Yellow Card brusquely in the following terms: 'I do not consider that the court should have any regard to the "Yellow Card," which the Attorney-General chose not to include among the relevant facts and of which the court cannot take judicial notice.'

It is respectfully submitted that the learned judges, and Justice MacDermott in particular, could just as easily have concluded that minimum force, as prescribed by the Yellow Card, was the appropriate standard which soldiers had to observe when they resorted to the use of lethal force. The general legal principles governing the use of force, discussed earlier, clearly established that lethal force could be justified only as a last resort in order to protect someone against a specific and imminent threat of death or serious injury. This would seem to be more in line with the standard set by the Yellow Card than that set by the courts in the McElhone case. Indeed, in his dissenting judgment in the Court of Appeal in the McElhone case Lord Justice McGonigal specifically described the procedure for opening fire as set out in the Yellow Card as a factor to be taken into account when deciding whether reasonable force had been used in the shooting of McElhone. The fact that the soldier had not followed the prescribed procedure seemed to weigh heavily on his conclusion that the force used was unreasonable in the circumstances. However his was, and remains, a lone voice crying in the wilderness.[62] It is therefore difficult to avoid the conclusion that the courts were unduly lenient in favour of soldiers on the ground when defining the circumstances in which they could resort to lethal force in the course of duty in Northern Ireland. The inevitable consequence, of course, was that the soldiers would be encouraged to ignore their own internal standards and rely on the greater leniency of the law. In other words the strictures of the Yellow Card would simply be ignored.[63]

European Convention on Human Rights

The argument that the Northern Irish courts have adopted an unduly lenient standard on the lawful use of lethal force by the security forces would appear to receive support from the European Convention for the Protection of Human Rights and Fundamental Freedoms. The convention has been binding on the United Kingdom in international law since 1953. Accordingly the United Kingdom is legally obliged to ensure that its laws satisfy the standards set out in the convention.[64] An individual who feels that his or her rights under the convention have been infringed by the government of the United Kingdom can pursue a case against the government before the institutions of the convention in Strasbourg. Equally it can be expected that when a court in the United Kingdom has to choose between two possible interpretations of domestic law it will prefer, where relevant, that interpretation which accords with the United Kingdom's obligations under the convention.[65]

For the purposes of this chapter the most significant provisions of the convention are to be found in Article 2, which protects the right to life and defines the conditions in which the deprivation of life will not infringe the convention. It reads:

1. Everyone's right to life shall be protected by law. No one shall be deprived of his life intentionally save in the execution of a sentence of a court following his conviction of a crime for which this penalty is provided by law.
2. Deprivation of life shall not be regarded as inflicted in contravention of this Article when it results from the use of force which is no more than absolutely necessary:
    (a) in defence of any person from unlawful violence;
    (b) in order to effect a lawful arrest or to prevent the escape of a person lawfully detained;
    (c) in action lawfully taken for the purpose of quelling a riot or insurrection.

Signatory states are permitted to enter a derogation from many of the convention rights in time of war or other public emergency threatening the life of the nation.[66] No such derogation is permitted with respect to Article 2, however, apart from deaths resulting from lawful acts of war. Moreover states are obliged under the convention to provide remedies for any breach of the right to life by servants of the state, including members of the security forces. The relevant provision is Article 13, which reads: 'Everyone whose rights and freedoms as set forth in this Convention are violated shall have an effective remedy before a national authority notwithstanding that the violation has been committed by persons acting in an official capacity.' The question therefore arises of whether the interpretation and application of the law governing the use of force by the security forces in Northern Ireland by the courts in Northern Ireland and the House of Lords are compatible with the United Kingdom's obligations under the European Convention on Human Rights.

Critically, the use of lethal force is compatible with Article 2 of the convention if it is absolutely necessary for self-defence, in order to effect an arrest or in order to quell a riot or insurrection. This would appear to be a higher standard than the reasonableness standard applied by the courts in Northern Ireland. An opportunity to test the standard required by Article 2 in the context of Northern Ireland was presented during the *Farrell* case. When Mrs Farrell's civil action against the Ministry of Defence was dismissed by the House of Lords she lodged a case against the United Kingdom under the convention. The basis of her case was that by resorting to lethal force in order to arrest her husband and the other unarmed robbers, the security forces had used more force than was absolutely necessary. In particular she argued that (1) as there had been no threat to the soldiers concerned, the convention did not allow the use of fatal force to prevent crime; (2) the courts failed to draw a distinction between the case where a person is resisting arrest and that where a person is fleeing from arrest without resistance; and (3) the trial judge's direction to the jury that a fleeing suspect was believed to be 'likely to commit actual crimes of violence if he succeeded in avoiding arrest' gave soldiers the power to execute people summarily for crimes which might be committed in the immediate or remote future.[67] The European Commission on Human Rights ruled the case admissible and proceeded to hear legal arguments on the substantive issue. However a friendly settlement was reached between the two sides before it went to judicial determination or full argument before the European Court of Human Rights.

In *Kelly v United Kingdom*[68] the European Commission on Human Rights was presented with the opportunity to deliver an opinion on whether it was a breach of Article 2 for soldiers to shoot dead a suspected terrorist in order to prevent his escape. In that case a UDR patrol had set up a road checkpoint with the aim of stopping a stolen car whose occupants had been acting suspiciously near the home of a member of the security forces. The driver of the car had made desperate efforts to drive through the checkpoint. Believing that the occupants of the car were terrorists and were getting away, members of the patrol had opened fire, killing the driver and wounding two of the passengers. The parties sued the Ministry of Defence for unlawful assault, battery and negligence in respect of the death and injuries. They lost at first instance in the Northern Ireland High Court, which accepted that the soldiers had used reasonable force in order to prevent the suspects from escaping. In other words the soldiers had acted reasonably to prevent crime and/or arrest the suspects. An unsuccessful appeal in the Court of Appeal followed and leave to appeal to the House of Lords was refused. The father of the deceased driver brought an application to the European Commission on Human Rights under Article 2.

The major difficulty for the British government in defending the application was that Article 2 does not recognise the prevention of crime as a ground upon which an individual can be lawfully killed, and the only offence for which the soldiers could lawfully have arrested the suspects was the unlawful taking of the car. Surprisingly, perhaps, the commission took the view that the soldiers had not been acting in the prevention of crime but for the purpose of effecting a lawful arrest, which happens to be one of the grounds recognised by Article 2 as justifying the use of lethal force. Bizarrely, however, the Commission went on to find that the soldiers had been justified in resorting to lethal force in order to effect the arrest in this case because the harm that would be averted by preventing the escape of the supposed terrorists, 'namely the freedom of the terrorists to resume their dealing in death and destruction', outweighed the harm caused by the shooting. It is not at all clear what arrestable offence the Commission had in mind. A soldier's power of arrest in Northern Ireland can be exercised only in respect of a specific offence. He has no power to arrest for unspecified acts of terrorism that may be committed at some time in the future. As it happened the deceased and his passengers had been 'joyriders' who had chosen to crash through the roadblock rather than be apprehended. It therefore follows that the commission's decision in *Kelly* afforded very little protection to the right to life of individuals whom the security forces suspect to be escaping terrorists.[69] In that it is consistent with the domestic law as declared by the Northern Irish courts in *McNaughton* and the McElhone case, and by the House of Lords in the latter.

The question of whether the use of plastic baton rounds (plastic bullets) as a riot control weapon was in breach of Article 2 was raised in *Stewart v United Kingdom*.[70] In that case a 13-year-old boy had been hit on the head and killed by a plastic bullet fired by a British soldier. The victim's mother's action for compensation was rejected in the High Court by Lord Justice Jones, who found that the plastic bullet had been fired by the soldier in a riot situation where he had had reason to believe that he was using no more force than reasonably necessary to protect himself and his fellow soldiers from the risk of serious injury. The applicant took her case to the European Commission where she argued, *inter alia*, that even if there had been a riot situation (which she disputed) the use of plastic bullets, which were known to inflict grievous and sometimes fatal injuries, had been a totally disproportionate response to the threat or risk of injury confronting the soldiers. The Commission, however, proceeding on the basis of the facts as found by Lord Justice Jones, concluded that the use of plastic bullets in the circumstances surrounding the death of Brian Stewart amounted to no more force than had been absolutely necessary for the purpose of quelling a riot, and as such was not in violation of Article 2. It is worth noting that when assessing the proportionality of the soldier's response the Commission took the following into account:

> the events took place in Northern Ireland which is facing a situation of continuous public disturbance that has given rise to much loss of life. Moreover, rioting of the kind which occurred in the present case is a frequent occurrence and gives rise to the apprehension, as adverted to by Lord Justice Jones, that the disturbance will be used as a cover for sniper attack, although no claim has been made in the present case that the patrol actually came under such attack.[71]

This decision does not exactly inspire confidence in the capacity of Article 2 to provide a remedy for the use of lethal force in a Bloody Sunday type situation.

The first and so far only Article 2 case to reach the European Court of Human Rights from the conflict in Northern Ireland was *McCann v United Kingdom*.[72] In this case the court was invited to find that the standard of 'such force as is reasonable in the circumstances fell short of the standard demanded by Article 2 of the convention, namely that which is 'no more than absolutely necessary'.[73] The case concerned the fatal shooting of three members of the IRA by the SAS while in Gibraltar on a reconnaisance mission with a view to planting a bomb in the area where the Royal Anglian Regiment was to assemble to carry out the changing of the guard. The governments of the United Kingdom, Spain and Gibraltar had been aware of the terrorist plans well in advance and had the victims under surveillance. At the time they were shot dead the three victims had been unarmed and no bomb had been found in the vehicle they had parked in Gibraltar. The SAS soldiers who had carried out the shootings, however, had been informed by their superiors that the car contained a bomb which could be detonated by the mere flick of a switch on a remote control device. They had also been told that the victims would not hesitate to detonate the bomb the moment they were challenged. The soldiers claimed that when called upon to halt, each of the victims had made a movement which they had interpreted as being consistent with an attempt to detonate the bomb. The soldiers, in accordance with their training, had responded by shooting until they were satisfied that each one of the targets had been immobilised.[74] Only then had it been discovered that the victims were unarmed and did not possess a remote control device and that there was no bomb. Indeed the 'facts' conveyed to the soldiers had been no more than suspicions or at best dubious assessments on the part of their superiors.

The Court rejected the argument that the law governing the use of lethal force in Gibraltar (and by analogy the law in Northern Ireland) was incompatible with the convention simply because it was framed on the basis of what was *reasonably justifiable* in the circumstances as opposed to what was *absolutely necessary*. While it accepted that the convention standard appeared at face value to be stricter than the national standard, the Court concluded that the difference between the two standards was not sufficiently great to amount to a violation of Article 2. In reaching this conclusion the Court emphasised that it was not its role to examine *in abstracto* the compatibility of national provisions with the requirements of the convention. It follows that the law governing the use of lethal force in Northern Ireland is not *per se* in breach of Article 2. Nevertheless, it is still possible that the Court of Human Rights could find that the circumstances of a fatal shooting are such as to amount to a breach of Article 2 even though a Northern Irish court has found no breach of domestic law in that case.

On the facts of *McCann*, as established by the European Commission on Human Rights, the court concluded that there had been no premeditated plan to kill the three victims. It is worth noting in particular that the court was not persuaded by the argument that the use of SAS soldiers was in itself indicative of a decision to use more force than was absolutely necessary in the circumstances, even though the evidence clearly established that members of the SAS are trained to shoot to kill at the merest hint of a threat. With respect to the actions of the individual soldiers the Court concluded that, in the light of the information they had been given, they had been entitled to consider that it was absolutely necessary to shoot the victims in order to safeguard innocent lives. Accordingly they had not acted in breach of Article 2. The fact that their information proved subsequently to be mistaken did not alter this situation as their actions had been based on a belief which they honestly and reasonably held.

The Court's exoneration of the soldiers did not dispose of all the Article 2 issues in the McCann case. There was also the question of the manner in which the whole operation had been planned and controlled by the authorities in Gibraltar. The Court was careful to point out that when determining whether there had been a breach of Article 2 it must take into consideration not only the actions of the state agents who had administered the force but also all the surrounding circumstances, including such matters as the planning and control of the actions under examination. In reviewing the surrounding circumstances of the shootings in this case the court found that the authorities had made serious errors of judgment in deciding not to arrest the victims as they entered Gibraltar and in their failure to make sufficient allowances for the possibility that their intelligence assessments might be erroneous in some respects. When these failures were added to the choice of SAS personnel, with their training to shoot to kill once they had opened fire, the Court concluded that the authorities had failed to establish that the use of force had been no more than absolutely necessary in defence of persons from unlawful violence. Accordingly the government of the United Kingdom was in breach of Article 2 of the convention. This has been the only occasion to date on which the United Kingdom has been found to be in breach of Article 2 of the convention with respect to fatal shootings by security forces in connection with events in Northern Ireland.

The European Court's decision in *McCann* has major significance for the events of Bloody Sunday. A very cogent argument can be made to the effect that the government of the United Kingdom was in breach of Article 2 of the convention in respect of those shot dead on Bloody Sunday. Just like the SAS, those in the 1st Battalion of the Parachute Regiment are trained to shoot to kill at the first hint of a threat. Indeed Lord Widgery specifically adverted to this when discussing the soldiers' interpretation of the rules governing when to open fire:

> In the Parachute Regiment, at any rate in the 1st Battalion, the soldiers are trained to take what may be described as a hard line upon these questions. The events of 30 January and the attitude of individual soldiers whilst giving evidence suggest that when engaging an identified gunman or bomb-thrower they shoot to kill and continue to fire until the target disappears or falls. When under attack and returning fire they show no particular concern for the safety of

others in the vicinity of the target. They are aware that civilians who do not wish to be associated with violence tend to make themselves scarce at the first alarm and they know that it is deliberate policy of gunmen to use civilians as cover. Further, when hostile firing is taking place the soldiers of 1 Para will fire on a person who appears to be using a firearm against them without always waiting until they can positively identify the weapon. A more restrictive interpretation of the terms of the Yellow Card by 1 Para might have saved some of the casualties on 30 January, but with correspondingly increased risk to the soldiers themselves.[75]

To deploy such a regiment in the front line to maintain public order at the Bloody Sunday march surely displays a very scant regard for the safety of the participants and residents. If violence did break out, and if gunmen did take advantage of the situation to fire at the security forces, it was highly probable that the soldiers in this particular battalion would return fire with little regard for the safety of innocent civilians in the vicinity. Indeed Lord Widgery effectively said as much:

> [W]here soldiers are required to engage gunmen who are in close proximity to innocent civilians they are set an impossible task. Either they must go all out for the gunmen, in which case the innocent suffer; or they must put the safety of the innocent first, in which case many gunmen will escape and the risk to themselves will be increased. The only unit whose attitude to this problem I have examined is 1 Para. Other units may or may not be the same. In 1 Para the soldiers are trained to go for the gunmen and make their decisions quickly. In these circumstances it is not remarkable that mistakes were made and some civilians hit.[76]

In the McCann case the European Court of Human Rights considered that the decision to deploy the SAS was not *per se* a breach of Article 2 because the authorities in that case had been responding to a bomb threat posed by individuals who were known to be dangerous terrorists and probably armed. It is submitted that the Court would not have reached the same decision with respect to the deployment of the 1st Battalion of the Parachute Regiment to control a large protest march simply because there was a theoretical risk that unidentified gunmen would use the occasion to attack the security forces. In any event the Court in *McCann* went on to hold that the deployment of the SAS, interpreted in the light of the negligence in the planning of the overall operation, amounted to a breach of Article 2. Given the negligent decisions which were taken in the actual planning and execution of the Bloody Sunday operation, there are substantial grounds for saying that the European Court of Human Rights would also conclude that deployment of the 1st Battalion of the Parachute Regiment constituted resort to force which was more than absolutely necessary in the circumstances.

The Widgery interpretation

One might reasonably have expected that a tribunal of inquiry into the events of Bloody Sunday would consider the law governing the use of lethal force by the security forces in Northern Ireland. This expectation is considerably strengthened by the fact that the tribunal was chaired by the lord chief justice. Surprisingly, however, Lord Widgery gave the matter scant attention. He interpreted the tribunal's remit as being confined to 'the events which led to the shooting of a number of people in the streets of Londonderry on the afternoon of Sunday 30 January'.[77] Even this exceptionally narrow interpretation of the terms of reference would not preclude an analysis of the law governing the use of lethal force. Indeed Lord Widgery went on to explain that while the tribunal was not concerned with making moral judgments, it would 'try and form an objective view of the events and the sequence in which they occurred, so that those who were concerned to form judgments would have a firm basis on which to reach their conclusions'.[78] It is submitted that in order to form an objective view of the events it is necessary to have a clear understanding of the circumstances in which soldiers are lawfully justified in opening fire against civilians. This element provides an essential foundation upon which to sift out the relevant from the irrelevant when piecing together an objective account of what happened. It is as much a part of the context as the description of matters such as the details of the army deployment in Derry that day, the contents of the army plan to contain the march and the legality of the march itself. It is certainly much more relevant than the security events in Derry over the previous six months, to which the Widgery Report devoted six paragraphs.

Lord Widgery himself implicitly acknowledged the relevance and importance of the law governing the use of lethal force at several points in the report. In paragraph 54, for example, after having considered eye-witness accounts of some of the shootings, he said: 'To those who seek to apportion responsibility for the events of 30 January the question "Who fired first?" is vital.'[79] The importance of this question lies in the fact that if soldiers come under fire they normally have a good claim to self-defence if they fire back and kill or seriously injure a gunman. The applicability of this defence, of course, depends very much on the nature of the threat posed by the initial firing and the scale and extent of the soldiers' firing. In the context of Bloody Sunday, when soldiers had fired 108 shots in a crowded, built-up area, killing 13 unarmed civilians and wounding 15 others, the relevant legal principles required careful consideration before the significance of 'who fired first' could be determined. Incredibly Lord Widgery did not even advert to the legal principles at this juncture, let alone discuss them in the context of the events that unfolded on Bloody Sunday. This of course enabled him to attach undue prominence to the narrow issue of 'who fired first'. It also meant that an excellent opportunity to clarify the law on when armed soldiers can open fire in a crowded situation was squandered.

Later in the report Lord Widgery turns his attention to the conduct of the individual soldiers who had fired shots and the circumstances in which each individual had been shot dead. In this section he immediately homed in on one of the vital issues:

> The Army case is that each of these shots was an aimed shot fired at a civilian holding or using a bomb or firearm. On the other side it was argued that none of the deceased was using a bomb or firearm and that the soldiers fired without justification and either deliberately or recklessly.

Once again this raises the self-defence argument. Unfortunately, however, Lord Widgery did not preface his analysis of the evidence about the circumstances in which each of the victims had been killed or wounded with an exposition of the law on when soldiers are justified in opening fire in self-defence. It follows that the basic principles upon which the actions of the soldiers had to be assessed were not defined in advance. These would include vital issues such as whether soldiers have a duty to take advantage of an opportunity to withdraw and/or take cover rather than return fire in an area crowded with innocent and unarmed civilians; whether an absolute, objective or subjective standard applies with respect to whether a victim of a shooting was carrying a firearm; and whether a lawful shooting requires the victim to have been using a firearm for offensive purposes.

Lord Widgery's failure to address these issues in advance was reflected in his analysis of the fatal shootings. In most of these cases

Lord Widgery confined himself to an analysis of what each victim had been doing at the time he was shot, coupled with the nature of the forensic evidence. Scant attention was paid to the role of the individual soldiers involved. This of course can be explained by the fact that the evidence in most cases was not sufficiently adequate to connect individual soldiers with individual deaths or injuries. That in itself, however, brings into stark relief the significance of Lord Widgery's failure to address the legality of soldiers resorting to the use of lethal force to the extent they did in the circumstances prevailing on Bloody Sunday. In the few cases where it was possible to match up individual soldiers with individual victims, Lord Widgery was equally silent on the relevant legal principles he was applying to assess responsibility. In the case of Patrick Doherty, Lord Widgery was of the opinion that the fatal shot was most likely to have come from Soldier F, who claimed that he had fired at a man who had been firing shots from a pistol. He also concluded that if Soldier F had fired with such a belief he had been mistaken. Nevertheless Lord Widgery did not proceed to consider the legal significance of this finding. Soldier F was one of only two soldiers who could definitely be identified as having fired a fatal bullet. The forensic evidence established that the bullet which killed Michael Kelly had come from Soldier F's gun. He claimed that he had fired at a man who was attempting to throw what appeared to be a nail bomb. Lord Widgery concluded that Kelly had been neither armed nor throwing a bomb at the time he was shot. Once again, however, Lord Widgery did not proceed to consider the legal implications of these findings. The same comment can be applied to the finding that Soldier P had probably fired the shot which killed William Nash. Soldier P claimed that he had fired at a man who was firing a pistol from the barricade on Rossville Street. Lord Widgery contented himself with the conclusion that 'it is possible that Soldier P has given an accurate account of the death of Nash'. Finally there is the case of Sergeant K, whom Lord Widgery considered to be the likely source of the bullet which killed Kevin McElhinney. Although Lord Widgery reached the loaded conclusion that Sergeant K had 'obviously acted with responsibility and restraint', he made no attempt to support his dubious conclusion by elucidating the legal principles upon which Sergeant K's actions had to be assessed.

After considering the factual circumstances surrounding each fatal shooting, Lord Widgery finally turned to the critical issue of 'were the soldiers justified in firing?' Here at last was the opportunity to consider the relevant legal principles governing the use of lethal force and their application to soldiers, both individually and collectively, in the sort of circumstances prevailing on Bloody Sunday. Bizarrely Lord Widgery confined his analysis of this vital issue to the contents of the Yellow Card. Not once did he advert to the law. It is not immediately obvious why Lord Widgery should have chosen to assess the shootings relative to the standards set by the Yellow Card, which as has been seen has no legal standing, and failed to assess them relative to the standards set by the law. Given how the law has been developed subsequently by the courts it might be considered that Lord Widgery's focus on the Yellow Card would actually have militated in favour of the victims. The reality, however, was that Lord Widgery did not treat the Yellow Card as laying down absolute standards governing the use of lethal force. Instead he highlighted possible ambiguities and anomalies in the rules and the restrictive limitations they imposed on soldiers who had to make snap decisions on whether to open fire when under threat from a hostile mob or when a gunman fired at them from the protection of a crowd of civilians. He further undermined the relevance of the Yellow Card rules by subordinating their objective standards to their subjective interpretation by individual soldiers:

> Soldiers will react to the situations in which they find themselves in different ways according to their temperament and to the prevailing circumstances. The more intensive the shooting or stone-throwing which is going on the more ready they will be to interpret the Yellow Card as permitting them to open fire. The individual soldier's reaction may also be affected by the general understanding of these problems which prevails in his unit. In the Parachute Regiment, at any rate in the 1st Battalion, the soldiers are trained to take what may be described as a hard line upon these questions. The events of 30 January and the attitude of individual soldiers whilst giving evidence suggest that when engaging an identified gunman or bomb-thrower they shoot to kill and continue to fire until the target disappears or falls. When under attack and returning fire they show no particular concern for the safety of others in the vicinity of the target. They are aware that civilians who do not wish to be associated with violence tend to make themselves scarce at the first alarm and they know that it is the deliberate policy of gunmen to use civilians as cover. Further, when hostile firing is taking place the soldiers of 1 Para will fire on a person who appears to be using a firearm against them without always waiting until they can positively identify the weapon. A more restrictive interpretation of the

terms of the Yellow Card by 1 Para might have saved some of the casualties on 30 January, but with correspondingly increased risk to the soldiers themselves.[80]

Quite incredibly, Lord Widgery would appear to be saying that the standards imposed by the Yellow Card ultimately depended on how individual soldiers interpreted them in the light of their training and the prevailing ethos in their unit.[81] The sheer absurdity of this approach is exposed in the very same paragraph in which it was espoused and in the succeeding paragraphs. In effect it meant that the soldiers of the 1st Battalion of the Parachute Regiment could rely on the card to justify their resort to maximum force without any particular concern for the safety of others in the vicinity, merely by believing, without being sure, that their target was carrying a weapon. The actual terms of the card, by contrast, prescribed the use of minimum force only, and even then it should only be used without warning against a person actually using a firearm offensively or carrying it in circumstances where there was reason to think that it would be used offensively. Lord Widgery's interpretation would appear to render the Yellow Card virtually useless for the very purpose for which it was intended. Further confirmation of this is provided by his cursory dismissal of admitted infringements of the card on the ground that they did not 'seem to point to a breakdown in discipline or to require censure'.[82] In other words the individual requirements of the card were always subordinate to a subjective assessment of their implications for general discipline.

Having given the Yellow Card an interpretation so exceptionally sympathetic to the interests of a trigger-happy soldier it was almost inevitable that Lord Widgery would conclude that the actions of the soldiers had been justified. In doing so he accepted, most controversially, that the soldiers had generally told the truth about the circumstances in which they had opened fire. It has already been seen that Lord Widgery's conclusions were fundamentally flawed on account of his reliance on the veracity of the soldiers' evidence. In the current context, however, it is worth noting that they were also flawed by virtue of the fact that he considered justification exclusively within the ambit of his peculiar interpretation of the standards required by the Yellow Card. At no point did he attempt to define the legal principles governing the use of lethal force by the security forces and how those principles should be interpreted and applied in the circumstances of Bloody Sunday. It follows, of course, that the actions of the soldiers were not assessed with respect to the standards imposed by the law.

However Lord Widgery's conclusion that the soldiers had been justified in firing, along with the manner in which it was reached, conveys the impression that the soldiers had acted lawfully. The reality is that Lord Widgery made no attempt to assess the legality of the soldiers' actions.

Prosecutions

The disappointing failure of the Widgery Tribunal to offer an interpretation of the law governing the use of lethal force by the security forces was compounded by the decision not to prosecute any of the soldiers involved in the Bloody Sunday shootings. Had there been prosecutions the courts would have been presented with an opportunity to pronounce upon the relevant legal principles and their application to the actual circumstances of Bloody Sunday. The decision not to prosecute was taken by the DPP (with the support of the Attorney General) on the ground that there was insufficient evidence to warrant the prosecution of any soldier. It appears that this decision was based primarily on the separate investigation into the shootings carried out by the RUC. Little is known about the manner in which the RUC conducted this investigation. It is not clear, for example, whether they interviewed the soldiers concerned or simply accepted statements through their legal advisers. Equally, it is not clear whether they had access to the original statements made by the soldiers to the military police on the night of Bloody Sunday. In the light of the findings of the Widgery Tribunal and the contents of the original statements offered by the soldiers concerned on the night of Bloody Sunday it seems strange that prosecutions were not launched. Indeed the failure to initiate prosecutions in the light of the evidence available indirectly sheds some light on what the authorities perceived the relevant law to be. It also reinforced the general perception that the security forces were effectively above the law in taking measures which they considered necessary to achieve an objective of security policy. Accordingly it is worth highlighting at this point the findings of the Widgery Tribunal which, in themselves, might have justified prosecutions.

Despite Lord Widgery's conclusion that 'in the majority of cases the soldier gave an explanation which, if true, justified his action' the reality is that he made a number of findings in individual cases which would have warranted the prosecution of the soldiers concerned. Equally there were several cases in which he doubted the veracity of the explanatory accounts offered by the soldiers in circumstances which should have exposed the soldiers to prosecution.

Lord Widgery's conclusion in the case of Patrick Doherty for example was that he had not been carrying a weapon, and if Soldier F had shot Doherty in the belief that he had had a pistol that belief had been mistaken. This finding by itself does not mean that Soldier F was guilty of murder. It all depends on the honesty of his mistaken belief that Doherty had been firing a pistol. Lord Widgery made no finding on this point and the extraneous evidence was such as to cast serious doubt on the veracity of Soldier F's belief. This, therefore, would appear to be a case in which a prosecution would have been warranted. Soldier F might also have been charged with the murder of Michael Kelly on the basis of Lord Widgery's conclusion that, contrary to the explanation offered by Soldier F, Kelly had not been throwing a bomb at the time he was shot. Once again, of course, the issue is whether Soldier F honestly believed that Kelly had been throwing a bomb.

Glenfada Park and a concerted action

By far the most compelling argument in favour of prosecution on the basis of Lord Widgery's findings alone concerned the fatal shooting of James Wray, Gerald McKinney, Gerald Donaghy and William McKinney in Glenfada Park. Lord Widgery dealt with these four cases together because he considered the evidence 'too confused and contradictory to make separate consideration possible'.[83] Nevertheless he went on to make some very damaging findings against the soldiers concerned, namely soldiers E, F, G and H. The two key findings were as follows:

1. it seems to me more probable that the civilians in Glenfada Park were running away than that they were seeking a battle with the soldiers in such a confined space;[84]
2. the balance of probability suggests that at the time when these four men were shot the group of civilians was not acting aggressively and that the shots were fired without justification.[85]

Significantly Lord Widgery went on to find support for these two conclusions from Soldier H's patently false account of his actions. He claimed that he had fired a shot at a gunman operating from the window of a flat on the south side of Glenfada Park. The gunman had withdrawn and soldier H had fired another shot at him when he reappeared. This pattern allegedly repeated itself 19 times, with a break for Soldier H to change his magazine. Lord Widgery's view of this account was that:

It is highly improbable that this cycle of events should repeat itself 19 times; and indeed it did not. I accepted evidence subsequently given, supported by photographs, which showed that no shot at all had been fired through the window in question. So 19 of the 22 shots fired by Soldier H were wholly unaccounted for.[86]

On the basis of these facts and conclusions alone it is difficult to fathom why prosecutions for murder were not taken with respect to the events in Glenfada Park. One possible explanation concerns the difficulty of associating individual soldiers with individual fatalities. The basic argument here is that a soldier cannot be charged with murder simply on the basis that he has fired a shot in a location where a civilian has been killed by a soldier's bullet. It may not even be sufficient that there are grounds to believe that the soldier has not offered a truthful account of the circumstances in which he fired the shot. Not only would it have to be established that the victim was killed unlawfully, but there would have to be some evidence to connect the soldier's act in firing with the bullet which killed the civilian. This evidence may be lacking where a number of soldiers, and perhaps others, have fired shots in the immediate vicinity at the relevant time. In the absence of forensic evidence connecting the fatal bullet with the gun of an individual soldier it may not be possible to prove which soldier shot the civilian. Certainly this could have been a critical factor in the decision not to prefer murder charges with respect to many of the deaths outside Glenfada Park. In all but one of them the fatal bullets had not been recovered from the bodies of the victims. Moreover in most of these cases the eye-witness accounts and circumstantial evidence were not sufficiently strong to connect individual soldiers with individual victims. The shootings in Glenfada Park, however, were different.

In Glenfada Park it was firmly established that the only shots fired had been those fired by soldiers E, F, G and H. There was also cogent evidence to suggest that they had acted in concert in causing the four deaths. It follows that even if there was some doubt about which soldier had killed which civilian in the park, there were grounds for charging all four soldiers with the murder of all four civilians on the basis that when they had opened fire they had been acting in concert. Charging them on the basis of a concerted action, it is submitted, relieved the prosecution of the burden of proving which individual soldier had shot which individual victim. Admittedly there was no exact precedent for soldiers to be charged on the basis of a concerted action in such circumstances.[87] That, however, is hardly a justification for deciding not to test the possibility in the courts given that the evidence of serious criminal wrongdoing on the part of the soldiers was so strong. A major loophole in the law would be exposed if it transpired that the four victims had been unlawfully killed by the four soldiers in the course of a joint operation, but no convictions for homicide could be secured because it was impossible to prove which soldier had killed which victim. There are, of course, other possible but less satisfactory alternatives. Each soldier could have been charged with the murder of a person or persons unknown on the basis of their statements and in the light of the evidence that none of their possible victims had been lawfully killed. This is hardly satisfactory given that the names of all of their possible victims were known. Another complicating factor is that in addition to the four fatalities there had been three woundings in Glenfada Park. An argument could be mounted with respect to each of the four soldiers that there was a reasonable chance that his bullets had merely wounded his target or targets. This, of course, could result in all four murder prosecutions being lost as it could not be proved beyond a reasonable doubt that any one of the four soldiers had killed any of the four victims. Other possibilities are attempted murder and shooting with intent to murder. Each of them, however, carries problems of its own.

The other shootings and a joint enterprise

The difficulty of linking individual soldiers to individual victims presents greater problems for the prospect of murder charges arising out of the other shootings on Bloody Sunday. For the most part these did not occur in circumstances where all of the shots and all of the fatalities could be traced to a small, finite group of soldiers who had acted in concert within a confined area. With one or two exceptions, which will be noted later, prosecutions for murder in respect of the shootings outside Glenfada Park would have to be based on the notion that the whole operation was a joint enterprise. While there can be no doubt that all of the shootings occurred in the context of a planned security operation, that in itself would not be sufficient to provide the basis for prosecutions based on a joint enterprise. It would have to be established that the participants embarked upon a common venture in which each of them contemplated that there was a real or substantial risk that one or more of them would use unlawful lethal force. The obstacles which would have to be overcome in establishing murder by joint enterprise in the context of Bloody Sunday are immense, but by no means so impossible as to be dismissed out of hand.

The first obstacle, of course, is Lord Widgery's finding that the soldiers were generally entitled to regard themselves as acting individually as opposed to collectively for the purposes of the Yellow Card. The significance of this finding, however, is confined to the fact if they were acting collectively they could not fire without an order from their commander on the spot, while if they were acting individually they could fire on their own initiative. It does not determine the question whether the soldiers were acting in the course of a joint enterprise for the purposes of the criminal law. It was concerned with a different matter altogether, namely the extent to which the soldiers could be expected to wait for the orders of their commanders before opening fire. The question with respect to a joint enterprise is whether the soldiers embarked on the operation with a common purpose in which it was contemplated that they would use lethal force regardless of whether there was any immediate threat of serious injury or whether it was necessary to prevent crime or effect an arrest.

There was certainly some evidence to suggest that one of the planned objectives of the Bloody Sunday operation was to stem the IRAs' influence in the general Bogside area and prevent that influence from spreading further towards the city centre. The tactics adopted to achieve this objective appear to have been the use of maximum force against rioters, and any one who might be considered to pose a threat to the life or personal safety of the soldiers. An integral part of these tactics would appear to have been an understanding that the soldiers should shoot first and ask questions later. If this does reflect the substance of the operational policy and tactics adopted for Bloody Sunday there may be a basis for preferring murder charges not just against those who fired the shots but also against all the soldiers who took part in the operation as well as their commanders and those who took part in the formulation and adoption of the policy. It must also be said, however, that further legal uncertainties would have to be determined in favour of the prosecution before convictions could be secured on this basis.

Even if it can be proved that the soldiers embarked upon a joint enterprise in which it was contemplated that unlawful force would be used, it does not necessarily follow that they committed murder by shooting dead in the course of the operation individuals who were unarmed and not posing a threat when they were shot. The prosecution would also have to prove that one or more of the victims were killed unlawfully. Surprising as it may seem to the layperson, that is not achieved simply by establishing that the victims were innocent. The prosecution would actually have to prove that one or more of the soldiers who fired the fatal shots did not genuinely believe that their targets were presenting a serious threat to the life or person of themselves or their colleagues. This in turn would depend primarily on what credence can be attached to the explanations offered by the individual soldiers as to the circumstances in which they opened fire. Significantly Lord Widgery concluded that:

> in the majority of cases the soldier gave an explanation which, if true, justified his action. A typical phrase is 'I saw a civilian aiming what I thought was a firearm and I fired an aimed shot at him.' In the main I accept these accounts as a faithful reflection of the soldier's recollection of the incident; but there is no simple way of deciding whether his judgment was at fault or whether his decision was conscientiously made.[88]

Lord Widgery's qualified trust in the honesty of the soldiers' evidence in the witness box must now be assessed in the light of the critique of that evidence offered in Chapter 5. Nevertheless the very fact that he stopped short of accepting the full truth of the soldiers' explanations of individual decisions to open fire leaves room for the possibility of a court reaching a different conclusion in a criminal trial.

It is worth emphasising in this context that it is only necessary to establish that one of the victims was killed unlawfully. The essential concept of a joint enterprise is that all who participate in it are jointly responsible for any consequences which can be considered to have been within the scope of the enterprise. It will be no defence to any one of the joint parties that another of his partners fired the fatal shot, if he knew that lethal force without lawful justification might be used in the course of the joint enterprise. In other words if it can be shown that at least one of the victims shot dead on Bloody Sunday was killed unlawfully, all of those who participated in the joint enterprise will be criminally liable for the death. Given Lord Widgery's conclusion that the shots fired in Glenfada Park were fired without justification, it would appear that there is at least a basis upon which prosecutions for murder in the course of a joint enterprise might be brought.

All of this analysis must be qualified by the admission that there is no exact precedent for prosecutions for murder on the basis of a joint enterprise in circumstances such as those prevailing on Bloody Sunday. That, however, does not amount to a compelling argument against a prosecution being brought. Given the substantial evidence that at least some of the soldiers acted unlawfully in resorting to lethal force on Bloody Sunday, it would seem reasonable to expect that the authorities would at least test the law by launching a prosecution.

Individual prosecutions

The Widgery Inquiry produced sufficient forensic, eye-witness and photographic evidence to warrant consideration of individual prosecutions in a few cases. It would therefore seem appropriate to consider each of these cases in turn, particularly in the light of the original statements made by the soldiers on the night of Bloody Sunday.

The forensic evidence established that the bullet which killed Michael Kelly had been fired from Soldier F's gun. Kelly was one of those shot at the barricade on Rossville Street. In his evidence to the Tribunal Soldier F claimed that he had seen a person at the barricade about to throw a nail bomb. He had fired a single shot at this person and hit the target. Lord Widgery found that the lead particle density on Kelly's right cuff was above normal and consistent with his having been close to someone using a firearm. However Widgery went on to conclude that Kelly had been neither firing nor throwing a bomb at the soldiers at the time he was shot. This finding alone suggests that Soldier F had been mistaken if he believed that Kelly had been firing a nail bomb. The next question, therefore, is whether there is any evidence that Soldier F may not have been telling the truth about his belief. It has been seen in Chapter 5 that Soldier F's original statement on the night of Bloody Sunday differed in many substantial respects from the evidence he later gave to the tribunal. For example he did not even mention shooting a nail bomber, or anyone else, at the barricade. Even when he amended his statement a short time afterwards he still failed to mention this shooting. It was only when his formal statement of evidence was taken some months later by the Treasury Solicitor acting for the tribunal that there was mention of this shooting. This was only one of the major discrepancies between Soldier F's original statements and the evidence he gave to the tribunal. The others are dealt with fully in Chapter 5. For the moment it is sufficient to note that he was one of the soldiers involved in the Glenfada Park shootings. Taking all of these factors into account it would seem that there is at least a case to answer with respect to the honesty of Soldier F's belief in the shooting of Michael Kelly. This, together with Lord Widgery's findings, lays a solid foundation for Soldier F to be charged with the murder of Michael Kelly.

The only other case in which forensic evidence could connect the fatal bullet with an identifiable soldier was the shooting of Gerald Donaghy by Soldier G. This was one of the shootings in Glenfada Park. As has already been seen, Lord Widgery concluded that the four civilians, including Donaghy, shot dead in Glenfada Park had not been acting aggressively and that the shots which killed them had been fired without justification. He also intimated that the soldiers responsible for the shootings in Glenfada Park were not telling the truth about the circumstances of the shootings. These findings, combined with the forensic evidence, should have been sufficient to warrant the prosecution of Soldier G for the murder of Gerald Donaghy. This conclusion is supported by the unsatisfactory nature of Soldier G's several accounts of the circumstances in which he had opened fire in Glenfada Park, which are recounted in Chapter 5. However there was one complication with respect to his shooting of Donaghy, namely the discovery of four nail bombs in Donaghy's pockets. As has been seen, Lord Widgery found, perversely it is submitted, that it was more likely than not that the nail bombs had been in Donaghy's pockets at the time he was shot.[89] The significance of this finding in the current context is that it might be thought that it provides justification for the failure to charge Soldier G with the murder of Gerald Donaghy. As explained earlier, however, the prosecuting authority is not confined to Widgery's findings when deciding whether or not to prosecute. He must look at all the evidence and form his own decision on whether it warrants a prosecution. It is submitted that a closer analysis of the circumstances in which the bombs were found in Donaghy's pockets, coupled with the unsatisfactory nature of Soldier G's evidence, neutralises them as an obstacle to the prosecution of Soldier G for the murder of Gerald Donaghy.

Nevertheless before a charge of murder could be preferred against Soldier G in respect of Gerald Donaghy's death there would have to be some evidence that he fired the fatal bullet without lawful justification. In his evidence to the tribunal Soldier G claimed that he had fired three shots at one of two men who were carrying rifles in the southwest corner of Glenfada Park. He also said that F had fired at the same time. Both gunmen had fallen and his impression was that he had hit one and F had hit the other. Strangely he identified his target as John Young. This of course contradicts the forensic evidence to the effect that the person he had shot in Glenfada Park was Gerald Donaghy. In any event, John Young had actually been shot at the Rossville Street barricade and Soldier G had not been among those whom Lord Widgery identified as the possible sources of that fatal bullet. In his original statement on the night of Bloody Sunday Soldier G's account of the shooting in Glenfada Park did not differ materially from the account he gave in evidence. Bizarrely, however, he also signed a photograph of John Young as the person he had shot and stated that he had been throwing nail bombs. This blatantly contradicted his state-ment that he had fired at one of two men carrying rifles. About two weeks later it appears that Soldier G made a supplementary statement. In this he claimed that he might have shot both gunmen in the south-west corner of Glenfada Park and that perhaps Soldier F had shot a third, who had been found nearby. By the time he came to give evi-dence he repudiated this part of the supplementary statement and said that he did not recall saying those words despite the fact that he did recall the statement being read back to him before he signed it. He also said in evidence that he did not remember saying that the person he shot had been throwing nail bombs. There is more than enough in these contradictions to question the veracity of Soldier G's claims about the circumstances in which he had fired the shot which killed Gerald Donaghy. When this is combined with Lord Widgery's finding that all four civilians shot dead in Glenfada Park had been shot without justifi-cation there would appear to be a very strong case at least to charge Soldier G with the murder of Gerald Donaghy.

Although there were no other cases, apart from those of Michael Kelly and Gerald Donaghy, where the forensic evidence could connect fatal bullets with identifiable soldiers, there are some cases in which the evidence is sufficiently strong to link certain soldiers with individ-ual deaths. In the case of Patrick Doherty, for example, Lord Widgery felt that the evidence pointed to Soldier F as having fired the fatal bul-let.[90] Doherty had been shot between the rear of Block 2 of Rossville Flats and Joseph Place while crawling along the ground holding a handkerchief over his face. He had been hit from behind by a bullet which entered his buttock and proceeded through his body almost par-allel to his spine. Lord Widgery found that he had not been carrying a weapon when he was shot. In his evidence Soldier F claimed that he had fired two shots at a man who had been crouching and firing a pis-tol from the spot where Doherty's body was later found. The issue, therefore, was whether Soldier F honestly believed that his target had been firing a pistol. Soldier F, it will be remembered, was the same sol-dier who had shot Michael Kelly at the Rossville Street barricade. It has already been seen that his account of that shooting was highly suspect. Not surprisingly the same applies to his account of the shooting of Patrick Doherty. Indeed in his original statement to the military police on the night of Bloody Sunday he failed to mention that he had fired two shots at an alleged gunman (Patrick Doherty) between Block 2 of Rossville Flats and Joseph Place. He later made a supplementary state-ment which substantially amended the original statement. Once again he failed to make any reference to the shooting of Patrick Doherty.

This did not appear until weeks later when his formal statement of evidence was taken by the Treasury Solicitor acting on behalf of the tribunal. This, combined with other serious discrepancies in soldier F's statement, which are considered in more detail in Chapter 5, are sufficient to raise a doubt about the veracity of his account. It is therefore submitted that there was a sufficient basis for Soldier F to be charged with the murder of Patrick Doherty.

Kevin McElhinney had been shot while crawling along the pavement on the west side of Block 1 of Rossville Flats. The bullet had entered his buttock. Although any one of three soldiers, L, M or K, might have fired the fatal bullet, Lord Widgery concluded that it was most likely to have been Sergeant K. He was a senior NCO and a qualified marksman, and he had fired a rifle fitted with a telescopic sight. Sergeant K claimed that he had fired one shot at a man crawling from the barricade to the flats at or around the spot where McElhinney was shot. Sergeant K claimed that his target had been carrying a rifle. Although Lord Widgery declared himself much impressed by sergeant K's evidence, saying that he obviously acted with responsibility and restraint, he stopped short of concluding that his shooting of Kevin McElhinney had been justified.[91] Indeed Lord Widgery accepted that the lead particles detected on the back of McElhinney's left hand and on the back of his jacket did not establish that he had fired a gun. Moreover no rifle had been recovered from his body. It is also worth noting that K's identification of the rifle was highly speculative. He could not establish positively that it had been a rifle. Ultimately the key issue is likely to be whether Sergeant K had genuinely believed that Kevin McElhinney had been carrying a rifle. While it is accepted that the basis for a murder charge in this case may be weaker than in some of the others, it is nevertheless submitted that there is sufficient doubt about the veracity of K's account to justify a prosecution.

The forensic evidence concerning the other fatal shootings was not sufficient to connect an individual soldier or soldiers with individual victims. Although the soldiers gave accounts of the circumstances in which they had fired each shot and the targets at which they had fired, it was not possible to connect any of the other victims with the accounts offered by any of the soldiers. It follows that criminal charges with respect to the other fatalities would have to stand or fall on the possibility of murder charges based on joint enterprise, attempted murder or shooting with intent to murder.

Lord Widgery did not deal specifically with the shooting of those who did not die from their wounds. Two exceptions were the shooting of Damien Donaghy and John Johnson by soldiers A and B. These two

shootings were separate in both time and place from the other shootings and the circumstances were such that it was feasible to consider
charging the soldiers with attempted murder or shooting with intent
to murder. Lord Widgery accepted that both victims had been entirely
innocent individuals going about their lawful business. Soldier A
claimed in evidence that he had fired two shots from inside a building
at a man lighting what he had believed to be a nail bomb. The first had
missed but the second had hit its target. Soldier B, who had been operating from a different floor of the same building, said in evidence that
he had fired three shots at a man who had been about to light what
appeared to be a nail bomb. The first had missed but the second and/or
the third must have struck the target. In both cases the soldiers claimed
that the body had been dragged away by a crowd. Although each
claimed to have fired at only one target it was not clear whether both
had shot Donaghy and Johnson or whether one had shot Donaghy
and the other had shot Johnson. While there was no doubt that both
Johnson and Donaghy had been shot by soldiers A and/or B it was not
possible to establish who had shot Donaghy and who had shot
Johnson. Indeed it was even possible that only one of them had shot
both. While that may have posed a difficulty for a charge of murder
had either or both victims died it is submitted that it is irrelevant in
the case of a charge of attempted murder or shooting with intent to
murder. What is required here is evidence that the soldiers fired one or
more shots at a target in circumstances where they did not genuinely
believe that lives or personal safety were at risk. It is not necessary to
establish the identity of the target. The question, therefore, is whether
there is reason to doubt the veracity of the accounts offered by soldiers
A and B.

Lord Widgery accepted that soldiers A and B had actually believed
that missiles, including nail bombs, were being thrown at their building, although he did not feel able to determine whether their belief
had been well-founded. He also accepted that they had believed,
rightly or wrongly, that their respective targets had been 'engaged in
suspicious action similar to that of striking a match and lighting a nail
bomb'. He was more ambiguous, however, about whether the soldiers
had been lawfully justified in firing in the circumstances which they
had believed to exist:

> The soldiers fired in the belief that they were entitled to do so by
> their orders. Whether or not the circumstances were really such as
> to warrant firing there is no reason whatever to suppose that either

Mr Johnson or Mr Donaghy was in fact trying to light or throw a bomb.[92]

It has already been seen in Chapter 5 that when the evidence offered to the tribunal by soldiers A and B is examined in the light of their original statements, there are substantial grounds for suspecting that their accounts to the tribunal were embellished in order to conceal the truth about the shootings. This, coupled with the failure of Lord Widgery to find that there was lawful justification for their actions, would seem to provide a reasonable basis for criminal charges.

Conclusion

It is a gross injustice to those who were wounded on Bloody Sunday, and to the relatives of those who were shot dead, that no prosecutions were brought against those responsible. Even on the basis of the Widgery Report itself there are clear grounds for believing that at least some of the soldiers fired without lawful justification at civilians who were unarmed and posing no threat at the time they were shot. Consideration of the whole evidence that was available to the tribunal of inquiry suggests very strongly that Widgery's conclusions grossly underestimated the extent of the soldiers' culpability and the numbers who were culpable. Indeed there is also a case for arguing that all those involved in the planning and execution of the Bloody Sunday operation are guilty of murder in the course of a joint enterprise. In considering whether to initiate prosecutions for the events of Bloody Sunday the prosecution is not confined to the contents and findings of the Widgery Tribunal of Inquiry. It can and should consider all the available evidence and it should carry out whatever further inquiries it considers necessary.

Of course it is important not to underestimate the potential legal minefield which would have to be negotiated before convictions could be secured. It is freely acknowledged, for example, that the application of the joint enterprise concept to an operation planned and executed by the security forces is quite a novel proposition in the context of Bloody Sunday. Equally it cannot be stated with any degree of confidence that the courts would be prepared to apply the concerted action concept to a situation where the joint partners fired shots at more than one target. These are issues of law which have yet to come before the courts for determination. All the more reason, therefore, that the state should have been prepared to test them through the medium of criminal prosecutions in the wake of Bloody Sunday. Given the issues at stake, clarity in the law governing such matters would seem to be a vital priority.

The uncertainty is compounded by the fact that the state did not offer any explanation for the decision not to prosecute in respect of the deaths and injuries resulting from Bloody Sunday. Of course this is not unusual. It is standard practice not to give reasons for a decision to prosecute. Nevertheless occasional exceptions have been made.[93] Given the uniqueness of what happened on Bloody Sunday, it was imperative for the state to offer an explanation of its decision not to prosecute. The failure to do so merely fuelled a widespread belief that the victims had been murdered by the agents of the state in the knowledge that the state would not render them accountable to the law for their actions. If, by contrast, the decision not to prosecute was based on the notion that there were insuperable legal obstacles in the path of securing convictions, then this should have been explained.

7
Law and Security Policy since Bloody Sunday

Law and justice

Central to the concepts of law and justice is that everyone within the state, no matter how powerful, is subject to the law.[1] The agents of the state and their political masters do not receive any special exemption from the law because of their official status or political power. Indeed a critical indicator of the health of a democracy based on the rule of law is the extent to which those who wield power in the state are answerable to and governed by the law. A distinct characteristic of common law jurisdictions such as the United Kingdom is the notion that public officials and public bodies do not generally enjoy special legal privileges on account of their status as servants or agents of the state. They are subject to the same laws in exactly the same capacity as the ordinary citizen. The rule of law and democratic legitimacy in such common law jurisdictions draw their strength from the fact that the highest and mightiest in the land are subject to the law to exactly the same extent as the poorest and least powerful. Dicey illustrated the point very succinctly when he said that 'every official from the Prime Minister down to a constable or collector of taxes, is under the same responsibility for every act done without legal justification as any other citizen'.[2]

The need to demonstrate that the law applies equally to everyone without fear or favour is at its most acute when agents of the state have used lethal force to eliminate opponents of their political masters. When this takes the form of the armed forces of the state engaging in the public mass slaughter of unarmed civilians participating in a public protest against the security and political policies of the government, it is absolutely imperative that the law is applied, and is seen to be applied, vigorously and impartially to those responsible. Any weakness

215

or failure in this regard will have devastating consequences for public confidence in the rule of law and the very legitimacy of the state. The worst possible scenario is that the law will be used as a tool by the political masters of the armed forces to ensure not only that those directly responsible are not brought to justice for their deeds but that their actions are given some sort of spurious legitimacy. When this happens the very currency of the law is debased. It loses its aura as a steady and unquenchable fountain of impartial justice and becomes just another tool to be used by those in power to achieve partisan security and political objectives. The rule of law is inevitably set to one side in this process. The danger, of course, is that it will be destroyed altogether, with all the consequences that implies for the legitimacy of the state.

It is submitted that the events of Bloody Sunday, coupled with the Widgery Inquiry and the failure to prosecute those responsible, inflicted irreparable damage on the rule of law. A crushing blow was dealt to the nationalists' confidence in the capacity of the law to protect them and their lives against the oppressive policies and strategies of a hostile state and its armed forces. Any vestige of legitimacy the state might have held for them was dissipated. It must be remembered in this context that in the immediate three years preceding Bloody Sunday, as outlined in Chapter 2, the law had failed to protect nationalists against shootings and brutality at the hands of the security forces. Indeed in the case of arbitrary arrests, searches, curfews, detentions, oppressive interrogations and internment the law had actually provided the necessary authority and support. In the fifty years preceding that the law had functioned more as a vehicle for, as opposed to a check against, the discriminatory and oppressive political, economic, cultural and security policies of the Northern Irish government. The events of Bloody Sunday therefore provided nationalists with unequivocal proof that the law was primarily a tool used by the state to crush their dissent and a means of providing a spurious legitimacy to whatever security policies the state deemed necessary to achieve that objective.

The question that must be considered now is whether Bloody Sunday can be interpreted retrospectively as a turning point, or whether it was merely the most heinous and despicable example of the law being hijacked by the executive in order to secure its immediate security and political objectives in Northern Ireland. Unfortunately a brief survey of security policy and the law since Bloody Sunday will reveal that the broad strategy which prevailed up to and including Bloody Sunday has continued in one form or another right up to the present. Critically the one constant throughout this period has been the benign role of the law in facilitating this strategy even when, as was often the case, it involved the gross denial of fundamental rights and freedoms, including the right to life, at the hands of the security forces. This chapter will survey the dominant features of this process by outlining the relevant legislative framework, the security policies and practices pursued on the basis of this framework and the manner in which the courts have responded to the legal challenges mounted against the policies and practices.

The legislative framework

When the Stormont government was prorogued of its security powers shortly after Bloody Sunday hopes were high that Bloody Sunday would in fact prove to be the decisive turning point. Law and its enforcement would revert to their intrinsic functions of protecting the citizen and the state against unjust attack irrespective of the source of attack, punishing wrongdoers irrespective of their identity or status and generally upholding the rule of law for the benefit of all in society. These hopes were further fuelled when the Stormont government was suspended in March 1972 and Northern Ireland was brought under direct rule from Westminster. Apart from a brief interlude in 1974 Northern Ireland has continued to be governed directly from Westminster right up to the present, although the good Friday Peace Agreement makes provision for the establishment of a power-sharing administration. Since the demise of the Stormont government, executive power in Northern Ireland has been exercised primarily through a secretary of state appointed by the British prime minister. Legislation is enacted through Orders in Council issued by the queen on the advice of the secretary of state.[3]

One of the first moves of the British government was to promise the repeal of the Special Powers Act. This more than any other individual decision signalled that there was to be a new dawn of law and justice for all. Many of the objectionable security policies and practices prior to Bloody Sunday could be traced back to the Special Powers Act. The broad discretionary powers that it conferred on the executive and security forces were directly responsible for internment, arbitrary arrests, detentions and searches, curfews and restrictions on the freedom of assembly, association and expression. Indirectly the Act could also be blamed for brutal interrogations, the use of excessive force to deal with public order situations and ultimately the use of lethal force. It was a source of immeasurable relief to the nationalist community, therefore, when it was eventually repealed in 1973. What was not initially appreciated was that the repeal would be accompanied by the enactment of replacement legislation which would bear many of the hallmarks of the Special Powers Act and would remain in force in one form or another for more than a quarter of a century. During this period it would be supplemented and strengthened by further measures. A brief survey of the origins, content and development of this legislation will starkly illustrate how Northern Ireland has continued to be governed since Bloody Sunday on the basis of draconian emergency legislation which has conferred broad discretionary powers on the security forces. This survey will also reveal how these powers were primarily designed to serve the immediate needs of the security forces and the overall security policies and objectives of the government.

The British government's early promise to repeal the Special Powers Act was backed up by moves to phase out internment through a programme of ministerial releases of internees. In the first few months of direct rule about 500 persons were released by order of the secretary of state.[4] During this period an IRA truce was in force and secret negotiations were being held in Britain between the British government, IRA leaders and nationalist politicians with a view to securing a political resolution to the violence.[5] Some of the nationalist participants in these talks, including Gerry Adams and Martin McGuinness, were actually released temporarily from internment and flown secretly to Britain for the purpose. However the talks were inconclusive and the IRA truce broke down. The British government had meanwhile embarked upon a strategy of seeking changes in the criminal justice system which would enable it to be used, in preference to internment, as the primary means of taking suspect terrorists out of circulation. This strategy has had a profound impact on the shape of the criminal justice system in Northern Ireland over the past 25 years.

The Diplock Report

There were several obstacles in the path of using the ordinary courts to secure the conviction of persons who were believed to be guilty of serious terrorist offences. The first of these, particularly in the case of IRA suspects, concerned the admissibility of confessions. It has already been seen that the sort of interrogation methods used by the security forces against such suspects inevitably rendered consequential confessions inadmissible.[6] Cases were thrown out by the Northern Irish courts on this basis and several prosecutions were abandoned by the authorities for the same reason. Other problems cited by the authorities concerned jury intimidation and jury prejudice for or against the defendant, as well the legal difficulties involved in proving a charge of possession where a firearm was found in circumstances where it could have been in the possession of any one of a finite group of persons, all of whom denied any knowledge of it.

The government responded to these difficulties by establishing a commission under the chairmanship of Lord Diplock with a remit to consider:

> what arrangements for the administration of justice in Northern Ireland could be made in order to deal more effectively with terrorist organisations by bringing to book, otherwise than by internment by the Executive, individuals involved in terrorist activities, particularly those who plan and direct, but do not necessarily take part in, terrorist acts; and to make recommendations.[7]

These very terms of reference clearly signalled an intent to subordinate law and the justice process to the immediate needs of security policy. Lord Diplock did not disappoint. After an inquiry which took only three months to complete, in a short report he recommended: detention without trial; broad discretionary powers of stop, question, search, arrest, detention and interrogation for the police and army; serious restrictions on the right to silence; stringent restrictions on the granting of bail; a fundamental change to the common law rules on the admissibility of confessions; imposing an obligation on persons found in possession of firearms or explosives to prove that they were not aware of their presence; the abolition of the jury; and the continuation of detention without trial. Even the Stormont government had not dared to effect such a realignment in the whole balance and structure of the criminal trial. Nevertheless the bulk of the Diplock recommendations were accepted with alacrity by the British government and enacted in the form of the Northern Ireland (Emergency Provisions) Act 1973, the very same act which repealed the Special Powers Act. Prior to that, however, the British government had moved to place the internment provisions on a quasi-judicial footing by introducing the Detention of Terrorists Order (Northern Ireland) 1972. The contents of this order were subsequently incorporated into the 1973 Act. Less than a year later the 1973 Act was supplemented by the Prevention of Terrorism (Temporary Provisions) Act 1974 which was enacted in great haste in response to the Birmingham bombings, which killed 21 people and injured 184 on 21 November 1974. While the 1973 Act applied solely to Northern Ireland, the 1974 Act applied to the whole of the United Kingdom. The following outline of the emergency legislation applicable in Northern Ireland must therefore take account of both measures.

To complicate matters further each Act has been amended and replaced on several occasions. The 1973 Act was first supplemented by the Northern Ireland (Emergency Provisions) (Amendment) Act 1975 before both were replaced by the Northern Ireland (Emergency Provisions) Act 1978. The 1978 Act was later amended and supplemented by the Northern Ireland (Emergency Provisions) Act 1987 before both were replaced by the Northern Ireland (Emergency Provisions) Act 1991. This act has since been replaced by the current version, the Northern Ireland (Emergency Provisions) Act 1996, which in turn has been amended by the Northern Ireland (Emergency Provisions) Act 1998. The Prevention of Terrorism (Temporary Provisions) Act 1974 was replaced by the Prevention of Terrorism (Temporary Provisions) Act 1976. The 1976 Act was replaced by the Prevention of Terrorism (Temporary Provisions) Act 1984, which in turn was replaced by the Prevention of Terrorism (Temporary Provisions) Act 1989. For the most part these amended and replacement versions resulted from judicial inquiries into the operation of the respective Acts. The Northern Ireland Emergency Provisions legislation was considered by the Gardiner Committee in 1975,[8] the Baker Inquiry in 1984[9] and the Rowe Inquiry in 1995.[10] The Prevention of Terrorism legislation was examined by the Shackleton Inquiry in 1978,[11] the Jellicoe Inquiry in 1982[12] and the Rowe Inquiry in 1995.[13] Both Acts have also been the subject of annual reviews by a 'commissioner' who reports to parliament. In 1996 Lord Lloyd examined both Acts in the context of the 'future need for specific counter-terrorism legislation in the United Kingdom if the cessation of terrorism connected with the affairs of Northern Ireland leads to a lasting peace, taking into account the threat from other kinds of terrorism, and the United Kingdom's obligations under international law.[14] The Northern Ireland (Emergency Provisions) Act 1996 and the Prevention of Terrorism (Temporary Provisions) Act 1989 were both amended and supplemented by the terms of the Criminal Justice (Terrorism and Conspiracy) Act 1998, which was enacted in the wake of the Omagh bombing atrocity. Both Acts are set to be replaced by a single act in the year 2000.[15]

Rather than deal with each Act and their successors separately, attention will focus on their impact on the key elements of the criminal justice process. While attention will focus on the contents of the measures which have been introduced specifically as 'emergency' or 'temporary' provisions, it is worth noting that they have been supplemented by a substantial body of coercive measures which have been introduced as 'ordinary' legislation. These measures include draconian inroads into the right to silence,[16] freedom of movement, freedom of association, freedom of expression, freedom of assembly and the right to march.[17]

Criminal offences

Before outlining the main provisions affecting police and army powers and criminal procedure, it might be worthwhile drawing attention to two new offences created by the emergency legislation.[18] These are particularly significant because their existence gives a much broader scope to police and army powers than might otherwise have been the case. The first of these offences is membership of a proscribed organisation.[19] The secretary of state enjoys the statutory power to proscribe organisations by order. The current list of organisations proscribed in this way includes all the paramilitary organisations which have been active in Northern Ireland in recent years. Membership of any of these listed organisations is a criminal offence. The nature of the offence, however, is such that it can be committed simply through a state of being. It is not necessary for the offender to do anything. Moreover anyone who merely professes to be a member of a proscribed organisation or gives support of any kind to such an organisation also commits a criminal offence. A person suspected of membership, or of any of these associated offences, is subject to police or army arrest. Clearly this leaves extensive discretion in the hands of the individual police officer or soldier.

The second offence arises when a person has information about an act of terrorism or people involved in terrorism and fails or refuses to disclose it to the authorities without reasonable excuse.[20] The existence of this offence enables the police and army to arrest a very wide range of individuals who have absolutely no involvement in terrorism. The obvious and most immediate candidates are relatives of an individual who has been convicted of a terrorist offence or is believed to have been involved in an act of terrorism.

Detention without trial

The detention without trial provisions first introduced by the Detention of Terrorists Order (Northern Ireland) 1972 were designed to replace internment at the arbitrary diktat of the executive with a process of administrative detention in which the case against an individual would have to be considered by an independent and impartial commissioner before any final decision on his detention could be taken. Commissioners were appointed by the secretary of state and had to be judicially qualified. Although they had to follow set rules of procedure, they were not bound by the rules of evidence applicable in an ordinary criminal court.

The process began with the making of an interim custody order against a person suspected of having been concerned in the commission or attempted commission of any act of terrorism or in the direction, organisation or training of persons for the purpose of terrorism.[21] Such an order could be made only by the secretary of state or his or her ministerial deputies. It authorised the detention of suspects for a period of 28 days. If during that period the chief constable of the RUC made further orders referring the cases to a commissioner for determination, the suspects could be held indefinitely until their cases were finally determined. Such determinations were made by the commissioner after formal private hearings in the presence of the suspects and their legal advisors, where relevant. For the purposes of the hearing the suspects were supplied with a formal statement of the nature of the terrorist activity alleged against them. Apart from the requirement to make a formal record of the proceedings, commissioners exercised control over the procedure at the hearings, including the power to exclude the suspects and their legal representatives in the interests of public security or the safety of any person. Before commissioners could make a determination to detain individuals they had to be satisfied, after enquiring into the case, that the suspects had been concerned in the commission or attempted commission of any act of terrorism or in the direction, organisation or training of persons for the purpose of terrorism and that detention was necessary for the protection of the public. When commissioners were not satisfied that the grounds for detention were established they had to order the release of the suspects.

When a Commissioner issued a detention order, the suspect concerned had the right to appeal to an appeal tribunal, comprising at least three legally qualified persons appointed by the secretary of state. The powers and procedure applicable at the appeal hearing were similar to those for the initial hearing. Beyond that there was a requirement that the case of each detained person should be reviewed within twelve months from the date of the relevant detention order, and thereafter at six-monthly intervals. These reviews were conducted by a Commissioner under the same rules governing the initial hearings. In a review hearing, however, the issue for the commissioner was whether the suspect's continued detention was necessary for the protection of the public. If not the suspect had to be discharged.

Superficially this detention procedure was more judicialised than its predecessor under the Special Powers Act. That, however, does not conceal the fact that it represented an almost total subversion of the individual's right to be deemed innocent until proven guilty in accordance with the law. Despite the judicialised trappings it was still essentially an exercise in locking people up on the basis of what they were suspected of having done rather than on the basis of a criminal conviction handed down by a court after a trial conducted in accordance with due process. Indeed the Diplock Report made no attempt to conceal the fact that the detention procedure was designed first and foremost to serve the objectives of security policy, as opposed to the individual's right to due process:

> We are thus driven inescapably to the conclusion that until the current terrorism by the extremist organisations of both factions in Northern Ireland can be eradicated, there will continue to be some dangerous terrorists against whom it will not be possible to obtain convictions by any form of criminal trial which we regard as appropriate to a court of law; and these will include many of those who plan and organise terrorist acts by other members of the organisation in which they take no first-hand part themselves. We are also driven inescapably to the conclusion that so long as these remain at liberty to operate in Northern Ireland, it will not be possible to find witnesses prepared to testify against them in the criminal courts, except those serving in the army or the police, for whom effective protection can be provided. The dilemma is complete. The only hope of restoring the efficiency of criminal courts of law in Northern Ireland to deal with terrorist crimes is by using an extra-judicial process to deprive of their ability to operate in Northern Ireland, those terrorists whose activities result in the intimidation of witnesses.[22]

The Detention of Terrorists Order was introduced just before the Diplock Commission reported. Its contents, however, were incorporated into the Northern Ireland (Emergency Provisions) Act, which was enacted to give effect to the Diplock recommendations in 1973. Although, as will be seen later, a policy decision was taken in 1975 to dispense with detention without trial, the relevant powers were not dropped from later versions of the legislation until 1998.

Police and army powers

Apart from the detention without trial provisions, the 1973 Act introduced sweeping new summary powers for police and soldiers to replace those lost by the repeal of the Special Powers Act. Section 10 of the 1973 Act empowered members of the RUC to arrest without warrant any persons whom they suspected of being a terrorist. A terrorist is defined elsewhere in the Act as 'a person who is or has been concerned in the commission or attempted commission of any act of terrorism or in directing, organising or training persons for the purposes of terrorism'.[23] In turn terrorism is defined as 'the use of violence for the purpose of putting the public or any section of the public in fear'.[24] Any person arrested under this provision could be held without charge for up to 72 hours. The cardinal features of this power, apart for the period for which the suspect could be held without charge, were that it could be exercised in the absence of reasonable suspicion and that it was not tied to any specified criminal offence. Indeed it is apparent that this power was designed to be used as the start of a procedure leading to questioning, followed by detention without judicial trial.[25] It will be seen later, however, that it was used regularly throughout the 1970s and 1980s to bring suspects before the courts for terrorist offences and to establish and maintain intelligence information on individuals and whole communities. In the 1978 version of the Act it became Section 11, and it was eventually dropped from the 1991 version.

Section 11 of the 1973 Act conferred a more specific power of arrest on members of the RUC. It permitted them to arrest without warrant anyone whom they suspected of committing, having committed or being about to commit a 'scheduled' offence or an offence under the act which was not a scheduled offence. What constituted a 'scheduled' offence will be dealt with in more detail later. For the moment it is sufficient to note that it corresponded roughly with the sort of offences against the person, property and the state which were most commonly associated with terrorism. The current version of the Section 11 power is to be found in Section 18 of the 1996 Act and is based, since 1987, on the objective 'reasonable grounds to suspect' standard. Persons arrested under Section 18 can be detained without charge for up to 48 hours.

Another surviving arrest power from the original legislation is to be found in Section 14 of the Prevention of Terrorism (Temporary Provisions) Act 1989. This appeared first as Section 7 of the 1974 Act. It empowers members of the RUC to arrest without warrant anyone whom they reasonably suspect to be a terrorist, or to have been concerned in the commission, preparation or instigation of acts of terrorism. Unlike the powers under the Northern Ireland (Emergency Provisions) Acts this power can be exercised only on the basis of reasonable suspicion. Suspicion, however, need not be tied to a specific offence. Of greater importance in practice is the fact that anyone arrested under this power can be held without charge for a period of 48 hours, which can be extended for up to five more days at the discretion of the secretary of state. The right of access to a solicitor for persons detained in police custody under the emergency legislation can be denied for the first 48 hours of detention.[26] The significance of this restriction is considerably enhanced by the serious inroads into the right to silence of suspects in police custody effected by the Criminal Evidence (Northern Ireland) Order 1988.[27]

Soldiers enjoy a specific power of arrest under Section 19 of the Northern Ireland (Emergency Provisions) Act 1996. First introduced in Section 12 of the 1973 version it permits soldiers on duty to arrest without warrant anyone whom they reasonably suspect of committing, having committed or being about to commit any offence. The huge scope of this power is reflected by the fact that it may be exercised for any offence known to the criminal law. Prior to 1987 it did not even have to be based on a reasonable suspicion. Soldiers effecting the arrest will satisfy the formalities governing lawful arrest merely if they state that they are making the arrest as a member of Her Majesty's Forces. Persons arrested, however, may be detained for no more than four hours. This power arose from the recommendations of the Diplock Report in 1972. At that time there were areas of Northern Ireland which were accessible only to the army, as distinct from the RUC. The Diplock Commission felt that it was essential that soldiers should have the power to arrest suspects whom they encountered within these areas. The sole purpose of such a power would be to render the suspects amenable to the RUC. Accordingly there was no need to grant the army an extended period in which to interrogate persons arrested under the power. Four hours would be sufficient to take suspects into safe custody, establish their identity and, if appropriate, transfer them into the custody of the RUC.

Both police officers and soldiers enjoy the power to stop, question and search persons at random on the street. Currently these powers are found in Sections 20(6) and 25 of the Northern Ireland (Emergency Provisions) Act 1996, although they were first introduced in the 1973 version. Members of the RUC or soldiers on duty may stop and question any person for the purpose of ascertaining that person's movements and identity and what he or she knows about any recent explosion or any other incident endangering life, or about any person killed or injured in any such explosion or incident. It is a summary offence to refuse to answer or fail to answer any question to the best of one's knowledge and ability. Persons and vehicles stopped at random may also be searched for explosives, firearms, ammunition or wireless transmitters. The key feature of these powers is that their exercise does not depend on suspicion. Police officers and soldiers can exercise them against anyone wherever and whenever they deem it necessary.[28] The subordination of the rights and freedoms of the individual to executive power is complete. In effect the availability of these powers make police officers and soldiers the undisputed masters of the streets.

Before leaving the powers of stop and question it is worth mentioning the special provisions applicable at ports for persons travelling *within* the United Kingdom and Ireland.[29] The Prevention of Terrorism legislation makes provision for a number of ports to be designated. The captains of ships and aircraft must ensure that passengers and crew who embark and disembark at these ports do so in accordance with the procedures approved by examining officers (police officers, immigration officials and customs officials). This may involve filling in personal information on embarkation and disembarkation cards. Examining officers have extensive powers to stop and examine passengers and search baggage. No prior suspicion is required if the examination is carried out for the purpose of checking whether a person is subject to an exclusion order (see later), whether there are grounds for suspecting that he or she is in breach of an exclusion order or whether the person is or has been involved in terrorism. In effect this is a power of random examination. Nevertheless the person concerned can be detained for up to 12 hours for the purpose of the examination, and is obliged to give any information duly required by the examining officer. If the officer reasonably suspects that the person is involved in terrorism the latter can be detained for a further 48 hours for further examination. This period can be extended by an additional five days on the authority of the secretary of state. It is worth noting that a person detained under these powers is not formally arrested and is not necessarily being investigated on suspicion of a criminal offence.

Both police officers and soldiers enjoy special powers of entry and search. These are to be found primarily in Sections 17–24 and 26 of the Northern Ireland (Emergency Provisions) Act 1996, although they were first introduced in the 1973 version. RUC officers and soldiers can enter any place, apart from a dwelling, without a warrant in order to conduct a search for arms and communications equipment. The sweeping scope of this power is reflected in the fact that no prior suspicion is needed. Apart from dwelling houses, therefore, the police and army control over persons on the streets extends to private property. Indeed it is worth noting that the powers to stop, question and search can also be used against any person found on the property being searched, although persons found on private property may be searched for arms only on the basis of reasonable suspicion. Dwelling houses can also be entered and searched without a warrant for arms and communications equipment, but only if there is reasonable suspicion that the items are present. This objective standard was introduced in the 1987 version. It is also worth noting that police officers and soldiers have the power to enter and search private property in association with the exercise of their power of arrest and to look for persons unlawfully imprisoned on the premises. Documents and records found in the course of any of these searches may be examined if reasonably necessary to ascertain whether they contain information likely to be useful to terrorists. Persons on the premises during the course of a search can be detained for a period of up to four hours, which can be extended for an additional four hours.

This brief survey of the policing powers available to members of the RUC and the army reveals that the emergency legislation first introduced by the British government in 1973, and the Prevention of Terrorism legislation first introduced in 1974, continued the long tradition of draconian security powers in Northern Ireland.[30] In some respects the new legislation imposed more specific controls on the RUC and the army than had been the case under the Special Powers Act. In other respects they conferred coercive powers which even the Special Powers Act had not contemplated. The key feature is that for more than 25 years of direct British rule in Northern Ireland the security forces have been equipped with broad discretionary powers which can be used to deprive individuals of the fundamental rights to freedom of movement, liberty, bodily integrity, private property and privacy. In short, since its inception Northern Ireland has been and continues to be governed by force.

Exclusion orders

One particular instrument which illustrates the unbelievable lengths to which the British government has been prepared to go in prioritising political and security objectives over the most basic fundamental rights and freedoms is the exclusion order. First introduced by the Prevention of Terrorism (Temporary Provisions) Act 1974 the relevant provisions are now to be found in Sections 4–8 and Schedule 2 of the 1989 Act.[31] These enable the secretary of state to exclude an individual from Britain and/or Northern Ireland if he or she is satisfied that the person in question is or has been concerned in the commission, preparation or instigation of acts of terrorism, or is attempting, or may attempt, to enter the territory with a view to being concerned in such activity. The secretary of state may exercise the power in whatever way appears expedient to prevent acts of terrorism designed to influence public opinion or government policy with respect to affairs in Northern Ireland. This sweeping discretionary power is complemented and reinforced by the procedure involved. Prior to 1995 recipients received no advance warning that an order was being considered. Consequent on the decision of the Court of Justice of the European Communities in *R v Secretary of State for the Home Department, ex parte Gallagher*[32] it has been the practice of the secretary of state to serve written notice on the individuals concerned that he or she is considering the issue of an exclusion order. The secretary of state then refers the matter to one or more advisers to whom the individuals can make representation. While the individuals may be legally represented in a hearing before the adviser(s), the proceedings are not adversarial and they will not know the real substance of the case against them. The secretary of state takes the advice of the adviser(s) into account when making a final decision. If an exclusion order is made it lasts for three years and can be renewed. The net effect is that the individuals concerned are removed from (and banned from entering) Britain and/or Northern Ireland, as the case may be, despite the fact that they may have set up home there with their family. Failure to comply with an exclusion order is a criminal offence.

The draconian nature of this power of exclusion exceeds even the executive power under the Special Powers Act, which could be used to restrict an individual's freedom of movement to a defined locality in Northern Ireland. The exclusion order represents a full frontal attack not just on freedom of movement, but also on liberty, property rights and the most fundamental right of a family to live together. The fact that British citizens, or those ordinarily resident in Northern Ireland, cannot be excluded completely from the United Kingdom does little to curb the excessive nature of this power. Similarly the fact that an order expires after three years is of little significance as there is nothing to prevent an individual from being the subject of successive orders. Indeed the flavour of this exclusion power was best captured by Lord Jellicoe, who described it as 'in many ways the most extreme of the

Act's powers: in its effect on civil liberties [it] is … more severe than any other power in the Act; in its procedure and principles it departs more thoroughly from the normal criminal process.'[33] However the British government revoked all subsisting exclusion orders in October 1997 and announced its intention to repeal the relevant legislation permitting the issue of new orders.

Diplock Courts

Probably the most fundamental innovations introduced by the emergency legislation concern the criminal trial. The major features here are the abolition of the jury trial and the replacement of the common law rule on the admissibility of confessions by a statutory test. First introduced by the Northern Ireland (Emergency Provisions) Act in 1973 they continue to constitute a dominant feature of the criminal justice process.[34] Each will be considered in turn.

Trials on indictment for scheduled offences are normally conducted by the court without a jury. These courts are known generally as 'Diplock Courts' in order to distinguish them from their ordinary counterparts, which continue to function for non-scheduled offences and the trial of descheduled offences. The list of scheduled offences has been amended on several occasions. Currently it includes the common law offences of murder, manslaughter, riot, kidnapping and false imprisonment; and certain offences under the Offences against the Person Act 1861, the Explosives Substances Act 1883, the Prison Act (Northern Ireland) 1953, the Theft Act (Northern Ireland) 1969, the Protection of Property Act (Northern Ireland) 1969, the Criminal Damage (Northern Ireland) Order 1977, the Criminal Law (Amendment) (Northern Ireland) Order 1977, the Firearms (Northern Ireland) Order 1981, the Taking of Hostages Act 1982, the Nuclear Material (Offences) Act 1983, the Prevention of Terrorism (Temporary Provisions) Act 1989, the Aviation and Maritime Security Act 1990, the Channel Tunnel (Security) Order 1994, the Northern Ireland (Emergency Provisions) Act 1996 and certain hijacking offences.[35] If, however, a person is charged with both a scheduled offence and an ordinary offence the latter can be treated as scheduled. On the other hand the director of public prosecutions (DPP) has the discretion to deschedule offences in individual cases if they were not committed in circumstances connected with terrorism. This would enable him or her to deschedule serious offences, such as murder, committed by members of the security forces in the course of operational duties. In practice, however, they are normally tried as scheduled offences in the Diplock Courts.

The key feature of the Diplock Courts is that the judge sits to hear and determine the case without a jury.[36] He is the arbiter of all questions of law and fact. This can prove particularly contentious in a trial where the accused has contested the admissibility of a confession. In an ordinary trial the jury will be excluded from the court while evidence is called and arguments presented over the admissibility of the confession. If the judge decides as a matter of law that the confession is inadmissible he or she excludes it, the jury is called back and the trial proceeds without the jury ever being made aware that the accused has made a confession. This protects the accused against the unfair prejudice which would result if the fact-finder was aware, and therefore might be influenced by, the inadmissible evidence. In a Diplock trial, however, the judge will normally proceed with the trial after having heard the evidence about a confession which he has ruled inadmissible. When he comes to make a determination on guilt he reminds himself not to take into account the fact that the accused has actually confessed to the crime. The obvious prejudice that can result in this situation can be avoided by the judge stepping down from the trial. In practice, however, this rarely happens.

When giving his judgment in a Diplock Court the judge is obliged to give reasons for a conviction. The accused is granted an unlimited right of appeal against both conviction and sentence. Apart from these matters the Diplock Court has the same powers, including the power to sentence, that are available to the ordinary Crown Court.

The abolition of the right to jury trial in Diplock Courts is undoubtedly the most public manifestation of the extent to which the judicial process has been subordinated to security needs. In practice, however, the replacement of the common law rules on the admissibility of evidence by a statutory test has probably made a much greater contribution to denying the accused a fair trial. Under the common law rule a confession could be admitted in evidence only if it was relevant and voluntary. Voluntary in this context meant that the prosecution had to establish beyond reasonable doubt that in making the confession the accused was not acting under a fear of prejudice or hope of advantage exercised or held out by a person in authority or oppression.[37] It has already been seen that one of the primary reasons why the authorities could not resort to the ordinary courts to secure convictions against suspect terrorists was because the interrogation methods used in many cases would not satisfy this basic common law test. What was required by the state, therefore, was a test which accepted much more forceful interrogation methods. Lord Diplock formulated a suitable test, which was first enacted in 1973. This statutory test is now applied to all trials in the Diplock Courts. The common law test continued to apply in the ordinary courts up to 1989, when it too was replaced by a statutory test. This test, however, is substantially different from the Diplock test, which continues to apply in the Diplock Courts.

The Diplock test, in its current formulation, reads as follows:

(1) In any criminal proceedings for a scheduled offence or for two or more offences at least one of which is a scheduled offence, a statement made by the accused may be given in evidence by the prosecution in so far as –

    (a) it is relevant to any matter in the proceedings, and

    (b) it is not excluded by the court in pursuance of subsection (2) or in the exercise of its discretion referred to in subsection (3) (and has not been rendered inadmissible by virtue of such a direction as is mentioned in subsection (2)(iii).

(2) Where in any such proceedings –

    (a) the prosecution proposes to give, or (as the case may be) has given, in evidence a statement made by the accused, and

    (b) prima facie evidence is adduced that the accused was subjected to torture, to inhuman or degrading treatment, or to any violence or threat of violence (whether or not amounting to torture), in order to induce him to make the statement, then, unless the prosecution satisfies the court that the statement was not obtained by so subjecting the accused in the manner indicated by the evidence, the court shall do one of the following things, namely –

        (i) in the case of a statement proposed to be given in evidence, exclude the statement;

        (ii) in the case of a statement already received in evidence, continue the trial disregarding the statement; or

        (iii) in either case, direct that the trial shall be restarted before a differently constituted court (before which the statement in question shall be inadmissible).

(3) It is hereby declared that, in the case of any statement made by the accused and not obtained by so subjecting him as mentioned in subsection 2(b), the court in any such proceedings as are mentioned in subsection (1) has a discretion to do one of the things mentioned in subsection 2(i) to (iii) if it appears to the

court that it is appropriate to do so in order to avoid unfairness to the accused or otherwise in the interests of justice.[38]

In its original formulation the test did not make it clear that the use of any violence or the threat of violence would also result in the exclusion of a resultant confession. Later it will be explained more fully how judges have interpreted this test. Broadly speaking, however, the effect of the statutory provisions is that a confession will be admitted unless the prosecution fail to satisfy the court that it has not been obtained by torture, inhuman or degrading treatment or the use of violence or threat of violence. This will be referred to generally as the torture, inhuman or degrading treatment test.

A number of other changes have been effected to the pretrial and trial procedures in order to make them more user-friendly to the state. For the most part these concern bail, committal proceedings and rules of evidence in firearms cases. It is not necessary, however, to describe them in any detail. Initially the emergency legislation imposed a presumption against the granting of bail in scheduled offence cases. Now, however, there is relatively little difference between the formal principles governing bail in these cases and those applicable to ordinary offences, apart from the fact that bail can be granted only by a High Court judge in scheduled offences. The emergency legislation abolished the right to a full oral hearing at the committal proceedings, during which the accused previously had the opportunity to contest the substance of the case against him or her through the examination and cross-examination of witnesses. In scheduled offences the committal proceedings normally consist of a hearing based on written testimony, in which the function of the magistrate is largely confined to deciding whether there is a case to answer. The emergency legislation also facilitates the prosecution by placing an evidential burden of proof on the accused in the case of firearms offences in certain circumstances. In the case of those charged with possession of firearms, the court may accept as evidence of their possession the fact that they were found in the same premises or vehicle as the firearm or that they were the owner, occupier or habitual user (otherwise than as a member of the public) of the premises or vehicle in question.[39]

Conveyor-belt justice

All these radical changes to trial procedure, combined with the extensive police and army powers, have produced a criminal process which differs radically from due process norms.[40] The whole balance of this process has been dramatically altered in favour of the state. The traditional image of the criminal process as a series of checks or obstacles to ensure that convictions are obtained only in respect of individuals against whom the state can positively prove guilt has been replaced by a process which is designed to facilitate the incarceration of those whom the state merely suspects of being guilty. The obstacle course has been replaced by the conveyor belt in order to cater for the immediate and narrow requirements of security policy. Basic concepts such as the independence and impartiality of law and justice and the fundamental rights and freedoms of the individual have been peremptorily swept aside in order to cater for the immediate and narrow requirements of security and political objectives. This is not what had been anticipated when the British government took up the reins of direct government in Northern Ireland in the aftermath of Bloody Sunday with the promise of abolishing the Special Powers Act. The question that must be considered now is what impact these legislative measures have had in practice, particularly in respect of the contents of security policies and practices since Bloody Sunday.

Security policies and practices

In a brief review of security policies and practices from 1972 to the present it is possible to identity certain trends. For example the period 1972–75 can be associated with a continuation of the military strategy which had commenced in earnest in 1970. The period 1975–79 can be associated with a criminalisation policy. A dominant feature was the use of brutal interrogation practices aimed at extracting confessions which would secure convictions on a large scale in the Diplock Courts. This was combined with a prisons policy which was geared towards treating those convicted in the Diplock Courts as ordinary criminals. From 1979 to 1985 a policy of reliance on accomplice evidence prevailed; known generally as the supergrass policy. The period from the early to late 1980s can be associated with a shoot to kill policy by the security forces. From the late 1980s to the mid 1990s the dominant theme was collusion between the security forces and loyalist terrorists in the execution of republicans suspected by the security forces of being engaged in terrorism. A distinctive feature of this period were the allegations that elements within the RUC pursued a practice of intimidating and making threats against the lives of lawyers representing suspected republican terrorists. Two lawyers who complained about such threats were shot dead by loyalist terrorists.

This attempt at superimposing a neat classification on security policies over the past 27 years must be qualified by the acknowledgement
that it offers no more than a convenient generalisation. It is not meant
to suggest that the policy assigned to any particular period of time
operated only during that period. In practice, virtually all of the policies and practices identified have been deployed to some degree
throughout the whole period. The classic example, of course, is shoot-
to-kill. Ill-treatment in the police interrogation centres is also a recurrent theme,[41] as is the oppressive use of police and army summary
powers to stop and question individuals in public and to enter and
search private property.[42] Others, such as the use of exclusion orders
and broadcasting bans,[43] were not dominant during any distinct period
as they primarily operated in the background as an integral part of
security policy. All that is being suggested by the classification is that
particular policies and practices were dominant during certain periods.
For the purposes of exposition, therefore, it will be convenient to follow the classification.

Continuation of the military strategy

The imposition of direct rule from London in the wake of Bloody
Sunday did not result in the early abandonment of the military strategy. Quite the contrary, following the breakdown of the IRA truce in
July 1972 the reformed internment provisions were put into full effect
in conjunction with the arrest, detention and interrogation powers
conferred by the Northern Ireland (Emergency Provisions) Act 1973.
Suspects would be arrested under Section 10 of the Act and taken for
interrogation to the joint army/RUC Special Branch centre at Castlereagh
in Belfast. If the interrogation produced sufficient evidence to warrant
the prosecution of the suspects through the Diplock Courts they would
be duly charged. If not they would be considered for an interim custody order. It would appear that the recommendation for such an order
could and often was passed directly to the secretary of state by army
intelligence officers. Moreover most suspects were held in detention for
at least five or six months before their cases became the subject of the
limited judicial consideration provided for in the legislation. When
their cases were heard they found that the charges were usually confined to statements of general allegations with no supporting evidence,
the case against them was often presented by witnesses from behind a
curtain who relied heavily on hearsay and even information from
informers whose identities were unknown. The judicial commissioners
could and did authorise detention orders without determining exactly
what contribution to terrorism the person concerned had made.[44]

Given the nature of the hearings, the mere fact that the judicial commissioners ultimately rejected the case made out by the security forces in a substantial proportion of cases provides the clearest indication of the extent to which these draconian powers were being abused. After June 1973 the proportion of rejections to approvals remained at a constant one third. Compared with the normal rate of acquittals in the courts this was a remarkably high figure. Boyle *et al.* summed up the significance of these figures as follows: 'The fact that the security authorities continued to present cases for the Commissioners' determination with such a high failure rate would...be a further indication of the extent to which traditional legal values were eroded by the pursuit of the "military security" approach.'[45]

The military strategy was also very evident on the streets. Nationalist areas continued to be policed by armed soldiers in full battle fatigues on foot and in heavily armoured vehicles and troop carriers. Heavily fortified military bases and posts were established in these areas, some even being located at the top of high-rise residential buildings. Relying on their emergency powers of stop, question and search, soldiers regularly stopped civilians going about their business, particularly in nationalist areas. Such individuals would be asked for evidence of their identity and details of their movements and their bags would be routinely searched. They would often be spreadeagled against a wall or army vehicle for the purpose of a body search. Frequently whole residential streets or areas were cordoned off and all vehicles and persons entering or leaving were searched. Sometimes these cordons were a prelude to house searches in the streets or areas concerned. The practice here was for each house to be searched by a team of soldiers. The systematic and comprehensive nature of the searches suggest that little attention was paid to the statutory requirement that searches of dwellings should be based on reasonable suspicion. In the course of the search floorboards and walls were routinely ripped out and furniture destroyed, and the residents were confined to a single room for the duration of the search.

Since the early 1970s the search operations have become more 'civilised'. The typical scenario in the 1980s was recounted in the case of *Kirkpatrick v Chief Constable of the RUC and Ministry of Defence*.[46] An army search team arrived at the house. Its composition in the Kirkpatrick case was a leader, two soldiers for upstairs, two for downstairs and one to keep records. An initial cursory search of the entire house was made, the doors were locked, the curtains drawn and the occupants assembled in one room under 'house arrest'. In the presence of the occupants the leader searched the other soldiers and he was searched by the record keeper. The occupants were then formally asked whether they possessed any munitions or transmitters. The team leader invited the head of the household to make a tour of inspection to record preexisting damage. Only then did the search proper commence, with the occupants confined to one room.

Closely related to the house-to-house searches was the practice of 'census-taking'. This consisted of a patrol of soldiers calling at each house in an area to record details of each person present in the house and details of wall coverings, floor coverings and soft furnishings. On the next visit a few months later the same details would be recorded and compared with those recorded on the previous visit. The householder would be required to account for any significant changes, such as an increase or decrease in the persons present or a change of wall covering or floor covering. Failure to give a satisfactory answer could result in walls and floors being ripped out in the course of a thorough search for concealed firearms. The overall purpose of the exercise was to develop and maintain detailed intelligence banks on the residents of nationalist areas. Just like the systematic house searches it would appear that the soldiers had no power to compel the cooperation of householders in the census-taking. In practice, however, most people considered themselves powerless to resist the demands.

The abuse of powers by the military was also reflected in the practice of 'screening'.[47] Typically this involved a mobile patrol of soldiers swooping on a house in the early hours of the morning. The occupants, including children, would be woken up and herded into a room, where they would be held as prisoners while the house was subjected to a cursory search.[48] One of the occupants would then be arrested under the army's four-hour power and taken away in an armoured vehicle to the local army base. There he or she would be searched, given a quick medical examination and imprisoned in a small cubicle until it was time to be interviewed by a military intelligence officer.[49] The questioning could last for anything from 15 to 90 minutes. Almost invariably it would be focused on the personal details, occupation and interests of the individual concerned including, on occasion, details about members of his or her family and associates. Rarely would the questioning involve the commission of a specific criminal offence in terms that suggested the individual was a suspect. All answers would be noted painstakingly in writing. The objective quite clearly was to develop and maintain low-level intelligence on the individuals and communities concerned. Huge numbers of individuals from nationalist areas experienced this 'screening' process. Many experienced it on a regular basis. The legality of the practice, however, was highly suspect. The army's four-hour power of arrest could be exercised only on suspicion of a specific criminal offence. Even then it was only intended as a means of enabling the army to go into a dangerous area to arrest a suspect, who would then be passed on to the RUC for further arrest, interrogation and charge. It was never envisaged that the army would use the power to conduct their own arrests and interrogations with a view to gathering intelligence.

These military policing practices perpetuated a sense of military rule which had been a feature of the nationalist areas in question since 1970. This was reinforced by the extent to which the army resorted to the use of lethal force in these areas between Bloody Sunday and 1975. During this short period the security forces shot dead no fewer than 55 civilians, the vast majority of whom were unarmed.[50] Most appear to have been innocent civilians shot dead by the army in nationalist areas. Only six prosecutions were taken against the soldiers responsible. Of these, all but one were acquitted. The one conviction, on a charge of manslaughter, was overturned on appeal.[51]

Interrogation and confessions

A 'criminalisation' or 'Ulsterisation' policy was gradually introduced from about 1975 and officially adopted in 1977.[52] In effect this meant that the IRA campaign against British rule and the loyalist violence would be treated as ordinary criminal activities. Detention without trial would be abandoned in favour of pursuing convictions in the Diplock Courts. Individuals convicted and sentenced to imprisonment by these courts would henceforth be treated as ordinary prisoners rather than as 'special category' prisoners, as had been the practice. Primary responsibility for the formulation and implementation of law enforcement policy would revert to the RUC, with the army providing back-up force when needed.

The successful implementation of this criminalisation policy depended heavily on the RUC being able to secure enough evidence against suspects to ensure their conviction in the Diplock Courts. In the case of republican terrorism, however, the normal processes of police investigation and intelligence gathering, which relied on the cooperation of the community, were not available to the RUC. Such was the hostility to the RUC in nationalist areas that officers could not even enter without a heavy army presence in support. It followed that the necessary evidence would have to come primarily in the form of confessions obtained from suspects through an arrest and interrogation process. The emergency legislation, of course, provided the necessary broad powers of arrest, coupled with very lengthy periods of detention. It also made the necessary changes in trial procedure to ensure that confessions obtained from oppressive detention and interrogation practices would not be ruled inadmissible. All that was needed, therefore, was a policy decision to put this machinery into full effect, and the provision of the necessary infrastructure to cater for the large numbers of suspects who would be arrested, detained and interrogated over extended periods. The policy decision was taken in 1977 and the infrastructure was put in place in the form of Castlereagh Holding Centre in Belfast, the Gough Barracks in Armagh, the Strand Road RUC Station in Derry and the Omagh RUC station.[53]

It was not long before the first complaints of ill-treatment began to emerge from these centres. Suspects who were detained for up to three days or seven days, depending on the particular power of arrest used, complained of repetitive and exhausting interrogation sessions by teams of detectives, lack of sleep, denial of access to legal advice and medical treatment, being held incommunicado, being subjected to threats against themselves and members of their families and, increasingly, being subjected to varying degrees of physical brutality.[54] As the 1970s progressed the volume and gravity of these complaints increased disturbingly until it was quite apparent that these interrogation centres were being run as confession factories with little or no limit to the brutality of the methods being used. The chief police surgeon at Castlereagh eventually resigned in protest at the sort of injuries he was witnessing on suspects coming out of the interrogation cells. The leaders of the four main churches in Northern Ireland publicly expressed their concern at what was happening and two members of the Police Authority for Northern Ireland resigned in protest. As public concern grew Amnesty International visited Northern Ireland for the second time to investigate interrogation practices. It concluded that 'maltreatment of suspected terrorists by the RUC has taken place with sufficient frequency to warrant the establishment of a public inquiry to investigate'.[55] The British government begrudgingly responded by establishing a private inquiry under the chairmanship of Judge Harry Bennett with a remit to examine police interrogation practices for scheduled offences, as opposed to the actual truth of the allegations. By the time the Bennett inquiry reported in February 1979 with a large body of important recommendations, the torrent of complaints had virtually dried up.[56] Clearly the belated establishment of the inquiry had been sufficient to cause a change of policy.

Perhaps the most disturbing feature about the interrogation practices between 1975 and 1979 was not so much what happened in the interrogation room as the effect they had in the courtroom. In each of these years an average of about 1000 individuals were charged with scheduled offences. Over 90 per cent were convicted either on a plea of guilty or after trial in the Diplock Courts. Research carried out in 1979 established that in over 85 per cent of cases the evidence against persons charged with scheduled offences consisted either substantially or exclusively of a confession obtained in the interrogation centres.[57] These statistics, considered in the light of the nature of the interrogation practices employed, give serious cause for concern about the justness of the convictions. This concern is accentuated by the exceptionally long prison sentences which were regularly handed down in these cases. Did the courts shelter behind the torture, inhuman and degrading treatment test to admit into evidence confessions that should not have been admissible in any civilised democracy based on the rule of law? It will be seen later that the courts did not exactly cover themselves in glory in this critical matter.

The supergrass strategy

Even while they were winding down their brutal arrest and interrogation policy the security forces were laying the groundwork for its successor, the supergrass policy. Once again the key legal instruments were the emergency powers of arrest and interrogation. Towards the end of the 1970s the RUC began to use its arrest and detention powers for the purpose of gathering low-level intelligence on individuals and whole communities in much the same way as the army used its statutory power of arrest and detention.[58] The RUC's powers, however, permitted detention without charge for up to three days or seven days depending on the particular power used. The typical pattern was that a joint police and army squad would swoop on the house of the target early in the morning. The occupants would be ordered from their beds and herded into a room, where they would be held while a cursory search of the dwelling was conducted. The target would then be arrested and taken to an RUC interrogation centre, usually Castlereagh or Gough Barracks. The procedure there was identical to that described above in respect of the arrests and interrogations for the purpose of securing confessions, apart from the fact that the individuals concerned were not usually subjected to physical ill-treatment aimed at securing a confession.[59] In fact the critical feature of these interrogations was that the persons detained were not normally interrogated about their suspected involvement in specific criminal offences. Instead they were questioned about their backgrounds, political views, recreational interests, employment, family circumstances, individual family members and associates, as well as persons, political activity and terrorist activity in their neighbourhood. Written notes would be taken of the question and answer sessions in the normal manner. The detained persons would then be released without charge, usually well short of the maximum period for which they could have been held under the power of arrest used. This general practice is reflected in the fact that about 90 per cent of those arrested under the emergency powers during this period were released without charge.[60]

The low-level intelligence gathered by the RUC through this process could be added to their other sources of intelligence to build a very detailed picture of life in some communities and of the lives of some individuals in particular. In general they knew which individuals in a community were experiencing domestic problems of a marital or financial nature, who suffered from alcohol or drug dependency, who were desperately concealing secrets about their personal sexual lives, who were engaged in criminal activities, who were engaged in terrorist activities and who were cheating on their criminal or terrorist associates. With access to this sort of information the RUC was able to identify the weaknesses of individuals in these communities; weaknesses that could be used to pressurise such individuals into acting as informers and ultimately as witnesses against suspect terrorists in their communities.

The procedure was quite simple. The RUC would target vulnerable individuals, whom they would arrest and detain under their three-day or seven-day powers. The period in detention would be used to play on the weakness or fears of the individuals by offering an appropriate reward. Depending on the individual the proffered reward could be money, a job, a new life elsewhere or immunity from prosecution. If individuals were involved in terrorist activity the RUC might offer them a way out by promising immunity in return for their cooperation against their accomplices. They might also apply pressure by threatening to pursue members of their family. A common tactic used here was to threaten to arrest and charge a spouse and have the couple's children taken into care. In any case where the target actually confessed to terrorist activity the RUC had a much stronger hand in offering immunity in return for cooperation.

These tactics were used to devastating effect. It is not possible to put a precise figure on the number of persons that the RUC managed to persuade to act as informers with a view to giving evidence in the

Diplock Courts against their alleged accomplices. However the scale of the operation can be gauged from the fact that between 1980 and 1985 no fewer than 499 terrorist suspects were charged either wholly or partly on the evidence of a former accomplice, or 'supergrass' as they were known. Two hundred and forty nine of these were tried in the Diplock Courts and 190 convicted at first instance.[61] Significantly, many of the supergrasses were confessed terrorists who had been granted immunity for their own terrorist offences. In some cases immunity was even granted for murder. Inevitably there was a strong temptation for such individuals to exaggerate the extent of their knowledge about the activities of terrorist suspects. Their value to the RUC and their bargaining power in terms of immunity were closely connected to their capacity to implicate in serious crimes individuals against whom the RUC was keen to secure convictions.

The manner in which these supergrasses were initially identified and 'turned' was a serious abuse of police power in itself. However the abuse did not stop there. The supergrasses had to be taken under police protection. In some cases this meant that individuals and even whole families disappeared overnight and were not seen again until the committal proceedings months or, in some cases, years later. Attempts by relatives to contact them or establish their whereabouts proved fruitless. It would also appear that many of the supergrasses were coached in the art of giving evidence while being held under police protection. In several cases the supergrass spent days in the witness box giving evidence of scores of offences allegedly committed by many individuals over a period of years. Very few of them cracked under the strain. None had any difficulty in recalling the events in question and most remained unscathed from several days of intense and searching cross-examination. In the case of supergrass Christopher Black, for example, there were 38 defendants, the indictment contained over 184 charges spanning 45 separate incidents in a 14-month period, 550 witnesses gave evidence at the trial, there were 70 000 pages of trial papers and Black was in the witness box for 15 days. When finding all the defendants guilty the trial judge was moved to describe supergrass Black as 'one of the best witnesses I have ever heard'.[62]

The supergrass strategy faded in the mid 1980s after a string of decisions by the Court of Appeal overturned scores of convictions which had been secured on the basis of supergrass evidence. By that time, however, most of those who had been convicted on the tainted evidence had spent long periods in prison, both on remand and after sentencing. Significantly the primary reason given by the Court of Appeal for overturning the convictions was that the trial judges had erred in being too willing to believe the supergrass evidence and had paid insufficient attention to the specific weaknesses which had been exposed by the defence.[63] The irony behind this is that most of the judges who sat on these appeal hearings had themselves convicted at first instance on the uncorroborated evidence of supergrasses. One can only speculate why the judges were so willing to convict at first instance on evidence which they would find flawed on appeal.

The prisons strategy

The whole issue of prisoners is and has always been one of the most sensitive factors in the Northern Ireland conflict over the past 28 years. From the mid 1970s to the early 1980s it was particularly volatile. The government's policy decision to abandon internment and switch from a military strategy to a criminalisation strategy had major implications for the treatment of prisoners.[64] Individuals who had been interned since 1971 were treated as political prisoners. They were housed separately from ordinary prisoners and were permitted to organise themselves after the fashion of prisoners of war. They were also granted a range of privileges which were not available to convicted prisoners, such as wearing their own clothes. Similar privileges were granted to members of paramilitary organisations who were convicted and sentenced to terms of imprisonment for terrorist offences. These were referred to as 'special-category status' prisoners.

The abandonment of special category status was an integral part of the criminalisation strategy. Accordingly a policy decision was taken to treat individuals convicted in the Diplock Courts from February 1976 onwards as ordinary prisoners. Republican and, to a lesser extent, loyalist prisoners refused to accept that they were ordinary criminals. In their eyes the offences for which they were sentenced had been politically motivated, and as such they believed that they should be treated as political prisoners. The first convicted republicans to be denied special category status immediately embarked on a protest which entailed refusing to wear prison clothes, breaking prison furniture and refusing to conform to ordinary prison regime. The authorities, in turn, were determined to break the prisoners' resistance and impose the criminalisation policy upon them. The prisoners were left without beds or furniture in their cells during the day, were denied ordinary privileges such as food parcels and visits, were subjected to regular spells of solitary confinement and had nothing to wrap themselves in but a blanket. If they wished to leave their cells for any purpose they either had to do so in prison clothes or naked. The prisoners responded by refusing to come out of their cells to wash, shave and slop out. Over a period of months their hair and beards grew long and matted and they smeared the walls of their cells with excrement. Needless to say, photographs of the prisoners in these conditions and clothed only in a blanket provoked strong protest from the nationalist community on the outside. Still the British government, under Margaret Thatcher, refused to budge. An application on behalf of the prisoners to the European Commission on Human Rights also failed. Their ultimate form of protest was the hunger strike, which eventually resulted in the death of Bobby Sands on 5 May 1981, followed at intervals by nine more republican prisoners.[65]

The impact of the hunger strikes on the nationalist community was dramatic. Once again mass demonstrations were organised on the streets, not just in protest against British policy but also at the funerals of the hunger strikers. Bobby Sands was elected a Westminster MP for Fermanagh-South Tyrone. Fellow hunger striker Kieran Doherty and blanket protestor Paddy Agnew were elected members of the Irish parliament. The depth of nationalist alienation was reflected in the establishment of Sinn Fein as a serious political organisation, which has since gone from strength to strength. Long after the protest ended, largely as a result of action by the families of the hunger strikers, the legacy of the hunger strikes has continued to reverberate. Indeed it would be no exaggeration to say that to this day events within the prisons have had a decisive impact on the stance taken by the paramilitary organisations and their political associates on the outside.

Shoot-to-kill

As the supergrass strategy faded a 'shoot-to-kill' policy began to assume greater prominence. This refers broadly to the policy of resorting to the use of lethal force in circumstances where such action would appear to have been excessive. Of course 'shoot-to-kill' had been a regular component of security strategy since the violence broke out in 1969. Bloody Sunday itself was the most extreme example. Throughout the remainder of the 1970s and the 1980s a steady stream of individuals were shot by the security forces in circumstances where the use of lethal force appeared unjustified. The most poignant, perhaps, were the seven children shot dead by plastic bullets.[66] From the early 1980s to the early 1990s, however, it would appear that the security forces used lethal force with particular enthusiasm. Between November 1982 and September 1992 the security forces in Northern Ireland shot dead 75 civilians in over 50 separate incidents in circumstances which suggested that a shoot-to-kill policy was in operation.[67] Some of these incidents involved the ambush of suspected terrorists, who were shot dead in circumstances where arrest would appear to have been a viable option. In several of these cases the suspects were unarmed, and in some cases they turned out to be ordinary criminals or innocent civilians. Other examples included the shooting of individuals at close range with plastic bullets in a riot situation, the shooting of joyriders at roadblocks and the shooting of innocent civilians in disputed circumstances.

Both the British Army and the RUC participated in this shoot-to-kill policy. Many of the army shootings were carried out by members of the SAS, who are trained to respond with maximum fire-power against any threat to life. Significantly, many of the RUC shootings were carried out by their E4A undercover squad. This is a unit within the RUC which has been specially trained by the SAS to respond with maximum firepower against any threat to life. Neither their training nor their special status in the army and the RUC conferred any legal immunity on the members of the SAS or the E4A for their actions. It follows that if they resorted to the use of maximum firepower in any instance where that amounted to the use of excessive force they would be guilty of murder if their victim died. Despite this, prosecutions for murder or manslaughter were initiated in respect of only nine of the fatal shooting incidents mentioned above, resulting in the conviction of four soldiers for murder.

Public concern about the alleged use of a shoot-to-kill policy, coupled with pressure from the Irish government, resulted in the establishment of an inquiry into six of the ambush deaths that were alleged to have resulted from the policy in the early 1980s. Officially the inquiry was established by the chief constable of the RUC, who called in the deputy chief constable of Greater Manchester, John Stalker, to head it up in May 1984. Sensationally, Stalker was removed from the inquiry three days before he was due to complete what he described as the last and most important part of his investigation. His removal resulted from an unprecedented decision to suspend him from his duties as deputy chief constable while weak and vague disciplinary allegations against him were investigated by Colin Sampson, the chief constable of the West Yorkshire Police. He was eventually cleared of all of the allegations, but by that time the RUC inquiry had been handed over to Colin Sampson for completion. John Stalker subsequently published a book on his experiences at that time.[68] His book offers a shocking and sinister account which leaves the reader with little doubt not only that a shoot-to-kill policy was in operation, but also that very senior police and political figures were prepared to ensure that the truth was not disclosed. Equally disturbing is the fact that Sampson's report was never published. The attorney general did report subsequently to parliament that the report disclosed serious offences of obstructing and perverting the course of justice on the part of several RUC officers.[69] He went on to say that the DPP had decided that it would not be proper to institute criminal proceedings. The basis for this decision appears to have been considerations of public interest and, in particular, national security. Once again the security forces were receiving a loud and very clear message that they were above the law in the methods they adopted in the name of combatting terrorism.

Amnesty International's investigation of killings by the security forces between 1982 and 1986 highlights the problem posed by these killings:

> The pattern that has emerged, and that causes concern, is one of repeated allegations that suspects are arbitrarily killed rather than being arrested, that members of the security forces believe they can operate with impunity, and that this is reinforced by government failure to take steps to prevent unlawful killings. The government evades responsibility by hiding behind an array of legal procedures and secret inquiries which serve to cloud the issues. These issues are: whether there is a policy at any official level to kill government opponents rather than to detain them (this includes allegations of collusion between the security forces and Loyalist armed groups), whether legislation acts as an effective deterrent to unlawful killings, whether disputed incidents are thoroughly and impartially investigated and whether perpetrators of unlawful killings are brought to justice.[70]

Collusion with loyalist paramilitaries

Ever since the establishment of the Provisional IRA in 1970 there have been allegations of collusion between the security forces and loyalist paramilitaries. Given the close affinity between the loyalist community and the local security forces, namely the RUC, the B Specials and their successors, the Ulster Defence Regiment (now designated the Royal Irish Regiment of the regular British Army), it was always inevitable that there would be contact and even cooperation between members of the security forces and loyalist groupings.[71] In the late 1960s members of the B Specials took part in the loyalist attacks on civil rights demonstrations. Several members of the UDR have been charged and convicted of the sectarian murder of innocent Catholics. There have also been very strong suspicions that the British Army and intelligence services assisted loyalist paramilitaries in committing some major atrocities such as the bombings in Dublin and Monaghan, in which 33 civilians were killed and 100 injured,[72] and the murder of the members of the Miami Showband. It is becoming increasingly apparent that the security forces cultivated a number of informers within loyalist organisations, ostensibly to counter terrorist activities by loyalists. In practice it would appear that this also involved the security forces turning a blind eye to several loyalist attacks on republicans in which these informers were involved. The most notorious of these informers would appear to have been Brian Nelson. The truth about his terrorist activities against nationalists, committed with the connivance of the British Army, is only beginning to surface.

Public concern about the extent of collusion between the security forces and the loyalist paramilitaries was fuelled in the late 1980s and early 1990s when confidential security intelligence about republican suspects increasingly began to surface in loyalist paramilitary circles.[73] Many of those identified in the security documents were targeted by loyalist paramilitaries in terrorist actions which resulted in the death of more than one hundred individuals between 1990 and 1994 alone. Evidence of security force involvement in these executions is mounting steadily.[74] Indeed the circumstances surrounding many of the killings followed a similar pattern. It would begin with the victim being stopped and questioned by the RUC on a regular basis and being arrested and interrogated frequently. He would allege that RUC detectives often threatened him on these occasions and that he had not got long to live as he would be set up for assassination by loyalist paramilitaries. This would be followed by official warnings from the RUC that his life was in danger as details from his security file had fallen into the hands of loyalist paramilitaries. In the days preceding his shooting he would be subjected to close surveillance by the RUC, or there would be heightened security force activity in the area where he lived immediately prior to the shooting. The security presence would suddenly be withdrawn just before the arrival of the loyalist gunmen. Almost invariably the terrorists were able to enter the area where their victim lived, carry out the shooting and leave without being apprehended. The subsequent RUC investigation of the murder often proved deficient in one or more respects. Generally it contrasted markedly with the lengths to which the RUC would go to secure convictions against republicans for the murder of members of the security forces.[75] Indeed they even went as far as to seek a judicial review of a coroner's decision to prevent an inquest from hearing evidence which would expose serious inadequacies in their investigations, and to prevent the inquest record from including material about the victim's complaints about being threatened with death at the hands of loyalists while in RUC custody.[76] In addition to all this, loyalists are now freely admitting that they received intelligence reports on republican suspects from elements within the RUC on an almost daily basis.[77]

Collusion between the security forces and loyalist paramilitaries coincided with the complaints that elements within the RUC were systematically intimidating and harrassing lawyers representing republican suspects. Indeed there are good grounds to believe not only that such intimidation and harrassment has been and continues to be a serious problem, but also that it was linked to collusion with loyalist paramilitaries.[78] A typical complaint is that RUC detectives interrogating suspects in their custody will harangue the suspects with allegations about their chosen solicitors. These allegations include assertions that the solicitor in question is a member of the IRA and therefore the suspect must also be a member,[79] is incompetent and gives bad advice, is responsible for many of his or her clients being convicted and sentenced to long terms of imprisonment, and is only interested in his or her fee. Clients have also reported that interrogating officers regularly make abusive remarks about and death threats against their solicitors.[80] The general objective seems to be to scare suspects away from experienced defence solicitors.

The most sinister aspect of the intimidation of defence lawyers is the link between it and loyalist paramilitary death squads. Two solicitors who were favourite targets of abuse by some RUC detectives were shot dead by loyalist terrorists in circumstances which raised serious concern about collusion with the RUC. Patrick Finucane, a Belfast solicitor who featured prominently in the defence of republican suspects, was shot dead in 1989 in his home in front of his wife and children. Although a loyalist paramilitary organisation claimed responsibility for his murder there has always be a strong suspicion of RUC involvement.[81] In the few months before the shooting, clients of his who had been interrogated by the RUC reported that RUC detectives had made death threats against him. No prosecutions have ever been brought in respect of his killing despite the fact that an inquiry conducted by the deputy chief constable of Cambridgeshire is thought to have produced sufficient evidence for charges to be brought.[82] The RUC investigation of Finucane's murder reflects many of the deficiencies associated with their investigation of the execution of republican suspects by loyalist terrorists. In this case they did not even bother to interview Finucane's wife, who was both a victim of and an eyewitness to her husband's murder. The RUC's handling of the investigation has itself been the subject of an investigation by Param Cumaraswamy, the UN special rapporteur on the independence of judges and lawyers. In his report to the UN Commission on Human Rights he called on the British government to appoint an independent judicial inquiry to investigate the outstanding questions which remain in respect of the murder of Patrick Finucane.[83] The British government very swiftly rejected this request. Since then, however, the chief constable of the RUC has invited the former deputy chief constable of Cambridgeshire, John Stevens to re-open the inquiry into Patrick Finucane's murder. At the time of writing, that inquiry is ongoing and to date has resulted in charges being preferred against one individual.

The second case was that of Rosemary Nelson, who acquired a high profile in the 1990s because of her representation of the nationalist community on the Garvaghy Road[84] and her defence of some prominent republican suspects.[85] She alleged that she had been assaulted, spat upon and directly threatened on several occasions by RUC officers. Her clients have also stated that detectives told them she was supplying sex to her clients and 'must be good in bed'. She was blown up by a bomb planted under her car by loyalists terrorists in March 1999. Once again there are strong suspicions of RUC collusion. In the months prior to her death Nelson voiced fears for her safety as a result of the threats made against her by RUC detectives. The chief constable of the RUC called in the chief constable of Kent to assist in the investigation of her murder. At the time of writing he has effectively been replaced at the head of the investigation by the Deputy Chief Constable of Norfolk, Colin Port. It remains to be seen how that investigation will be conducted. If the RUC investigation into her complaints of intimidation and harassment is anything to go by, it is most unlikely that it will bring to justice all those culpable for her death. The Independent Commission for Police Complaints, which supervised the RUC investigation into her complaints, has presented a damning indictment of the manner in which it was conducted. In particular it found that: (1) the value of the interviews of the police officers concerned was undermined by the fact that they had been prompted to prepare statements in advance of their interviews; (2) '[t]he ill-disguised hostility to Mrs Nelson on the part of some of the police officers was indicative of a mindset which could be viewed as bordering on the obstructive'; (3) when drafting the report of the investigation the chief inspector made 'a number of assertions which constitute judgments on the moral character of Mrs Nelson and others'; (4) the chief inspector carrying out the investigation 'appeared to have difficulty in cooperating productively with the independent supervision of the investigation'; (5) another senior officer equated the evidence of Mrs Nelson with that of her clients, whom he deemed unreliable; and (6) concerns raised by the independent supervisor during the course of the investigation were 'either not addressed or addressed unsatisfactorily'.[86] The commission was so concerned with the manner in which the investigation was being handled that it took the unprecedented step of conveying its concerns to the secretary of state. This resulted in the RUC being removed from the investigation and replaced by Commander Niall Mulvihill of the London Metropolitan Police. The commission has declared itself satisfied with the latter inquiry, the results of which have not been published.[87]

The courts and the law

The nature and extent of the abuse described above inevitably raise questions of legality. Despite the very broad powers conferred on the security forces by the emergency legislation it is difficult to imagine that many of these practices were lawful. The question that must be asked now, therefore, is what was the response of the law? From the outset it must be emphasised that, unlike the Republic of Ireland, Northern Ireland does not have a written constitution protecting fundamental rights. Nor does it have an entrenched bill of rights against which the legality of police and security practices can be tested.[88] Instead, allegations of abuse by the security forces must be tested through the normal civil and criminal processes. The courts have therefore played a vital role in determining what is and what is not acceptable practice by the security forces in the exercise of their emergency powers, just as they were the arbiters of what was acceptable under the special powers legislation. As a generalisation it must be said that they do not appear to have been any more active in curbing the excesses of the security forces since Bloody Sunday than they were before it. The pattern has been very similar, with the courts adopting an exceptionally passive and supine stance when called upon to uphold the fundamental rights of the individual and due process values against the immediate interests of the security forces. This will now be illustrated by a brief survey of judicial decisions in cases which tested the scope of police and army powers that were central to the primary practices described above, namely powers in respect of army screening arrests, police arrests, interrogation and the use of lethal force. It must also be said that at least part of the explanation for the judicial failure to prevent or punish these abuses can be laid at the door of the police and prosecution agencies, which did not initiate prosecutions in many cases where prosecution would appear to have been warranted.

Stop and search

The police and army powers of summary stop, question and search have rarely featured in reported case law. The scope of the powers are so broad that it is difficult to mount a serious challenge to them in the Northern Irish courts. In *Carlisle v Chief Constable of the RUC*,[89] however, it was accepted that routine stops and frisk searches were not permitted. The searching officer or soldier must genuinely be searching the individual for munitions or transmitters. However, this does not alter the fact that no prior suspicion is required to stop and search any individual.

House searches have featured occasionally in reported case law but this has not led to any more protection of the human rights and civil liberties of the occupants than is the case with individuals stopped, questioned and searched on the streets.[90] Even the European Commission of Human Rights rejected a claim that the detention of the occupants during the search of a dwelling was in breach of the European Convention on the Protection of Human Rights and Fundamental Freedoms.[91]

Army screening arrests

In *Murray v Ministry of Defence*[92] the plaintiff had been arrested under the army's four-hour power at her house by a squad of armed soldiers. She had been taken to the nearest army 'screening centre' where she had been questioned purely about her private life and about her brother, who had been convicted for gun-running in the United States. She had not been questioned directly about her suspected involvement in a criminal offence. Clearly hers was the classic example of a screening arrest. Indeed the details of the question and answer session were even recorded on a standard army form, headed 'Screening Proforma'. Part one of this form related to personal details and Part II to details of offences.

It was explained earlier that the four-hour power was conferred on soldiers for the purpose of enabling them to go into areas or situations to arrest individuals who would otherwise be inaccessible to the RUC.

Once the individuals had been arrested and their identity established they were handed over to the RUC. The power was never meant to be used for the purpose of interrogating the arrested individuals in order to gather intelligence, although that was the primary use to which it was put by the army.

Murray challenged the legality of her arrest on several grounds, including that she had not been genuinely suspected of a criminal offence. The court was therefore being offered an opportunity to declare unlawful the standard army practice of using the four-hour power for screening purposes. Instead it upheld the legality of the arrest by accepting that the officer who had effected the arrest had had a genuine suspicion, based upon what she had been told by intelligence officers, that the plaintiff had committed a criminal offence. The court went on to hold that the mere fact that the motive of the intelligence officers in ordering the arrest had been to pursue matters unconnected with any offence the plaintiff may have committed did not invalidate the arrest itself. The implication is that it was quite lawful for the army to use the four-hour power for screening purposes as long as it went through the motions of planting a genuine suspicion in the mind of the arresting officer. If ever there was an example of a technicality getting in the way of justice, this was it. The court clearly bent over backwards to avoid imposing a substantive restriction on the oppressive manner in which the army used this four-hour power. It is worth remarking, indeed, that the judicial decision in this case reflects even greater deference to the primacy of security interests over individual rights than that shown by the Diplock Commission (which first recommended the power), the British government (which proposed it) and parliament (which enacted it into law).

Mrs Murray also challenged the legality of the army's action on the ground of false imprisonment. When the soldiers had arrived at her house at 7 am the whole family had been in bed. Her husband and children had been ordered out of their beds and held captive in a room by armed soldiers while other soldiers had checked out the house and taken Mrs Murray into another room to get dressed. Although she had twice asked whether she was under arrest she had received no answer until 7.30 am, when she had been taken away. The Court of Appeal accepted that had she or any members of the family attempted to leave the house at any time between 7.00 am and 7.30 am they would have been restrained by the soldiers. Bizarrely, however, the court also found that she had not realised that she was not free to go, and therefore was not a victim of the tort of false imprisonment. The House of Lords overruled the Court of Appeal on this point, holding that it was not necessary for a prisoner to be aware of his or her imprisonment in order to satisfy the tort of false imprisonment. Nevertheless the House of Lords upheld the Court of Appeal's ultimate decision in favour of the army on the basis that it had been reasonable to imprison her husband and children in one room and delay the arrest of Mrs Murray until the soldiers had been ready to leave. In other words it was reasonable to subordinate an individual's fundamental liberty and privacy in his or her own home to military expediency. This is neatly summed up in the following statement by Lord Justice Griffiths on the imprisonment of Mrs Murray's husband and children in one room:

> I also regard it as an entirely reasonable precaution that all the occupants of the house should be asked to assemble in one room. As Cpl Davies explained in evidence, this procedure is followed because the soldiers may be distracted by other occupants in the house rushing from one room to another, perhaps in a state of alarm, perhaps for the purpose of raising the alarm and to resist arrest. In such circumstances a tragic shooting accident might all to easily happen with young, often relatively inexperienced, armed soldiers operating under conditions of extreme tension.[93]

Similarly, on the issue of delaying the formal arrest beyond the point where Mrs Murray was actually a prisoner, the learned lord justice said:

> It was in my opinion entirely reasonable to delay the words of arrest until the party was about to leave the house. If words of arrest are spoken as soon as the house is entered before any precautions have been taken to search the house and find the other occupants, it seems to me that there is a real risk that the alarm may be raised and an attempt made to resist arrest, not only by those within the house but also by summoning assistance from those in the immediate neighbourhood.[94]

What Lord Justice Griffiths considered entirely reasonable in these circumstances represented a significant development in what the law had always been understood to be. Moreover his concept of reasonableness was heavily coloured by the immediate requirements of the military and not at all by the interests of innocent individuals being secure and free in their own homes from intrusive harassment at the hands of armed agents of the state. Nevertheless the British government was happy to adopt the judicial lead.[95] The Emergency Provisions Act 1991 empowered the police to require any person in a building (including a dwelling) being searched to remain in a part of the building for a period of up to four hours. This could be extended by a further four hours.[96] The current power is contained in Section 19(4) of the 1996 Act.

It must also be acknowledged that some judicial decisions on the four-hour power went against the military. In *Walsh v Ministry of Defence*,[97] for example, the plaintiff had been arrested under this power because she was believed to have associated with a member of an illegal organisation. The court held that associating with a member of an illegal organisation did not constitute a criminal offence, and as such the arrest was unlawful. Exemplary damages were awarded in this case. As welcome as this decision was it lost much of its significance in the light of the decision in the Murray case. The plaintiff succeeded only because the army had been careless about satisfying the prerequisites for a valid arrest. The victory had no substantive implications for the validity of using the arrest power for screening purposes. Another minor victory occurred in the Murray case itself. The plaintiff had been frisk searched, as was the normal practice in these arrests, but the legislation did not confer a specific power of search in these circumstances. The Court of Appeal held that in the absence of a specific statutory power authorising the search it was unlawful as it had be carried out without good reason. Damages of £250 were awarded.

Such victories can be classified as minor or technical in the context of defeat on the major issue. Indeed, they reflect the pattern evident in the days of the Special Powers Act, when the courts were prepared to rule against the security forces and the executive in minor matters but upheld the legitimacy of their actions on major matters of concern to the fundamental rights and freedoms of the individual.

Police arrest powers

The judicial approach in the Murray case was consistent with that applied to the RUC's emergency powers of arrest. The net effect was to ensure that the police could resort to arrest as a convenient and flexible tool when investigating suspect terrorists. It will be remembered that the seven-day power under the prevention of terrorism legislation and the old three-day power under the emergency provisions legislation could be exercised on the basis of a reasonable suspicion of terrorism. There was no need for the suspicion to be connected to a specific identifiable offence. Despite the tremendously broad scope of such powers the courts managed to extend them further by a very loose interpretation of what constitutes reasonable suspicion. In *R v Officer in Charge of Police Office, Castlereagh, Belfast, ex parte Lynch*,[98] Lord Chief Justice Lowry ruled in the Court of Appeal that it would be sufficient for a constable making an arrest under the seven-day power to have a general suspicion that the individual concerned was somehow involved in terrorist activity. The fact that the constable did not know the nature of the terrorist activity nor the extent to which the individual was involved in it was irrelevant. The RUC could use this power as a means of starting its investigation into these matters. Such an interpretation effectively emasculated the protection that reasonableness was meant to secure for the liberty of the individual in the face of a police investigation. The Lynch case also established that the requirement to inform individuals of the grounds for their arrest under the seven-day power would be satisfied by telling them that they were being arrested under the statutory provision in question because they were suspected of involvement in terrorist activities.

The ability of the RUC to use their emergency powers of arrest to gather intelligence received a major boost from the decision of the House of Lords in *McKee v The Chief Constable for Northern Ireland*.[99] In that case the plaintiff had been arrested by an RUC officer in a pre-planned, joint army–RUC swoop on his house. The arresting officer, as was typical in these cases, had been acting on instructions from his superior officer. He had had no knowledge about the plaintiff that would have been sufficient to form a reasonable suspicion that the plaintiff was involved in terrorist activities. His suspicion had been based solely on information he had been given by his superior officer. Nevertheless the House of Lords ruled that the arresting officer could have formed the necessary reasonable suspicion in such circumstances. The sting in the tail was a further ruling that the court would not investigate the superior officer's suspicion to see if it had been based on reasonable grounds. The explanation for this judicial reticence was that it was the suspicion of the arresting officer alone which was relevant. Since the superior officer had not effected the arrest his suspicion was irrelevant. The net effect of this ruling, therefore, was that if a senior RUC officer instructed his subordinate that he had reason to believe that a named individual was or had been engaged in a certain terrorist activity and the subordinate officer then formed a suspicion that the individual was so engaged, the latter could proceed to arrest the named individual. Not only would the arrest be perfectly lawful, but the court would refuse to consider whether the senior officer had genuinely entertained the necessary suspicion against the individual concerned and whether that suspicion had been based on reasonable grounds. Since most RUC intelligence-gathering arrest operations have been conducted in the manner featured in the McKee case it would appear that they are virtually unchallengeable. The courts have freed the RUC of even the limited constraints imposed by the legislation.

The full implications of the decision in the above cases are illustrated in the later case of *O'Hara v The Chief Constable for Northern Ireland*.[100] In this case the arresting officer had attended a briefing session by a senior officer in which he had been told that the plaintiff was suspected of being involved in a murder. The purpose of the briefing session had been to plan the arrest and search operation, in the course of which the officer was to arrest the plaintiff. Like the McKee case, this case went all the way to the House of Lords, where the central question considered was whether the officer could have formed the requisite reasonable suspicion in these circumstances. The House of Lords confirmed that the critical issue was what had been in the mind of the arresting officer.[101] As long as he had sufficient information to afford him reasonable grounds for his suspicion the arrest would be lawful. This information could have come from his senior officer and it would not matter that it subsequently proved to be inaccurate. In this case the only material before the court about the information available to the arresting officer was that he had been told that the plaintiff was suspected of a recent murder. Nevertheless the trial court held that this was sufficient to afford reasonable grounds for the suspicion. The House of Lords saw no reason to interfere with this finding. A judicial decision more sympathetic to the interests of the security forces and prejudicial to the liberty of the individual would be difficult to find. Once again the courts failed to interpret and apply the law in a manner which afforded even minimal protection to the liberty of the individual when pitched against the needs of the security forces.

Admittedly there have been some minor victories for the rights and freedoms of the individual on the arrest and detention front. In *Clinton v Chief Constable of the RUC*,[102] for example, it was held that if a person questioned his or her arrest under the seven-day power on suspicion of involvement in terrorism the police must supply information 'in general terms' of the matters which constituted reasonable grounds for the suspicion. Moreover even if an arrest for questioning was initially lawful the subsequent detention would become unlawful if the suspect was assaulted during questioning. Accordingly in *ex parte Gillen*[103] the court ruled that the applicant, who had suffered a perforated eardrum due to ill-treatment during questioning, could be granted a writ of *habeas corpus* to secure his release. If persons have been detained unlawfully they are entitled to monetary compensation even if the period of unlawful detention has been relatively short. In *Petticrew v Chief Constable of the RUC*,[104] for example, the plaintiff had been arrested and detained for questioning under the emergency legislation. Before being released she had been further detained for a medical examination. The court held that the legislation did not permit the police to detain the individual against her will for the purposes of offering her a medical examination. She was awarded £300 in damages. Similarly in *Moore v Chief Constable of the RUC*[105] a suspect who had been arrested and detained under the emergency legislation was awarded £150 in damages for the one or two hours of detention which the police failed to justify. The relevant rate went up in 1993, when the court ruled that £600 per hour would be appropriate for the first twelve hours of unlawful detention, with a lesser sum being appropriate for each hour thereafter if it appeared that the distress caused had lessened.[106] Welcome as these decisions were, it is submitted that they have since done little to soften the impact of the extensive and oppressive use of the police and army powers of arrest and detention and the associated powers of entry and search.

Access to a solicitor

Access to a solicitor (as well as family members and so on) has always been severely limited in the case of persons arrested under the emergency legislation. It used to be the case that the RUC regularly refused access until the suspect had made a full confession. The Bennett Committee, however, recommended that there should be an absolute right of access after 48 hours in detention. This meant, of course, that the RUC adopted a policy of absolute refusal for the first 48 hours. Indeed the emergency legislation since 1987 has stipulated that the police may delay access (during the first 48 hours of detention) on certain grounds, including if they consider that granting access would interfere with the gathering of information about an act of terrorism, or would result in persons being alerted, thereby making it more difficult to prevent an act of terrorism or apprehend a person involved in a terrorist act.[107]

For many years the RUC took full advantage of the scope for delay, particularly in cases where terrorist suspects requested a solicitor against whom the RUC was hostile. Initially the courts were very supportive. In *R v Harper*,[108] for example, the Court of Appeal held that it was sufficient to deny access to a solicitor if the police reasonably believed that there was a real risk of a legal adviser being used as an unwilling agent to convey information of interest to terrorists. In *In re Kenneway's Application*[109] the court even accepted the unlikely argument that the RUC was justified to deny access if it was thought that a solicitor could be kidnapped and forced to release information against his or her will. It must also be said that the courts have displayed an increased willingness to examine evidence put forward by the RUC to justify denial of access. Even more important in practice, perhaps, is their acceptance that a refusal of access is amenable to judicial review,[110] and that interim relief may be granted to prevent the interrogation of a suspect pending a judicial review of an RUC decision to deny access.[111] The net result is that the RUC has been more judicious in the exercise of its power to deny access.[112] It is also worth noting that the European Court of Human Rights has now ruled that a denial of immediate access to legal advice, when coupled with the court's power to draw adverse inferences from the suspect's silence during police interrogation, violated the fair trial provisions of Article 6 of the European Convention.[113]

By contrast the courts have been distinctly more reticent about recognising and enforcing a suspect's right to have his or her solicitor present during police interrogation. The courts have moved from a position of refusing to recognise the right to be present to one of treating each application on its merits. However the RUC routinely denies applications for solicitors to be present and there is no evidence of a willingness on the part of the courts to second-guess such decisions.[114] In *In re Russell's Application*, for example, Lord Chief Justice Hutton said that it was the general intent of parliament that the police should be able to 'create a situation in which a guilty man is more likely than he would otherwise have been to overcome his initial reluctance to speak and to unburden himself to his questioners'.[115] While the lord chief justice accepted that the police had a discretion to permit a solicitor to be present during the interrogation it should be exercised only in exceptional circumstances. The issue went all the way to the House of Lords *in R v. Chief Constable of the RUC, ex parte Begley*.[116] The applicants in that case argued that the House of Lords should develop the common law so as to recognise a suspect's right to have a solicitor present during questioning in police custody under the emergency legislation. They argued that this was necessary to help offset prejudice to the accused which may result from the provisions of the Criminal Evidence (Northern Ireland) Order 1988 which permits the court to draw adverse inferences from the failure of the accused to mention certain facts when questioned in police custody. Their Lordships, however, declined the invitation. In his opinion (which was adopted by the other members) Lord Browne-Wilkinson considered that the express intention of Parliament was to deny suspects in Northern Ireland the services of their solicitor when being questioned in police custody under the emergency legislation. This was despite the fact that suspects in the rest of the UK did enjoy such a right by statute even when being questioned in custody under the Prevention of Terrorism legislation.

Interrogation and the admissibility of evidence

Despite the brutal interrogation methods that were undoubtedly used in the RUC interrogation centres in the mid to late 1970s not one prosecution was taken against the police officers involved. In one celebrated case the Police Authority for Northern Ireland exercised its power to require the chief constable to refer a complaint of ill-treatment to a tribunal. The case in question concerned Joseph Rafferty, who had been arrested by the RUC under its emergency powers and interrogated in the Omagh RUC station over a period of three days in November 1976.[117] Upon his release he had been taken by the RUC to Omagh hospital. He had complained that he had been subjected to severe physical ill-treatment at the hands of his RUC interrogators. Medical examinations by the police doctor, his own doctor and at the hospital all confirmed that he had been physically abused. Afterwards a local councillor and member of the police authority had unsuccessfully attempted on five occasions to raise the case with the police authority, but had eventually resigned in disgust at its inaction. Indeed the authority did not direct the chief constable to set up the tribunal until two years after the event, and the tribunal itself did not get down to the substance of the case until December 1980. During the proceedings an RUC chief superintendent admitted that detectives must have assaulted Rafferty and that the only issue was the identity of the detectives involved. It also emerged that in the initial RUC internal investigation into the complaint the detectives had refused to take part in an identification parade. A similar attitude was displayed at the tribunal proceedings and 28 detectives refused to give evidence. The High Court ruled that it had no power to compel the officers to give evidence to the tribunal.[118] The net result was that the case collapsed in the face of an RUC wall of silence.

Despite the fact that concern about the physical ill-treatment of suspects in the interrogation centres has continually been voiced over the past 20 years, there have been no successful prosecutions of the police officers involved.[119] This of course is partly due to the failure of the DPP to institute proceedings against police officers in cases such as *ex parte Gillen*,[120] where the suspect's eardrum had been perforated in the course of his interrogation. Prosecutions of police officers were brought in the case of the 'UDR Four',[121] four members of the UDR who had been convicted in 1986 of the sectarian murder of a Catholic. They claimed that their confessions had been obtained by oppressive interrogation methods. Their convictions were eventually referred back to the Court of Appeal by the secretary of state. The court, in quashing the convictions in the case of three of them, found that RUC officers had lied under oath and had altered written evidence. Prosecutions were taken subsequently against four of the officers involved, but these resulted in acquittal.[122]

The courts were also called upon to denounce the brutal interrogation practices in challenges to the admissibility of confession evidence in those cases which went to trial on the basis of confessions obtained by the use of such methods. The primary obstacle to overcome was the torture, inhuman and degrading treatment test, which had been introduced by emergency legislation to facilitate the conviction of suspected terrorists. The critical issues were how the courts would interpret the new admissibility test and whether they would believe the allegations of ill-treatment in the face of repeated police assertions that interrogations were carried out with the utmost regard for the rights and comfort of the suspect. The courts' performance on these matters might be described as their greatest failure to protect the individual against oppressive security policies. From the outset they interpreted the test in a manner which afforded maximum discretion to the interrogators, and reached conclusions which displayed a disturbing lack of appreciation of the effects of the detention and interrogations practices inflicted on the suspects.

In *R v McCormick*,[123] one of the leading cases on the interpretation of the test, Lord Justice McGonigal explained that the 'torture, inhuman and degrading treatment' threshold would appear to permit 'a degree of physical violence which could never be tolerated by the courts under the common law test' and would free an interrogator to 'use a moderate degree of physical maltreatment for the purpose of inducing a person to make a statement'. Subsequent judicial decisions, and statutory enactment, make it clear that confessions obtained pursuant to the use of physical violence or threat of violence would not be admitted under the test. Nevertheless it is quite plain that Lord Justice

McGonigal's interpretation leaves substantial scope for interrogators to resort to oppressive methods without running the risk of a confession being excluded. Repetitive and exhausting interrogation sessions, for example, would not be sufficient in themselves. Neither would shouting, the use of abusive language,[124] threats to arrest and interrogate other family members, threats to arrest the suspect repeatedly until he or she confessed, and denial of access to a solicitor.

Even if the accused has been subjected to torture or inhuman or degrading treatment it does not follow that any consequent confession will be excluded. In *R v McGrath*,[125] for example, the accused had been arrested and interrogated for the same offence in June 1976, again in March 1977 and again in November 1977, when he finally confessed. He argued that the repeated arrests and interrogations, which seemed set to continue until he did confess, amounted to mental torture and inhuman treatment. Not only did the court decide that the accused had not suffered torture and inhuman treatment but it went on to rule that the statutory test was aimed at discouraging the *deliberate* infliction of torture, inhuman and degrading treatment. It was not concerned with police conduct or practices which were not intended to subject the suspect to such treatment. It would seem to follow that if the accused confessed after being subjected to torture, inhuman and degrading treatment his confession would not be excluded automatically if it transpired that the RUC had not meant to subject him to treatment of that nature. Furthermore in both the McGrath case and *R v Milne*[126] the courts emphasised that the torture, inhuman and degrading treatment must have been inflicted *for the purpose of securing a confession*. It would seem to follow, therefore, that if the interrogators abused a suspect in order to avenge the death of a colleague and the suspect confessed to a serious crime in the hope that it would end the abuse, his confession would not be excluded automatically.

Probably one of the most astounding decisions to have been handed down by the courts during this phase was that in *R v McKearney*.[127] In this case the accused was interrogated on 33 occasions over a seven-day period. In the course of the first 13 interrogations he allegedly admitted membership of an illegal organisation. The trial judge, Justice Murray, excluded this confession on the ground that the prosecution had not satisfactorily proved that it had not been induced by physical ill-treatment. During interrogations 14 to 16 the accused allegedly admitted complicity in a murder. Justice Murray admitted this statement as the accused had not alleged that this second statement had been made as a result of further ill-treatment or fear of further ill-treatment. One might consider that this would have been unnecessary. The accused had still been in the custody of the very individuals who had ill-treated him in the earlier sessions. It was only to be expected that his mind would continue to be affected by that experience at least until he had been released. However Justice Murray gave this notion short shrift in the following terms:

> Even if any conduct on the part of the detectives at any of the earlier interviews had created in the mind of the accused a fear or a sense of oppression, the time that had passed since those interviews and the proper form and tone of the interviews … had completely dissipated any such fear or sense of oppression.

Even if Justice Murray's interpretation of the situation was an accurate reflection of McKearney's state of mind in this case, it is respectfully submitted that his approach fell below even the minimum standard necessary for a fair trial. In any liberal democracy based on the rule of law a criminal trial must not only be fair but must be seen to be fair to the accused. Surely most people would be disturbed to find that a conviction for murder could be returned on the basis of a confession the accused had made when being interrogated by RUC officers in the same room of the same RUC station where he had been seriously ill-treated by RUC officers earlier in the same period of detention. Attempting to justify the admission of the confession on the basis that the effects of the earlier ill-treatment had worn off risks the appearance of being oversensitive to the interests of the prosecution at the expense of fairness to the accused.

Clearly the mere fact that a confession is not voluntary will not be sufficient in itself to warrant its exclusion. In *R v Dillon and Gorman*,[128] for example, the court ruled that a confession would be admissible under the torture, inhuman and degrading treatment test even though the accused had not wished to speak and had only confessed as a result of his will being broken by periods of searching questioning. In common law such methods would result in the confession being excluded on the ground of oppression. The courts have accepted, however, that the involuntariness of a confession is a factor which may be taken into account when deciding whether to exercise their discretion to exclude it under the torture, inhuman and degrading treatment test.[129] Unfortunately they have not resorted to this discretion as a device to leaven the severity of their interpretation of what is permitted under the heading of torture, inhuman or degrading treatment.[130] The enormity of the task involved in persuading judges that they should exercise their discretion to exclude confessions in Diplock cases is illustrated by the facts of *R v Tohill*.[131] The accused in that case was a fifteen-year-old youth who had been arrested and interrogated on suspicion of being a look-out during a fatal bomb attack on soldiers. He had been held in police custody from 3.30 am to 1.05 pm on the same day and interrogated for four hours with only a short break in between. The confession had been made at 12.45 pm. The trial judge found that the interrogation had been persistent and pressing and at times the police had become aggressive and angry and expressed in forceful language their disbelief of the accused's protestations of innocence. The judge also accepted that there had been a breach of Rule V of the Judges' Rules. Nevertheless he refused to exercise his discretion to exclude the confession. Fortunately, due to diligent work on the part of the accused's lawyer two vital and impeccable witnesses were traced in the United States. They had been visiting Belfast when the bomb attack took place and the accused claimed that not only had he been in their company at the time but also their whereabouts would have rendered it impossible for him to have assisted the bombers. The witnesses agreed to travel to Belfast to testify and their testimony supported the accused's account of his movements. The trial judge subsequently ruled that there was sufficient circumstantial evidence for there to be reasonable doubt about the truth of the confession and the accused was acquitted.

R v Milne[132] is one of the few examples of judges being persuaded to exercise their discretion to exclude a confession. In that case Lord Justice McGonigal felt that the accused's mental confusion when he had made the confession and the fact that he had been interrogated for 39 hours out of a total of 72 hours in custody were sufficient to justify the exercise of the discretion. One can only despair that being interviewed for 39 hours out of the 72 hours spent in custody was not branded as inhuman treatment. As a general rule, however, judges have refused to accept that lengthy and persistent interrogation by itself is sufficient to warrant the automatic exclusion of a confession under the statutory admissibility test.[133] In *R v Cowan*[134] Lord Justice MacDermott rejected the suggestion that the discretion could be exercised if a police officer had offered an inducement in order to encourage a suspect to confess, such as a lighter sentence, resettlement or financial support. He was prepared to accept, however, that it could be exercised if a confession had been obtained by trickery. Breach of the Bennett guidelines or the codes of practice for the interrogation of suspects would not *per se* give grounds for the exercise of the discretion.[135]

Not surprisingly, very few confessions have been excluded because the prosecution failed to satisfy the court that they had not been obtained by torture, inhuman and degrading treatment. This is most disturbing given the extent to which the RUC resorted to brutal interrogation methods, particularly in the mid to late 1970s. Equally disturbing is evidence that in the second half of the 1970s the courts became increasingly reluctant to acquit in Diplock cases. Boyle et al. attribute this trend to case-hardening among the judges.[136] Their theory is that the small group of judges who presided over the Diplock trials heard the same allegations being made by one defendant after another and the same denials being made by the same officers. They became increasingly more sceptical of the allegations, particularly as the officers concerned became more practiced at coping with cross-examination. Walsh found evidence of this trend continuing into the 1980s.[137] *R v Brophy*,[138] one of the few cases in which a confession was successfully challenged, offers some idea of how difficult it could be to persuade a judge in the Diplock Court that a confession had been obtained by torture inhuman or degrading treatment.[139]

Brophy had been arrested under the seven-day power and interrogated about the 1978 bombing of the La Mon House restaurant, in which 12 people had died in horrific circumstances. He had signed statements of admission on the third day of interrogation and made verbal statements confirming them on the fourth. At his trial for murder he alleged that he had only confessed because he could no longer endure the ill-treatment to which he had been subjected over the three-day period. Medical evidence supported many of his disturbing claims, which ranged from being repeatedly punched to being sexually assaulted. Nevertheless the trial judge was reluctant to believe him. Only Brophy's exceptional astuteness and memory, combined with very unsatisfactory police evidence, ultimately persuaded the judge to exclude the confession. Brophy had been careful to memorise the names of his interrogating officers and the various times at which each of them had interrogated and ill-treated him. At his trial he was able to point out the culprits, who just happened to be in the courtroom on other business. It transpired that some of them were not even on record as having interrogated him. They claimed that they had been engaged in other activities that would have made it impossible for them to have been interrogating Brophy at the times cited by Brophy. When their duty rosters were checked, however, not only were their claims proved false but it was revealed that they had all been available at the interrogation centre at exactly the times Brophy claimed that they had interrogated and ill-treated him. The coincidences were so great that the judge had no alternative but to accept that there was sufficient truth in Brophy's account to exclude his confession. It must be said, however, that there are very few individuals with the strength of character and presence of mind to be able to remember the details remembered by Brophy while detained and ill-treated for several days, cut off from the outside world without even a watch to keep track of time.

It is submitted that this brief survey of Diplock cases on the interpretation and application of the statutory test for the admissibility of confessions reveals an unusually quiescent judiciary in the face of interrogation practices which should find no place in a trial process based on respect for fundamental rights, the dignity of the individual and fair procedures. It was not as though there was no other route open to the judges in the face of the bare words of the statutory test. Judges in the common law world, including Northern Ireland, have an honourable tradition of interpreting legislation in a manner which eases its adverse impact on the fundamental rights and freedoms of the individual. The judges in the Diplock Courts could have given an expansive interpretation of 'torture, inhuman and degrading treatment' to ensure that the more oppressive interrogation practices fell foul of it. Instead they adopted an approach which probably resulted in confessions getting through in circumstances which even the legislature may not have intended. When combined with their equally supine interpretation of police powers of arrest under the emergency legislation it is difficult to avoid the conclusion that their judicial inactivity encouraged the police to believe that their arrest and interrogation strategy had the support of the judicial system as well as that of the security and political establishments. Once again the law was bending to the expediency of security policy.

The only significant judicial contributions which might have the effect of ameliorating the interrogation methods used under the umbrella of the torture, inhuman and degrading treatment test are the retention of the judicial discretion to exclude confessions,[140] the ruling to the effect that assaulting suspects during questioning renders their detention unlawful and the ruling that a decision to delay access to a solicitor for a suspect in detention is amenable to judicial review. These might be considered relatively weak and indirect contributions. Indeed the executive has had a more substantial input. In 1979 it implemented most of the recommendations of the Bennett Committee. In 1992 it established an office of independent commissioner to make random visits to the interrogation centres for the purpose of overseeing the conditions under which suspects were held. This was followed by the publication of a draft code on the detention, treatment and questioning of persons arrested under the emergency legislation. The current version was adopted in 1996 under Section 52 of the 1996 Emergency Provisions Act. Although this code lacks the force of law, police officers who fail to comply with it may become subject to disciplinary proceedings. There is no provision in the code or the 1996 Act for the audio or video recording of interrogations. While these measures fall short of those designed to protect suspects in the ordinary criminal process, they nevertheless contrast with the judicial failure to impose more stringent controls on the RUC.

Judicial inactivity in the face of abuse by the security forces is equally apparent in the supergrass strategy, where the basic tenets of a fair trial were surely stretched beyond breaking point.[141] Despite the fact that many of the supergrasses had bought immunity from prosecution by agreeing to testify against their alleged accomplices, the courts ruled their evidence admissible. Indeed it would be no exaggeration to say that judicial manipulation of the complex rules on the admissibility of accomplice evidence played a critical role in saving supergrass evidence from exclusion.[142] Even when it transpired that accomplices had committed very serious crimes, including murder in some cases, and had a track record of lying and double-crossing, the courts did not move to exclude their evidence. The obvious possibility that some of these supergrasses might have been motivated to exaggerate and even manufacture their evidence against suspects in order to secure immunity did not seem to weigh heavily with the judges. In fact in some cases the judges seemed to be almost hypnotised by the manner in which the supergrasses gave evidence in the witness box; mistaking this for proof of their reliability rather than the more likely probability that they had been extensively coached in the giving of evidence by their RUC minders.

The judicial willingness to accept and act upon supergrass evidence is reflected in the fact that between 1980 and 1985 no fewer than 190 accused persons were convicted at first instance in the Diplock Courts either wholly or partly on the evidence of a former accomplice. A bizarre feature of these trials, which added substantially to their inherent unfairness, was the fact that very large numbers were tried together on the evidence of a single supergrass. In the Gilmour case, mentioned earlier, 35 persons were tried together on 180 separate counts. The only evidence against them was the word of supergrass Raymond Gilmour.

The sense of incredulity aroused by such spectacles was compounded by the fact that 66 convictions were subsequently overturned in the Court of Appeal by judges who themselves had been happy to convict at first instance on the sort of evidence they subsequently deemed insufficient on appeal. Perhaps it was no coincidence that the appeal decisions were handed down in an environment where intense political pressure was being applied in the context of the Anglo-Irish Agreement to clean up the supergrass strategy. Indeed it is disturbing to discover the extent to which the judges were willing to redefine their positions on the admissibility of supergrass evidence from trial to appeal. This was accentuated by their willingness to reproach each other for placing too much trust on the evidence of witnesses whose characters were heavily discredited and who had a strong motivation to concoct evidence. All this, of course, merely underlines the extent to which the initial judicial receptivity to supergrass evidence reflected an unacceptable preference for the needs of the security forces over the fundamental rights of the individual and fair procedures.

Lethal force

The judicial interpretation of the law governing the use of lethal force by the security forces in Northern Ireland was laid down primarily in decisions arising out of the fatal shootings in the 1970s. It has already been seen in Chapter 6 that this interpretation favoured military expediency over an individual's right to life. Perhaps because of this judicial attitude the DPP failed to bring prosecutions in the many cases in the 1980s when prosecution would appear to have been warranted.[143] This failure was particularly marked in many of the cases involving death by plastic bullet.[144] Perversely, in the one plastic bullet case when a prosecution was brought there was clear video evidence of the victim wielding a stick while running at police officers when the bullet was fired.[145] Such evidence was patently lacking in many of the cases in which little children, old men and women were shot dead, but no prosecutions were brought in these cases.

However the failure of the law to prevent and punish the excessive use of lethal force by the security forces in the 1980s cannot be explained fully by the actions or inaction of the DPP. Once again the courts had a part to play in that they interpreted and applied the law in a manner which appeared to be unduly sympathetic to the security forces. Since 1969 more than 350 persons have been killed by the security forces, most of them in hotly disputed circumstances. Nevertheless only four soldiers have been convicted of murder and one of manslaughter in prosecutions arising out of these shootings.[146] No police officer has been convicted. The manner in which the judges have interpreted the powers of the security forces to use force against suspect terrorists, as detailed in Chapter 6, is in large part responsible for this low conviction rate. An additional factor, however, is the manner in which the judges have applied this law in practice. Two cases in particular are worth mentioning in this context. The first is *R v Robinson*.[147]

In December 1982 Seamus Grew and Roddy Carroll, both suspected members of the INLA, were travelling after dark in a car near Grew's home in Armagh when they were intercepted by an unmarked police car. Constable Robinson emerged from the police vehicle and fired 15 shots at Carroll in the passenger seat. He was hit by seven or possibly nine bullets, most of which came from behind and to his right. Robinson then reloaded and ran around the front of the car in the glare of the headlights to the driver's side, where he shot Grew. Grew was hit by seven bullets, most of which entered from behind and to his left. Both men were unarmed. It transpired that Robinson had been part of a team from the RUC's heavily armed undercover Special Support Unit and E4A which had been expecting Grew to rendezvous with Dominic McGlinchey, one of the most notorious terrorists being sought by the security forces at that time. Indeed both Grew and Carroll had been followed by the RUC on their journey from a family funeral into the Republic of Ireland and back again towards Grew's home.

At his trial for murder Robinson claimed that he had fired in self-defence. In support of this claim he asserted that the suspects had driven through a roadblock, injuring a policeman as they did so. Under cross-examination, however, he admitted that this version had been concocted in consultation with senior officers to conceal the fact that they had been engaged in a planned operation based on intelligence information in concert with army surveillance teams. Although Robinson also claimed in evidence that he heard gunfire from the car, when conducting tests on the vehicle forensic scientists did not succeed in producing any sound similar to gunshots. The forensic evidence also established that Grew could not have been shot through the car door, as had been claimed by Robinson. In fact he had been shot from a distance of 30–36 inches when trying to get out of the car through an open door. This point was vital as Robinson was trying to argue that he had believed Grew to be armed when he shot him. If the door had been closed at the time of the shooting this would have provided some support for Robinson's belief as he would not have been able to see that Grew was in fact unarmed. In the event, however, he would have had a clear view of him.

The facts that emerged at the trial, coupled with information which has emerged since, strongly suggest that the death of Grew and Carroll was the result of a planned execution by the security forces. Most disturbingly, it has transpired that another officer fired several shots at the vehicle, but neither he nor a Special Branch inspector who was present and witnessed the whole incident were called to give evidence. Nevertheless, it was apparent that at the very least Constable Robinson's account of acting in self-defence was false in several respects. Indeed one might reasonably have expected a conviction to have resulted even on the basis of the evidence presented. Instead Justice MacDermott found Robinson not guilty as he was not satisfied that the prosecution had proved that Robinson had not acted in self-defence.

The really incredible feature about the judgment was the process through which Justice MacDermott sought to justify this conclusion. First of all he recited the law on self-defence, taking care to emphasise that the court must treat Constable Robinson on the basis of the facts as he believed them to be, even if his belief turned out to be mistaken. However he then proceeded to dismiss with exceptional perfunctoriness the evidence which suggested that Robinson may not have been telling the truth about his belief. The forensic evidence that the car could not be made to produce a sound like a gunshot was explained on the ground that 'a clinical test of that nature does not however mean that there could not have been a noise which the accused reasonably thought was a gunshot'. The critical conflict between the forensic evidence and Robinson's account of having fired through the closed door caused little difficulty for the learned judge. He concluded that Robinson's recall 'in relation to this part of the incident is and will remain disturbed and he is not lying or seeking to conceal something'. He went on to surmise that, notwithstanding Robinson's own version of events, he had in fact opened the door before firing the fatal shots. This disposed of the awkward conflict with the forensic evidence. Throughout all of this Justice MacDermott did not seem to take into consideration the fact that Robinson's credibility as a witness was seriously undermined by his participation in the conspiracy to conceal the facts of what had really happened and to perjure himself in the witness box. Nor was he concerned that the prosecution called as witnesses members of the security forces who had not witnessed the shootings and failed to call a witness who had actually participated in the shootings and another who had witnessed the whole incident and played a critical part in setting it up.

The cumulative effect of these individual factors, coupled with the outcome of the case, leaves little room for confidence in the likelihood of the legal process punishing members of the security forces for the excessive use of lethal force in operational situations. The courts, in particular, seemed to be infected with an unshakeable belief in the integrity of the security forces in their dealings with terrorist suspects. Indeed this is clearly evident in the judgment of Lord Justice Gibson in the second case, which bears many of the hallmarks of the first.

In *R v Montgomery*[148] three suspected terrorists were travelling in a car in Lurgan, County Armagh, in November 1982 when they were all shot dead by members of the RUC's E4A unit. One hundred and nine bullets were fired at the car and 56 hit the targets. Once again the police attempted to mislead by claiming that the suspects' car had driven through an ordinary police checkpoint and concealing the fact that the suspects had been under surveillance right up to the shooting. Three members of the unit were subsequently charged with murder. At their trial they claimed that they had opened fire on the car after it drove through their checkpoint. Believing that fire had been returned they had continued to shoot until the car had come to a halt. At that point they had heard a gun being cocked so they opened fire again. In fact the three deceased had been unarmed. At the end of the prosecution's case, however, Lord Justice Gibson took the unusual step of acceding to the defence's submission of no case to answer and entering an acquittal. Comments made by the learned lord justice when giving his reasons suggest very strongly that the courts would not stand in the way of the security forces resorting to the use of maximum firepower and aggression when dealing with suspected terrorists:

> I wish to make it clear that having heard the Crown case I regard each of the accused as absolutely blameless in this matter. That finding should be put in their record *along with my own commendation for their courage and determination in bringing the three deceased men to justice, in this case, the final court of justice* (emphasis added).

Lord Justice Gibson went on to castigate the authorities for bringing the prosecution, referring to the confusing effect their actions would have on police officers and soldiers who were sent out to arrest dangerous criminals on the basis of an order to bring them back dead or alive.

By any standard these were very disturbing words from a judge in whom primary responsibility for impartially upholding the rule of law was entrusted.

The judicial attitude evident in the Robinson and Montgomery cases has contributed to a perception in some quarters that judges are unduly sympathetic to the security forces in shoot to kill cases.[149] Further evidence for this can be found in the contrasting approaches of judges to the manner in which evidence relevant to a shooting is taken from security force personnel and civilians, both as suspects and witnesses.[150] Soldiers being investigated for a fatal shooting are not arrested and interrogated under the seven-day power of detention. Indeed the RUC is not normally given access to them until they have consulted a lawyer of their choice and prepared a statement with the assistance of the lawyer. It is normal practice for soldiers to be accompanied by their lawyer throughout the questioning by the RUC. This, of course, contrasts markedly with the procedure adopted for the investigation of civilians suspected of a fatal shooting. Judges, however, have never commented adversely on the disparity nor even acknowledged that there is a disparity. Moreover in at least one case where civilian witnesses to a fatal shooting by soldiers gave their statements through a solicitor, as opposed to the RUC, the trial judge drew adverse inferences about the reliability of the witnesses from the fact that they had not given their statements directly to the RUC.[151] He was quite unsympathetic to the suggestion that the civilians in question had adopted this course of action because they had had absolutely no confidence in the RUC to carry out a thorough and impartial investigation. The judge's stance was critical to the outcome of the case as there was a fundamental conflict between the evidence of the civilians with respect to the shooting and the evidence of the soldiers. The net result was that the judge preferred the soldiers' versions, even though he accepted that they were not truthful witnesses. It is therefore difficult to avoid the conclusion that security force personnel were treated more leniently than civilians.

The contrasting judicial approaches to the manner in which evidence was obtained was also reflected in the judicial approach to the assessment of the evidence. The judicial approach in the Robinson case, for example, can be contrasted with that in many of the 'casement trials' which resulted from the murder of two British soldiers. In these trials some of the judges displayed a disturbing readiness to draw inferences that were adverse to the accused from incomplete evidence from television footage and videotape filmed from a helicopter. The approach in the Robinson case was also reflected, albeit to a lesser extent, in other cases in which members of the security forces were acquitted of homicide charges. In *R v Elkington and Carrington*,[152] for example, Lord Chief Justice Hutton accepted the improbable evidence of two soldiers who claimed that they had fired at the rear of a car to defend a colleague whom they believed was being carried away on the front of the car. The lord chief justice preferred the soldiers'evidence to the conflicting evidence of civilian witnesses, despite the fact that he also believed that the soldiers were not truthful witnesses. Similarly in *R v Hegarty*[153] Justice Hutton, as he then was, accepted without reservation the evidence of the accused that he had acted in reasonable defence of two colleagues when he had fired a plastic bullet at an individual who was running towards them from behind wielding a stick or a pole. The learned judge was not deterred by the fact that the only spot where the accused's colleagues were vulnerable to injury was a small space between the bottom of their helmets and the top of their bullet-proof vests. He also swept aside the fact that the accused had given false information in his statement to the police in an apparent attempt to bolster his defence.

Even those few cases which have resulted in conviction for murder have not reflected the adoption of more stringent judicial controls on the security forces. They are notable, moreover, for excessive leniency on the part of the executive with respect to the terms of imprisonment actually served by the soldiers in question. In *R v Thain*[154] the deceased had been one of a group of youths drinking cider on the street. The youths had become involved in an altercation with soldiers in an army foot patrol. The deceased had run off and the accused (a member of the army patrol) had called three times for him to halt. On the third occasion the accused had fired one shot, killing the youth. At his trial the accused pleaded self-defence because he had thought that the youth had been turning to fire a gun at him or members of the patrol. The youth, who had been stripped to the waist, had been unarmed. The court rejected the self-defence claim on the facts and convicted the soldier of murder. His appeal to the Court of Appeal was unsuccessful. However the soldier was released to rejoin his regiment after serving only four years and three months of his life sentence, thereby confirming the impression that there was one law for the security forces and another for civilians.

Another case, *R v Clegg*,[155] concerned the fatal shooting of 16-year-old Karen Reilly, who had been the front seat passenger in a car driven by a joyrider. In an earlier case, *Magill v Ministry of Defence*,[156] it had been held that shooting at the 15-year-old driver of a car which had driven through a vehicle checkpoint had been reasonable use of force in the prevention of crime. In the Clegg case, however, the accused soldier relied solely on self-defence. He claimed that the car had hit a soldier at a checkpoint and that he had fired to prevent the car from injuring or killing his colleagues. In fact the car had not struck a soldier. The members of the patrol had deliberately inflicted an injury on one of their colleagues in order to make it appear that he had been struck by the car. Moreover it transpired that the car had actually passed the checkpoint and was no longer a danger to any of the soldiers at the time the fatal shot was fired. On the basis of these facts the court convicted the accused of murder. Appeals to the Court of Appeal and the House of Lords were unsuccessful. In fact the only significant feature about the appeals was the defence's attempt to persuade the House of Lords to change the law on self-defence so that a conviction for murder could be reduced to manslaughter in a case where the use of some force was reasonable but not the lethal force actually used by the accused. The House of Lords, however, considered that such a change in the law was a matter for parliament alone.[157] The net effect is that when members of the security forces use lethal force in self-defence when preventing crime they will either be guilty of murder or nothing at all. There is no half-way house.[158]

Clegg was released from his life sentence after only three years, at which point he rejoined his regiment. His conviction was eventually quashed after the case was referred back to the Court of Appeal by the secretary of state. At the subsequent retrial the judge found Clegg not guilty of murder as he could not be certain that Clegg had fired the fatal shot. He was, however, found guilty of attempted wounding. Nationalists have been quick to contrast the treatment of Clegg and Thain with that of IRA and INLA members convicted of similar offences.

The third case in which convictions for murder were secured concerned the shooting of 18-year-old Peter McBride.[159] McBride had been stopped by a British Army foot patrol at about 10 am one September morning as he was walking from his sister's house to his own house in the New Lodge Road area of Belfast. After being searched an altercation had developed between himself and members of the patrol, as a result of which he had run off. In the course of giving chase two members of the patrol, Scots Guardsmen James Fisher and Mark Wright, had fired five shots at McBride, two of which had hit and killed him. The soldiers argued in their defence that they believed that McBride had been carrying a 'coffee jar bomb' which he might throw at the patrol. One of them also claimed that he had thought McBride was armed and had fired a shot at the soldiers. In fact McBride had had neither a gun nor a bomb. After an incisive and detailed analysis of the evidence of the accused soldiers and civilian witnesses, Lord Justice Kelly concluded that there was no reasonable possibility that the soldiers had honestly believed that McBride had been carrying a bomb or that the lives or safety of the patrol had been in jeopardy. In effect they had fired at him simply in order to apprehend him, despite the fact that he was not suspected of being engaged in terrorist activity. Not only, therefore, had the soldiers not acted in self-defence but they had used more force than had been reasonably necessary to effect an arrest. They were convicted of murder and given the automatic penalty of life imprisonment. However, as with their predecessors, Thain and Clegg, they were released to rejoin their regiment after serving only six years of their sentences.

The European Convention on Human Rights

Since the United Kingdom is a signatory to the European Convention on the Protection of Human Rights and Fundamental Freedoms, and accepts the right of individual petition under the convention, it is necessary to consider why the convention was not used effectively to prevent the sorts of abuse described in this chapter. Certainly there has been a steady stream of applications under the convention challenging abuses by the security forces and aspects of the emergency legislation. The results, however, have been mixed.

The most notable success, and the one which perhaps fuelled false hopes about what the convention could achieve in this context, was the Irish government's case against the United Kingdom in the early 1970s. It is best remembered for the fact that the Court of Human Rights found the UK government in breach of the convention's prohibition on the use of inhuman and degrading treatment. This part of the case concerned the interrogation methods used against many of those arrested in the context of the internment operations which commenced in August 1971. The second success did not come until *Brogan v United Kingdom*[160] in 1988. In that case the Court ruled that the police power under the prevention of terrorism legislation to detain suspects without charge for up to seven days was in breach of Article 5(3) of the convention, which stipulates that everyone arrested or detained on suspicion of a criminal offence must be brought promptly before a judicial authority. The Court considered that the executive detention of a person without judicial authorisation for a period of even four days and six hours would be in breach of this provision. This success was followed in 1990 when the Court held in *Fox et al. v United Kingdom*[161] that the arrest of the three applicants on suspicion of terrorism had not been based on reasonable suspicion, as required by Article 5(1). Success in the McCann case, discussed in Chapter 6, was followed by further success in *John Murray v United Kingdom*.[162] In the latter case the Court ruled that denying legal advice for 48 hours to a suspect in police custody, when coupled with the adverse inferences that could be drawn in a criminal trial from the suspect's failure to mention certain matters during questioning, amounted to a breach of the right to a fair trial guaranteed by Article 6 of the convention.

These successes were overshadowed by other applications being rejected by the European Commission and European Court of Human Rights. Indeed even successful cases incorporated a number of critically important rejections. The *Ireland v United Kingdom* case, for example, was about much more than the brutal interrogation practices for which it is best remembered. The Irish government also challenged the sweeping powers of arrest, detention and internment and the fatal shooting of nine civilians as being incompatible with diverse articles in the convention. As will be seen in Chapter 8, it also challenged the Bloody Sunday shootings themselves as a breach of the convention. While the Court accepted that the arrest, detention and internment measures were in clear breach of several provisions of Article 5 of the convention it felt compelled to reject this part of the Irish government's application because the UK government had lodged a derogation from several articles of the convention, including Article 5, in respect of the situation in Northern Ireland (derogation is explained below). The Irish government's application in respect of the fatal shootings was declared inadmissible on the ground that the prerequisite of exhausting domestic remedies had not been satisfied.

The applicant's success in the Brogan case was tempered by the Court's rejection of the argument that terrorism did not constitute a sufficiently specific or identifiable offence upon which to base a power of arrest within the scope of Article 5(1). Similarly in the Fox case the Court rejected the argument that the power to arrest and detain a suspect for 72 hours on the basis of subjective suspicion of involvement in terrorist activity was automatically in breach of Article 5(1). Even though Article 5(1)(c) requires arrests to be based on reasonable suspicion, the Court considered that the power at issue in this case was not in breach of the convention as long as it had been exercised on the basis of an honest and *bona fide* suspicion that the person arrested was a terrorist. Moreover the state would satisfy its obligations under Article 5(1)(c) by furnishing some facts or information capable of satisfying the Court that the arrested person had been reasonably suspected of having committed the alleged offence. The state would not be required to disclose confidential sources of information:

> Certainly, Article 5(1)(c) of the Convention should not be applied in such a manner as to put disproportionate difficulties in the way of the police authorities of the Contracting States in taking effective measures to counter organised terrorism.... It follows that the Contracting States cannot be asked to establish the reasonableness of the suspicion grounding the arrest of a suspected terrorist by disclosing the confidential sources of supporting information or even facts which would be susceptible of indicating such sources or their identity.

In this case the Court accepted that the police authorities had reasonably suspected the applicants simply on the basis that they had questioned them in custody about specific offences. It went on to hold that there had been no breach of the requirement in Article 5(2) for persons arrested to be informed promptly of the reasons for their arrest. The Court concluded that this could be satisfied by the arrested persons being questioned about one or more specific offences while in custody subsequent to the arrest.

Even the success in the McCann case was tempered by the Court's finding that the law governing the use of lethal force in Northern Ireland was not necessarily incompatible with Article 2. Similarly the applicant's success in *John Murray v United Kingdom* was tempered by the Court's refusal to find that the provisions in the Criminal Evidence (Northern Ireland) Order 1988 which permitted a court to draw adverse inferences from a suspect's refusal to give an explanation for his or her actions when demanded during police questioning were in themselves a violation of Article 6.

These partial failures were complemented by a number of applications which were substantially or wholly rejected by the court and/or the European Commission. Those pertaining to the use of lethal force have already been covered in Chapter 6. There are several other examples concerning, *inter alia*, inhuman and degrading treatment, personal liberty and privacy. In *McVeigh et al. v United Kingdom*,[163] for example, the Commission found that the sweeping powers of arrest, detention, search and examination of persons travelling through internal ports between Britain and Ireland were not in breach of the provisions on the right to liberty laid down in Article 5(1) of the convention and the provisions on the right to respect for private life set out in Article 8.[164] Similarly in *Murray v United Kingdom*[165] the Court found that the applicant's rights under Article 5(1) and Article 8 had not been infringed in the course of her arrest under the army's four-hour power, despite the fact that it had all the hallmarks of a screening arrest. The Court accepted that the applicant had been arrested on reasonable suspicion of raising money for the purchase of arms by the IRA in the United States. The basis for this was the fact that the arresting officer had honestly held the requisite suspicion and that the applicant had travelled to the United States, where she had contacted two of her brothers who had been convicted in the United States of attempting to purchase arms for the IRA. No further basis for the reasonableness of the suspicion was disclosed, although the UK government declared that it had further grounds for suspicion but could not disclose these for security reasons. The Court stated that it was prepared to attach some credence to the government's declaration by finding that there had been no breach of Article 5(1).

The appalling conditions in which protesting prisoners were confined during the H-Block dirty protests were the subject of an unsuccessful application to the Commission in *McFeeley et al. v United Kingdom*.[166] The Commission rejected the argument that the conditions and the disciplinary punishments amounted to a breach of the Article 3 prohibition on torture, inhuman and degrading treatment. It reasoned that the conditions were largely the result of protest action by prisoners and could not be attributed to any positive action on the part of the government. The Commission also considered that the disciplinary punishments imposed had not been sufficiently severe to amount to a breach of Article 3. Equally it was not persuaded that the degree of humiliation and debasement involved in routine strip and rectal searches was sufficient to invoke Article 3.

The relative weakness of the European Convention on Human Rights in the face of what would appear to be gross violations of basic human rights and freedoms by the security forces in Northern Ireland over the past thirty years requires some explanation. At least part of the reason can be ascribed to the derogation provision in Article 15, which permits states to derogate from their obligations under several articles of the convention during times of war or other public emergency that threatens the life of the nation. There can be no derogation from the Article 2 protection for the right to life (except in respect of deaths resulting from lawful acts of war), the Article 3 protection against torture, inhuman and degrading treatment, the Article 4 protection against being held in slavery or servitude, and the Article 7 protection against retroactive criminal laws. However states can derogate in appropriate circumstances from all their other obligations under the convention, including those concerning the right to liberty and security of the person (Article 5), the right to a fair trial (Article 6), the right to privacy (Article 8), the right to freedom of thought and conscience (Article 9), the right to freedom of expression (Article 10) and the right to freedom of assembly and association (Article 11).

The UK government lodged notice of derogation under Article 15 in respect of the sweeping powers of arrest, detention and internment under the special powers legislation. This notice was subsequently updated to cover the relevant provisions of the emergency legislation which were introduced from 1972 onwards, including those establishing the no-jury Diplock Courts. As seen above, this derogation played a vital role in protecting the UK government from being found in breach of several provisions of the convention. By 1984, however, the government considered that there was no further need for the derogation. In other words it judged that the emergency legislation and the practices of the security forces at that time did not infringe the provisions of the convention. This judgment, of course, was found to be defective in the Brogan case, where the Court found that the power to detain arrested suspects for seven days without bringing them before a judicial authority was in breach of Article 5. The government responded by lodging a notice of derogation in respect of the seven-day power.

The ease with which the UK government has been able to elude some of its basic obligations under the convention focuses attention on the scope of the derogation provision. It seems that just when the fundamental rights and freedoms protected under the convention are most at risk they receive the least protection. Indeed the Court itself must carry some of the blame for this situation on account of its unwillingness to second-guess the subjective decision of the state that there is a public emergency justifying a derogation and the extent of the measures required to contain it. In *Brannigan & McBride v United Kingdom*,[167] for example, the applicants challenged the UK government's resort to the derogation in the wake of the Brogan decision. The government's claim that there had been a public emergency in Northern Ireland which threatened the life of the nation looked particularly weak in this case given that it had just lifted the derogation which had been in force up until 1984. Nevertheless the Court ruled that the state enjoyed a 'wide margin of discretion' when determining whether it faced a public emergency within the scope of Article 15 and in the measures it considered necessary to cope with that emergency. It went on to accept the United Kingdom's belated declaration of a public emergency in 1988 and its justification for the retention of the seven-day power of detention without judicial control.

The Court's supine attitude towards the state's assertion of a public emergency was matched by its approach to the question of whether the measures introduced to deal with the emergency went beyond what was strictly required by the exigencies of the situation. In *Ireland v United Kingdom*, for example, the Irish government accepted that there was a public emergency but challenged the draconian measures under the special powers legislation as being out of all proportion to what was required. The Court, however, always gives the derogating state the benefit of the doubt in such matters:

> It falls in the first place to each Contracting State with its responsibility for 'the life of [its] nation' to determine whether that life is threatened by a 'public emergency' and, if so, how far it is necessary to go in attempting to overcome the emergency. By reason of their direct and continuous contact with the pressing needs of the moment, the national authorities are in principle in a better position than the international judge to decide both on the presence of such an emergency and on the nature and scope of derogations necessary to avert it. In this matter Article 15(1) leaves these authorities a wide margin of appreciation.

In the event the Court concluded that even the virtually unlimited power of arrest under Regulation 10, and the detention without trial and internment provisions were justified in the circumstances prevailing in Northern Ireland. It must be said, however, that the reasoning which led to the Court's decision on these matters bordered on the unreal. In seeking to justify the arrests under Regulation 10, for example, it said:

> This sort of arrest can be justifiable only in a very exceptional situation, but the circumstances prevailing in Northern Ireland did fall into such a category. Many witnesses could not give evidence freely without running the greatest risks...; the competent authorities were entitled to take the view, without exceeding their margin of appreciation, that it was indispensable to arrest such witnesses so

that they could be questioned in conditions of relative security and not be exposed to reprisals. Moreover and above all, regulation 10 authorised deprivation of liberty only for a maximum of 48 hours.

This conveys the spectacle of the state actually doing witnesses a service by arresting and detaining them for up to 48 hours so that they can assist the state.

The relative weakness of the convention in the face of the emergency legislation and security force excesses in Northern Ireland can also be traced to the marked reluctance of the Court and the Commission to take a tough line against national measures which the state seeks to justify as necessary in its fight against terrorism. In many of the cases emanating from Northern Ireland the Court and the Commission were prepared to accept the most blatant and draconian intrusions into fundamental rights and freedoms on the basis that they were necessary to combat terrorism. In other words the British government was effectively relieved of the politically embarrassing obligation to resort to Article 15 derogations to protect these measures. In *McVeigh et al. v United Kingdom*,[168] for example, the Commission said:

> The existence of organised terrorism is a feature of modern life whose emergence since the Convention was drafted cannot be ignored any more than the changes in social conditions and moral opinion which have taken place in the same period. It faces democratic Governments with a problem of serious organised crime which they must cope with in order to preserve the fundamental rights of their citizens. The measures they take must comply with the Convention and the Convention organs must always be alert to the danger in this sphere adverted to by the Court, of 'undermining or even destroying democracy on the ground of defending it (*Klass* case ...) However as both the Commission and the Court observed in that case, some compromise between the requirements for defending democratic society and individual rights is inherent in the system of the Convention, specific requirements of the situation facing the society in question must be taken into account.'

Accordingly the Commission found that the arrest and detention of the applicants for 45 hours under the prevention of terrorism legislation for the purpose of a security check or screening process had not been in breach of the convention despite the fact that they had not actually been suspected of any offence or breach of the law. Moreover, the Commission also concluded that no breach of the convention had occurred when the applicants had been searched, questioned about their private lives, fingerprinted and photographed. Nor did any breach ensue from the fact that the state had retained the records of the examination, including the fingerprints and photographs, after the applicants' release. Despite the fact that the applicants had not been suspected of having committed or being in the course of committing a criminal offence, the convention proved incapable of protecting them against these gross and arbitrary restrictions on the exercise of their fundamental rights and freedoms.

The disappointing result in the McVeigh case was by no means an exception. The relative weakness of the convention in protecting human rights and fundamental freedoms in the face of the antiterrorist measures adopted by the British government in Northern Ireland was also reflected in cases such as those of McFeeley and Fox. In explaining its interpretation of what constituted a 'reasonable suspicion' for the purpose of a lawful arrest, the Court had this to say in the Fox case:

> As the Government pointed out, in view of the difficulties inherent in the investigation and prosecution of terrorist-type offences in Northern Ireland, the 'reasonableness' of the suspicion justifying such arrests cannot always be judged according to the same standards as are applied in dealing with conventional crime.

In other words, should the government claim that extraordinary measures were necessary to combat terrorism the Court could apply a lesser standard than would normally be appropriate in its interpretation of the convention.[169] Even in those few cases where the applicants had some measure of success, both the Commission and the Court displayed a distinctly progovernment line in the interpretation of the convention. In the Brogan case, for example, the Commission was prepared to accept that the period of detention of four days and eleven hours had been compatible with the convention 'given the context in which the applicants were arrested and the special problems associated with the investigation of terrorist offences'. While the Court differed from the Commission in its conclusion, it too accepted that a lower standard for the protection of human rights was acceptable where the government could justify the impugned measures as necessary to combat terrorism:

> The investigation of terrorist offences undoubtedly presents the authorities with special problems.... The Court takes full judicial

notice of the factors adverted to by the government in this connection.... The Court accepts that, subject to the existence of adequate safeguards, the context of terrorism in Northern Ireland has the effect of prolonging the period during which the authorities may, without violating Article 5(3), keep a person suspected of serious terrorist offences in custody before bringing him before a judge or other judicial officer.

Finally, it is worth noting that it is important not to have too high an expectation of what the European Convention on Human Rights and Fundamental Freedoms can achieve in combatting excesses by the security forces and the implementation of draconian emergency legislation. It was drafted to reflect a standard of protection to which all the signatory states felt able to subscribe to and comply with. Inevitably it reflected the lowest common denominator. Moreover, since the success of the convention depends on the voluntary cooperation of all of the states, the Commission and the Court have had to be sensitive in their interpretation and application of its provisions, particularly in the context of an internal threat to the security of the state. It should come as no surprise, therefore, to find that the degree of protection of human rights and fundamental freedoms afforded under the convention is not always of a higher order than that available within the domestic legal system.

Conclusion

The disturbing conclusion to be drawn from this survey of law and security policy in Northern Ireland since Bloody Sunday is that there has been little change. The requirements of security policy have remained paramount. The executive and the legislature have been active throughout in equipping the army and the police with extensive and draconian powers. These have been matched with the imposition of severe constraints on the freedom of the individual and curbs on the basic due process requirements. For the most part neither the courts nor the criminal process generally have been as active or as vigilant as they might have been in punishing abuses and imposing some measure of legality on the practices of the security forces and the state generally. The net result is that the security forces patently do not feel any more threatened or constricted by the limits of the law than they did at the time of Bloody Sunday. Mercifully, with one or two notable exceptions, this has not resulted in more examples of mass killings at the hands of the state. It has, however, provided the basis for the heinous practices outlined in this chapter. Not only have these practices inflicted immense suffering on the thousands directly affected, but they have done immense damage to public confidence in law and justice in Northern Ireland. Restoring that confidence is a vital prerequisite for the success of any proposals aimed at achieving a political settlement.

8
The Path to Justice

Introduction

Arguably Bloody Sunday presents the ultimate example of law and justice being set to one side in order to serve the narrow interests of the security forces and their political masters. Not only did the law fail to protect 28 innocent civilians from being shot dead or wounded by the soldiers, but it also appears that the judicial process was deployed to cover up the full extent of the culpability of the soldiers and their military and political masters. It cannot be assumed, however, that Bloody Sunday was totally unique. While the scale of the slaughter that day has not been surpassed by the security forces in any other operation in Northern Ireland, the failure of the law either to protect the victims or to deliver justice is all too familiar. Indeed at one level Bloody Sunday might be considered as the worst example of the rule of law being shamelessly prostituted in the service of the partisan security and narrow political interests of the state. Since 1969 at least, the security forces have been able to perceive the law and the criminal justice process as supports for, rather than controls on, the immediate demands of security policy. Their use of arbitrary arrest, detention, interrogation, imprisonment, search, seizure and force, including lethal force, has been supported by legislative and executive action and abuses have rarely been penalised in the courts. The net effect has been to convey an image of the security forces as being the law as opposed to being subject to the law.

In the light of the Good Friday Peace Agreement it would appear that efforts are finally being made to lay the foundations for restoration of the rule of law and justice in Northern Ireland. For the present, the emergency legislation and much of the security apparatus remains in place. Nevertheless the prolonged ceasefire by the dominant paramilitary organisations, coupled with progress on the political front, have created an environment in which the impact of the emergency legislation and security apparatus is considerably reduced. Indeed the implementation of certain measures in the peace agreement holds out the prospect of a repeal of the emergency legislation and fundamental reform of the police and the criminal justice process.

While these developments are essential for the restoration of peace and the rule of law in Northern Ireland they will not deliver justice retrospectively for Bloody Sunday, nor will they do much to heal the deep wounds inflicted by the events of that day. This factor is of the utmost significance for the successful implementation of the agreement and the establishment of institutions of law and government in which all sections of the community can have confidence and respect. The failure of law and justice encapsulated by Bloody Sunday is so fundamental in its nature and extent that it is seared into the collective consciousness of the nationalist community. It, more than any other individual incident, law or practice, has instilled in the nationalist community a fundamental distrust in the capacity of the law and judicial process to protect them against hostile forces within the province of Northern Ireland. If justice is finally done with respect to Bloody Sunday, it is reasonable to suppose that nationalists will be more willing to place their trust in the promise of equal citizenship and the new political, social and cultural environment inherent in the peace agreement. It is therefore interesting that moves to heal the wounds inflicted by Bloody Sunday are running in an almost uncanny parallel with the peace process.

The struggle for justice

The legal options in 1972

The legal options available to those wounded on Bloody Sunday and the relatives of the deceased in the immediate aftermath of the Widgery Report were limited. Ideally the attorney general (subsequently the DPP) would have preferred criminal charges against some or all of the personnel responsible. Even on the basis of the highly selective findings of the Widgery Tribunal there were at least some grounds for the preferring of charges. The RUC conducted its own investigation into the Bloody Sunday deaths and woundings. Its file was passed to the DPP on 4 July 1972. Ultimately the DPP, with the support of the attorney general, decided that there was insufficient evidence to warrant the prosecution of any member of the security forces who participated in the Bloody Sunday operation.[1] For all practical purposes that removed the option of criminal prosecution, leaving the victims with the challenge of pursuing a civil action for damages.

Civil actions for damages were taken by the relatives of the deceased in the High Court. The government, however, responded by issuing a public statement that on the basis of the Widgery findings it accepted that 'all of the deceased should be regarded as having been found not guilty of the allegation of having been shot whilst handling a firearm or bomb'. The statement went on to say that 'in a spirit of goodwill and conciliation towards the relatives and friends of the deceased and on an *ex gratia* basis Her Majesty's Government have agreed to pay to the relatives of each of the deceased' certain specified sums.[2] It remained the government's position, however, that neither the British Army nor the Ministry of Defence were under any legal liability with respect to the deaths. Pursuant to legal advice the relatives received they withdrew their civil claims in the light of this statement and offer. It is worth making the point, however, that the payments the relatives received were so paltry that they only added to their sense of loss and grievance.

A judicial review to quash the findings of the Widgery Tribunal might be considered to have been a possible option largely on the basis of the flaws in the inquiry itself and its report, as explained in Chapters 3 and 4. Many of these flaws, however, would not have been known to the victims before the time limit for a judicial review expired. In any event there was no precedent for the successful challenge to the findings of such a tribunal of inquiry by way of a judicial review. Technically the tribunal merely conducted an inquiry with a view to establishing the facts of what had happened in disputed circumstances. It made no determination that affected the legal rights or liabilities of any individual. It is highly unlikely, therefore, that the High Court in 1972 would have accepted that the findings of such a tribunal would have been amenable to challenge by way of a judicial review.

An inquest into the 13 deaths was held on 21 August 1973. An inquest by itself, of course, could not provide a remedy for the relatives of the victims.[3] Its role was confined to determining the identity of the deceased and how, when and where they died. Its verdict on each of the deaths had to take one of the following forms: (1) died from natural causes; (2) died as a result of accident or misadventure; (3) died by his own act; (4) died by execution of sentence of death; or (5) open verdict (where none of the other options applied). The coroner could not commit any person for trial on a charge of murder or manslaughter. Nor could he or the jury express an opinion on matters of criminal or civil liability. Moreover, if a person was suspected of causing the death he could not be compelled to attend and give evidence. It is hardly surprising, therefore, that the inquest into the deaths on Bloody Sunday did not make any significant progress in establishing the full facts of what had happened on that day or in advancing the cause of justice for the victims. In the event the jury returned open verdicts on all the deaths. The following day, however, the coroner was quoted in the *Irish Times* as saying:

> It strikes me that the Army ran amok that day without thinking what they were doing. They were shooting innocent people. The people may have been taking part in a march that was banned but that does not justify the troops coming in and firing live rounds indiscriminately. I would say without hesitation that it was sheer, unadulterated murder. It was murder.[4]

The reported comments of the coroner, of course, had no legal standing. Nevertheless they did serve to strengthen the resolve of the victims in their quest for justice.

The last option for the victims was to seek a remedy in international law. The European Convention for the Protection of Human Rights and Fundamental Freedoms offered the potential to challenge the legality of the shootings and the subsequent failure of the UK authorities to prosecute those responsible. The United Kingdom became party to the convention in 1953 and it has accepted the right of individual petition. In practice this meant that an individual could utilise the machinery of the convention to take a case against a signatory state alleging that the state had infringed the rights of the individual under the convention. Equally, one signatory state could take an action against another signatory state alleging that the latter had infringed its obligations under the convention.

In the event the Irish government exercised the state's right of initiative under the convention to take a case against the United Kingdom alleging that the latter was in breach of, *inter alia*, Article 2 of the convention.[5] This case was part of a broader action alleging that the United Kingdom and its security forces were in breach of several articles of the convention in respect of their laws and actions, respectively, in Northern Ireland in 1970–72. In particular the Irish government targeted the Special Powers Act, the regulations made under the Act, the operation of internment, the arrest, detention and interrogation practices associated with internment and the fatal shooting of nine civilians. In the immediate aftermath of Bloody Sunday the Irish government included the 13 deaths on that day as part of their case.[6]

The basis of the Irish government's case with respect to the deaths was that the UK authorities were pursuing an administrative practice which failed to protect life, contrary to Article 2, and that this practice had been responsible for the death of the 22 persons concerned. In order to succeed the Irish government first had to establish that its complaint was admissible under the convention. In particular it had to show that the domestic remedies available in Northern Ireland in respect of the deaths had been exhausted. The Irish government had hoped to circumvent this requirement by virtue of the case law of the European Commission and the European Court, which had established that it would not be necessary to exhaust domestic remedies if the basis of the complaint was an administrative practice. The Irish government claimed that the 'deaths showed a failure by government, as a matter of administrative practice, to protect by law the right to life of persons within their jurisdiction in Northern Ireland.' The Commission ruled, however, that it would not be sufficient merely to assert that there was an administrative practice in order to benefit from the exclusion of the domestic remedies rule. The existence of the alleged measures or practices would have to be established by means of substantial evidence. In this case the Commission ruled that the Irish government had failed to produce the necessary evidence. Accordingly it was not relieved of the requirement to exhaust the available domestic remedies such as a civil action in the courts. Since these remedies had not been exhausted the Commission declared the Irish government's case inadmissible insofar as it asserted a breach of Article 2 in respect of the 22 deaths, including the 13 on Bloody Sunday.

In 1972 an action under the European Convention on Human Rights was the only practical remedy open to the victims in international law. The possibility of submitting a complaint to the United Nations' Special Rapporteur on Summary and Arbitrary Executions was not initiated by the United Nations Commission on Human Rights until March 1982.

The campaign for a new inquiry

For the remainder of the 1970s and the 1980s the calls for justice from the relatives of the Bloody Sunday victims fell largely on deaf ears. Nevertheless they refused to give up. Driven by the belief that the

Widgery Report seriously distorted the truth of what had actually happened on Bloody Sunday in a cynical attempt to cover up the full extent of the wrongdoing by the soldiers and the British military and political establishments, they came together in April 1992 to establish the Bloody Sunday Justice Campaign. Their primary objective was to persuade the UK government to establish a new and independent inquiry into Bloody Sunday. Their efforts to this end were supported by the work of the Bloody Sunday Trust, which provided professional and financial support. The campaign has also benefited from the active support of the British Irish Rights Watch.[7]

The application to the European Commission of Human Rights

On 24 January 1994 the relatives of those shot dead on Bloody Sunday wrote to the UK prime minister setting out the major flaws in the Widgery Inquiry and Report. The prime minister's undersecretary replied to this submission on 17 February 1994, stating the government's conventional position that it would not be right, after a Tribunal of Inquiry had already reported, to set up a further inquiry into events which had taken place 22 years previously. In the meantime British Irish Rights Watch had submitted, on behalf of the relatives, a report on Bloody Sunday to the United Nations Special Rapporteur on Summary and Arbitrary Executions.

On 18 August 1994 the relatives submitted an application against the United Kingdom to the European Commission of Human Rights. They claimed that the deceased had been intentionally and wrongfully deprived of their right to life, contrary to Article 2 of the European Convention on Human Rights. In particular they submitted that Article 2 imposes a positive duty on the state to protect the right to life and that the UK government had failed to discharge that duty with respect to those killed on Bloody Sunday. They further claimed that the failure to examine thoroughly and impartially the circumstances of the death of the deceased and to take criminal or other proceedings against those involved in the killings constituted a continuing breach of that duty. They also submitted that the only domestic remedy open to them was to persuade the UK government to reopen the inquiry.

Once again the crunch issue was admissibility. An application under the convention must be brought within six months of the exhaustion of domestic remedies. In a case of this nature this would ordinarily mean within six months of the decision not to prosecute, the failure of a civil action against those responsible, the outcome of the inquest or the report of the inquiry, whichever was the latest in time. The relatives sought to circumvent the time limit by arguing that they were the victims of a continuing breach in that the UK government was guilty of continuing to refuse to carry out an effective investigation into the deaths. The Commission, however, ruled that a continuing violation in this context was confined to a state of affairs whereby continuous activities by or on the part of the state were rendering the applicants victims. In this case the complaint was based on specific events which had occurred on identifiable dates, namely the decision not to prosecute, the publication of the Widgery Report and so on. Accordingly the six months ran from the last of those dates.

The relatives' however, argued that the time limit should run from the date of the prime minister's decision to refuse to hold a new inquiry, namely 17 February 1994. For this argument to succeed the request to hold a new inquiry would have to be considered an effective remedy for the purpose of the rule requiring the exhaustion of domestic remedies. The Commission was not persuaded. It did not consider that a request to reopen the inquiry submitted to the executive 22 years after the original tribunal published its findings could be considered an effective remedy for this purpose. Accordingly the application was rejected as inadmissible on the ground that it had been brought after the expiry of the time limit.[8]

New evidence

The first significant breakthrough for the justice campaign came in August 1995. While examining the few records on Bloody Sunday which were open to public inspection in the Public Records Office in London, the director of British Irish Rights Watch came across the confidential memo of the meeting between the prime minister, Lord Chief Justice Widgery and the Lord Chancellor on 31 January 1972, the evening before the inquiry was formally established by a resolution of both Houses of Parliament. Not only was this memo of devastating importance in its own right but its existence suggested that there must be further material on the Widgery Inquiry which was not in the public domain. The solicitors for the Bloody Sunday Trust and British Irish Rights Watch pursued the matter with the Public Records Office and the Home Office until eventually it was discovered that the Home Office had custody of a substantial volume of material relating to the inquiry. In all there were 13 categories of documents which were closed to public inspection for periods of 30 to 75 years. Eventually 12 categories were released to the solicitors for the Bloody Sunday Trust. The category which was held back consisted of the medical records of the injuries suffered by those shot dead. The Home Office sought to justify this exclusion by stressing the need to respect the privacy of the victims and their families. The significance of the exclusion of these documents is discussed later. It is also worth noting at this point that, despite the Home Office's assertion that it was not in possession of any further material relating to the inquiry, it is apparent from the contents of some of the documents released that they are incomplete. It was seen in Chapter 5, for example, that some of the statements by the soldiers referred to earlier statements they had made, but the earlier versions were not included in the documents released by the Home Office.

Despite the omissions, the newly released documents opened up a whole new vista for the campaign for a new inquiry. Included among them were memos from the tribunal secretary to Lord Widgery commenting upon issues and arguments that had arisen in the public hearings, strategic documents relating to evidence which had been given and potential witnesses, early drafts of parts of the tribunal's report and summaries of Widgery's response to some of these comments. Also included, of course, were the original statements given to the military police on the night of Bloody Sunday by those soldiers who had fired bullets, as well as supplementary statements made by some of the soldiers in the succeeding days and weeks and their formal statements to the legal team servicing the tribunal (the Treasury Solicitor). The documents also included a record of who had received what documentation at the time of the inquiry. This was important as it illustrated the huge discrepancy between the range of documentation supplied to Lord Widgery and the tribunal's legal team compared with that supplied to the legal team for the victims and their relatives. Of critical significance in this context was a record of the former having been supplied with the original statements by the soldiers on the night of Bloody Sunday, while the latter had not been supplied with this vital documentation.

In September 1996 the solicitors for the Bloody Sunday Trust engaged the author to examine the new documents in the light of the transcript of the tribunal proceedings and additional material which had been gathered independently. In particular he was asked to consider the statements the soldiers had made on the night of Bloody Sunday in the light of their testimony to the tribunal. He was also asked to draw any pertinent conclusions for the credibility of the inquiry and the legal culpability of the soldiers for their actions on Bloody Sunday.

The results of this examination are set out in Chapter 5. Originally, however, they were presented as part of a broader report entitled *The Bloody Sunday Tribunal of Inquiry: A Resounding Defeat for Truth, Justice and the Rule of Law*. This report exposed fundamental flaws in the inquiry and its report including, in particular, the unreliability of the soldiers' evidence, upon which the inquiry's conclusions were substantially based, the inquiry's failure to examine fully the circumstances in which each soldier had fired and the circumstances in which each non-fatal victim had been wounded, the apparent bias which permeated the inquiry and the proceedings being conducted on an adversarial as opposed to an inquisitorial basis.

The author's report was launched at an international press conference organised by the Bloody Sunday Justice Campaign on 30 January 1997, the twenty-fifth anniversary of Bloody Sunday. It attracted widespread interest and added significantly to the growing national and international concern about the events of Bloody Sunday and the manner in which the UK government had responded to them. The Bloody Sunday Justice Campaign adopted the report as a vital part of their strategy to secure a new inquiry. At one point they even applied for a judicial review to quash the report of the Widgery Tribunal on the basis of the author's report. This strategy, however, was never likely to succeed on account of the very strict time limits applicable to an application for judicial review. Ultimately the application was withdrawn. Instead, as will be seen below, the campaign used the author's report and the results of other research to persuade the Irish government to apply political and diplomatic pressure on the UK government to call a new inquiry.

The release of the new materials coincided with the conduct of another major piece of research on Bloody Sunday. In late 1995 Don Mullan rediscovered the hundreds of statements which had been collected from civilian eyewitnesses to Bloody Sunday by the Northern Ireland Civil Rights Association in early 1972. These are the statements of the witnesses whom Lord Widgery refused to call to give evidence at the inquiry. Mullan had a particular interest in these statements as he had been present as a boy on Bloody Sunday and had actually made one of the statements himself back in 1972. While examining the contents of these statements in the course of 1996 he began to form the theory that some of the shots fired on Bloody Sunday must have come from one or more positions in the vicinity of the Derry Walls. The Widgery Tribunal, however, had failed to investigate the possibility of firing from the Walls. Accordingly, if it transpired that some of the dead and wounded had been shot from the walls the credibility of the inquiry and its findings would be fatally flawed.

Mullan's theory could have found substantial support in the medical reports on the injuries of the victims, which had been made available to the Widgery inquiry. Significantly, however, these are the only category of documents which the Home Office withheld when it released the other materials. This deprived Mullan of vital material to test his theory. Nevertheless he was able to access the inquest reports, which contained the reports of the postmortem examinations carried out on those who had been shot dead on Bloody Sunday. These confirmed his suspicions that at least some of the victims had not been shot by soldiers on the ground but by soldiers firing from positions in the vicinity of the Derry Walls. He derived further support for his theory from discussions with Dr Raymond McClean, who had been in attendance at the postmortems. In November 1996 he obtained an opinion from a ballistics expert in New York, Mr Robert J. Breglio, to the effect that three of the deceased had been shot from a position in the vicinity of the Derry Walls. Mullan also found support for his theory in the transcripts of police and army radio messages sent during the shooting on Bloody Sunday. These suggest that at least some shots had been fired from a position in the vicinity of the Derry Walls.

In January 1997, just a few weeks short of the twenty-fifth anniversary of Bloody Sunday, Mullan published his research in a book entitled *Eyewitness Bloody Sunday: The Truth*. For the most part this consisted of an edited collection of a broad sample of the statements given by the civilian eyewitnesses on Bloody Sunday. In addition, however, Mullan aired his theory about the shooting from one or more positions in the vicinity of the Derry Walls. His book attracted widespread media interest and was adopted by the Bloody Sunday Justice Campaign as another vital component in their quest for a new inquiry.

Naturally the twenty-fifth anniversary of Bloody Sunday in January 1997 offered a convenient focal point for renewed media interest in Bloody Sunday and the report of the Widgery Tribunal of Inquiry. This interest was fuelled by the publication of Mullan's book and the author's report. Investigative reporters, particularly from Channel 4 News, the BBC 'Newsnight' programme and the *Sunday Business Post*, carried out further research into what had actually happened on Bloody Sunday. This in turn resulted in further witnesses coming forward to give evidence which fundamentally contradicted the official version offered by the Widgery Inquiry. Some of these witnesses purported to be soldiers who had participated in the Bloody Sunday operation.

The Irish government's report

The Anglo-Irish Agreement, which was signed in 1985, signalled the dawn of a new era in relations between the Irish and the UK governments with respect to Northern Ireland. For the first time the latter formally acknowledged that the former has a legitimate interest in making representations on behalf of the nationalist minority in Northern Ireland. The establishment of the Anglo-Irish Secretariat in Belfast provided a formal mechanism through which the concerns of the nationalist minority could be conveyed to the Irish government and from there to the UK government. The Bloody Sunday Justice Campaign took full advantage of the secretariat to press their claim for a new inquiry. While the Irish government shared the relatives' lack of confidence in the report of the Widgery Tribunal it had very little success in persuading the UK government. While the latter was prepared to acknowledge that those who had been killed should be considered innocent of the allegation that they had been shot while handling firearms or explosives, it refused to entertain the notion that the Widgery Tribunal's report was flawed. It stuck rigidly to its official position that Bloody Sunday had been fully investigated by the Widgery Tribunal, and that in the absence of significant new evidence there was no basis upon which the matter could be reopened.

In early 1997 the Bloody Sunday Justice Campaign was able to approach the Irish government with an impressive dossier of new evidence attacking the credibility of the Widgery Report. This new evidence consisted of five primary components. The first was Don Mullan's book, *Eyewitness Bloody Sunday*, including evidence in support of his thesis that some of the fatal shots had been fired from a position in the vicinity of the Derry Walls. The second was the author's report, *The Bloody Sunday Tribunal of Inquiry: A Resounding Defeat for Truth, Justice and the Rule of Law*. The third consisted of Channel 4 interviews with individuals who were believed to have been soldiers on duty in Derry on Bloody Sunday. These interviews supported Mullan's thesis that shots had been fired from the vicinity of the Derry Walls and asserted that military command and control had been absent for a period, during which 'shameful and disgraceful acts' had been perpetrated. They also claimed that officials working for the Widgery Tribunal had changed the version of events presented by at least one soldier. The fourth was a *Sunday Business Post* interview with an individual claiming to have been a member of the 1st Battalion of the Parachute Regiment and present in Glenfada Park when his colleagues had shot and wounded several victims. He claimed that his colleagues had killed unarmed and fleeing civilians, some of whom had already been wounded. He also claimed that the staff of the Widgery Tribunal had fabricated aspects of his original statement in an apparent attempt to justify the killings. The fifth was a collection of 101 statements from eyewitnesses to the events of Bloody Sunday which had been taken by the Irish government in 1972.

The Irish government formulated its own assessment of this new material after subjecting it to a thorough examination. It then proceeded to deconstruct the Widgery Report on the basis of this assessment. The results were subsequently published under the title, *Bloody Sunday and the Report of the Widgery Tribunal: The Irish Government's Assessment of the New Material*. The very fact that the Irish government embarked upon a deconstruction of the report of a Tribunal of Inquiry set up by the UK government under the Tribunals of Inquiry (Evidence) Act 1921 was, of course, highly unusual in itself. What must be unprecedented, however, was the unrestrained and forceful manner in which the Irish government presented its damning indictment of the credibility of the Widgery Report:

> As is evident from the foregoing assessment, it can be concluded that the Widgery Report was fundamentally flawed. It was incomplete in terms of its description of the events on the day and in terms of how those events were apparently shaped by the prior intentions and decisions of the authorities. It was a startlingly inaccurate and partisan version of events, dramatically at odds with the experiences and observations of civilian eyewitnesses. It failed to provide a credible explanation for the actions of the British Army units in and around Derry. It was inherently and apparently wilfully flawed, selective and unbalanced in its handling of the evidence to hand at the time. It effectively rejected the many hundreds of civilian testimonies submitted to it and opted instead for the unreliable accounts proffered by the implicated soldiers. Contrary to the weight of evidence and even its own findings, it exculpated the individual soldiers who used lethal force and thereby exonerated those who were responsible for their deployment and actions.
>
> Above all it was unjust to the victims of Bloody Sunday and to those who participated in the anti-internment march that day in suggesting that they had handled fire-arms or nail bombs or were in the company of those who did. It made misleading judgements about how the victims met their death. The tenacity with which these suggestions were pursued, often on flimsy or downright implausible

grounds, is in marked contrast to the many points where significant and obvious questions about the soldiers' behaviour, arising from the Report's own narrative, are evaded or glossed over.

Given these conclusions it is hardly surprising that the Irish government proceeded to call for the establishment of a new inquiry. Significantly, it supported its case by reference to the need to remedy the profound injustice that both Bloody Sunday and the Widgery Report had inflicted on the victims and their families and on the rule of law. The events of Bloody Sunday and the response of the British political and legal establishments were so deeply seared into the consciousness of the nationalist community that, even after 25 years, they still constituted a major impediment to rebuilding trust and confidence in the rule of law in Northern Ireland:

> There have been many atrocities in Northern Ireland since Bloody Sunday. Other innocent victims have suffered grievously at various hands. The victims of Bloody Sunday met their fate at the hands of those whose duty it was to respect as well as uphold the rule of law. However, what sets this case apart from other tragedies which might rival it in bloodshed, is not the identity of those killing or killed, or even the horrendous circumstances of the day. It is rather that the victims of Bloody Sunday suffered a second injustice, this time at the hands of Lord Widgery, the pivotal trustee of the rule of law, who sought to taint them with responsibility for their own deaths in order to exonerate, even at that great moral cost, those he found it inexpedient to blame.
>
> The new material fatally undermines and discredits the Widgery Report. A debt of injustice is owed to the victims and their relatives to set it unambiguously aside as the official version of events. It must be replaced by a clear and truthful account of events on that day, so that the poisonous legacy can be set aside and the wounds left by it can begin to be healed. Given the status and currency which was accorded to the Widgery Report, the most appropriate and convincing redress would be a new Report, based on a new independent inquiry.

The new inquiry

The Irish government presented its report to the UK government in June 1997. The expectation was that once the latter had had time to consider the report, plus the new evidence and the analysis upon which it was based, it would move swiftly to establish a new inquiry. The election of a new Labour government on 1 May 1997 with an unassailable parliamentary majority, coupled with its declared commitment to pursue a lasting peace in Northern Ireland, gave grounds for optimism that at long last justice would be done. As the months passed, however, it became apparent that there were strong forces within the British establishment who were implacably opposed to any reopening of the Bloody Sunday question.

With the twenty-sixth anniversary of Bloody Sunday approaching and no sign of a new inquiry the Irish government embarked upon a bold strategy which would apply pressure on the UK government. It let it be known that the publication of its report on the Widgery Inquiry was imminent. Unquestionably the UK government would find it very difficult to defend publicly its failure to establish a new inquiry given the strength of the new evidence and analysis presented in the Irish government's report. It was hardly a coincidence, therefore, that the UK government announced the establishment of a new public judicial inquiry on the eve of the twenty-sixth anniversary, the same day that the Irish government published its report.

The terms of reference of the new tribunal of inquiry are to inquire into 'the events of Sunday, 30th January 1972 which led to loss of life in connection with the procession in Londonderry on that day, taking account of any new information relevant to events on that day'. These are identical to the terms of reference of the Widgery Inquiry, apart from the reference to taking account of any new information relevant to events on that day. The new inquiry, however, cannot be considered in any sense an appeal from the Widgery Inquiry. It is a totally separate and *de novo* inquiry into the same events investigated by the Widgery Inquiry. Indeed the new inquiry enjoys exactly the same legal status as the Widgery Inquiry. The establishing instrument stipulates that the Tribunals of Inquiry (Evidence) Act 1921 applies to it and its proceedings. Accordingly, just like the Widgery Tribunal of Inquiry, the tribunal enjoys all of the powers, rights and privileges of the High Court or a judge of the High Court in respect of compelling witnesses to attend and submit to examination, compelling the production of documents and the examination of witnesses abroad. Any person who refuses to attend when summoned, refuses to take an oath required by the tribunal, fails to answer any question or produce any document required by the tribunal or does any other thing which amounts to a contempt of court is at risk of being proceeded against for contempt in the High Court. A witness before the tribunal is entitled to the same immunities and privileges to which he or she would be entitled as a witness in civil proceedings in the High Court. Just like the Widgery Tribunal, the new tribunal must sit in public, although it does have the power to exclude the public or a section of the public in certain circumstances. It also has the power to authorise or refuse legal representation to any person appearing before it.

It is worth emphasising that the remit of the new inquiry focuses very tightly on the events of Bloody Sunday and the background to those events. It has no jurisdiction to examine how the Widgery Inquiry was conducted or to make any findings on the reliability of its conclusions. In effect the report of the new inquiry will constitute a second official account of what actually happened on Bloody Sunday and will exist side by side and with equal status to the account offered by the Widgery Tribunal.

While the Widgery Tribunal of Inquiry was chaired by the lord chief justice sitting alone, the new tribunal is presided over by three judges. The chairman, Lord Justice Saville, was appointed a High Court judge in 1985, a lord justice of appeal in 1993 and a lord of appeal in ordinary in 1997. As a High Court judge he was most closely associated with commercial matters and between 1994 and 1996 he chaired a Department of Trade and Industry committee on arbitration legislation. He enjoys a reputation as a moderniser within the senior judiciary. Lord Saville accepted the chairmanship of the Bloody Sunday Inquiry at the invitation of the lord chancellor. In marked contrast to the Widgery experience the government did not seek in any way to influence him on how he should conduct the inquiry or what conclusions he should reach. Indeed Lord Saville did not discuss any aspect of the inquiry with any member of the government, apart from the lord chancellor.

Significantly the other two judges on the tribunal are from outside the United Kingdom. The legacy of the Widgery Inquiry has been such that the relatives of the victims would have found it very difficult to have confidence in another tribunal of inquiry headed by a single British judge. The inclusion of two judges from outside the United Kingdom can therefore be interpreted as a concession designed to allay their fears. The two judges in question are Sir Edward Somers, formerly a judge of the Court of Appeal of New Zealand, and Mr Justice William Hoyt, who was the chief justice of the Province of New Brunswick in Canada at the time of his appointment to the tribunal. The lord chancellor consulted Lord Saville on the choice of these two members of the tribunal.

The Saville Inquiry opened in Derry on 3 April 1998. The choice of venue is, of course, significant. Moreover in contrast to the Widgery Inquiry it was announced that most of the oral hearings would be held in Derry. Another important announcement at the opening concerned the identity of the inquiry's back-up team. As explained in Chapter 3 the Widgery Inquiry's reliance on the Treasury Solicitor gave the appearance of a possible conflict of interest. The secretary to the Saville inquiry initially was Ann Stephenson, a senior administrator in the Department of Health. She has since moved on and has been replaced by Adrian Shaw. The solicitor to the inquiry initially was Philip Ridd, a senior legal adviser to the Inland Revenue. He has since moved on and has been replaced by John Tate. Counsel to the inquiry is Christopher Clarke QC assisted by Alan Roxborough BL and Jacob Grierson BL. Lord Saville personally selected the secretary, the solicitor and leading counsel. In making his selections he was clearly intent on securing the necessary talent for the inquiry without running into the possible conflicts of interest which affected the Widgery Inquiry.

The preliminary hearings were held in Derry on 20–21 July 1998 and again on 27 November 1998. The first item to be discussed was the critical issue of legal representation. The standard practice in such tribunals of inquiry is that any individuals who are likely to be the subject of damaging allegations in the course of the tribunal's proceedings are granted legal representation. The purpose of such representation is to protect the right to natural justice of the individuals concerned and, in particular, to help them prepare and present their defence against any such allegations. This must be distinguished from the role of legal representation in trial proceedings, where the lawyers for each side engage in adversarial combat on behalf of their clients with a view to having the case decided in their favour. The function of a tribunal of inquiry, however, is not to decide a case in favour of one side or another. Rather its aim is to establish and present the truth of what actually happened in a situation or incident which has given rise to serious public controversy. It adopts an inquisitorial rather than an adversarial approach to its task. Accordingly the primary burden of ferreting out the truth falls not on the lawyers acting for one or more individual who is likely to be the subject of damaging allegations but on the lawyers for the tribunal itself. As explained in Chapter 3, one of the major defects of the Widgery Inquiry was that its proceedings were conducted primarily on an adversarial basis with an underresourced legal team representing the interests of the victims, the families of the deceased and the nationalist people of Derry against a very well-resourced legal team representing the interests of the

British Army. By comparison the legal team for the tribunal adopted a predominantly passive role throughout the public hearings.

Initially it seemed that the Saville Tribunal was not going to make the same error on legal representation as the Widgery Tribunal. Its strategy was to conduct the proceedings on an inquisitorial basis, with the legal team for the tribunal playing a dominant role in actively seeking out and testing the credibility of evidence of what actually happened on Bloody Sunday. This meant that the legal teams for the respective parties would be relieved of much of this burden and as such could be kept quite small. In the case of the families of the victims the tribunal gave a provisional ruling to the effect that one leading and two junior counsel would be sufficient. The legal representatives of the families, however, argued vehemently for substantial legal representation to be granted to the families of the victims. They were acutely conscious of the unlimited resources available to the British Army. The experience of the Widgery Tribunal was such that they simply were not willing to take the risk of participating in the inquiry without the support of substantial legal representation. Moreover the additional material available to the legal team for the victims in 1998 was such that an adversarial approach to the proceedings could hardly disadvantage them to the extent that it had in 1972.

In the event the tribunal was persuaded by the argument that, in the light of the Widgery experience, the level of legal representation afforded to the victims and their families would have a critical bearing on the extent to which justice was being seen to be done. Accordingly it granted the victims and their families a composite legal team of five leading counsel and five junior counsel in addition to the services of their solicitors. Separate legal representation was subsequently granted to the family of James Wray, one of those shot dead. It is also useful at this point to note that several of the soldiers whose actions and decisions on Bloody Sunday are central to the inquiry are represented by leading and junior counsel on the instructions of the Treasury Solicitor. Given the fact that the Treasury Solicitor actually serviced the Widgery Tribunal, it is submitted that this arrangement is far from satisfactory. To make matters worse the Ministry of Defence, which is separately represented at the inquiry, is also being advised by the Treasury Solicitor.

Another important issue that the inquiry had to address at the preliminary hearings was the question of self-incrimination. It can be anticipated that a significant number of individuals will be reluctant to come forward or participate fully in the inquiry for fear of incriminating themselves. Witnesses appearing before the tribunal have the same rights and privileges as those who give evidence before an ordinary court. They can refuse to answer questions on the ground that their answers may be used against them in a criminal prosecution. This of course could present a major impediment to the work of the tribunal in searching out the truth. Accordingly the tribunal made a recommendation to the attorney general and the DPP for a ruling to the effect that nothing said to the tribunal by any person either before or at the oral hearings could or would be used in subsequent criminal proceedings against that person. This is not quite the same as immunity from prosecution. Any individual giving evidence to the tribunal could still be prosecuted. It is just that any statement they make to the tribunal or document they produce cannot be used in evidence against them. However there is nothing to stop such statements or evidence being used in the prosecution of another party.

Closely related to the question of self-incrimination is the issue of the anonymity of witnesses. Several individuals might fear for their personal security if their identities became known as a result of giving evidence in public to the tribunal. In July 1998 the tribunal indicated that anonymity would be granted to any soldier who could satisfy it that he had a genuine and reasonable fear of the potential consequences of the disclosure of his personal details. Several soldiers applied for anonymity. In December 1998 the tribunal ruled that the soldiers could not refuse to reveal their names, although their present addresses and other personal details could be kept secret. In the case of soldiers who admitted firing live rounds only the surnames had to be revealed. The tribunal also ruled that individual soldiers could apply for complete anonymity on the basis of special circumstances. Four soldiers mounted a challenge in the High Court to the tribunal's refusal to grant them complete anonymity. The High Court upheld their application largely on the basis that the tribunal had erred through its failure to give sufficient weight to the nature and extent of the security threat to the soldiers in question and on the basis that it had misled the soldiers on the basis upon which it would be prepared to grant anonymity.[9] Subsequently all those soldiers who had fired live rounds on Bloody Sunday lodged applications for anonymity. These were considered at a tribunal hearing on 26 and 27 April 1999.

In its ruling on the second application the tribunal declared that its fundamental objective was to establish the truth about Bloody Sunday. As such, it regarded itself as under a duty to carry out its investigative function in a way that demonstrates to all concerned that it is engaged in a thorough, open and complete search for the truth. In the absence of compelling countervailing factors it ruled that this duty, which it traced back to the fundamental principle of open justice in a democratic society, entails that those who gave evidence to the tribunal should do so under their proper names. To withhold the names of those in the army who were implicated in the shootings would detract from an open search for the truth and would require justification of an overriding kind. The fact that anonymity would not actually hamper the tribunal in its search for the truth was not the issue. Accordingly the tribunal refused to grant blanket anonymity to the soldiers, although it did rule that only their second names should be published. It also ruled that any individual soldier could apply for anonymity on the basis of special circumstances when the time came to give evidence in public.[10]

The Saville Inquiry's stand on anonymity was in total contrast with that of the Widgery Tribunal. The latter had given the soldiers an assurance that 'subject to some compelling unforeseen circumstance' they would enjoy anonymity with respect to their evidence so long as there was any danger of reprisals being taken against them or their families. This, of course, raised the question of whether the Saville Inquiry would be bound to respect that assurance. The Saville Inquiry, however, ruled that the establishment of a second inquiry with substantially the same terms of reference as the Widgery Inquiry was a 'compelling unforeseen circumstance'. As such it cancelled out the 'Widgery assurance'. In any event the Saville Inquiry felt that the assurance was no longer sufficient in itself to override the inquiry's duty to conduct its investigation openly. While the inquiry accepted that there were grounds for the soldiers assertion that they had genuine and reasonable fears of reprisals, it ruled that these were not of sufficient substance to override its duty to conduct an open investigation.

Once again the soldiers went to the High Court to challenge the legality of the inquiry's ruling on anonymity and once again they were successful, although on this occasion only by a two to one majority.[11] Normally the High Court will only interfere with the substance of a decision taken by a tribunal within its jurisdiction where the decision was so unreasonable in the relevant circumstances as to be perverse or bordering on the absurd. In this case, however, the High Court ruled that where a tribunal's decision interfered with fundamental human rights the appropriate test to be applied by the court on a review was whether a reasonable tribunal could reasonably conclude on the material before it that such interference was justifiable. The Court also ruled that where the fundamental human rights of the individual would be affected by the decision of a tribunal the law gave precedence to those rights.

Accordingly, those rights should prevail unless the threat of infringement as a result of the tribunal's decision was slight or there was a compelling reason why they should yield. In this case the Court found that if the soldiers were refused anonymity their lives and the lives of their families, as well as their private and family lives, would be exposed to a real risk. As against that, the only benefit which could be achieved by refusing anonymity would be greater openness at the inquiry. The Court considered that the inquiry's fundamental task of discovering the truth would not be impeded if anonymity was granted to the soldiers. Accordingly, the Court concluded that the inquiry had erred by favouring greater openness over the fundamental rights of the soldiers and their families to life, security of the person and respect for private and family life.

The inquiry appealed to the Court of Appeal which upheld the decision of the High Court.[12] Since it was accepted that the security fears of the soldiers were based on reasonable grounds, the Court of Appeal ruled that the correct approach was to consider whether there was any compelling justification for naming the soldiers. The inquiry felt that its duty to carry out an open public investigation which would capture the confidence of the public generally, and the families of the deceased and injured in particular, provided sufficient justification. The Court of Appeal, however, considered that the inquiry had failed to appreciate the extent to which it was already discharging its duty of discovering the truth and establishing public confidence in its deliberations. It was sitting in public, the names of the soldiers concerned were known to the inquiry, the officers who were in control on Bloody Sunday were named, any of the individual soldiers could be named if that was considered necessary and the inquiry would ultimately present a full report which would be published. The inroads on the openness of the inquiry which would ensue from granting anonymity would be very limited. The soldiers would still have to give their evidence in public. The only thing which would be concealed would be their names. The Court concluded that by refusing anonymity the inquiry had failed to attach sufficient weight to the right to life of the soldiers and their families. In the light of this ruling the Saville Inquiry has felt compelled to grant anonymity to all soldiers who played a part in relation to Bloody Sunday.

Since the decision of the Court of Appeal was handed down it has become public knowledge that the senior judge sitting on the appeal, namely the Master of the Rolls Lord Woolf, had been a captain in the Royal Hussars and a member of the British army's legal services.[13] Lord Woolf had also sat on the Court of Appeal which ruled against the inquiry in the first anonymity appeal. On neither occasion had he declared his former links with the British Army. Given the subject matter of the appeals it is arguable that Lord Woolf's participation raises an appearance of bias. It must be said immediately that there is absolutely no suggestion of even the merest hint of bias in Lord Woolf's treatment of the issues in either appeal. Not only is he one of the finest judges sitting on Court of Appeal, but his commitment to justice and fairness is impeccable. The issue, however, is one of appearance as opposed to substance.

Earlier this year an appearance of bias was sufficient to persuade the House of Lords to take the unprecedented step of setting aside its decision that General Pinochet, the former Chilean dictator, had no immunity in Britain against arrest and prosecution for crimes against humanity.[14] In that case the appearance of bias stemmed from the failure of Lord Justice Hoffman, one of the judges who sat on the case, to declare his links with Amnesty International. Amnesty had been active in the campaign to have General Pinochet prosecuted. It can be argued by analogy that the Court of Appeal's decision on anonymity should be set aside as a result of the Master of the Rolls failing to declare his past links with the British Army. Admittedly, the anonymity case can be distinguished from the Pinochet case on the basis that Lord Woolf's connections with the British Army were in the past and were of a professional or commercial nature, while Lord Hoffman's links with Amnesty are current and of a personal nature. Such distinctions, however, may not be sufficient to assure those whose confidence in the British judiciary has been shaken by the experience of the Widgery Inquiry.[15]

Since it was established the tribunal has been engaged in the laborious process of identifying and tracking down witnesses, taking witness statements, compiling documentary evidence, carrying out further investigations and generally preparing the groundwork for the public hearings in which evidence will be formally presented and tested. Initially it had some difficulty identifying and contacting the soldiers who had participated in the events of Bloody Sunday and persuading them to come forward. Moreover the Ministry of Defence sought to rely on the provisions of the Data Protection Act to refuse to reveal the names and addresses of those receiving pensions. The tribunal responded by threatening to issue subpoenas to force the disclosure of the names and addresses of any soldiers who failed to come forward voluntarily. At the time of writing the tribunal was in receipt of some 60 000 pages of text, 2500 photographs, 19 videotapes and 22 audiotapes. It had taken 420 statements from those present at the events of

Bloody Sunday. One hundred and fifty local people had still to be interviewed. One hundred and fourteen soldiers had come forward voluntarily, while the Ministry of Defence forwarded the names of 3000 soldiers who would have to be checked out for involvement. Thirty journalists had also been identified as potential witnesses. The oral hearings are scheduled to commence in March 2000.

Restoring confidence in the rule of law

In a state governed by the basic principles of democracy and the rule of law it is the law which provides individuals and minorities with the ultimate protection against the worst excesses of a hostile government. If the law cannot protect their fundamental human rights from being trampled upon in order to serve some partisan political objective, the very legitimacy of the state itself will be called into question. One of the most disturbing aspects of Bloody Sunday, therefore, is the dismal failure of the law and the legal system to prevent the killings and woundings from happening in the first place and to deliver justice to the victims and the broader community after the event. This failure was compounded over much of the succeeding 26 years by the persistent failure of the legal system to prevent or provide a remedy for a whole series of excesses by the security forces, as outlined in Chapter 7. The inevitable effect was profound damage to the nationalists' confidence in justice and the rule of law in Northern Ireland. This in turn created and sustained an environment in which the violent overthrow of the state could be presented not just as a plausible strategy but also as the only realistic means of redress for those at the receiving end of the security policies and practices. The violence against the state provoked a response in kind, and so the cycle continued until the ceasefires of 1994 and 1997 created a breathing space in which the representatives of the various factions in Northern Ireland were able to explore a political settlement in conjunction with the British and Irish governments. It is, to say the least, fortuitous that the Saville Inquiry has been established at the same time as determined efforts are afoot to address the fundamental problems at the source of the conflict in Northern Ireland. Resolution of the Bloody Sunday issue will not be sufficient in itself to convince nationalists that they will secure justice and equality of treatment and respect in Northern Ireland. Equally the prospect of a political settlement will remain very slim for as long as the injustices of Bloody Sunday are allowed to fester.

A political settlement

Unquestionably a political settlement, such as that reached in the Good Friday Peace Agreement, is essential if the cycle of terrorist violence and state oppression is to be broken permanently in Northern Ireland. Indeed it is significant that the agreement directly addresses many of the political, economic and social grievances which have been alienating the nationalist community from the province of Northern Ireland since its establishment in 1921. Under the terms of the agreement, for example, nationalists are effectively guaranteed the opportunity to participate in the government of Northern Ireland as a distinct entity within the United Kingdom.[16] Their political, social and cultural attachment to Ireland will be reflected in the establishment of, and the opportunity for them to participate in, all-Ireland bodies for the implementation, on an all-Ireland basis, of certain executive responsibilities of mutual interest to both governments on the island.[17] Equally the agreement provides for the development of new social and economic policies to address, *inter alia*, the problems of a divided society, social exclusion, a strengthening of fair employment legislation, the progressive elimination of the differential in unemployment rates between the two communities and action to support the development and use of the Irish language.[18]

While all of these measures are undoubtedly essential to combat the sources of alienation and promote the development of an inclusive society in Northern Ireland, a vital prerequisite for the success of the agreement itself is the restoration of nationalist confidence in the rule of law. The very fact that a second inquiry into Bloody Sunday has been established will, of course, make an important contribution to this end. However, as is evident from Chapters 2, 6 and 7, further more general reforms will be required in the criminal justice system as a whole if the weaknesses which allowed Bloody Sunday to happen and to go unremedied for so many years are to be removed. Significantly the basis for such reforms is written into the agreement itself, primarily in the form of enhanced protection of human rights, the dismantling of the security apparatus and the establishment of a commission on policing. It is worth outlining the progress made on each of these in turn.

The protection of human rights

The Good Friday Peace Agreement commits the parties to mutual respect for the civil rights and religious liberties of everyone in the community.[19] The UK government, in particular, is committed to the incorporation of the European Convention for the Protection of

Human Rights and Fundamental Freedoms into Northern Irish law.[20] This will include provision for the courts to overrule Northern Irish Assembly legislation[21] on the grounds of inconsistency with the convention. In addition there is provision for the establishment of a new independent Northern Ireland Human Rights Commission, the membership of which must reflect the community balance.[22] Its role will include frequent review of the adequacy and effectiveness of laws and practices pertaining to human rights, making recommendations to the government on such matters, providing information and promoting awareness of human rights, considering draft legislation referred by the assembly and, in appropriate cases, bringing court cases on its own initiative or assisting individuals to bring such cases. It will also be invited to consult and advise on the scope for defining, in Westminster legislation, rights supplementary to those in the European Convention on Human Rights to reflect the particular circumstances of Northern Ireland.[23] These additional rights will reflect the principles of mutual respect for the identity and ethos of both communities and parity of esteem between them. The commission must also address itself to the formulation of a general obligation on government and public bodies fully to respect, on the basis of equality of treatment, the identity and ethos of both communities; and a clear formulation of the rights not to be discriminated against and to equality of opportunity in both the public and private sectors. Together with the European Convention on Human Rights, these additional rights will constitute a Bill of Rights for Northern Ireland. Clearly the Northern Ireland Human Rights Commission is meant to function as a dynamic mechanism for the promotion and protection of human rights as an essential element in tackling some of the fundamental grievances which lie at the heart of the conflict in Northern Ireland.[24]

Dismantling the security apparatus

The damage which has been done to public respect for the rule of law by the catalogue of security force excesses which have gone unremedied over the past thirty years will not be repaired by a reawakening of respect for human rights alone. The sources of the damage must also be tackled. These can be traced to the immense security powers and resources which have been placed at the disposal of the executive, the courts, individual soldiers, police officers and other state officials, coupled with the relative failure of the courts to ensure that such powers and resources are not used oppressively against individuals and communities. If confidence is to be restored in the rule of law and the capacity of the courts to provide a remedy against abuse by the security forces, there is no substitute for the dismantling of the broad discretionary powers which have been enjoyed by the executive and the security forces as a result of emergency legislation since Northern Ireland was established nearly 80 years ago. The importance of this issue is recognised in the provisions of the peace agreement which deal with the reform of the security and justice arrangements, including the RUC in particular.

Under the heading of security the agreement acknowledges the opportunity presented by the overall terms of the agreement for the development of a peaceful environment, leading to the normalisation of security arrangements and practices.[25] In this context the British government undertakes to make progress towards normal security arrangements by removing security installations and reducing the numbers and role of the armed forces to levels compatible with a normal peaceful society.[26] Critically it also undertakes to remove the emergency powers. Progress on these matters is linked to the level of threat posed by terrorist organisations. Indeed the stability of the ceasefires by the main terrorist organisations has already borne fruit in the form of significant reductions in the number of troops stationed in Northern Ireland, a significant scaling down of the number of patrols by the armed forces and the dismantling of some major military installations. Although it does not come under the heading of security in the agreement, it is also worth noting the significant progress which has been made in the release of prisoners convicted of scheduled offences.[27] The practical importance of this issue in securing the peace process and creating confidence in the criminal process is reflected in the fact that a separate section is devoted to it in the peace agreement.[28] Without such releases it would never be possible for the communities from which the prisoners come to accept that there really had been a normalisation of the security and justice arrangements.

Police reform

The agreement itself specifically recognises the central importance of policing and the need for 'a new beginning to policing in Northern Ireland with a police service capable of attracting and sustaining support from the community as a whole'.[29] Indeed it is no exaggeration to say that the success of the entire agreement could depend on its capacity to resolve the policing problem. As explained in Chapter 2, policing has been an active and vital issue at the very heart of the conflict, at least since the establishment of Northern Ireland as a separate entity in 1921. Broadly speaking, one community has always identified the RUC as their primary protection against internal and external subversion from nationalist/Irish sources. The other has perceived it as the mailed fist protecting and upholding the unionist/British ethos of a state which has denied them equality of treatment and respect. If confidence in the rule of law is to be restored it is absolutely essential that these perspectives on the police in Northern Ireland are replaced with the perception and reality of a police service that is geared to serve the needs of all sections of the community without favour or distinction on the grounds of political or religious identity. Indeed it is worth quoting in full what the parties to the peace agreement consider are the basic principles upon which the new police service should be built:

> The participants believe it is essential that policing structures and arrangements are such that the police service is professional, effective and efficient, fair and impartial, free from partisan political control; accountable, both under the law for its actions and to the community it serves; representative of the society it polices, operates within a coherent and co-operative criminal justice system, which conforms with human rights norms. The participants also believe that those structures and arrangements must be capable of maintaining law and order including responding effectively to crime and to any terrorist threat and to public order problems. A police service which cannot do so will fail to win public confidence or acceptance. They believe that any such structures and arrangements should be capable of delivering a police service, in constructive and inclusive partnerships with the community at all levels, and with the maximum delegation of authority and responsibility, consistent with the foregoing principles. These arrangements should be based on principles of protection of human rights and professional integrity and should be unambiguously accepted and actively supported by the entire community.[30]

Agreeing these principles was one thing; devising agreed policing arrangements which would satisfy them was quite another. The pragmatic solution was an agreement to establish an independent commission to make recommendations for future policing arrangements in Northern Ireland.[31] The peace agreement went on to set out in some detail the terms of reference of the commission. These are broadly encapsulated by the first two paragraphs of the terms of reference, as set out in the agreement:

> Taking account of the principles on policing as set out in the agreement, the Commission will inquire into policing in Northern Ireland

and, on the basis of its findings, bring forwards proposals for future policing structures and arrangements, including means of encouraging widespread community support for those arrangements.

Its proposals on policing should be designed to ensure that policing arrangements, including composition, recruitment, training, culture, ethos and symbols, are such that in a new approach Northern Ireland has a police service that can enjoy widespread support from, and is seen as an integral part of, the community as a whole.[32]

Clearly, it was envisaged that the commission would bring forward proposals for a complete reform and overhaul of policing in Northern Ireland with a view to the establishment of a policing system which is rooted in the community as a whole, capable of commanding the support, trust and cooperation of the whole community, responsive to the needs of the whole community, governed by and fully accountable to the law and informed by respect for human rights and internationally accepted norms on policing standards.

Given this clear signal that fundamental reform in the governance and ethos of policing in Northern Ireland was a vital issue in the context of the overall peace settlement, it is surprising that the UK government should have proceeded with legislative proposals on the governance of the police in Northern Ireland. These proposals, which were still at an early stage of the legislative process when the peace agreement was signed, aimed at extending to Northern Ireland many of the important changes in the governance of the police first introduced in England and Wales in 1994, as well as the establishment of an independent police complaints system based on an ombudsman model. They can therefore be interpreted as a not very subtle attempt to set the agenda for the Independent Commission on Policing. Indeed when defending the proposals on the second reading of the Police (Northern Ireland) Bill 1997 in the House of Lords, Lord Dubs intimated that the government viewed the bill as a foundation upon which it expected the commission to build.[33] The Bill has since been enacted as the Police (Northern Ireland) Act 1998.[34]

The Independent Commission on Policing for Northern Ireland was established in June 1998 under the chairmanship of Chris Patten, former governor of Hong Kong and one-time Conservative government minister for Northern Ireland.[35] Its terms of reference are identical to those set out in the peace agreement and the target date for its report was the summer of 1999. In the course of its work the commission invited and received a substantial volume of submissions from the public and interest groups. It also conducted a whole series of public meetings in all parts of Northern Ireland in order to meet ordinary people in their own communities and hear their thoughts on policing.

The substance and intensity of the views expressed at some of these meetings, coupled with the huge contrast in such views from one community to another, reflect just how sensitive and important the whole subject of policing is for the success of the peace agreement. Certainly the commission was left with no doubt about the complexity of the task facing it in bringing forward proposals on police reform which would fulfil its terms of reference under the agreement and at the same time command widespread support throughout the community.

The Commission reported in September 1999 with far-reaching proposals for the reform of policing in Northern Ireland. If these proposals are implemented in full they will go a long way towards creating a police service which should cater without distinction for the civil policing needs of both communities in Northern Ireland. Critical recommendations which should help to overcome the nationalists' traditional distrust of and alienation from the RUC include: the designation of the police service as the Northern Ireland Police Service (in place of the RUC), the adoption of a new badge and symbols, the abolition of the practice of flying the Union flag above police stations, the rewording of the constable's oath and the commitment to attract substantial numbers of nationalists into the new police service in order to make it representative of the whole community. In addition there are a large number of proposals aimed at building community confidence in the new police service. These include: placing respect for human rights at the heart of policing, the reform of police accountability structures, the devolution of police management, the development of community policing structures and practices and the civilianisation of education and training.

At the time of writing the British government is engaged in a public consultation process with respect to the Patten recommendations. It is encouraging that the recommendations have not been rejected out of hand by nationalists despite the fact that they do not go so far as to recommend the total disbandment of the RUC. Opposition is being organised, however, from elements within the unionist community who wish to hold on to the traditional image and role of the RUC. The response of the British government will ultimately prove critical in determining whether Northern Ireland will shortly benefit from a civil policing service which caters for the needs of the whole community and captures the respect and support of that community.

Criminal justice reform

The section of the agreement dealing with policing also makes provision for a wide-ranging review of the criminal justice system as a whole apart from policing and those aspects relating to the emergency legislation.[36] Despite the exclusions this review will have an important role to play in promoting other changes necessary to ensure that the criminal justice system caters for and is responsive to the whole community's needs for a fair and impartial system of justice.[37] Just as important is the need for the system to be perceived as being able to cater for and respond to the needs of the whole community.

The review is currently being carried out by a Criminal Justice Review Group, established in June 1998. It is composed of a small team of officials representing the secretary of state for Northern Ireland, the lord chancellor and the attorney general,[38] assisted by a number of independent assessors with expertise in the field of criminal justice.[39] The terms of reference of the review are as follows:

> Taking account of the aims of the criminal justice system as set out in the Agreement, the Review will address the structure, management and resourcing of the publicly funded elements of the criminal justice system (other than policing and those aspects of the system relating to emergency legislation) covering such issues as:
>
> - the arrangements for making appointments to the judiciary and magistracy, and safeguards for protecting their independence;
> - the arrangements for the organisation and supervision of the prosecution process, and for safeguarding its independence;
> - measures to improve the responsiveness and accountability of, and any lay participation in, the criminal justice system;
> - mechanisms for addressing law reform;
> - the scope for structured cooperation between the criminal justice agencies on both parts of the island; and
> - the structure and organisation of criminal justice functions that might be devolved to an Assembly, including the possibility of establishing a Department of Justice, while safeguarding the essential independence of many of the key functions in this area.

In August 1998 the Review Group published a consultation paper, and the review itself is scheduled for completion by the autumn of 1999. At the time of writing it had not appeared.

It follows that by the time the report of the Saville Inquiry appears it will already be apparent whether Northern Ireland has been set on course for a future in which peace, equality and respect for the rule of law can thrive. Much will depend, of course, on progress in the implementation of the Patten recommendations, the establishment of a devolved government and cross-border bodies, the decommissioning of arms and dismantling of terrorist organisations, the reform of the criminal justice system and the equality agenda.

Conclusion

Using Bloody Sunday as the prime example this book has attempted to expose how the law and justice system in Northern Ireland has failed to provide a remedy for the worst excesses of the security forces. An underlying theme which surfaces again and again is the cynical manner in which the political and military establishments have been willing to hijack the law and justice system as an integral part of their effort to crush mass opposition to the sectarian policies of the state and, later, the sustained attempt to overthrow the state by violence. The combined effect inevitably has been to undermine public confidence, particularly among the nationalist community, in the capacity of the legal process to deliver justice impartially and fairly in any situation where the immediate interests of the security establishment in Northern Ireland are involved. In short the manipulation and abuse of the law and justice system has had a profoundly damaging effect on the health of the rule of law, which is one of the fundamental pillars upon which rests the legitimacy of the state. If that pillar falls, not only will the legitimacy of the state be called into question, but the process to rebuild it will be long, slow and arduous.

The process of restoring the law and justice system to its proper status and function in a Western liberal democracy has begun with the adoption of the peace agreement. The full implementation of the terms of the agreement will go a long way towards eradicating the major nationalist grievances which have fuelled passive and violent opposition. The recommendations of the Independent Commission on Policing and the Review Group on the Criminal Justice System, the dismantling of the security apparatus and the abolition of the emergency legislation will also have a vital role to play in determining whether nationalists confidently accept that the dark days of oppression and fear are over. Equally important and timely is the Saville Inquiry into Bloody Sunday. While it is neither possible nor proper to speculate on the outcome of the inquiry, there can be little doubt that the very fact of its establishment has made a useful contribution to confidence building in the nationalist community.

It must be remembered, of course, that peace, justice and the rule of law in Northern Ireland cannot be secured simply by redressing long-standing nationalist grievances and reforming the security apparatus and criminal justice system. The state and the unionist community have also suffered, primarily from nationalist violence, for at least the last thirty years. Unlike the nationalist community, however, they have been able to rely on the law and justice system and harsh security measures in response. If these tools are to be taken away, they too will need a guarantee that their rights and interests will be equally protected. There is also the problem of violence from unionist paramilitaries, primarily targeted against the nationalist community. The peace agreement, of course, makes a substantial contribution towards resolving these difficulties. Of particular significance in this context is the planned removal of the Irish government's constitutional claim over Northern Ireland,[40] and the commitment of all parties to the agreement to exclusively democratic and peaceful means of resolving political differences and their opposition to any use or threat of force for any political purpose.[41] In addition the agreement records the commitment of all the parties to the total disarmament of all paramilitary organisations.[42] The full implementation of these obligations will create a situation in which loyalist violence will cease and both the state and the unionist community will be able to look to the future with confidence that their legitimate rights and interests are secure.

As of very early 2000, there are very sound reasons for believing that, at long last, the Good Friday Peace Agreement will be implemented in full. A power-sharing executive has been established, cross-border bodies are operational and the IRA has taken the first concrete steps on a process of decommissioning. Admittedly, there is no guarantee that the whole project will not come unstuck at some point in the future over an issue such as policing or decommissioning. Nevertheless, only three years ago it would have been foolhardy in the extreme to believe that the current developments could have been realised before the end of the twentieth century. For the first time in the history of Northern Ireland nationalists can feel a sense of joint ownership, while unionists can look forward to a future of peace and political stability. It may take a little longer to restore confidence in the rule of law. If justice is to become a reality for all then it is vitally important that the work of the Northern Ireland Human Rights Commission should be complemented by the full implementation of the Patten recommendations on policing, the normalisation of security arrangements, the reform of the criminal justice system and, of course, the truth about Bloody Sunday.

Notes and References

1 Bloody Sunday

1 See Chapter 2.
2 See 'Report of an Inquiry into the Events on 30 January 1972 which led to Loss of Life in Connection with the Procession in Londonderry on that Day' (London: HMSO, 1972) (the Widgery Report), para. 29, quoting from the brigade log.
3 Ibid., para. 94.
4 Ibid., para. 24.
5 Ibid., para. 29.
6 The 13 shot dead were Patrick Doherty (aged 31), Gerald Donaghy (17), John Duddy (17), Hugh Gilmore (17), Michael Kelly (17), Michael McDaid (20), Kevin McElhinney (17), Bernard McGuigan (41), Gerald McKinney (35), William McKinney (26), William Nash (19), James Wray (22) and John Young (17).
7 The Widgery Report only lists 13 wounded (including John Johnson and Damien Donaghy). The list of those admitted to Altnagelvin Hospital with gunshot wounds actually runs to 15 persons. One person was run over by a military vehicle.
8 John Johnson and Damien Donaghy.
9 See the summary of conclusions at the end of the Widgery Report.

2 The Road to Bloody Sunday

1 N. Mansergh, *The Irish Question 1840–1921*, 3rd edn (London: George Allen & Unwin, 1975), ch. 1.
2 See, generally, A. T. Q. Stewart, *The Ulster Crisis* (London: Faber & Faber, 1967); J. Lee, *Ireland: 1912–85* (Cambridge: Cambridge University Press, 1989), pp. 11–24.
3 Suspensory Act, 1914.
4 Lee, op. cit., pp. 38–43; C. Campbell, *Emergency Law in Ireland 1918–1925* (Oxford: Clarendon Press, 1994), ch. 2; J. Bowyer Bell, *The Secret Army: The IRA*, 3rd edn (Dublin: Poolbeg Press, 1998), chs 1 and 2.
5 P. Buckland, *Irish Unionism Vol. 2: Ulster Unionism and the Origins of Northern Ireland 1886–1922* (Dublin: Gill and Macmillan, 1973); J. McColgan, *British Policy and the Irish Administration 1920–1922* (London: George Allen & Unwin, 1983), chs 2 and 3; Mansergh, op. cit., ch. 6.
6 The provisions of the treaty were given legal effect by the Irish Free State (Agreement) Act 1922.
7 See C. Palley, 'The Evolution, Disintegration and Possible Reconstruction of the Northern Ireland Constitution', *Anglo-American Law Review*, vol. 1 (1972), p. 385 for a criticism of this characterisation of the Northern Irish administration.
8 H. Calvert, *Constitutional Law of Northern Ireland* (Belfast, 1968).

9 Ibid., pp. 162–72.
10 See Palley, op. cit., pp. 388–450, for an overview of the government's performance.
11 P. Buckland, *The Factory of Grievances: Devolved Government in Northern Ireland 1921–39* (Dublin: Gill & Macmillan, 1979), ch. 12; Calvert, op. cit.
12 Calvert, op. cit.
13 R. Byrne and P. McCutcheon, *The Irish Legal System*, 3rd edn (Dublin: Butterworths, 1996), pp. 28–40; V. T. H. Delany, *The Administration of Justice in Ireland* (ed. C. Lysaght) (Dublin: Institute of Public Administration, 1979), ch. 3.
14 Calvert, op. cit.
15 Report of the Working Party on Public Prosecutions, Cmnd 554 (Belfast: HMSO, 1971), pp. 13–16.
16 Prosecution of Offences Act (Northern Ireland) 1972.
17 See Palley, op. cit., pp. 368–83, for a useful overview of the division and how it culminated in the constitutional arrangements devised between 1920 and 1922.
18 N. Mansergh, *The Government of Northern Ireland* (London: George Allen & Unwin, 1936), p. 126 (quoting L. Worthington Evans, minister without portfolio 1920–21, in 1920).
19 See Palley, op. cit., pp. 393–5.
20 This result was further secured by additional factors such as the gerrymandering of electoral boundaries, the imposition of a three-year residence requirement for eligible voters and the retention of university and business constituencies.
21 Article 44, removed in 1972.
22 Articles 2 and 3. These are set to be amended in the light of the constitutional referendum of May 1998. The effect of the amendment is to remove the legal claim to Northern Ireland.
23 Buckland, *Irish Unionism*, op. cit.
24 See, generally, M. Farrell, *Northern Ireland: The Orange State* (London: Pluto Press, 1982); *Disturbances in Northern Ireland: Report of the Commission appointed by the Governor of Northern Ireland*, Cmd 532 (Belfast: HMSO, 1969), ch. 12 (hereafter Cameron Report); Palley, op. cit.
25 Local Government Act (Northern Ireland) 1922.
26 See Sunday Times Insight Team, *Ulster* (Harmondsworth: Penguin Special, 1972), pp. 34–5 (hereafter *Sunday Times Insight*); Farrell, op. cit., pp. 83–6; *Cameron Report*, op. cit., ch. 12; Palley op. cit., pp. 404–6; Buckland, *The Factory of Grievances*, op. cit., ch. 10.
27 This became particularly marked in the period of economic regeneration in Northern Ireland from the early 1970s; see Farrell, op. cit., pp. 240–3.
28 *Sunday Times Insight*, op. cit., pp. 29–30, 36; Farrell, op. cit., pp. 90–2.
29 Although Northern Ireland's fair employment legislation and machinery are often lauded as ranking among the most developed in the world, they have not managed to eradicate anti-Catholic discrimination in employment. Further measures are now envisaged in the wake of the 1998 peace agreement.
30 *Cameron Report*, op. cit., ch. 12; Farrell, op. cit., pp. 87–9.
31 *Campbell & Casey v Dungannon RDC. Cameron Report*, op. cit., ch. 3.

32 He went on to become a founding member of the main nationalist party, the Social Democratic and Labour Party (SDLP). He later left this party to joint the Fine Gael party in the Republic of Ireland, where he is an elected member of the lower house of parliament (the Dail).

33 Farrell, op. cit., pp. 246–7; *Cameron Report*, op. cit., ch. 4; *Sunday Times Insight*, op. cit., pp. 49–54.

34 See Farrell, op. cit., ch. 5.

35 K. Boyle, T. Hadden and P. Hillyard, *Law and State: The Case of Northern Ireland* (London: Martin Robertson, 1975), pp. 12–13; Palley, op. cit., pp. 398–9; *Sunday Times Insight*, op. cit., at p. 34.

36 D. Walsh, *The Irish Police: A Legal and Constitutional Perspective* (Dublin: Round Hall Sweet & Maxwell, 1998), pp. 101–6.

37 C. Ryder, *The RUC 1922–1997: A Force under Fire* (London: Mandarin, 1997), p. 38; McColgan, op. cit.

38 The following account of the establishment of the special constabularies and the RUC in Northern Ireland is taken primarily from M. Farrell, *Arming the Protestants: The Formation of the Ulster Special Constabulary and the Royal Ulster Constabulary* (London: Pluto Press, 1983). See also Buckland, *The Factory of Grievances*, op. cit., chs 8 and 9.

39 For a totally different perspective on the B Specials see their official history, A. Hezlet, *The 'B' Specials: A History of the Ulster Special Constabulary* (Belfast: Mourne River Press, 1997).

40 Subsequently it fell as low as 6 per cent.

41 An orange lodge confined to members of the RUC was formed in 1923. Its membership soon encompassed one tenth of the force. See C. Ryder, *The RUC 1922–1997: A Force under Fire* (London: Mandarin, 1997), p. 61. See also Farrell, *Arming the Protestants*, op. cit., pp. 191–2.

42 Each member of the force had to take an oath to *well and truly serve our Sovereign Lady the Queen [and her government in Northern Ireland] in the office of*.

43 For an account of policing in Northern Ireland during these years, see Ryder, op. cit., ch. 3, and Farrell, *Arming the Protestants*, op. cit., ch. 12.

44 *Report of the Advisory Committee on Police in Northern Ireland*, Cmd 535 (Belfast: HMSO, 1969) (hereafter *Hunt Report*).

45 Farrell, *The Orange State*, op. cit., pp. 93–4.

46 See Campbell, op. cit., ch. 4, for a detailed account of the use of the legislation in the early years of the State. See *Cameron Report*, op. cit., appendix III.iii, for the substance of the Act and regulations in force in 1969.

47 Many of these powers were in breach of articles of the Universal Declaration of Human Rights, in particular Article 10 (arbitrary arrest), Article 12 (the right to be presumed innocent until proven guilty), Article 13 (interference with personal privacy, home and correspondence) and Article 20 (freedom of opinion and expression); see *Cameron Report*, op. cit., para. 9.

48 Regulation 12(1).

49 Palley, op. cit., p. 400.

50 See generally, Farrell, *The Orange State*, op. cit.

51 L. Donohue, *Emergency Powers and Counter Terrorism Laws in the UK* (Dublin: Irish Academic Press, 2000), ch. 3.

52 *McEldowney v Forde* (1969), 3 WLR 179.

53 Boyle *et al.*, op. cit., p. 15.

54 For accounts of the birth and development of the civil rights Movement in Northern Ireland, see *Sunday Times Insight*, op. cit., chs 3 and 4; *Cameron Report*, op. cit., ch. 15. Their basic demands were (1) one-man-one-vote in local elections, (2) the removal of gerrymandered electoral boundaries, (3) laws against discrimination by local government and the provision of machinery to deal with complaints, (4) allocation of public housing on a points system, (5) repeal of the Special Powers Act, (6) disbanding of the B Specials.

55 Public Order Act (Northern Ireland) 1951, s. 2(1).

56 Ibid., s. 2(2).

57 Public Order (Amendment) Act (Northern Ireland) 1970, s. 2.

58 *Cameron Report*, op. cit., ch. 3

59 Ibid., ch. 4

60 Ibid., chs 5 and 6.

61 Ibid., ch. 7.

62 Ibid., ch. 8. It must be said that the Cameron Commission actually commended the police for preventing the outbreak of serious violence. The use of excessive force by the police to disperse Catholics who were throwing stones at unionists returning to their buses in a Catholic area was described as 'a few isolated incidents of indiscipline and misconduct'. The brutality of the police in these incidents contrasted with their passivity in the face of the armed unionist mob in threatening a breach of the peace.

63 See *Cameron Report*, op. cit., ch. 9; *Sunday Times Insight*, op. cit., ch. 4.

64 See Farrell, *The Orange State*, op. cit., pp. 249–52.

65 See *Cameron Report*, op. cit., ch. 10.

66 *Sunday Times Insight*, op. cit., ch. 4.

67 A subsequent investigation into the death of Samuel Devenny by a detective from Scotland Yard met with a wall of silence from the RUC. No one was ever charged. An internal investigation of police action in the Bogside that day recommended charges against some RUC officers but no action was ever taken.

68 *Violence and Civil Disturbances in Northern Ireland in 1969: Report of Tribunal of Inquiry*, Vol. 1, Cmd 566 (Belfast: HMSO, 1972) (hereafter *Scarman Report*); *Sunday Times Insight*, op. cit., chs 6–8; Farrell, *The Orange State*, op. cit., ch. 11.

69 *Scarman Report*, op. cit.

70 Based on the transcripts of the Scarman Tribunal, the Sunday Times Insight Team concluded that on the night of 14–15 August 1969 the RUC used firearms with such freedom as to disqualify it from being called a police force. *Sunday Times Insight*, op. cit., pp. 126–7.

71 Farrell, op. cit., p. 265; Boyle, *et al.*, op. cit., p. 30.

72 *Sunday Times Insight*, op. cit., ch. 3.

73 Farrell, op. cit., pp. 272–82; *Sunday Times Insight*, op. cit., chs 12–14; Bowyer Bell, op. cit., chs 18 and 19.

74 *Sunday Times Insight*, op. cit., ch. 11.

75 Farrell, op. cit., pp. 273–4; Palley, op. cit., p. 413; *Sunday Times Insight*, op. cit., ch. 12.

76 Farrell, op. cit., p. 279; *Sunday Times Insight*, op. cit., ch. 15.

77 *Sunday Times Insight*, op. cit., ch. 15. It had been introduced earlier in August 1969 but was abrogated on the order of the British home secretary shortly after British soldiers were deployed in Northern Ireland.

78   Farrell, op. cit., ch. 12.
79   Boyle *et al.*, op. cit., pp. 48–52; *Report of the enquiry into allegations against the security forces of physical brutality in Northern Ireland arising out of events on the 9th August, 1971*, Cmnd 4823 (London: HMSO, 1971) (hereafter *Compton Report*).
80   *Ireland v United Kingdom*, application no. 5310/71, *Yearbook of the European Convention for the Protection of Human Rights and Fundamental Freedoms*, vol. 15 (The Hague: Kluwer Law International, 1972), pp. 77–256.
81   Farrell, op. cit., p. 288.
82   Walsh, *The Irish Police*, op. cit., ch. 3.
83   S. A. De Smith, *Constitutional and Administrative Law*, 2nd edn (Harmondsworth: Penguin, 1973), ch. 8 and pp. 513–14.
84   Cited in Palley, op. cit., footnote 214.
85   De Smith, op. cit., pp. 513–15.
86   Northern Ireland. Text of a Communiqué and declaration issued after a meeting held at 10 Downing Street on 19 August, 1969, etc. Cmnd 4154 (London: HMSO), See also *Scarman Report*, op. cit., ch. 6.
87   See text of a communique issued following discussions between the secretary of state for the Home Department and the Northern Ireland government in Belfast on 9 and 10 October 1969, Cmnd 4178 (London: HMSO, 1969).
88   One of these was John Hume, an SDLP member of the Stormont parliament and later to become the leader of the SDLP and Nobel Peace Prize Laureate.
89   *Reg. (Hume) v Londonderry Justices* [1972–73], NI 91. The issue was also raised unsuccessfully in an application for *habeas corpus* before the High Court in London by persons who had been detained under the Special Powers Act; *In re Keenan & Another* (1972–73), NI 118. In that case Judge Ackner ruled that the Government of Ireland Act did not prevent the minister for home affairs extending the relevant regulation to members of the armed forces. His decision was upheld on appeal, albeit on the different ground that the British courts had had no jurisdiction to hear *habeas corpus* applications from Ireland since 1782 or 1783; [1972] 1 QB 533.
90   Northern Ireland Act 1972.
91   *In re McElduff* [1972] NI 1, p. 9.
92   Ibid., p. 10.
93   Regulations 4, 5, 6 and 7.
94   Regulation 4. See also Regulation 34, which gives the executive authority absolute power of entry to any land and buildings.
95   Regulation 19.
96   [1972] NI 1.
97   *Christie v Leachinsky* [1947] AC 573.
98   Boyle *et al.*, op. cit., p. 133.
99   One individual who escaped from custody after having been unlawfully arrested during this episode successfully defended criminal charges associated with his escape on the ground that it was not an offence to escape from unlawful custody; see *R v Meehan* (1973) NIJB. However Lord Chief Justice Lowry overruled this decision in *R v Gorman* [1974] NI 152, when he ruled that the Northern Ireland Act 1972 retrospectively validated the unlawful arrest so that an escape which was lawful at the time it was

effected (because the custody was unlawful at that time) became an unlaw-ful escape because the unlawful arrest was retrospectively validated.

100 See R. Cross, *Cross on Evidence*, 6th edn (London: Butterworths, 1985), pp. 533–9, for an account of these rules. The common law rules have been replaced by a statutory test in both Northern Ireland and Britain.

101 Belfast City Commission, 24 May 1972; see also *R v Gargan* (Belfast City Commission, 10 May 1972), where the accused had been detained in a tiny cubicle with room only for a wooden chair and questioned at inter-vals throughout the day and night for a period of 24 hours. In this case the judge ruled that the circumstances in which the accused had been detained and questioned were such as to sap the free will which must exist before a confession can be considered voluntary.

102 *Report of the Committee of Privy Councillors appointed to consider authorised procedures for the interrogation of persons suspected of terrorism*, Cmnd 4901 (London: HMSO, 1972).

103 See *Compton Report*, op. cit.

104 *Ireland v United Kingdom*, application no. 5310/71, *Yearbook of the European Convention for the Protection of Fundamental Rights and Freedoms*, vol. 15, op. cit., pp. 77–256.

105 A committee under the chairmanship of Judge Brown was appointed in September 1971. By December it had recommended the release of 25 persons out of hundreds of cases. The minister acted on these recommen-dations. See Boyle *et al.*, op. cit., p. 58.

106 Belfast City Commission, 16 December 1971.

107 See Chapter 6 for an analysis of the law.

108 For further details see *Shoot to Kill? International Lawyers' Inquiry into the Lethal Use of Firearms by the Security Forces in Northern Ireland* (Dublin: Mercier Press, 1985).

3 The Widgery Inquiry

1 *Report of the Tribunal appointed to inquire into events on Sunday, 30th January 1972, which led to loss of life in connection with the procession in Londonderry on that day by The Rt. Hon. Lord Widgery, O.B.E, T.D.* (London: HMSO, 1972) (hereafter *Widgery Report*), para. 1.

2 Ibid., para. 2.

3 Ibid., para. 2.

4 Ibid., para. 8.

5 This act also applies in Ireland, as amended by the Tribunals of Inquiry (Evidence) Act, 1979.

6 Tribunals of Inquiry (Evidence) Act 1921, s. 1(1).

7 *Report of the Royal Commission on Tribunals of Inquiry* (London: HMSO, 1966) (hereafter *Salmon Report*), para. 28.

8 Tribunals of Inquiry (Evidence) Act 1921, s. 1(2).

9 Ibid., s. 1(3).

10 Ibid., s. 2(a).

11 Ibid., s. 2(b).

12 *Salmon Report*, op. cit., para. 32.

13 Ibid., para. 48.

14 Ibid., para. 49.
15 Ibid., para. 28.
16 S. A. De Smith, *Judicial Review of Administrative Action*, 3rd edn (London: Stevens & Sons, 1973), ch. 5.
17 The confidential memo was eventually discovered (misplaced in a publicly accessible file) in 1995 by Jane Winter, Director of British Irish Rights Watch.
18 *Widgery Report*, op. cit., para. 5.
19 *Violence and Civil Disturbances in Northern Ireland in 1969*, Cmnd 566 (Belfast: HMSO, 1972) (hereafter *Scarman Report*).
20 *Salmon Report*, op. cit., para. 87.
21 See for example *Farrell v Ministry of Defence* [1980] 1 All ER 166.
22 *Widgery Report*, para. 8.
23 Dr McClean has written a book about his personal experience of Bloody Sunday; see R. McClean, *The Road to Bloody Sunday*, originally published in 1983 it has since been reprinted (Derry: Guildhall Press, 1997).
24 *Widgery Report*, para. 71.
25 Ibid., para. 8.
26 Ibid., para. 2.
27 *Salmon Report*, para 49.

4   A Flawed Report

1 *Widgery Report*, paras. 10–14.
2 Ibid., para. 11.
3 See also B. McMahon, 'The Impaired Asset: A Legal Commentary on the Widgery Tribunal', *La Domaine Humain* (The Human Context) vol. VI, no. 3 (1974), p. 683.
4 *Widgery Report*, paras 61–104.
5 Ibid., paras 89–104.
6 Ibid., para. 102.
7 Ibid., Summary of Conclusions 1.
8 McMahon, op. cit., p. 685.
9 *Widgery Report*, paras 31–4.
10 Ibid., para. 33.
11 Ibid., para. 34.
12 Ibid., para. 95.
13 Ibid., para. 102.
14 Ibid., para. 94.
15 A dum dum bullet can be made by filing a cross on the head of a regular bullet. The bullet shatters on impact and causes massive internal damage.
16 See also *Bloody Sunday and the Report of the Widgery Tribunal: The Irish Government's Assessment of the New Material* (presented to the British Government in June 1997), pp. 20–23.
17 *Widgery Report*, para. 54.
18 Ibid., para. 97.
19 Ibid., para. 104.
20 Ibid., para. 85.
21 Ibid., para. 64.

5 The Soldiers' Statements

1 *Widgery Report*, para. 97.
2 See Report No. 2 from Counsel to Tribunal, http://www.Bloody-Sunday-Inquiry.org.uk.
3 Ibid., para. 36.
4 Ibid., para. 98.
5 Ibid., para. 54.
6 Ibid., para. 59.
7 Ibid., para. 79.
8 Ibid., para. 82.
9 Ibid., para. 85.
10 Ibid., para. 85.
11 Ibid., para. 88.
12 For further detail on the Donaghy episode, see M. O'Connell, *Truth: The First Casualty* (Dublin: Riverstone, 1993), pp. 35–40.
13 See *Widgery Report*, para. 8; and Tribunal Schedule of Evidence.

6 Lethal Force and the Law

1 A. V. Dicey, *An Introduction to the Study of the Law of the Constitution*, 10th edn (London: Macmillan, 1965), ch. 9, p. 193.
2 See J. Smith, *Smith and Hogan: Criminal Law*, 8th edn (London: Butterworths, 1996), ch. 12.
3 Ibid., p. 360.
4 Ibid., pp. 377–87.
5 See for example *R v Foxford* [1974] NI 181.
6 Firearms Act (Northern Ireland) 1969, s. 14.
7 *R v Clegg* [1995] 1 All ER 334; *Yip Chiu-cheung* [1994] 2 All ER 924.
8 *R v Fisher & Wright* (Belfast Crown Court, 10 Feb. 1995).
9 *Smith and Hogan*, op. cit., pp. 147–50.
10 Ibid., p. 263.
11 *R v Duffy* [1967] 1 QB 63; *R v Fisher & Wright* (Belfast Crown Court, 10 Feb. 1995); *R v Hegarty* [1986] NI 343; *R v Elkington & Carrington* (Belfast Crown Court, 21 Jan. 1993).
12 Report of the Criminal Law Revision Committee, Cmnd 2659 (London: HMSO, 1965), para. 23.
13 See Lord Justice Jones in *Attorney General for Northern Ireland's Reference* [1976] NI 169, 177. Also Hutton J. in *R v Hegarty* [1986] NI 343.
14 *R v Hegarty* [1986] NI 343, at 354.
15 [1971] AC 814, 832.
16 See for example *R v Rose* (1884) 15 Cox CC 540; *R v Chisam* (1963) 47 Cr App Rep 130.
17 *R v Fennell* [1970] 3 All ER 215.
18 Ibid., p. 217.
19 *Devlin v Armstrong* [1971] NI 13.
20 [1973] NI 96.
21 Ibid., p. 106.
22 [1976] AC 182.
23 (1983) Cr App Rep 276.

24 [1988] 1 AC 130.

25 *R v Elkington & Callaghan* (Belfast Crown Court, 21 Jan. 1993); *R v Fisher & Wright* (Belfast Crown Court, 10 Feb. 1995).

26 For an analysis see J. Rogers, 'Justifying the Use of Firearms by Policemen and Soldiers: A Response to the Home Office's Review of the Law on the Use of Lethal Force', *Legal Studies*, vol. 18, no. 4 (1998) 486; S. Doran, 'The Use of Force by the Security Forces in Northern Ireland: A Legal Perspective' *Legal Studies*, vol. 7 (1987) 291.

27 *Palmer v R* [1971] AC 814; *R v Clegg* [1995] 1 All ER 334. The Australian courts adopted the manslaughter option temporarily; see *R v McKay* (1957) ALR 648; *R v Howe* (1958) 100 CLR 448; *R v Bufalo* (1958) VR 363; *R v Haley* (1959) 76 WNNSW 550; *R v Tikos* (1963) VR 285; *R v Tikos* (no. 2) (1963), VR 306. The law was eventually brought back into line with that in *Palmer v R* in *Zekevic v DPP for Victoria* (1987) 61 ALJR 375, when the High Court of Australia overruled its previous decision in *Howe*.

28 [1995] 1 All ER 334.

29 J. Smith, *Smith and Hogan: Criminal Law*, 8th edn (London: Butterworths, 1996), p. 262.

30 See J. Smith, 'The Right to Life and the Right to Kill in Law Enforcement', *New Law Journal*, vol. 144 (1994) 354. But see the opinion of the European Commission on Human Rights in *Kelly v United Kingdom*, application no. 17579/90 (1993).

31 [1971] NI 13.

32 Bernadette Devlin (now better known by her married name, Bernadette McAliskey), was a leading student activist in the civil rights movement in the late 1960s. She was elected a member of the Westminster parliament in 1969 and is famously remembered for crossing the floor of the House of Commons to slap the face of the home secretary, Reginald Maudling, on the day after Bloody Sunday. More recently her daughter Roisin McAliskey was the subject of a controversial extradition request by the German authorities to the British government.

33 By this time 108 civilians had been shot dead and two stabbed to death with a pitchfork by the security forces. The vast majority had been unarmed at the time they were shot.

34 Although the corporal was convicted at first instance, the conviction was quashed on appeal on the grounds of irregular conduct by prosecuting counsel; *R v Foxford* [1974] NI 181.

35 [1975] NI 203.

36 In between the Foxford case and this case there were three unsuccessful prosecutions of soldiers for murder and manslaughter. A soldier was acquitted of murder in *R v Ross* (1974) despite evidence that he had shot an unarmed man at a distance of 2 yards. In *R v Spencer* (1974) and *R v Nicholl* (1975) soldiers were acquitted of the manslaughter of unarmed civilians.

37 *R v Jones* (1975) 2 NIJB.

38 *Attorney General for Northern Ireland's Reference* [1977] AC 105.

39 *Attorney General for Northern Ireland's Reference* [1976] NI 169.

40 The other majority judge was Lord Justice Gibson, who agreed with the judgment handed down by Lord Justice Jones.

41 *Attorney General for Northern Ireland's Reference* [1976] NI 169, 180.

42 It was accepted that McElhone was not a member of the IRA and indeed was a totally innocent person. However it was also accepted that the accused believed that he might be a member of the IRA.

43 *Attorney General for Northern Ireland's Reference* [1976] NI 169, 193.

44 Ibid.

45 Ibid., p. 194.

46 *Attorney General for Northern Ireland's Reference* [1977] AC 105.

47 Ibid., p. 136.

48 [1980] 1 All ER 166.

49 The Court of Appeal ordered a new trial.

50 It has been suggested that this was tantamount to affording a defence of superior orders to soldiers who resort to the use of lethal force in such circumstances; see D. S. Greer, 'Legal Control of Military Operations – A Missed Opportunity', Northern Ireland Legal Quarterly, vol. 31, no. 2 (1980) 155.

51 (1978) 7 NIJB.

52 See Greer, op. cit., for criticism of the House of Lords approach.

53 The issue normally arises in the context of the liability of a corporation for the actions of its officers and servants; see Smith, *Smith and Hogan*, op. cit., pp. 188–90.

54 *R v Fisher & Wright* (Belfast Crown Court, 10 Feb. 1995).

55 Ibid.

56 See Hutton J. in *Lynch v Ministry of Defence* [1983] NI 216; and Carswell J. in *Kelly v Ministry of Defence* (Belfast Crown Court, 13 Jan. 1989).

57 *Kelly v United Kingdom*, no. 17579/90 (Jan. 1993).

58 This is set out in *Shoot to Kill?: International Lawyers' Inquiry into the Lethal Use of Firearms by the Security Forces in Northern Ireland* (Dublin: Mercier Press, 1985), pp. 75–6.

59 [1975] NI 203.

60 Ibid., 206.

61 (1975) 2 NIJB.

62 Interestingly, McGonigal LJ described the instructions in the Yellow Card as 'clear and explicit' while MacDermott J. castigated the card as 'to say the least of it a difficult document'.

63 See for example A. F. N. Clarke, *Contact* (London: Secker & Warburg, 1983), p. 98.

64 The convention has been incorporated into the domestic law of the United Kingdom pursuant to the terms of the Human Rights Act 1998 but it will not come fully into effect until October 2000. Up until then it can not be enforced in the UK courts.

65 *R v Secretary of State for the Home Department, ex parte Brind* [1991] AC 696.

66 European Convention for the Protection of Human Rights and Fundamental Freedoms, Article 15.

67 See T. Jennings, 'Shoot to Kill: The Final Courts of Justice', in T. Jennings, (ed.), *Justice in Error* (London: Pluto Press, 1990), p. 112.

68 Application no. 17579/90 (1993).

69 For trenchant criticism of the decision see J. Smith 'The Right to Life and the Right to Kill in Law Enforcement', *New Law Journal*, vol. 144 (1994) 354.

70   (1982) 7 EHRR 409.

71   Ibid., p. 459.

72   (1996) 21 EHRR 97.

73   The case actually concerned the use of lethal force under the law of Gibraltar. As with Northern Ireland, however, the law of Gibraltar adopts the standard of what is reasonably justifiable (as distinct from what is absolutely necessary) with respect to the use of force in self-defence or in order to effect an arrest; see Article 2 of the Gibraltar constitution.

74   McCann was hit by five bullets, Farrell by eight and Savage by 16, all from a distance of between three and six feet.

75   *Widgery Report*, para. 94.

76   Ibid., para. 102.

77   Ibid., para. 2.

78   Ibid., para. 2.

79   Ibid., para. 54.

80   Ibid., para. 94.

81   For an incisive critique of Lord Widgery's interpretation of the standards required by the Yellow Card, see B. McMahon, 'The Impaired Asset: A Legal Commentary on the Report of the Widgery Tribunal', *Le Domaine Humain*, vol. 4, no. 3 (1974), pp. 690–1.

82   *Widgery Report*, para. 98.

83   Ibid., para. 83.

84   Ibid., para. 85.

85   Ibid.

86   Ibid.

87   The closest precedent in Northern Irish case law was the case of *R v Fisher & Wright* (Belfast Crown Court, 10 Feb. 1995), where two soldiers were found to be acting in concert when both shot at the same person. The issue that would have to be decided in respect of Glenfada Park is whether this precedent can be extended to the situation where a group of soldiers fire at a group of civilians, all of whom are killed in circumstances where it is not possible to establish which individual soldier shot which individual victim or even which soldier targeted which victim.

88   *Widgery Report*, para. 102.

89   Ibid., para. 88.

90   Ibid., para. 70.

91   Ibid., para. 82.

92   Ibid., para. 39.

93   The attorney general cited public policy as a ground for his decision not to prosecute several RUC officers for serious offences against the administration of justice in the light of the Stalker/Sampson investigation into the alleged shoot to kill policy (see Chapter 7).

7   Law and Security Policy since Bloody Sunday

1   D. Lloyd, *The Idea of Law* (Harmondsworth: Penguin, 1981), ch. 6, pp. 142–4; J. F. McEldowney, *Public Law* (London: Sweet & Maxwell, 1994), pp. 102–4.

2   A.-V. Dicey, *Introduction to the Law of the Constitution*, 10th edn (London: Macmillan, 1965), p. 193.

3 See B. Dickson, *The Legal System of Northern Ireland*, 3rd edn (Belfast: SLS, 1993), pp. 54–55.

4 K. Boyle, T. Hadden and P. Hillyard, *Law and State: The Case of Northern Ireland* (London: Martin Robertson, 1975), p. 59.

5 M. Farrell, *Northern Ireland: The Orange State* (London: Pluto Press, 1980), p. 295.

6 See Chapter 2.

7 *Report of the Commission to Consider Legal Procedures to Deal with Terrorist Activities in Northern Ireland*, Cmnd 5185 (London: HMSO, 1972) (hereafter *Diplock Report*), para. 1.

8 *Report of a Committee to Consider, in the Context of Civil Liberties and Human Rights, Measures to Deal with Terrorism in Northern Ireland*, Cmnd 5847 (London: HMSO, 1975).

9 *Review of the Operation of the Northern Ireland (Emergency Provisions) Act 1978*, Cmnd 9222 (London: HMSO, 1984).

10 *Review of the Northern Ireland (Emergency Provisions) Act 1991 by JJ Rowe QC* (London: HMSO, 1995).

11 *Report of the Operation of the Prevention of Terrorism (Temporary Provisions) Acts 1974 and 1976*, Cmnd 7324 (London: HMSO, 1978). See also D. Schiff, 'The Shackleton Review of the Operation of the Prevention of Terrorism Acts', *Public Law* (1978) 352.

12 *Report of the Operation of the Prevention of Terrorism (Temporary Provisions) Act 1976* Cmnd 8803 (London: HMSO, 1983) (the *Jellicoe Report*) See also D. Bonner, 'Combating Terrorism – the Jellicoe Approach', *Public Law* (1983) 224; C. Walker, 'The Jellicoe Report on the Prevention of Terrorism (Temporary Provisions) Act 1976' *Modern Law Review*, vol. 46 (1983) 484.

13 John Rowe, *Report on the Operation in 1994 of the Prevention of Terrorism (Temporary Provisions) Act 1989* (London: HMSO, 1995).

14 Lord Lloyd of Berwick, *Inquiry into Legislation against Terrorism* (London: HMSO, 1996).

15 See, *Legislation Against Terrorism, Cm. 4178* (London: HMSO, 1998).

16 The Criminal Evidence (Northern Ireland) Order 1988, *inter alia*, permits the judge (or jury or magistrate) to draw inferences from a suspect's failure, under police interrogation, to mention facts which are material to his defence, and for the failure to account, at the earliest possible time, for the presence, marks or objects which connect him to the offence with which he is charged.

17 See for example Public Order (Northern Ireland) Orders 1981 and 1987.

18 Other offences specifically created by the emergency legislation include interfering with the closure of a road blocked by order of the secretary of state; directing the activities of terrorist organisations and racketeering.

19 Northern Ireland (Emergency Provisions) Act 1996, ss. 30–2 and Schedule 2; Prevention of Terrorism (Temporary Provisions) Act 1989, ss. 1–3 and Schedule 1. See C. Walker, *The Prevention of Terrorism in British Law* (Manchester: Manchester University Press, 1986), ch. 4; G. Hogan and C. Walker, *Political Violence and the Law in Ireland* (Manchester: Manchester University Press, 1989), pp. 138–43.

20 Prevention of Terrorism (Temporary Provisions) Act, 1989, s. 18.

21 See, generally, Boyle *et al.*, op. cit., ch. 5.

22   Diplock Report, op. cit., para. 27.
23   Northern Ireland (Emergency Provisions) Act, 1973, s. 28(1). See s. 58 of the 1996 Act.
24   Ibid.
25   D. Walsh, *The Use and Abuse of Emergency Legislation in Northern Ireland* (London: Cobden Trust, 1983), pp. 23–4.
26   Northern Ireland (Emergency Provisions) Act 1996, s. 47. Suspects have no right to have a solicitor present during interrogation, and in practice the RUC does not normally permit the presence of lawyers during the interrogation of terrorist suspects; see *Re Russell and Others Applications* [1996] NI 310.
27   The European Court of Human Rights has ruled that the power to draw adverse inferences from a suspect's silence during interrogation, as provided by the 1988 Order, coupled with the denial of access to a solicitor, violates the fair trial provisions of Article 6 of the convention; see *Murray v United Kingdom* (1996) 22 EHRR 29.
28   The only qualification with respect to the powers of search is that the search must be carried out for munitions or a transmitter; see *Carlisle v Chief Constable of the RUC* [1988] NI 307.
29   Prevention of Terrorism (Temporary Provisions) Act 1989, s. 16 and Schedule 5.
30   For a more detailed analysis of these provisions, see Brice Dickson (ed.), *Civil Liberties in Northern Ireland*, 3rd edn (Belfast: Committee on the Administration of Justice, 1997), chs 3 and 4.
31   See, generally, Walker, *The Prevention of Terrorism in British Law*, op. cit., ch. 5; A. Grimes and D. Bonner, 'Immigration and Freedom of Movement', in Dickson (ed.), op. cit.
32   [1996] 2 CMLR 851. In this case the British government's decision to exclude the applicant, a citizen of Ireland, was found to be in breach of the free movement of persons provisions in European Union law.
33   The Jellicoe Report, op. cit., para. 175.
34   See Northern Ireland (Emergency Provisions) Act 1996, ss. 10 and 11, for the current statutory basis.
35   Northern Ireland (Emergency Provisions) Act 1996, Schedule 1, as amended by Northern Ireland (Emergency Provisions) Act 1998, s. 2.
36   Northern Ireland (Emergency Provisions) Act 1996, s. 11. For empirical analyses of the operation of these courts see K. Boyle, T. Hadden and P. Hillyard, *Ten Years On in Northern Ireland: The Legal Control of Political Violence* (London: Cobden Trust, 1980), ch. 6; D. Walsh, *The Use and Abuse of Emergency Legislation in Northern Ireland* (London: Cobden trust, 1983). For a critical analysis and proposals for reform see D. Korff, *The Diplock Courts: A Fair Trial?* (London: Amnesty International, 1984); S. Greer and T. White, *Abolishing the Diplock Courts: The Case for Restoring Jury Trial to Scheduled Offences in Northern Ireland* (London: Cobden Trust, 1986), S. Doran and J. Jackson, *Judge without Jury: Diplock Trials in the Adversary System* (Oxford: Clarendon, 1995).
37   *Ibrahim v R* [1914] AC 599; *Callis v Gunn* [1964] 1 QB 495.
38   Northern Ireland (Emergency Provisions) Act 1996, s. 12.
39   Ibid., s. 13.

40 See D. Walsh, 'Emergency Justice', *Criminal Justice Matters*, vol. 13 (1993) 6.

41 See for example Amnesty International, *United Kingdom: Allegations of Ill-Treatment in Northern Ireland* (London, 1991).

42 See for example Human Rights Watch/Helsinki, *Human Rights in Northern Ireland* (New York, 1991), pp. 15–26.

43 Ibid., chs 7 and 8.

44 Boyle *et al.*, op. cit., pp. 69–71.

45 Ibid., p. 71.

46 [1988] NI 421.

47 See Boyle *et al.*, op. cit., pp. 43–5; Walsh, *The Use and Abuse of Emergency Legislation*, op. cit., pp. 38–40.

48 See for example the facts of the house arrest in *Murray v Ministry of Defence* [1988] 2 All ER 524.

49 For a typical example see *Murray v Ministry of Defence*, op. cit.

50 See details in *Shoot to Kill?: International Lawyers' Inquiry into the Lethal Use of Firearms by the Security Forces in Northern Ireland* (Dublin: Mercier Press, 1985).

51 *R v Foxford* [1974] NI 181.

52 G. Hogan and C. Walker, *Political Violence and the Law in Ireland* (Manchester: Manchester University Press, 1989), pp. 38–9.

53 The UN Human Rights Committee recommended the closure of the Castlereagh facility in 1995 as a matter of urgency owing to conditions there. See *Comments of the Human Rights Committee in Consideration of the Fourth Periodic Report of the United Kingdom of Great Britain and Northern Ireland* (Geneva: UN Human Rights Committee, 1995). The UN Committee against Torture expressed concern that conditions there may have been in breach of the UN Convention Against Torture. See *Consideration of Second Periodic Report of the United Kingdom of Great Britain and Northern Ireland* (Geneva: UN Committee Against Torture, 1996). Even the government-appointed independent commissioner for the holding centres reported that '[e]ach day that passes, the Government is in breach of its obligations to comply with the minimum standards for prisoners'. See *Fourth Annual (1996) Report of the Independent Commissioner for the Holding Centres (Police Offices)* (Belfast, 1997). Nevertheless the Castlereagh facility is still the one used most for the detention and interrogation of terrorist suspects.

54 See, generally, P. Taylor, *Beating the Terrorists? Interrogation in Omagh, Gough and Castlereagh* (Harmondsworth: Penguin, 1980); Walsh, *The Use and Abuse of Emergency Legislation in Northern Ireland*, op. cit., ch. 3.

55 *Report of a Mission by Amnesty International to Northern Ireland.*

56 See Taylor, op. cit., pp. 296–7, 332–3, 335.

57 K. Boyle, T. Hadden and P. Hillyard, *Ten Years on in Northern Ireland: The Legal Control of Political Violence* (London: Cobden Trust, 1980), p. 44.

58 See generally, S. Greer, *Supergrasses: A Study in Anti-Terrorist Law Enforcement in Northern Ireland* (Oxford: Clarendon Press, 1995); A. Boyd, *The Informers* (Dublin: Mercier Press, 1984).

59 Dermot P. J. Walsh, 'Arrest and Interrogation in Northern Ireland: 1981', *Journal of Law and Society*, vol. 19, no. 1 (1982) 37.

60 Ibid.

61 These statistics are taken from Greer, op. cit.

62 *R v Donnelly* (unreported, 1983), per Kelly J.

63   Greer, op. cit., pp. 173–4.

64   See generally, Boyle *et al.* (1980), op. cit., ch. 7.

65   For an account of the hunger strike see P. Bishop and E. Mallie, *The Provisional IRA* (London: Heineman, 1987), ch. 19.

66   Stephen Geddis (aged 10), August 1975; Brian Stewart (aged 13), October 1976; Paul Whitters (aged 15), April 1981; Julie Livingstone (aged 14), May 1981; Carol Ann Kelly (aged 12), May 1981; Stephen McConomy (aged 11), April 1982; and Seamus Duffy (aged 15), August 1989. See Helsinki Rights Watch, op. cit., Appendix D, for a complete list of the 15 persons shot dead by plastic bullets and the circumstances of the shootings.

67   See Committee on the Administration of Justice, *Inquests and Disputed Killings in Northern Ireland* (Belfast: CAJ, 1992), Appendix A, for a summary of most of these killings.

68   J. Stalker, *Stalker* (Harmondsworth: Penguin, 1988).

69   *Hansard*, H. L., vol. 126, cols. 21–23 (1988).

70   Amnesty International, *Political Killings in Northern Ireland* (London, 1994), p. 7.

71   For an account of collusion in practice see M. Urban, *Big Boys Rule: The Secret Struggle against the IRA* (London: Faber & Faber, 1992).

72   See 'The Forgotten Massacre', BBC First Tuesday programme, July 1993.

73   In 1989 the chief constable of the RUC responded to these concerns by appointing the deputy chief constable of Cambrideshire to carry out an investigation. The subsequent Stevens Report was never published in full, but a summary was published in 1990. See *Summary of the Report of the Deputy Chief Constable of Cambridgeshire, John Stevens, into Allegations of Collusion between Members of the Security Forces and Loyalist Paramilitaries*.

74   See for example Lawyers Committee for Human Rights, *Human Rights and Legal Defense in Northern Ireland* (New York, 1993) and *At the Cross Roads: Human Rights and the Northern Ireland Peace Process* (New York, 1996); Human Rights Watch/Helsinki, *To Serve Without Fear: Policing, Human Rights and Accountability in Northern Ireland* (New York, 1997); British Irish Rights Watch, *Alleged Collusion and the RUC* (London, 1996); Amnesty International, *Political Killings in Northern Ireland* (London, 1994).

75   Contrast, for example, the handling of the investigation and subsequent prosecution of 41 individuals for the murder of two plain-clothed British soldiers who got caught up in the 1988 funeral of the IRA man who had been killed by loyalist Michael Stone at the funeral of the three IRA members shot by the SAS in Gibraltar; Committee on the Administration of Justice, *The Casement Trials: A Case Study on the Right to a Fair Trial in Northern Ireland* (Belfast, 1992). See also the manner in which the prosecution used the evidence of a loyalist terrorist in order to secure the conviction of alleged IRA man Colin Duffy; *R v Duffy* (Court of Appeal, 24.9.96).

76   *An Application by the Chief Constable of the RUC for Judicial Review in the Matter of Patrick Shanaghan*, KERK2136.T.

77   See BBC series *Loyalists* (1999) by Peter Taylor. This is now published, see P. Taylor, *Loyalists* (Bloomsbury, 1999).

78   Human Rights Watch/Helsinki, *To Serve Without Favor: Policing, Human Rights and Accountability in Northern Ireland* (New York, 1997) ch. 6; Amnesty International, *Political Killings in Northern Ireland* (London, 1994); Lawyers

Committee on Human Rights, *At the Crossroads: Human Rights and the Northern Ireland Peace Process* (New York, 1996), ch. 3; *Report of the Special Rapporteur on the Independence of Judges and Lawyers: Mission to the United Kingdom of Great Britain and Northern Ireland* (Geneva: Office of the UN High Commissioner for Human Rights, 1998).

79 It would appear that there is a view in security and government circles that some solicitors sympathise with the IRA. In the committee stage of a debate on the prevention of terrorism legislation, for example, Douglas Hogg MP, parliamentary undersecretary for the Home Department, said: 'I have to state as a fact, but with regret, that there are in Northern Ireland a number of solicitors who are unduly sympathetic to the cause of the IRA.' These words were uttered and widely reported less than four weeks before the murder of solicitor Patrick Finucane by loyalist gunmen. See also John Stalker, op. cit., p. 49.

80 *Human Rights and Legal Defense in Northern Ireland*, pp. 26–31.

81 Lawyers Committee for Human Rights, *Human Rights and Legal Defense in Northern Ireland: The Intimidation of Defense Lawyers, the Murder of Patrick Finucane* (New York, 1993); Lawyers Committee for Human Rights, *At the Crossroads: Human Rights and the Northern Ireland Peace Process* (New York, 1996), pp. 107–15; Human Rights Watch/Helsinki, *Policing, Human Rights and Accountability in Northern Ireland* (New York, 1997), pp. 146–50; Amnesty International, *Political Killings in Northern Ireland* (London, 1994).

82 In 1993 Stevens was asked by the chief constable, at the behest of the DPP, to reopen his original inquiry into collusion, with specific reference to new evidence on the shooting of Patrick Finucane. This new evidence concerned the involvement of the army agent Brian Nelson in the murder, as recounted by Nelson himself. The results of the reopened inquiry have never been published.

83 UN Commission on Human Rights, *Report of the Special Rapporteur on the Independence of Judges and Lawyers: Mission to the United Kingdom of Great Britain and Northern Ireland* (Geneva, Office of the UN High Commissioner for Human Rights, 1998).

84 The nationalist community on the Garvaghy Road is at the centre of the current impasse over the attempts by Orangemen to march from Drumcree Church to Portadown via the nationalist estate on the Garvaghy Road.

85 Human Rights Watch/Helsinki, *To Serve Without Favor: Policing, Human Rights and Accountability in Northern Ireland* (New York, 1997), pp. 173–5.

86 See *Irish Times*, 24 March 1999, p. 8.

87 The RUC did release a summary of the conclusions to the press, seemingly in an effort to counteract the unfavourable publicity consequent on the criticisms of the ICPC report on the RUC investigation.

88 This will be remedied when the Human Rights Act 1998 comes fully into force in October 2000.

89 1988, NI 307.

90 See for example *Kirkpatrick v Chief Constable of the RUC* [1988] NI 421; *Murray v Ministry of Defence* (1985) 12 NIJB.

91 *O'Neill & Kelly v United Kingdom*, 17441/90 (1992).

92 (1985) 12 NIJB.

93 *Murray v Ministry of Defence* [1988] 2 All ER 521, p. 527.

94 Ibid.

95   The substantive power was actually introduced first as s. 21 of the Preven-
     tion of Terrorism (Temporary Provisions) Act 1989 in response to a County
     Court decision in *Oscar and Toner v Chief Constable of the RUC* (1988) that
     the detention of a family for four hours during a search of their home con-
     stituted false imprisonment. See Committee on the Administration of
     Justice, *No Emergency, No Emergency Law* (Belfast, 1995), p. 33.
96   Northern Ireland (Emergency Provisions) Act 1991, s. 19(4) and (5).
97   (1985) 4 NIJB.
98   [1980] NI 123.
99   [1985] 1 All ER 1.
100 [1997] 1 All ER 129.
101 See also *McKee v The Chief Constable for Northern Ireland* [1985] 1 All ER 1;
     Hanna v The Chief Constable of the Royal Ulster Constabulary [1986] NI 103;
     A. Barrister, 'Reasonable Suspicion and Planned Arrests', *Northern Ireland
     Legal Quarterly*, vol. 43, no. 1 (1992) 66. See also *Moore v Chief
     Constable of the RUC* [1988] NI 456; *Brady v Chief Constable of the RUC*
     (1991) 2 NIJB.
102 (1991) 2 NIJB.
103 [1988] NI 40.
104 [1988] NI 192.
105 [1988] NI 456
106 *Oscar v Chief Constable of the RUC* (1993) 2 BNIL.
107 The current provision is contained in Northern Ireland (Emergency
     Provisions) Act 1996, s. 47.
108 (1990) 4 NIJB.
109 (1992).
110 *In re Duffy's Application* (1992) 6 BNIL 41; *In re McKenna's Application* (1992)
     3 BNIL 54.
111 *In re McNearney's Application* (1991).
112 Committee on the Administration of Justice, *No Emergency, No Emergency
     Law* (Belfast, 1995), p. 43.
113 *John Murray v United Kingdom* (1996) 22 EHRR 29.
114 Human Rights Watch/Helsinki, *To Serve Without Favor: Policing, Human
     Rights and Accountability in Northern Ireland* (New York, 1997), p. 19.
115 [1996] NI 310.
116 [1997] 4 All ER 833.
117 *The Rafferty File* (Belfast: Northern Ireland Civil Rights Association, 1981).
118 *In re Sterritt* [1980] NI 234.
119 See for example *Report of the UN Committee for the Prevention of Torture*
     (Geneva, 1994). Four RUC officers were eventually prosecuted in the
     Rafferty case – four years after the initial submission was made to the DPP's
     office. However at the trial Lord Chief Justice Lowry accepted a defence
     submission of no case to answer on account of the conflicting and gener-
     ally unsatisfactory nature of the evidence proffered against the officers.
     See *R v Hassan et al.* (Belfast Crown Court, 27 Nov. 1981).
120 [1988] NI 40.
121 *R v Latimer, Hegan, Bell and Allen* (Court of Appeal, 29.7.92)
122 *R v Mitchell, Hetherington, Christie and Brown* (1994).
123 [1977] NI 105.

124 In *R v Mullan* (1988) 10 NIJB 36, Lord Chief Justice Lowry felt that the use of abusive language by interrogating officers in a threatening manner could render a confession inadmissible, but not on the facts of that case.

125 [1980] NI 91.

126 [1978] NI 110.

127 December 1978.

128 (1984) 11 NIJB. See also *R v Howells* (1987) 5 NIJB 10.

129 *R v Milne* [1978] NI 110.

130 See for example *R v McCormick*; *R v Milne*; *R v McCracken*; *R v Hetherington*; *R v Culbert*.

131 (1974) NIJB.

132 Op. cit.

133 See for example *R v McCracken*; *R v Hetherington*; *R v Culbert*.

134 (1978) 1 NIJB 15.

135 *R v Dillon and Gorman* [1984] NI 292.

136 Boyle *et al.*, *Ten Years On*, op. cit., pp. 59–62.

137 D. Walsh, *The Use and Abuse of Emergency Legislation in Northern Ireland* (London: Cobden Trust, 1983), p. 94.

138 [1981] NI 79 and (1980) 4 NIJB. For further detail see P. Taylor, *Beating the Terrorists?* (Harmondsworth: Penguin, 1980), pp. 305–15.

139 See also *R v Nash* (1992).

140 *R v Corey* (1973) NIJB 67. Even so the courts are careful not to apply the discretion so as to defeat the will of parliament in enacting the torture, inhuman and degrading treatment test into law; *R v Cowan* [1987] NI 338. The discretion is now specifically written into Section 12 of the Northern Ireland (Emergency Provisions) Act 1996.

141 See Amnesty International, *United Kingdom: Killings by the Security Forces and 'Supergrass' Trials* (London, 1988).

142 For an expert account see S. Greer, *Supergrasses: A Study in Anti-Terrorist Law Enforcement in Northern Ireland* (Oxford: Clarendon Press, 1995).

143 Human Rights Watch/Helsinki, *Human Rights in Northern Ireland* (New York, 1991), chs 3 and 4.

144 Ibid., pp. 62–8. Over one million pounds has been paid out in compensation to victims of plastic bullets and their families.

145 *R v Hegarty* [1986] NI 343.

146 These statistics do not include corporal Clegg, whose conviction for the murder of Karen Reilly was quashed after being referred back to the Court of Appeal by the secretary of state.

147 (1984) 4 NIJB.

148 (1984).

149 See for example R. Spjut, 'The "Official" Use of Deadly Force by the Security Forces against Suspected Terrorists: Some Lessons from Northern Ireland', *Public Law* (1996) 38; A. Jennings, 'Shoot to Kill: The Final Courts of Justice', in A. Jennings (ed.), *Justice Under Fire: Civil Liberties in Northern Ireland* (Winchester: Pluto Press, 1990), ch. 5.

150 See Lawyers Committee for Human Rights, *At the Crossroads: Human Rights and the Northern Ireland Peace Process* (New York, 1996), pp. 75–7.

151 See comments of Lord Chief Justice Hutton in *R v Elkington and Carrington* (Belfast Crown Court, 21.1.1993).

152 Belfast Crown Court, 21 Jan. 1993.
153 [1986] NI 343.
154 [1985] NI 457.
155 [1995] 1 All ER 334.
156 [1987] NI 194.
157 The Home Office did carry out a subsequent review of the law and proposed no change. See *Report of the Inter-Departmental Review of the Law on the Use of Lethal Force in Self-Defence or the Prevention of Crime* (London: Home Office, 1996). For a critique of the review and proposals for reform see J. Rogers, 'Justifying the Use of Firearms by Policemen and Soldiers: A Response to the Home Office's Review of the Law on the Use of Lethal Force', *Legal Studies*, vol. 18, no. 4 (1998) 486.
158 For a critical analysis see S. Doran, 'The Use of Force by the Security Forces in Northern Ireland: A Legal Perspective', *Legal Studies* vol. 7 (1987) 291.
159 *R v Fisher & Wright* (Belfast Crown Court, 10 Feb. 1995).
160 (1989) 11 EHRR 117.
161 (1991) 13 EHRR 157.
162 (1996) 22 EHRR 29.
163 (1981) 5 EHRR 71.
164 The Commission did find for the applicants in their complaint that the prohibition on communicating with their wives while detained was a breach of Article 8.
165 (1995) 19 EHRR 193.
166 Application no. 8317/78, decision 15 May 1980.
167 (1994)19 EHRR 539.
168 (1981) 5 EHRR 71.
169 See also *Murray v United Kingdom* (1995) 19 EHRR 193.

8   The Path to Justice

1 See attorney general's written answer to a parliamentary question – Hansard 1 Aug. 1972. Significantly, the attorney general went on to say: 'I have also decided that it would not be in the public interest to proceed further with charges of riotous behaviour which have been brought against certain civilians in respect of their participation in the events of that day; and accordingly direction will be given that no evidence be offered in support of charges already preferred and that the necessary steps be taken to apply to the court to withdraw such summonses as have been issued.' This decision closed off the possibility of any of the events of Bloody Sunday being reopened in court on a criminal prosecution of any civilians alleged to have been rioting that day.
2 The sums were as follows: Patrick Doherty, £16 575.35; Gerald Donaghy, £850; John Duddy, £2422; Hugh Gilmour, £250; Michael Kelly, £250; Michael McDaid, £250; Kevin McElhinney, £250; Bernard McGuigan, £3750; James McKinney, £13 770; William McKinney, £1350; William Nash, £250; James Wray, £1500; John Young, £250.
3 At the time of Bloody Sunday inquests were governed by the Coroners Act (Northern Ireland) 1959 and the Coroners (Practice and Procedure) Rules (Northern Ireland) 1963. See generally J. Lecky and D. Greer, *Coroners' Law and Practice in Northern Ireland* (Belfast: SLS, 1998), ch. 1.

4 *Irish Times*, 22 Aug. 1973.

5 *Ireland v United Kingdom*, no. 5310/71; *Yearbook of the European Convention of Human Rights*, vol. 15 (The Hague: Kluwer Law International, 1972), pp. 77–256.

6 The original application was submitted on 16 December 1971 (see *Yearbook on the European Convention of Human Rights*, vol. 14 (The Hague: Kluwer Law International, 1971), pp. 100–2). By two supplementary memorials, application no. 5451/72, the Irish government alleged further continuing breaches, including in particular the 13 deaths on Bloody Sunday. These were treated as part of the original application.

7 British Irish Rights Watch was formally established in 1992. Its objects are: (1) the promotion by means of education and research of the proper observance and maintenance of human rights in Britain and Ireland and elsewhere in the world with particular reference to the conflict in Northern Ireland; (2) the promotion and dissemination of knowledge, information and understanding of such human rights by writing, publishing and distributing articles, reports, books and other documents and assisting in the same, by arranging and providing lectures and seminars, and by all other means of providing and exchanging information; and (3) to procure the abolition of torture, extrajudicial executions and arbitrary arrest, detention and exile.

8 *McDaid and Others v United Kingdom*, application no. 25681/94, 22 EHRR CD197–198 (1996).

9 *R v The Bloody Sunday Tribunal of Inquiry, ex parte B, O, U and V* (High Court, 16 Mar. 99). The tribunal appealed unsuccessfully to the Court of Appeal against that part of the judgment which declared that the tribunal had misunderstood the nature and extent of the anonymity granted to the soldiers by Lord Widgery in 1972; see *R v The Bloody Sunday Tribunal of Inquiry, ex parte B; O; U and V* (Court of Appeal, 30 Mar. 99).

10 On the basis of the assessment of the security threat to which he would be exposed the Saville inquiry ruled that one RUC officer could give evidence while screened from the public view.

11 *R v Lord Saville and others, ex parte A and others* 149 NLJ 965.

12 *R v Lord Saville of Newdigate and others, ex parte A and others* (The Times 29 July 99).

13 Don Mullan 'Judge's army links lead to calls for quashing of Bloody Sunday ruling' *Irish Times*, 2 August 1999.

14 [1999] 1 All ER 577.

15 Don Mullan, author of *Eyewitness Bloody Sunday* and a prominent spokesman for the Bloody Sunday Justice Campaign, has argued the case for a rehearing of the appeal before a differently constituted court; see Don Mullan 'Irish Times' op. cit.

16 Agreement Reached in the Multi-Party Negotiations, Strand One.

17 Agreement Reached in the Multi-Party Negotiations, Strand Two.

18 Agreement Reached in the Multi-Party Negotiations, Rights, Safeguards and Equality of Opportunity: Economic, Social and Cultural Issues.

19 Agreement Reached in the Multi-Party Negotiations, Rights, Safeguards and Equality of Opportunity: Human Rights, para.1.

20 Ibid., para. 2.

21 The agreement provides for devolved government in Northern Ireland. This will take the form of a directly elected assembly, from which an executive

will be established. There is provision for broad legislative powers to be transferred to this assembly. In effect it is a return to the devolved government arrangements which prevailed in Northern Ireland from 1921 to 1972, with the critical difference that power sharing between the two communities is specifically built into the machinery; see strand one of the agreement.

22 Agreement Reached in the Multi-Party Negotiations, Rights, Safeguards and Equality of Opportunity: Human Rights, para. 5. The first chief commissioner is Professor Brice Dickson, a leading international expert on human rights law with a long track record of campaigning on human rights and civil liberties issues in Northern Ireland.

23 Agreement Reached in the Multi-Party Negotiations, Rights, Safeguards and Equality of Opportunity: Human Rights, para. 4.

24 The statutory basis and remit for the Commission are to be found in Sections 68–72 of the Northern Ireland Act 1998 and are broadly in line with the relevant provisions in the agreement.

25 Agreement Reached in the Multi-Party Negotiations, Security, para. 1.

26 Ibid., para. 2.

27 Northern Ireland (Sentences) Act 1998.

28 Agreement Reached in the Multi-Party Negotiations, Prisoners.

29 Agreement Reached in the Multi-Party Negotiations, Policing and Justice, para. 1.

30 Ibid., para. 2.

31 Ibid., para. 3. 'The Commission will be broadly representative with expert and international representation among its membership and will be asked to consult widely.'

32 Ibid., annex A.

33 *Hansard*, H. L. May 1998, vol. 589, col. 1379.

34 See Current Law Statutes Annotated 1998, c. 32 (London: Sweet & Maxwell, 1998).

35 The members of the Commission, in addition to Chris Patten, are Sir John Smith, a former deputy commissioner of the London Metropolitan Police with experience as one of HM inspectors of constabulary; Kathleen O'Toole, formerly of the Boston police and currently secretary for public safety; Peter Smith QC, with 20 years experience at the Northern Ireland bar; Dr Maurice Hayes a former senior civil servant and Ombudsman in Northern Ireland and author of *A Police Ombudsman for Northern Ireland?* (Belfast: NIO, 1997); Professor Clifford Shearing, director of the Centre of Criminology at the University of Toronto; Dr Gerald Lynch, president of John Jay College of Criminal Justice in the City University of New York, which is rated the number one criminal justice institute in the United States; and Lucy Woods, chief executive of British Telecom in Northern Ireland.

36 Agreement Reached in the Multi-Party Negotiations, Policing and Justice, para. 5.

37 Ibid., para. 4.

38 The officials are Jim Daniell, director of criminal justice at the NIO (leader of the group); Glenn Thompson, director of the Northern Ireland Court Service; David Seymour, legal secretary to the Law Officers; and Ian Maye, Criminal Policy Division of the NIO (secretary to the review).

39   The independent assessors are Professor Joanna Shapland, professor of crim-
     inal justice at Sheffield University and director of the Institute for the Study
     of the Legal Profession; Professor John Jackson, professor of public law and
     head of the Law School at Queen's University Belfast; Eugene Grant QC,
     founder and general secretary of the Criminal Bar Association (NI) and for-
     mer chairman of the General Council of the Bar of Northern Ireland; Dr Bill
     Lockhart, director of the Extern Organisation and director of the Centre for
     Independent Research and Analysis of Crime; and John Gower QC, a retired
     English judge.
40   Agreement Reached in the Multi-Party Negotiations, Constitutional Issues,
     annex B.
41   Agreement Reached in the Multi-Party Negotiations, Declaration of
     Support, para. 4.
42   Agreement Reached in the Multi-Party Negotiations, Decommissioning.

Table of Legislation and Cases

Legislation

Northern Ireland

United Kingdom

Ireland

International

Cases

Northern Ireland

Index